GUN-FIRE

An Historical Narrative of

The 4th Bde. C.F.A.

in the Great War (1914-18)

2nd Cdn. Div.

4th Cdn. Div.

Compiled by

The 4th Brigade, C.F.A. Association

Editor
LIEUT. J. A. MacDONALD
15th and 30th Btys., C.F.A.

Illustrations by
Lieut. S. T. J. Fryer
13th and 26th Btys., C.F.A.

To the memory of those of the 4th Brigade (Canadian Field Artillery) who made the supreme sacrifice, whose names are recorded herein, and engraved in our hearts as "Our Glorious Dead," this history is dedicated.

"Faithful to the Last!"

Contents

PREFACE—*By Lieut. John A. MacDonald*

INTRODUCTORY—*By Maj.-Gen. A. G. L. McNaughton, C.M.G., D.S.O,*

Book I

PART I—*(November 6th, 1914—May 21st, 1916)*

 Chapter 1. Mobilization.
 Chapter 2. England.
 Chapter 3. Arrival in Flanders.
 Chapter 4. Trench Warfare.
 Chapter 5. St. Eloi.

PART II—*(May 21st, 1916—March 17th, 1917)*

 Chapter 1. Sanctuary Wood and Hooge.
 Chapter 2. Courcellette.
 Chapter 3. Regina Trench.
 Chapter 4. Signal Communication.
 Chapter 5. In Front of Vimy.

PART III—*(March 7th, 1917—June 21st, 1917)*

 Chapter 1. Battle of Vimy Ridge.
 Chapter 2. Minor Operations.

PART IV—*(June 21st, 1917—May 28th, 1919)*

 Chapter 1. Siege of Lens.
 Chapter 2. Hill 70.
 Chapter 3. Passchendaele.
 Chapter 4. Return to Vimy.
 Chapter 5. Holding the Ridge.
 Chapter 6. Amiens.
 Chapter 7. The Hindenburg Line.
 Chapter 8. Canal du Nord.
 Chapter 9. Cambrai to Valenciennes.
 Chapter 10. Downfall of Germany.

Book II

(The 15th and 16th Batteries, 6th Bde., C.F.A.)

 Chapter 1. Operations, 1916.
 Chapter 2. Operations, 1917.
 Chapter 3. Operations, 1918.
 Chapter 4. The March to the Rhine.

RETURN TO "CIVIES"—*By Hon. Capt. R. F. Thompson, M.C.*

Appendices

1. The Honour Roll, 4th Brigade, C.F.A.
2. The Decoration List, 4th Brigade, C.F.A.
3. The Nominal Roll, 4th Brigade, C.F.A.
4. Skeleton History of each Unit.
5. Table of Officers Commanding.

Illustrations

1. Frontispiece.

2. Commanding Officers, 4th Brigade, C.F.A.

3. Inspection by Duke of Connaught, Exhibition Camp (Toronto), 1915.

4. N.C.O.'s, 15th Battery, C.F.A., Exhibition Camp (Toronto), 1915.

5. Officers 4th Brigade, C.F.A.

6. King George and Earl Kitchener inspecting 2nd Canadian Contingent, Beachborough Park, (England), August, 1915.

7. Arrival of Batteries at Trawsfynnd, Wales.

8. Battery Commanders, 4th Brigade, C.F.A.

9. Unveiling Monument to the Fallen of the C.F.A.—Vimy Ridge, 1918.

10. Tablet, 21st Howitzer Battery, Zonnebeke Church.

11. Armistice Day (Mons), November 11th, 1918.

Maps

1. Shorncliffe Training Area, 1915.

2. Ypres-Armentieres Sector, 1915-1916.

3. Kemmel Sector, 1915-1916.

4. The Somme, September-November, 1916.

5. Lens-Arras Sector, 1917.

6. Ypres Salient, October-November, 1917.

7. Amiens, August, 1918.

8. Drocourt-Queant Line, August-September, 1918.

9. Cambrai, September-October, 1918.

10. Valenciennes, October-November, 1918.

11. Advance to Mons, November, 1918.

Preface

This volume is offered in response to a request on the part of members and friends of the 4th Brigade, C.F.A., whose services to the Empire it describes. "Gunfire" is not intended as a general history of the Great War of 1914-18.

The whole story of the 4th Brigade, C.F.A., will never be told. Each participant had a different point of view, but it is hoped that the records and incidents that follow may call to mind the pleasant features of the period of training and the services in the battle areas, as well as the splendid heroism and self-sacrifice manifested on the part of all ranks.

There is a vast amount of material covering the work of the units of the Brigade which could not be embraced within the restricted confines of this book. The author trusts, however, that sufficient is included to satisfy those who are most interested.

Some repetition has been inevitable, but it is hoped that many of the incidents recorded will be source material for future battery histories.

Ten years had passed since the great conflict, when a reunion of the Brigade was first mooted. Some 350 members "answered the Roll-Call" at the Carls-Rite Hotel, Toronto, March 24, 1928, and renewed old comradeships. At that time the formation of an Association of all Batteries who served in this Unit overseas was decided upon.

A few months after the reunion dinner, it was proposed to compile an historical narrative of the 4th Brigade, C.F.A., and the writer immediately began to gather material. Thus came into being—"GUNFIRE."

After considerable difficulty, maps, photographs, and other data were secured. The "Historical" and "Records" sections of the Dept. of National Defence assisted me greatly in this work. The co-operation of Col. A. F. Duguid, D.S.O., and Col. F. Logie Armstrong, O.B.E., after many months tedious research work, made it possible to secure the War Diary, official data, nominal rolls, honour rolls, and decoration lists.

Lieut. S. T. J. Fryer must also be complimented on his fine cartoon illustrations of our life in the Army, and Major-Gen. A. G. L. MacNaughton, Brig.-Gen. W. B. M. King, Lt.-Col. M. N. Ross, Major C. Sifton, Major G. A. Drew, Lieut. A. C. Lewis, Lieut. M. A. Wilson, Lieut. F. C. Mayberry, Lieut. C. R. Avery, Capt. G. R. Gouinlock, Lieut. R. R. Sparling, Lieut. A. L. Vokes, and L. A. Catchpole for their valuable assistance in furnishing detail on various chapters.

I hope that members of the "Old Brigade" will find this volume of interest, and that when the next generation ask:—"What did you do in the Great War, Daddy?", they may read them this story, "GUNFIRE."

John A. MacDonald,

Lieut. 15th and 30 Bty's,

Canadian Field Artillery.

February 1st, 1929.

Introductory

by Maj.-Gen. A. G. McNaughton, C.M.G., D.S.O.

WHEN I consented to write a short preface to the history of the 4th Brigade, C.F.A., I received a suggestion from the energetic secretary of the Association that my article should cover—"Sniping guns; registration; the "Meteor," and how "Error of the Day" was calculated; "S.O.S." lines; drum fire; box and rolling barrages; gas shells; smoke screens; counter battery work, and any other interesting features I might think of."

Now this is what might be called a 'tall order' and I regret that I have neither the time, knowledge nor ability to comply with it; nor can I, at this distance from the Historical Records, make any particular contribution to the work of the 4th Brigade, C.F.A.

All that is attempted in the following article is an outline of the development of artillery during the Great War, with particular reference to our own Canadian Corps, and marked with a few figures of guns employed and ammunition expended. If little is said about the infantry and other arms of the Service, the reader will appreciate that this is not because undue importance is attached to the rôle played by the artillery; none realize better than the gunners themselves that they are not an independent arm, but that their task is to assist the infantry and that, in the last analysis, however well the way is prepared by the artillery and other arms, it is the infantry advance and their determination to apply the cold steel that captures ground and confirms success in battle.

The fire power now in the hands of the infantry themselves, by reason of the modern magazine-rifle and the machine-gun, usually renders direct assault impracticable for the infantry alone, while the vast numbers of troops placed in the field, in modern war, results in there being no flanks around which to manoeuvre.

These conditions, together with the increased power of resistance conferred on the defender, by reason of field entrenchments and wire entanglements, soon brought the war in Europe into a stable condition, where the opposing armies faced one another along continous lines from Switzerland to the English Channel.

Each attempt to break the deadlock and obtain power of manoeuvre resulted in prohibitive casualties to the attacker.

The obvious solution of the difficulty lay in a preponderance of artillery, sufficient to crush out of existence a wide section of the enemy's defensive system, entrenchments and defenders alike, thus creating a gap through which troops would be thrown to work around the exposed flanks.

The establishments of artillery, based on pre-war requirements, were far from adequate to permit of the accomplishment of this result, and quite early, all belligerents set to work to remedy this defect in their organization.

In the British Field Army we had to begin with the following natures of armament:

	Calibre	Weight of Shell	Range
Horse Artillery	3"	13 lbs.	5,500 yards
Field Artillery	3.3"	18 lbs.	6,500 yards
Field Howitzer	4.5"	35 lbs.	7,200 yards
Heavy Artillery	5"	60 lbs.	10,000 yards
Siege Artillery	6"	100/120 lbs.	6,000 yards

The allotment of artillery, per division, worked out at about fifty-four field guns, and four 60-pounders, and I believe that I am correct in saying, that in 1914, the whole Siege Train, capable of taking the field, consisted only of some three or four batteries of 6-inch "Hows." and an Armoured Train equipped with antiquadated 6-inch guns.

The total number of guns of all natures with the British Expeditionary Force, in the fall of 1914, was 486.

Some idea of the growth of the British Artillery during the War may be realized from the fact that, at the time of the Armistice, the British guns in batteries on the Western Front numbered 6,437, of which 2,211 belonged to the heavy artillery.

On numerous occasions the Canadian Corps has been supported by over 750 guns and howitzers, while in the last organized fighting in which we took part—the attack on Mount Houy and the capture of Valenciennes on November 1st, 1918—the advance of the 10th Infantry Brigade alone was supported by 248 guns and howitzers.

Not only did the number of our guns increase, but the range and shell power were also markedly improved.

IMPROVEMENT OF EXISTING PIECES

Type	Range in Yards		
	1914	1918	Future
18-pdr.	6,500	9,500	
60-pdr.	10,000	15,000	
6" How.	6,000	9,500	12,500

NEW WEAPONS INTRODUCED

Type	Weight of Shell, Lbs.	Range		Remarks
		Yards	Miles	
8" How.	200	12,000	7	Travelling Carriage
9.2" How.	290	13,000	7.5	Pedestal mounting
12" How.	750	14,000	8	Pedestal and railway
15" How.	1,400	10,500	6	Pedestal (obsolete)
6" gun	100	19,000	11	Travelling carriage
9.2" gun	380	23,000	13	Railway
12" gun	850	30,000	17	Railway
14" gun	1,586	34,000	20	Railway

NEW WEAPONS PROMISED

Type	Weight of Shell, Lbs.	Range		Remarks
		Yards	Miles	
18" How.	2,500	?	?	Railway
? gun			75/100	Fixed Emplacement
8" gun		40/50,000		Railway

Remarkable as these improvements were, the German gun designers had an initial lead which we were never able to make up, and at the end of the war their weapons still outranged ours, on the average gun for gun, by nearly 30 per cent.

COMPARISON OF SOME GERMAN AND BRITISH GUNS

German		British		Remarks
Type	Range	Type	Range	
10 cm. How.	11,000	4.5 How.	7,200	
15 cm. Gun	25,000	6" Gun	19,000	
35.5 cm.	68,000	14" Gun	34,000	
77 mm.	11,700	18-pdr.	9,500	
15 cm. H.	9,600	6" How.	9,500	Medium Howitzers of both armies approximately same.
21 cm. H.	11,000	8" How.	12,000	Advantage with British.

At the beginning, while our heaviest piece in the field was the 6-inch, the Germans had the 17-inch, and those who were in front of Ypres, in April, 1915, will remember what it felt like to be shot at by every calibre up to and including the 17-inch, with nothing to reply with, except a few field guns; and how exasperating it was to have German batteries come into action in full view and not be able to reach them, while their shells were exploding in and around our own battery positions.

Then, too, in the matter of ammunition the Germans had the lead. While we were under limitations of three rounds per gun, per day, for our field pieces, he appeared to have plenty of reserve stocks and he certainly used them.

I am afraid that in the early days, the artillery situation was not such as to inspire confidence in the minds of our infantry.

Picture to yourself the case of an infantry officer pointing out to a gunner the location of a nest of German machine-guns which are worrying the men in the line. The gunner admits it is a good target and that he would like to engage it. "Sorry!" No ammunition." The retort of the infantryman was likely to be, "What are you doing in the Great War anyway?" and the result, if the gunner was a bit touchy, permanently damaged liaison.

As the war went on, we got more and more ammunition, but, we suffered considerably from lack of standardization.

In the early Summer of 1915, we had four different types of shrapnel in our limbers at the one time, with a variation of range between them of anything up to 400 yards.

In 1916, in the 4.5 Howitzers, we had three types of propellant in use simultaneously—Cordite, Ballistite and N. C. T.—all with different temperature and moisture co-efficients and all giving results varying in a most obscure way with the wear of the howitzer.

Charges originally shipped in lots of similar manufacture got mixed up on the L. of C. Shells varied in weight, driving bands were of many varieties.

The battery officers have, in any event, to make corrections for—

> Temperature of air and charge.
> Barometer.
> Velocity and direction of wind.
> Wear of gun.
> Type of shell and fuze.

and when the already difficult task is further complicated by lack of standardization in propellant, driving band and shell, the task of exact shooting is rendered almost impossible.

By 1918 the lack of standardization had become one of the serious limiting factors in the tactical employment of artillery.

I mention these facts for the benefit of those who, in the event of another war, will be responsible for the manufacture of munitions and in the hope that, if this unfortunate event should come about, due attention will be given to the necessity for a more thorough standardization than was possible in the last war.

I think that those of us who were in the field never quite realized the enormous difficulties under which the manufacturers of munitions laboured, and what a wonderful achievement lies to their credit; but if we had had closer touch with them perhaps some of our difficulties would have been earlier recognized and cleared away.

As the number of guns available began to increase, the existing artillery units had to be expanded and new ones raised. Technical skill had to be developed and previous lessons and teachings modified to suit the changing conditions. The Field and Horse gunners, accustomed to fighting under circumstances which enabled them to observe every round, had to cease from scoffing at corrections for temperature, barometer, etc., and the Heavy Artillery, used to the utmost deliberation, had to learn speed. Accuracy of fire on unseen targets, and the ability to shoot close over the heads of our own infantry had to be acquired, and an organization built up which could effectively handle large masses of artillery.

At the Somme, in 1916, we had any quantity of guns and ammunition, but many of our battery officers and higher commanders were inexperienced. They could not be otherwise; our artillery intelligence organization was in its infancy; the methods of co-operation between aircraft and the artillery command, rudimentary. The type of shell was, in many instances, unsuitable for the task to be performed—those who were there will recollect their disheartening task of endeavouring to cut wire with field gun shrapnel. Although, as Ludendorff admits, we did considerable harm to the Germans, the results indicated that there was not that happy combination in the employment of the artillery in support of the other arms which leads to easy success in battle. The lessons were invaluable, but the cost in life was terrific.

It was largely because the British General Staff read these lessons correctly and had the courage of their convictions to effect the necessary re-organization that, later, we were able to beat the Germans, despite the fact that in the technical matters of guns and ammunition they still maintained their lead.

Put shortly, the situation in 1917 and onward is, that the Germans had the advantage in quality of artillery material, we in quantity, organization and methods of tactical employment.

General Byng, the Commander of the Canadian Corps, was one of the first to grasp the significance of the lessons of the Somme and, with Major-General Sir Edward Morrison, set about perfecting our artillery organization. The improvement was continued when Sir Arthur Currie succeeded General Byng in the command.

I feel safe in saying, that by 1917, the organization of the Canadian Corps Artillery and its ancillary intelligence and other services had reached an advanced state and that our lead over similar organizations was maintained to the end of the war. The credit for this is largely due to our Corps Commander, who, in developing his policy of giving his infantry the maximum of support, was invariably sympathetic in his attitude towards the Canadian gunners, and gave us the necessary means and encouragement to surmount the difficulties which from time to time faced us; not only this, but he developed and put into practice a very thorough system of co-operation between the artillery and infantry. It was always the object of the Canadian Corps to exploit its gun power to the limit for the purpose of saving the lives of our infantry.

I said in a previous paragraph that one of the greatest advantages we had over the Germans was in organization; this will be realized from the fact that the enemy artillery was invariably organized and fought on a Divisional Front; as a consequence, they experienced great difficulty in bringing to bear, at any given time or place, an adequate volume of fire.

So too, the enemy's artillery intelligence was collected and co-ordinated on a Divisional Front and they experienced difficulty in passing this information quickly to adjacent formations, and while their intelligence service undoubtedly acquired a great mass of valuable data, there did not appear to be a suitable chain of artillery command through which its value could be fully exploited.

During the battle, we, on the other hand, organized and fought as a Corps, with the result that the whole force of our artillery, within range, was immediately available to support any sector of our front, and the whole of our intelligence system was centered on those who had the means at their disposal to take immediate and effective action.

Artillery intelligence is required first, for immediate action, and secondly, for compilation, study and deduction with a view to subsequent action.

In the following paragraphs I will indicate the principal sources of artillery intelligence and outline in some detail the nature of the work they were able to do for us.

(a) Aeroplanes. From the advantageous position of the aeroplane, the observer is able to locate the position of conspicuous things, such as a flash or a body of troops or transport, with a considerable degree of accuracy. This information is embodied in a zone call sent out by wireless and may be picked up directly by the batteries and acted on at once.

By means of close reconnaissance it is often possible to detect new battery position's tracks, effect of shell fire, etc. The information so obtained is reported either by a message dropped at Corps Heavy Artillery or by phone, when the plane returns to its aerodrome. Under position warfare conditions, fully 30 per cent, of the counter-battery information is supplied by the R.A.F. and in more mobile operations this proportion is much increased.

Since the aeroplane is in continual motion and always liable to interference by hostile aircraft and anti-aircraft fire, the observation is, at best, intermittent, and the whole attention of the observer cannot always be given to his task.

(b) Aeroplane Photographs show the exact position of emplacements and, to a skilled interpreter, the appearance gives a good indication as to whether or not they are occupied. Tracks, routes of approach, signal routes, etc., can be plotted from them and so assist in determining the enemy's vulnerable points.

Camouflage can often be overcome through stereoscopic photos, through photos taken on special colour plate or by comparison of recent and old photos.

Favourable weather is required before photos can be taken, and usually the prints cannot be interpreted and the information circulated under 6 to 24 hours.

(c) Survey Sections have two or more "posts" situated on commanding ground, equipped with the finest type of surveying instruments and interconnected by phone with a Central Station. When one post locates a hostile battery firing, the bearing is reported to Central Station and the other post, or posts, put on approximately. Then phone communication is cut off and each post, as it sees the flash, corrects its bearing and presses a key which lights a corresponding lamp at Central Station. When all lamps there light up together, the operator may be fairly certain that all posts are on the same flash. Bearings are phoned in and plotted and the position determined with great precision (under favorable conditions to within 5 yards). Flashes of other guns appear to the right and left in the graticule, and so an accurate count of the 'number of guns firing' may be made.

In addition to locating active hostile batteries, survey posts act like other 'ground observers', with the added advantage that cross bearings can be obtained on anything visible from two or more posts, and thus an accurate location secured. For satisfactory counter-battery work, survey sections require a base of 6,000-10,000 yards and a minimum of 3 posts. Survey sections should be able to come into action within a few hours of the capture of commanding ground, using wireless as a temporary expedient until phone communication is established.

(d) Sound Ranging Sections consist of a Headquarters connected to three or more microphone stations distributed along the front about 1½ miles from the line; in addition, a listening post is located well forward of these. When the listener hears the report of an enemy gun, he presses a key which completes an electric circuit and sets in motion a recording apparatus and the other microphone in turn, is recorded. From the time intervals between microphones, the location of the source can be calculated. Similarly, when the shell bursts, the sound waves sent out ultimately reach the microphone and are recorded, and hence the target at which the hostile battery is firing can be located. Under favorable conditions a record can be taken, and the colculations made and reported, within 3 minutes and with an accuracy of between 35 and 100 yards. Adverse winds check and dissipate the sound wave, and changes of temperature and barometric pressure vary the velocity with which it travels; also, the shape of the ground and the various strata of the atmosphere cause reflections and distortion which cannot accurately be allowed for, and which reduce the precision of the "locations."

During bombardment the microphones are continually recording and it is not possible to separate out the waves of any particular piece. From the records, the exact time of flight is known, and as the location of the gun and of the shell-burst have been determined, the range is known; hence, reference to range table will give "calibre" and "nature of piece." Further, each piece has a characteristic wave shape from which a skilled sound-ranger will at once recognize it.

With "Hows.," the muzzle velocity is less than that of sound, so the shell is always behind the sound wave, but with guns there is a complication due to the fact that the shell is travelling faster than the sound of the gun and of the noises made in flight. As the shell loses velocity, it ultimately drops to that of sound and below, and the accumulated noises which it has been making pass on ahead of it, thus producing the "onde de Choc," the first part of the familiar double report heard when in front of a gun. The second report is the true gun wave, and is the one on which calculations are based.

It takes from 36 to 48 hours for a Sound-Ranging Section to change base; this method, therefore, is of very limited usefulness in mobile operations.

(e) Balloon Observation can furnish useful information only under favourable conditions of light. The long range medium gun has driven the ballon so far back, and the methods of attack by aircraft have been so perfected, that it is questionable whether the ballon is worth retaining. Balloons can give general information such as area shelled, groups of active batteries, train movement, etc. (and can locate the closer targets and range on them under suitable conditions).

(f) Ground Observers include the "F.O.O.'s" of Batteries and the special intelligence posts provided by the other arms. They are subject to the limitation that observation is only on a single line and while the direction of the target can be given with fair accuracy, location is largely a matter of estimation. From these posts come the mass of general tactical information which, when co-ordinated with the more exact intelligence derived from the air, survey sections, etc., forms the basis for the immediate counter battery and other artillery action required.

(g) Liaison Officers. Artillery officers are maintained at the H.Q. of the Infantry brigades for the purpose of keeping the infantry informed of the disposition and possibilities of the artillery covering them. They are responsible for collecting and transmitting to their commanders all information regarding the plans, intentions and progress of our own troops, together with any intelligence of the enemy derived through infantry sources.

In the case of hostile shelling they should report at once :—

1. Area shelled. Time and intensity of fire.

2. Nature and size of projectile.

3. Direction from which shells are coming.

4. Time when fire ceases.

This information is of great assistance in locating the hostile batteries engaged so that neutralizing fire may be opened. An artillery officer is detailed to R.A.F. Sqdrn. H.Q., to act as technical assistant to the Sqdrn. Commander and to represent the Counter-battery Staff Officer. This officer is responsible for investigating any cases of failure in "shoots" with R.A.F. observation and for promoting inter co-operation, generally.

(h) Officers' Patrols. There is only one way to ensure obtaining information in battle; that is to detail special personnel, whose sole business it is to collect and transmit it. This is particularly the case in mobile operations, when the routine of Stationery War breaks down. Under these conditions it is essential that artillery commanders should know the progress of the infantry from moment to moment, and it has been found by experience that the only satisfactory way to obtain this information is by officers' patrols, either mounted or dismounted, operating in definite sectors and in touch with prearranged Report Centres from which the information is forwarded by wireless, phone or dispatch-rider, according to circumstances. These patrols give advance information of the fight from which the future action required from the artillery may often be forecasted and arrangements prepared accordingly.

(i) Espionage and Repatries often give valuable information concerning supply dumps and other centres of activity, the presence of reinforcing artillery in back areas, reliefs, enemy intentions, etc. Sometimes locations of gun positions are given, but this information is usually vague. On the whole, intelligence derived from this source, takes too long to get through and concerns the area too far in rear to be of much use to artillery commanders.

(j) Captured Documents and Prisoners' Statements usually deal with what is past but are of use in checking up previous deductions and arriving at an estimate of the probable accuracy of future forecasts.

(k) Listening Sets. Police arrangements are usually so perfected that little of value is obtained. Most often the information gleaned is confined to indications of a change of formations.

(l) Intercepted Wireless. Wireless Compass Stations can locate, with fair accuracy, any sending station whether in the air or on the ground. The intercepted message may give some information of tactical value and a study of the wireless traffic between located stations gives some clue to the hostile dispositions. Track charts of aeroplanes using wireless give indications of the enemy's artillery policy. Wireless camouflage has, of course, to be reckoned with.

In order to make the intelligence derived from these sources immediately available to the artillery, very elaborate communications are required. In fact, the whole system evolved in the Canadian Corps was only possible because our Signal Corps was so thoroughly efficient.

In handling artillery in the field the first consideration is that its fire must do the utmost possible to assist our Infantry to get forward. Exact intelligence and a careful study of the enemy's dispositions enables the Artillery Commander to form his plan with this end in view. He must forsee just which factors of the enemy's defence organization are dangerous and when, hostile artillery, machine guns, trenches, wire, mortars, enemy reserves, etc., all must be given attention at the proper time. Whenever intelligence is indefinite, inaccuracy must be made up by volume of fire. In practice the various conditions are met about as follows :—

Initially and during the advance, the whole of the Field Artillery and a part of the Heavy are on barrage work, carrying out a plan issued by the G.O.C., R.A., of the Corps and co-ordinated with flanking Corps by the Army.

The inner fringe of the barrage is laid in front of the infantry and throughout the attack goes forward according to the pre-arranged plan. It usually consists of 18-pounder shrapnel fired directly over the heads of our troops, and in some of our operations has reached a density of one 18-pounder per 9 yards of front, firing four rounds per minute. You will appreciate the accuracy demanded from our Field Batteries when you realize that they are called upon to burst their shells so that the "mean point of impact" of their shrapnel bullets shall be 200 yards in front of our advancing infantry, the range being anything from 1,500 to 4,500 or more yards.

The 4.5 field howitzers, firing "H.E." are employed on machine-gun nests, strong points, etc., in rear of the 18-pounders—the 6-inch howitzers on similar targets, still further in the rear.

The idea of the barrage is to tie the enemy to the ground, to inflict casualties and to demoralize him and prevent his using his rifles, machine-guns, trench-mortars, etc., and to screen the advance of our infantry by a wall of bursting shell, smoke and dust.

The Heavy Artillery not scheduled for the barrage, work directly under the intelligence centre at the Heavy Artillery Headquarters, are engaged in dealing with the enemy's artillery, exploiting targets of opportunity, harassing the enemy's line of retreat, his reserve troops, his railheads where reinforcements may be arriving, his aerodromes, etc.

As the attack progresses, and the end of the pre-arranged barrages are reached, a portion of the Field Artillery reverts to the control of the Divisions and moves forward to work directly with the attacking infantry. The remainder goes into reserve.

The heavy artillery which has been employed in the barrage moves forward to be in position to deal with the enemy's artillery as soon as it again comes into action.

The artillery on counter-battery work initially, which has been sited well forward, becomes available as a reserve of fire-power to be turned on any threatened sector as required.

You will realize that the whole method of employment of artillery has been in continuous development and we have had a succession of limiting factors to contend with. At Vimy, in April, 1917, for instance, it was observation of fire and intelligence; at Hill 70, in August of the same year, life of guns; at Amiens, in August, 1918, available positions for deployment; and during the later phases of the advance, transportation of ammunition from railhead to guns. Throughout, as our artillery intelligence system was perfected, the need for increased accuracy was felt.

The policy of our Corps Commander was invariably to give his infantry the maximum possible of artillery support and never to employ men where shells would do the work. The motto of the Canadian artillery has been to shoot the "ultimate round," and how well our gunners achieved this task may be seen from the figures of ammunition expenditure for some of our major operations.

	Days	Field Guns	Heavy Guns	Total	Th. rds.	Tons	Tons /day
Vimy—1-8 April	8	...	...	...	553	13,005	1,625
9th April	1	618	238	856	212	4,299	4,299
9-14 April	6	...	...	...	540	11,337	1,889
Hill 70	11	275	158	433	665	15,623	1,420
Passchendaele	30	360	220	580	1,453	40,908	1,370
Amiens	16	408	236	644	409		
Monchy	6	504	270	774	300		
Drocourt-Quéant	27	528	234	762	786		
Bourlon	12	522	262	784	1,067		
Cambrai	23	334	262	596	519		
Valenciennes to Mons	12	312	174	486	215		
Amiens to Mons	100	...	...	...	3,296	73,100	731

The significance of an ammunition expenditure of 73,100 tons in the 100 days operations from Amiens to Mons, is difficult to realize. In order to help the reader to gain some comprehension of the relations of the artillery to the other arms, and to the results achieved, I set down in cold statistical form the following information concerning the last hundred days of the operations of the Canadian Corps in France and Belgium.

Maximum number of guns 784
Divisions, Canadian .... 4; British attached on the average 1
Average total strength of Corps 105,000
Guns per 1000 troops 7.5
Duration of operations .... 100 days
          (Includes time spent in marching.)
Ammunition expenditure, rds. 3,296,000
Ammunition expenditure, per day 32,960
Ammunition expenditure per day per 1000 troops (including reserves) 313
Average ammunition expenditure per gun per day 42
Battle casualties 45,830
Enemy killed and wounded .... Unknown
Prisoners 31,537
Guns 623
Machine-guns 2,842
Trench-mortars 336
Territory freed in square miles 500
Villages freed 228
German Divisions met and defeated 47
Other Enemy Divisions partially engaged 21
Casualties per German Division defeated 975
          (No allowance made for German Divisions partially engaged)
Total battle advance .... 86 miles

No Canadian need fear a comparison of these figures with the corresponding results obtained by any similar organization, allied or enemy. I know of no organization in the history of the War which was able to produce such a high ratio in shell to troops, nor any in which the price paid for victory was lower in personnel.

I may say that this enormous ammunition expenditure by the Canadian Corps, and the satisfactory results achieved, were only possible because our leaders arranged their plans of attack in such a way that the maximum artillery support could be developed in the intimate assistance of our assaulting infantry.

From an artillery point of view one of the most interesting operations of the Canadian Corps was the attack carried out on the morning of November 1st, 1918, by the 10th Infantry Brigade against Mount Houy, the key to Valenciennes. The 10th Brigade advanced with its left flank on the Canal D'l'Escaut, and its right covered by the advance of the XXII Corps. On a front of about 2,000 yards, the depth of penetration was some 4,000 yards, taking 190 minutes, including pauses. As the initial forming up line was on a slight salient, the direction of the advance was practically parallel to our own front.

The attack was supported by eight Brigades of Field Artillery and six Brigades of Heavy Artillery, or roughly one hundred and forty-four 18-pounders, forty-eight 4.5 howitzers and one hundred and four heavy guns and howitzers.

Some eighty machine-guns were also employed.

The ammunition expenditure was as follows:—

Field	56,200	620 tons
Heavy	31,500	1,520 tons
Total	87,700	2,140 tons

This is approximately one ton per yard of front, or one and one-half tons per infantry soldier employed. This was the most intense barrage ever employed in support of any of the operations of the Canadian Corps. All objectives were taken on time.

Enemy killed	800	Our killed	60
Wounded prisoners	75	Our wounded	380
Unwounded prisoners	1,379	Our missing	61
	2,254		501

I have gone rather at length into the capture of Valenciennes, because I regard that operation as a type of what we would have tried to do in the Campaign of 1919 had we been obliged to fight.

As a further illustration by which the comparative expenditure may be judged:— At Waterloo, in 1815, the expenditure was 9,000 rounds, having a total weight of 37 tons. Compare this with the average daily expenditure of the Canadian Corps at Passchendaele, 48,500 rounds weighing 1,370 tons.

In the South African war the expenditure was 273,000 rounds weighing 2,800 tons. This is not much in excess of our Valenciennes operation, or equal to about two average days of the Passchendaele fighting.

I have been talking about the artillery generally, and many British batteries, field, heavy and siege, and some Australian and South African have helped us from time to time. But I wish to add a special word about our own Canadian gunners.

Our people took naturally to gunnery; our battery commanders, section officers, N. C. O.'s and gunners developed extraordinary skill, efficiency and dependability, and, if in support of our infantry, there was ever a particularly difficult or dangerous task to be performed, a Canadian battery was called on to do it.

On one occasion, only, were any of our guns in German hands. This happened in Sanctuary Wood, in 1916, when two of our forward guns were taken after they had expended all their ammunition, at close range, into the German attack. These guns were recovered in the subsequent fighting.

I mention this as a tribute to the work of the infantry and as a reason for the confidence our gunners had when Canadian infantry were in front of them.

Part I

(Nov. 6th, 1914 - May 21st, 1916)

CHAPTER I

𝔐obilization

WHEN, toward the end of July of 1914, it appeared that Germany and Austria had definitely decided upon a European War against France and Russia, who had offered protection to Serbia, Great Britain took immediate steps to prevent hostilities through the mediation of its Foreign Secretary, Sir Edward Grey. For a time it seemed as if war would be averted, but, as all powers concerned had ordered mobilization of their military forces, and no guarantee could be secured from Germany that she would respect the neutrality of Belgium, Great Britain prepared to side with her Allies. Then events moved fast. On August 1st, Germany declared war on France and Russia, and immediately commenced the invasion of Belgium.

The British Empire seethed with excitement and patriotic fervour. All party differences passed out of existence. In normal times our Empire was considered a loose, friendly group of nations, more conscious of its looseness than its unity. The Boer War had given it a momentary solidarity of spirit; but, when peace was signed, each of the Dominions went busily on its own road, and appeared to the world as a weak alliance of independent nations.

In German eyes, Canada was thought to be drifting towards the U.S.A.; Australia, New Zealand, and South Africa towards complete separation; and India needed just such an excuse as the present conflict to refute British authority.

To Germany, empire meant a machine, where each part was under the direct control of a central power. To her, local autonomy seemed only a confession of weakness, and the bonds of kinship an idle sentiment. British conception of empire, on the other hand, was just the reverse. Liberty of the parts was necessary to the stability of the whole. Our Empire, which had grown "as the trees grow while men sleep," was a living organization far more enduring than any machine.

When war broke out, August 1st, the Dominion Government cabled the War Office that Canada would despatch a complete division of troops, in the event of Britain becoming involved in the conflict. Other offers followed from Australia, New Zealand, South Africa, India, and New-foundland. Thus the Overseas Dominions proved their loyalty. The Motherland, overwhelmed with such expressions of fidelity, replied that no urgency yet existed. On the 4th, however, the British Government declared war on Germany, and a few days later the offers of the Over-seas Dominions were accepted, and mobilization commenced.

Due to the thoroughness and despatch with which organization of the 1st Canadian Contingent was carried out, over 30,000 picked men, sixty per cent. of whom had already seen service in the British Army, were concentrated at Valcartier within a few weeks. This big camp, fifteen miles north of Quebec, was only a strip of open range when Sir Sam Hughes began the construction of huts, water mains, and rifle ranges.

After a few months' training, the Contingent embarked at Quebec, assembled at Gaspé Bay, and crossed the Atlantic in one grand fleet of nearly forty vessels—the largest shipment of troops since the Spanish Armada. Landing at Plymouth, England, the Canadians were given further seasoning at Salisbury Plains, and in February, 1915, finally reached the battle-front in France. In March, the Division was con-sidered ready for its tour in the line, and on the 3rd occupied 6,400 yards of trenches in the Fleurbaix-Bac St. Maur sector.

During the intervening period between the Declaration of War and the arrival of the first Canadian troops, the great strategical moves of the opposing forces had run their course. Germany, carrying out the plan prepared by the Chief of the General Staff, von Schlieffen, many years before, placed the strength of her army on the right, under von Kluck and von Bulow, and their advance followed exactly in accordance with the existing plan.

All the world thrilled to a story of the heroic defence of Liège, but the old-fashioned forts, upon which so much faith had been placed, were of little value against the great Austrian howitzers which had been supplied to the German Army in anticipation of Belgian opposition, and the slight delay the enemy advance experienced there was soon made up in the quick demolition of the supposedly strong fortresses of Namur and Maubeuge. With the fall of these forts, the Germans had succeeded in establishing open warfare, and their great enveloping movement pro-ceeded with tremendous rapidity. Their right had swung almost as far as Paris, and the German Higher Command confidently expected to envelope the French and small British force in a second Sedan before the Swiss frontier.

It was at this point that certain events happened which have been greatly misunderstood and which have been generally described as the "Miracle of the Marne." The end of the German advance and the open-ing of the Allied counter offensive, early in September, followed well-defined strategical events which the world, at that time, scarcely comprehended. The resistance of the small Belgian Army, which had

Lt.-Col. W. J. Brown

Col. C. H. L. Sharman, C.M.G.,
C.B.E.

Brig.-Gen. W. B. M. King,
C.M.G., D.S.O.

Lt.-Col. J. S. Stewart, C.M.G.,
D.S.O., Croix de Guerre

Lt.-Col. M. N. Ross, D.S.O., Bar

remained intact at Antwerp, also the unexpected speed of the Russian mobilization and subsequent advance into East Prussia, were the two main contributing factors which halted the pre-arranged advance of the German troops.

It is now known that the Kaiser, as Supreme War Lord of the German forces, who had for years been concerned about the possibility of a Russian advance into East Prussia, became unduly concerned about his Eastern army, and ordered the immediate detachment of two Army Corps from the forces on the West to proceed to the Russian front. Two more Corps were despatched to hold the Belgian Army at Antwerp and prevent the severing of the northern lines of communication. The detachment of these considerable forces which had not been contemplated in the German plan, resulted in the weakening of their right wing to such an extent that it became necessary for the enemy to change his plans.

It was at this point that Marshal Joffre executed one of the really great strategical moves of the war, when, under cover of darkness, he rushed great numbers of troops from his right wing to Paris. These troops, together with the Paris garrison and reserves, who had been assembling, were formed into a new Sixth Army, under General Gallieni, and made the famous taxi-cab advance from Paris. This so strengthened the French, who were facing von Kluck and von Bulow, that the German right was ordered to retire. Immediately, the Allies pressed their advantage with great skill, the five British Divisions then at the front being the first to cross the Marne, at Chateau Thierry. The advance continued to the heights of the Aisne, where the Germans finally took up defensive lines which established the general location of the trenches for some considerable time.

During this period there had been practically no engagements aimed at the Channel Ports, but, with the failure of the first plan, the Germans drove a great blow to the north, in the hope of seizing the vital ports along the channel and interfering with British assistance to France. This plan was upset by the magnificent stand of the "Old Contemptibles" in December of 1914, and from that time until the closing days of the war there was practically no more open warfare, as open warfare is generally understood. Both sides then dug in along the lines held, and the first winter of trench warfare had set in. Such were the conditions which existed when the 1st Canadian Division arrived on the Fleurbaix front, in February, 1915.

As soon as the 1st Contingent had embarked for England, the mobilization of the 2nd Contingent was begun. In view of the fact that training would be carried on during the winter, it was decided to estabish local training centres, rather than attempt to bring all the troops into one great camp, as had been done at Valcartier, As part of this plan, the Canadian National Exhibition Grounds were utilized by the Dominion Government for the concentration of units from Central Ontario. Militia regiments, batteries, and other branches of the service were authorized to carry on recruiting, and by the middle of November several thousand men had joined the colours.

Field batteries at London, Guelph, Brantford, Hamilton, St. Catharines, and Toronto signed on such men as were considered fit for artillery
work at the front, but owing to the scarcity of equipment and insufficient
accommodation at the recruiting centres, only one Brigade was ready
for service when the Second Contingent sailed, in May of 1915.

The organization of this Brigade was as follows :—

Unit	Date of Mobilization	Arrival in Camp	Units from which Recruited		Original O.C.
H.Q.	Dec. 7/14 (Toronto)	Dec. 7/14 (Toronto)			Lt. Col. W. J. Brown
13th Bty.	Nov. 16/14 (Hamilton)	Dec. 1/14 (Toronto)	32nd (How.) Bty (Brantford) 33rd (How.) Bty (Hamilton)		Lt. Col. A. S. Rennie Maj. G. E. Vansittart
14th Bty.	Nov. 6/14 (Toronto)	Nov. 25/14 (Toronto)	7th (Fld.) Bty. 9th (Fld.) Bty.	(St. Catharines) (Toronto)	Maj. W. H. Merritt
15th Bty.	Dec. 4/14 (Toronto)	Dec. 19/14 (Toronto)	4th (Fld.) Bty. 9th (Fld.) Bty.	(Hamilton) (Toronto)	Maj. L. E. W. Irving, D.S.O.
16th Bty.	Nov. 18/14 (London)	Dec. 8/14 (London) Jan. 23/15 (Guelph)	6th (Fld.) Bty. 16th (Fld.) Bty. 30th (Fld.) Bty.	(London) (Guelph) (Aylmer)	Lt. Col. W. J. Brown Maj. W. Simpson
Amm. Col.	Nov. 28/14 (St. Catharines)	Jan. 4/15 (Toronto)	7th (Fld.) Bty. 9th (Fld.) Bty.	(St. Catharines) (Toronto)	Capt. E. J. Lovelace Capt. G. V. Taylor

When a recruit presented himself at the recruiting depot for overseas service, he was closely interrogated as to previous service, if any,
vouched for by some references, and given a thorough medical exam-
ination. Many were refused on account of poor physique, defective
eye-sight, teeth, flat feet, and other ailments. Those who passed the
rigid tests were taken "on the strength" for the duration of the war,
and six months after, pledged their allegiance to the King and Empire,
and were despatched to the concentration camp at the Exhibition
Grounds. On arrival there, the recruit was issued with uniform and
kit by the Quartermaster-Sergeant and turned over to the N. C. O. in
charge of training.

With the exception of the 16th Battery, all the units of the Brigade
assembled at the Exhibition Grounds (Toronto), were equipped with
the old "twelve-pounders" with which most of their training was done
in Canada. The 16th Battery went into training at London, and was
moved to the armoury at Guelph in January of 1915. This unit
was fortunate enough to receive a complete equipment of "eighteen-
pounders."

During the winter and early spring, the usual routine was followed
and the whole Brigade were gotten into shape along the lines laid down
by Field Artillery Training. The Toronto batteries had the advantage
of being able to indulge in some live shell practice, as they were able
to fire at targets in the lake. This training was of considerable advantage to both officers and men in their fire discipline and experience in
handling live shells.

In both Toronto and Guelph, the troops were comparatively comfortable, although the accommodation was far from luxurious. In Toronto, the Artillery were quartered in the old cow-sheds and horse-stables which stand at the eastern end of the grounds. These buildings were fitted with double tiers of bunks and heated by three large stoves which were quite adequate to keep the place warm. The 16th Battery, at Guelph, were somewhat more comfortably situated, being quartered in the Armoury, which, with its steam heating and hardwood floors, was really quite cozy, as training quarters went.

A high percentage of the N. C. O.'s and men had had previous experience in the permanent force, the British Territorials, or the Canadian Militia, and this served them well in their training. For many others, however, it was an entirely new experience.

Perhaps one of the most novel features of the new routine to which the men were subjected, was the importance attached to keeping their kits intact. Each man had to account for the small belongings which in everyday life seem of trivial significance.

On the days of kit inspection, great coats, fatigue breeches and shirts, extra boots, extra socks, underwear, grey flannel shirt, bandolier, spurs, water-bottle, haversack, mess-tin, hold-all, house-wife, and knife, fork and spoon were all laid out for inspection with the greatest care, and the man who was unfortunate enough to lose one of these comparatively inexpensive parts of his equipment had the feeling of impending disaster, as not only was he obliged to pay for the lost article, but he was likely to find himself doing extra fatigue at a time when he was most anxious to be out of barracks.

At Toronto, meals were served under the large Grand Stand which all yearly visitors to the Exhibition know so well, and if they were not elaborate, at least the food was wholesome and good. Each unit detailed a certain number of men for cook-house fatigue, whose duty it was to assist the cooks in preparing vegetables, cutting meat, and doing, generally, a great number of things which do not usually go hand in hand with the stirring pictures of a gunner in the Field Artillery. In striking contrast to his former life of ease, many a new recruit was forced to do a great many menial jobs which a few weeks before he had never dreamed of undertaking. However, it was all a part of the work; no one seriously complained and the spirit in which these tasks were performed made the men forget any feeling of resentment they might otherwise have had.

The strict hours which were imposed on the men in training came as something of a shock to the younger lads, at first. They had been accustomed to roaming about at night very much as they pleased, and, for them, "Lights Out" came all too early. Even if one had "Late Leave" the time seemed very short, and there was always a guard at the gate to cause trouble for the late-comer on his return to camp. Some, of course, mostly "old soldiers," were successful in eluding the guards; if not, there was the almost certain prospect of "Seven days C. B.," and a lot of extra work for the erring one.

With the coming of spring it was possible to undertake Battery Tactics on a larger scale, and presently, when the weather became fine, combined manoeuvres of all the units in camp were carried out. In March the Toronto Batteries were finally equipped with "eighteen-pounders," and these guns were used in all training from that time on.

Long route marches were arranged; in order to accustom the units to active service conditions, they would remain over night, bivouacing at some point well outside the city. There was a sufficient number of skilled riders and gunners with all the Batteries to bring the training along very rapidly, so that by May the whole Brigade had reached a surprisingly high state of efficiency.

Early in May all the units in training at the Toronto Exhibition Camp were assembled and inspected by the Duke of Connaught, who, as Governor General, was Commander-in-Chief of the forces in Canada. This inspection placed the final stamp of certainty on the rumors which had been circulating for some days that the Second Contingent were soon to sail for England. Just about this time a very impressive route march, including all the overseas troops then in training at Toronto, warned the citizens that there was to be another large movement of troops.

On the 14th of May, 1915, the Infantry Battalions departed, and the next day the Cycle Corps, Medical Units, and the Ammunition Column of the 4th Brigade, C.F.A. followed. On May 19th, the 13th and 14th Batteries entrained, their coaches making up part of the train bearing the men of the 16th Battery from Guelph. They proceeded to Montreal and the next morning embarked on the S.S. "Missanabie," which also carried the 29th Battalion of Vancouver. It was not until the 29th of May, that the 15th Battery and the Brigade Base Details left their old training quarters and sailed on the S.S. "Northland."

As the troop-trains pulled into sidings near the Montreal docks, curious crowds, relatives, and friends, looked on at the detrainment of our units. Stores and equipment were unloaded and packed into lorries for transport to the waiting ship. The Batteries were lined up in parade formation, numbered off, and swung away in fours, carrying full kit and loaded down with last parcels from home.

The transport officer ticked off the name of each man as he mounted the gangway, and he was directed to quarters aboard by the N. C. O. in charge. The officers occupied first class cabins, the N. C. O.'s second class, and the men anywhere room could be found to place them. Usually eight men were allotted to an 8' x 8' third class stateroom, and slept on double tiered bunks similar to those at the Toronto Exhibition Camp, or in hammocks swung between decks.

With as short a delay as possible, lines were cast off, and the ship steamed out of port on her way down the St. Lawrence. The crowds yelled themselves hoarse; the bands on shore played a great send-off; our boys, waving caps and handkerchiefs, said good-bye. Many of them were destined never to see their dear country again, although mercifully they did not realize it then.

Soon Montreal was left astern. Most of the men went down to their staterooms and arranged their blankets, kits and belongings. Others toured the ship, and spent several hours in the engine room, crew's quarters, and even down in the bunkers, where stokers, stripped to the waist, heaved coal in the huge boilers.

The St. Lawrence River Trip, by steamer, is the most beautiful one could desire. On either shore quaint French farm-houses, villages and small towns stand amid the most picturesque scenery imaginable. Many rivers, large and small, empty into this great waterway. French-Canadian boatmen, canoeists and yachtsmen are passed on the way down the river, and recall to mind the voyageurs and "courieurs-du-bois" of early days.

Between Montreal and Quebec the shoreline is dotted with towns and villages all of which are historically famous. Occasionally, too, one comes across huge paper mills indicating the rapid expansion of this industry in Canada. Quebec, in antiquity and historical romance, outshines all these other settlements in point of interest. The ancient citadel, built upon Cape Diamond and commanding the country for many miles around, is dwarfed in appearance by the huge structure known as the "Hotel Frontenac." The Upper Town and Lower Town are easily distinguished by the steep streets that separate them.

At Quebec, river pilots were taken aboard and again the ship proceeded on her way, skirting the Isle of Orleans and dodging among the many shoals and treacherous channels of the lower river. As we neared Rimouski a pilot boat took off our guides. The ship's whistle sounded a shrill "au revoir," and again we were on our way. During the night we crossed the Gulf of St. Lawrence and, negotiating the Straits of Belle Isle, we set out across the plunging waters of the Atlantic.

Up to this point there had been no sign of sickness aboard; but for the next week or more the men were in misery. Tripe, salted fish, bacon, a rare slice of beef, bread, ship's biscuits, cheese, prunes and coffee were the daily foods offered, but few of the men answered the dinner bell.

Every man on board, sick or well, was put through physical drill daily, also life-boat drill and fire fighting. He was obliged to keep his life belt beside him always. Submarine guards were stationed on duty day and night. Dining-room fatigue, sanitary and other duties kept several men busy; the others did as they pleased. Some played cards and dominoes, others gathered around the "salon" piano and sang old-time songs, while still others visited the crew's quarters and gambled all they owned on "Crown and Anchor." This game, new to Canadians, was banned by the army authorities on account of its unfairness. The odds of this ancient, if not time-honoured game, were heavily in favor of the banker; consequently he very soon became possessed of all the money which unsuspecting newcomers chose to lay on the board. When the voyage was over the "Crown and Anchor" set was usually sold by the crew to the highest bidder, and another secured for the next ship-load of Canadians.

To make the time pass pleasantly, games and boxing bouts for soldiers and crew were organized, cash prizes being awarded to the winners. In these contests, gunners of the 4th Brigade, C.F.A acquitted themselves creditably and won several classes of the bouts. On the "Corinthian," which carried the Brigade Ammunition Column, our boys did well also, while Cpl. Main of the 15th Battery, on board the "Northland," won every class he entered.

One afternoon, when nearing the danger zone, rendered tragic by the sinking, only a few weeks previous of the "Lusitania," without warning the ship's siren sounded a raucous blast. All ranks swarmed up companionways from every quarter of the ship to their appointed stations at the life-boats, waiting, with quickened pulse, for the expected torpedo from the Hun submarine. It was with a feeling of inexpressible relief that we discovered it was merely a test.

A rather amusing incident occured during this harrowing experience. A prisoner was in the guard room when the siren sounded. At the blast the guards started for their respective stations. The N. C. O. in charge called out, "Come back! You can't leave the prisoner!" "To h— with the prisoner!" yelled the guard, and as the N.C.O. turned to perform the duty himself, he discovered the prisoner had made good his escape in the shuffle.

When within two hundred miles of Lands End, we were met by two British naval destroyers—the "Lucifer" and the "Legion." They appeared, first, as a mere speck on the horizon. The thought of German submarines flashed through our minds and in a moment the bulwarks were thronged with anxious faces peering across the tossing waters, already the grave of one majestic liner and destined to be the grave of many another. Who will ever forget the tense emotion, first of forboding, then as the British Naval Ensign was identified, of relief, changing into pride that held us, as we watched those grey-hounds of the ocean tear through the foaming waters, circle about our ship and take post for duty: or the wild cheer that burst from our ship as they passed us in their course and with gracious courtesy accommodated themselves to our paltry speed. Semaphore signals advised us that these ships were to be our escort, and we were now assured of protection from hostile submarines for the remainder of the voyage.

Before long we entered the English Channel, and, as darkness fell, approached the entrance to Plymouth Sound. We were soon the target for search-lights from the shore and in due time we entered the sound and lay-to in its quiet waters till daybreak.

Inspection by Duke of Connaught, Exhibition Camp (Toronto), 1915.

CHAPTER II

England

As the first flush of dawn appeared over the Hoe, our ship weighed anchor and proceeded slowly up the sound to her berthing at Devonport. Soon the decks were swarming with soldiers. The men talked little, but their eyes sought to take in everything. Many of them had never seen England before; others were returning to the land of their birth. As we passed the Hoe, we thought of the gallant Admiral Drake and his captains whose game of bowls had been interrupted by the appearance of the Spanish Armada, in the days of Queen Elizabeth.

To those who had never seen England before, the day will never be forgotten. They had heard it was a wonderful country, but none could have imagined the beauty of the scenes that passed before them. The sparkling waters of the sound, the peaceful city of Plymouth and surrounding villages with their quaint houses and tall church spires, the grass-covered cliffs and green foliage of the shore line, and the distant fortifications and shipping at Devonport, formed a picture which no words can adequately describe.

Soon after, we docked, had our last meal on board, and prepared to disembark. Blankets were rolled, kits packed, and the units lined up on deck, in heavy marching order. After a final roll call, we landed and were assigned to a troop train.

This train was a new type to Canadians, and looked like a toy compared with our great steel passenger coaches and giant locomotives. The four-wheeled freight car, or goods-van, is no larger than an ordinary moving truck; the passenger carriages, as they are termed in the Old Country, are divided into private compartments, first, second and third class, according to the grade of comfort desired.

Soon all was in readiness, and our train pulled out of Devonport. Gathering speed gradually, we raced along at forty-five miles per hour, passing through the beautiful southern counties of England, with their quaint villages, green fields, clipped hedgerows and stately woodlands— all in the full bloom of an English May. Time after time we were greeted by cheering crowds and smiles of welcome.

One incident may be mentioned here, in passing. As we stopped at one of the numerous stations enroute, a number of men, contrary to orders, swarmed out on the right hand track. They were being ordered back into their carriages when the shriek of a whistle was heard, and a special train, said to be that bearing Lord Kitchener, passed, travelling at terrific speed. Lieut Daw, of the 14th Battery, was almost struck by the flying monster, and barely saved himself by throwing his body under the footboard of our own train.

We reached London finally, and hoped this might be our destination. Much to our disappointment the train passed on through, leaving us with a hazy recollection of house-tops, chimney-pots, bridges, turrets, pinnacles, a large river, and dreams of a new world to discover.

It was night when our train slowed to a stop and word was passed along that we had arrived at our camp at last. Clambering out into the gloom, laden down with kits and luggage, we marched off. Almost immediately we came to a halt amongst a group of hutments near by. After seemingly endless confusion and delay we were assigned our quarters and soon were in the land of dreams.

We had hardly been asleep, it seemed, when reveille sounded. We awoke to find our camp located in the middle of a racecourse near a little hamlet called Westenhanger. Wooden huts of a standard type had been erected, all the units of the Brigade having been provided for. Separate huts for the officers were located on the opposite side of the parade ground.

Close by was the old "Castle" and ancient stables said to have been used as a banquet hall by Henry VIII. The church across the road, the station and a cluster of houses formed the hamlet of Westenhanger. Further off was the Drum Inn and the Royal Oak, where good English beer could be obtained for tuppence a glass. A few miles down the road was Hythe, and nine miles away the city of Folkestone. The whole area round about was occupied by troops of the 2nd Canadian Contingent.

By degrees the Brigade, with the precision of veterans, broke into the routine of training, consisting of foot drill and standing gun drill. Imperial Officers and N. C. O's were attached to whip us into shape and they sure did work wonders.

We thought we were fully trained when we left Canada, but we soon found out we had indeed a lot to learn. Talcum powder shaves, and half-hearted preparation for parade no longer sufficed. Everything had to be done on the double.

But the more interesting part of our work was yet to come.

One Sunday morning we were told off for special duty. Our mounts had arrived. Thus far, most of our work was done on foot. The horses we had used at the Exhibition Camp had been left behind. Now we were to function as mounted troops in earest. Our first job was to train the horses, for we had fallen heirs to a bunch of cayuses from the wild and woolly west. It proved to be an exciting task, for many of these re-mounts were halter broken only and reverted to their broncho blood and breeding at the first attempt to ride them. No sooner would a rider mount than he would be sent flying through the air to come up "eating grass." We used numnah pads in place of saddles until we got to know the various characteristics of our new wards.

A school of rough-riders was organized and some of the wilder mounts were assigned to its members for breaking. No buckeroo of the days of the open range ever got more thrills than our rough-riders got out of some of these long-eared friends, and they were real horsemen at that. A few of the horses proved to be absolute outlaws, and refused to be tamed. These were sent back to the remount depot. The rest yielded to discipline. Lead, centre and wheel teams were selected and matched. These were assigned to various drivers in the respective sub-sections, until at last the batteries were ready for mounted drill.

N.C.O.'s and signallers were allotted their horses and given thorough instruction in riding and mounted cavalry drill. Some of the Battery Commander's party specialized as director-men and range-finders, and learned how to lay out "lines of fire" and estimate distances. Others were trained to reel off wire from the saddle and keep up communication by phone, flag, helio and lamp with the rest of the unit.

Then began a series of practice route marches and manoeuvres. Batteries went through all these evolutions, at the walk, at the trot, and at the canter. Positions were selected by the Battery Commanders, observation-posts and communication established, and the guns ordered forward to engage the "enemy." Advancing in line upon the battery markers and with "Halt! Action Front!" the gunners unhooked, swung about gun trails and the teams trotted to the wagon-lines in rear. Series after series was gone through in record time, the signallers sending down corrections in morse code or semaphore from the observation post. Advancing to other positions, in "battery column," new targets were taken on and every phase of open warfare thoroughly covered. After a few weeks of this continual grind the complete personnel of the unit had a far better understanding of each other's duties.

Rifle practice was next in order and each man had to qualify at Hythe Ranges before he was considered fit for overseas service.

Then one day word was received that the whole Division was to be reviewed by His Majesty the King and Field Marshal Earl Kitchener. Beachborough Park, close to camp, was chosen for the inspection. To prepare for the event, hours of labour were necessary. A clothing parade was called to get everyone properly outfitted. By aid of brasso, blanco, saddle soap, burnishing brush and grooming kit, not only the men, but the horses and harness, were soon shining bright.

Lined up in battery formation the staff passed by, our officers were called out, and the C.O. 4th Brigade, C.F.A. was complimented on the fine appearance of his unit. You cannot keep a good brigade down. We felt certain we would leave for France shortly.

In the meantime we had explored Kent—in so far as our daily passes and purses would permit—Hythe, Folkestone, Dover, Canterbury, and Ashford. Buses ran in every direction and trains several times a day, but a bicycle ride through country lanes and quaint old-fashioned villages seemed to delight many of the men.

Those who could claim Great Britain as their birth place had been granted one week's leave shortly after our arrival in May. Now, however, this was extended to Canadian boys as well. Most of these lads made straight for London, and got no further, though their passes may have been stamped for the Midlands, Yorkshire or even Inverness. There was much to see in London and, for a stranger, six days' leave was much too short a time.

As one alighted from the train at Victoria Station, passed through its gloomy portals, and found himself in the bustling thoroughfares of the metropolis, he was immediately "lost"—unless he had some pre-arranged plan laid out as to what he would do.

Usually, indeed, our lads taxied to the Maple Leaf Club, or some hotel, registered, left their luggage and set forth to explore.

London, the largest city in the world, had plenty to show us. We were advised by the "Bobbies," who seemed to know everything and everybody of consequence, that a ride on the top of a bus was the best way to really size up the layout of the city, so we climbed aboard. The girl conductor collected a few pennies from us and advised us to stay on for a complete circuit of the run. These buses were gaily decorated with advertisements of all descriptions, brands of beer and whiskey predominating. Each held about twenty-five persons below and the same number above, with a spiral stairway leading to the top deck. Owing to the many narrow, curving streets running in all directions, traffic critics found the bus the only solution of moving the huge London throngs. Electric trams were impossible on the main thoroughfares.

We passed on the bus along the Strand, past Charing Cross, the Embankment, Trafalgar Square, with Nelson's monument towering above us, the Admiralty Arch, the Mall, and by following devious routes to the celebrated Piccadilly Circus and into Leicester Square—with its theatres and music halls. We saw the Houses of Parliament, London Bridge, Waterloo Station, the Tower Bridge and Whitechapel—noisy, shabby, but bustling with energy. We visited the fish market in Billings-gate, saw many quaint and curious old shops, and ended up in a typical English "pub" for lunch.

A day or two of this and we were soon fagged out. We then visited the theatres and cinemas. Who will forget the Maid of the Mountains, Chu Chin Chow, To-Night's the Night, Ziz-Zag, Razzle-Dazzle, Going Up, and the many other wartime shows that had such an attraction for us?

Luncheon at Simpson's, the Clovelly, Lyon's Corner House, dinner and rooms at the Strand Palace, Regent Palace or the Savoy, where "Jimmie" mixed the drinks.

After visiting the Parliament Buildings, Tower of London, the British Museum, Madame Tussaud's, the National Art Gallery, the Horse Guards, Hyde Park, Regent's Park, and the Zoological Gardens, we felt that we had seen London. In reality we had only had a glimpse of it.

Those of Scotch descent invariably paid a visit to the land of their forefathers. The "Flying Scotchman" made the 390 miles from London to Edinburgh in nine hours, only two or three stops being made on the way. Here one saw Princes Street, dominated by the frowning ramparts of Edinburgh Castle looking as if it had been hewn out of the rugged

SHORNCLIFFE TRAINING AREA—England

crag on which it perched, with its garrison of Black Watch Highlanders; the historic Holyrood Palace, reminiscent of the stirring tales of Scottish Kings and Princes; Mary Queen of Scots, and Bonnie Prince Charlie; the crawling cable cars, the celebrated bridge over the Firth of Forth, the city's stately pride and poverty, and the camaraderie of the Scotch lassies, all bringing new interest and surprise. The bustling, smoky, factory city of Glasgow on the Clyde, Loch Lomond, Loch Katrine, Ben Nevis, the glens of the Highlands, or the town of Ayr— the home of Burns—the Doon, Auld Kirk, and the Brigs of Ayr, the Tam O'Shanter Inn, and, of course, a "skettle of suds"—and one for the chauffeur who steered the skinny nag and ramshackle hansom that met you on your arrival—all these bring back memories of a pleasant tour on our first English furlough.

Some of the men got back to camp on time. They were not promoted to the rank of Field Marshall for so doing. Those who didn't were not promoted either. Not much point in getting back on time if a chap had only known—except for the difference of a little pack drill.

On the 29th of August we entrained, bag, nose bag and baggage, man and beast, for North Wales for three days firing practice and manoeuvres. This was to be the crucial test of fitness for the front.

Trawsfynydd was the name of the camp. A new kind of country, with stone fences, few trees, sloping fields on portions of hills rising almost to mountains with rocky crags covered with gorse and purple heather. There was too much rain.

Telephone lines were reeled out, miles of them. Guns were brought into action, "lines of fire" given, shells were loaded into breeches—not dummies this time—orders were "barked" out, and for the first time Batteries saw the eighteen-pounder in action.

The Brigade passed this "Ordeal of Fire" successfully, and it is now a matter of history that it set a record for speed in training that labelled it ready for immediate despatch to France.

On returning to Westenhanger, preparations were pushed forward with new energy. Medical examinations, kit inspection and clothing parades followed each other in rapid succession and all preparations were made for the long-expected, and now imminent, move to France.

About this time several changes were made among the officers. Lt. J. Ivan McSloy, 14th Battery, became Adjutant, and proceeded to France to make arrangements for billets for the brigade. Maj. L. E. W. Irving, D.S.O., (15th), Capt. A. M. Brown (16th), Capt. G. L. Drew (13th), Capt. C. Sifton (14th), Lt. H. H. Lawson (13th), and Lt. D. C. Greey were posted to the Reserve Artillery Brigade, Shorncliffe and Capt. F. F. Arnoldi assumed command of the 15th Battery.

In the dusk of Sept. 13th, 1915, the Brigade mustered for parade— men, horses and vehicles fully accoutred for war. Everyone was in high spirits. As we marched in column of route through the darkness of the night from Westenhanger camp to Shorncliffe station, songs were sung and jokes and stories were told as if war existed only within the covers of a novel, instead of being enacted in grim reality.

We entrained in the glaring light of acetylene flares and journeyed through the night to Southampton. There we embarked on a transport called the "Mona Queen," and joined a convoy of other mounted units of the 2nd Canadian Division. We were the only Artillery Brigade ready for the front, the 5th, 6th and 7th still undergoing training at Otterpool.

It was a memorable voyage that, from Southampton to Le Havre. In murky darkness and driving rain we plowed across the channel through a heavy swell. We slept where we could, on hay between decks, close to our restless mounts. The crew, black lascars, most of them, moved stealthily about, making no sound. Rain beat through the open hatches and swilled about our improvised beds. We slept fitfully and wretchedly—rain-soaked and cold—dreaming of submarines.

We awoke to find ourselves in the port of Le Havre and our baptism of fire now but a few days off.

Meanwhile the 4th Infantry Brigade (18th, 19th, 20th and 21st Battalions); 5th Infantry Brigade (22nd, 24th, 25th and 26th Battalions); and 6th Infantry Brigade (27th, 28th, 29th and 31st Battalions) had marched to Folkestone and embarked for Boulogne.

CHAPTER III

Arrival in Flanders

O UR first glimpse of France was a blurred vision of fog.

Disembarking at daybreak in a drizzling rain, we were ordered to pile our goods and chattles on the wharves. All was confusion. The drivers were directed to remove the horses from their cramped quarters aboard ship, and the gunners to assist in unloading the vehicles. At last the work was done—the animals fed, a hurried breakfast served, and the units "hooked in" the teams ready to move off.

With a command to "Walk March!" the Brigade wended its way through the busy, winding streets of Le Havre. Smiles of welcome greeted this new addition to the Allied cause, and many of our men tried their scant vocabulary of French upon the natives — with humourous results.

After climbing a steep hill, the head of the column reached the outskirts of the city. Soon we came in view of a big rest camp, consisting of row after row of tents, huts and field kitchens. Here we halted, unhooked, had lunch and spent the rest of the day grooming, cleaning harness, and checking over equipment.

Later in the day, marching orders were received. Packing up again, the column headed for the railroad station. At the loading platforms, long trains awaited us. Guns and wagons were roped down securely on flat cars, and the horses ushered into freight cars marked "Chevaux 8, Hommes 40." These were ideal for the purpose. A five foot doorway in the middle of each car allowed sufficient room for four animals at each end, with their heads to the centre. The space in the doorway was occupied by the drivers of each team, their harness, saddles, equipment and feed.

Having completed their arduous task of loading, the remaining personnel of the units were allotted to other freight cars, by subsections, and the officers to passenger coaches. As darkness set in, the long trains pulled out of Le Havre. Passing through Abbeville, where we first saw Indian cavalry, and Etaples, we finally reached St. Omer, where detrainment took place. On our way north, Sgt. Gailer, of the 14th Battery, accidently fell through an open door and was killed—our first casualty of many.

We were gradually getting closer and closer to the firing line and what feelings were running through us! Did we not feel we were about "to be led to the slaughter"?

On Sunday morning, Sept. 17th., the Brigade passed through Caestre en route to the front. The whole column was laden down with the kit of war, signallers with huge range finders, directors, lamps and phones parked on their sturdy steeds, gunners clinging to the caissons while the wheels of their vehicles bumped over the rough cobbled roads, and the heavy "G.S." wagons rumbling along in rear. Miles back of the danger zone our C.O. warned us not to whistle, sing or talk for fear the Hun might hear us. We expected to run the gauntlet of "hell-fire and brimstone" that day. Instead of having our ranks decimated, however, the Batteries reached Dranoutre where wagon-lines were established.

A few nights later we relieved the 146th Brigade, R.F.A., in the line south of Kemmel, by sections, and as soon as the guns were in position a few trial rounds were fired on the Bosche. Our part in the war had begun!

The gun-pits in these positions, built by R.F.A. Batteries, consisted of three sand-bagged walls, with timbered roofs, topped with sand-bags and sods. Here our men first learned what sand bags were and how to fill and use them as a protection against shell fire. Inside the pits the ammunition was laid out neatly in racks, high-explosives in one section and shrapnel in another.

The gun platforms were timbered and the whole interior of the pits were so cozy and clean that part of the crew used them as living quarters—the remainder utilized dug-outs alongside the positions.

Some of the gunners, with considerable repairing and new work to be done, and only six round-nosed No. 9 shovels available, spied a working party of civilians on the road nearby. At night a foraging party "found" a few of these small Belgian shovels, and not only completed the necessary improvements on the gun pits, but filled innumerable sand-bags for an enlargement of their sleeping quarters.

Our gun-pits were only 2,000 yards back of the line, and the men had been warned to keep out of sight. There had been no mention, however, that washing should not be hung out. Some of the 15th Battery, who thought themselves cleaner than the rest, strung a clothes line from one pit to another, and put their shirts and underwear in the sun to dry. Our first baptism of fire began just about the time these garments, waving in the breeze, drew the attention of the enemy.

Lt. C. K. C. Martin, of the 15th, was transferred to the Base as Officer in charge of records, and a few days later, Lieuts. Ryan, of the 13th, Townsley, of the 14th, Swift, of the 15th, and Auld, of the 16th were temporarily transferred to the 1st Brigade, C.F.A., and the following switched from 1st Brigade, C.F.A. to the 4th Brigade, C.F.A.: Lieuts. Gillies to the 13th, Thackeray to the 14th, Goodwin to the 15th and Boville to the 16th. All of these officers were returned to their original units a few months later.

Behind, and towering above us, was Mont Kemmel. From our "O.P." on this hill one could see far over the enemy lines.

To understand this sector thoroughly, it is necessary to describe the topography of the Wytschaete-Messines Ridge. From Mont Kemmel it appeared to be a formidable, though inconsiderable slope, merging on the north into the low spurs and hillocks east of Ypres, but breaking down in the south to the Lys Valley, in a steeper gradient. Clearly distinguishable were the ruins of the White Chateau—running from Hollebeke to Wytschaete—the debris of Wytschaete Village, and the tooth of the ruined Church of Messines.

Viewed from the British trenches below—in the swampy flats of the Steenbeek—it seemed much more imposing. The whole ridge was seamed with white trenches and honeycombed with machine-gun emplacements, strong points and dug-outs. In fact, the Hun felt secure and deemed his position impregnable. Curving along the foot of the slope, the enemy front line followed every advantage of the ground. Behind his lines were Hill 60, the mound at St. Eloi, Bois Quarante, Petit Bois and Grand Bois, each formidable obstacles that must be surmounted before the heights could be stormed. From his skilfully sited trenches and redoubts, flanking fire could be brought to bear upon any ground won by our attacking troops.

Everywhere the Germans were on high ground and had observation of our positions. From the ridges in front of us, enemy observers watched and fired on every movement. They could see for miles across our territory. Clearly distinguishable were the trenches, the tracks that led to the forward lines, the villages behind them, and the roads through the villages.

German batteries were so cleverly situated that fire could be brought to bear on any part of the salient. On many occasions our infantrymen have been under fire from the north, east and south. The city of Ypres was a "death-trap." This sector had seen no active fighting since October, 1914, when Allenby's Cavalry, assisted by Indian and British Infantry, had, for two days, made a gallant stand at Messines before they were forced to the flats, below; and it was the longest section of trench line any Division was holding at the time.

For several weeks the Canadian troops made many raids on the enemy positions. "Saps" were built out into "No-Man's Land" and everything possible done to convince Fritz that preparations were being made for an attack in force. Our Batteries fired into the German wire and trench lines continually, which served to keep the Hun always on the alert.

On September 25th, an attack was launched by British Troops at Loos, and with the diversion provided by the Canadian Corps, great numbers of the enemy's reserve troops, intended for the battle zone, were kept on our front in case of an emergency.

Having become nicely acquainted with the Kemmel sector, we were destined to be moved. We were like pawns in the hands of chess players, to be moved hither and thither at their will.

On October 8th we dragged our outfits through Dranoutre and Locre to Dickebusch, where the Batteries relieved the 2nd West Lancashire, R.F.A., in various hedges back of Vierstraat, covering the M., N., O. and P. trenches. We were now attached to the Lahore Batteries for tactics, and covered the 4th Canadian Infantry Brigade. On the same date Capts. A. M. Brown, G. L. Drew, C. Sifton and Lt. D. C. Greey reported for duty, the latter going to the 4th Brigade Ammunition Column and the others to their original units. A few days later Capt. Mortimer, our Paymaster, garnered some francs and was able to pay us a little of our $1.10. The money went for "French frites" and eggs, or on the old "mud hook," another name for "Crown and Anchor."

It was about this time that many of the boys were becoming acquainted with "cooties"—those dear, little, lingering friends that retreated to the most inaccessible seams of one's under garments. Many of our good, kind people at home sent out little camphor balls tied up in scarlet flannel bags, and tins of insect powder to drive away these troublesome "centipedes." These exterminators were always used according to directions, but to our consternation and wonder, they were useless. The "cooties" thrived overnight. They snuggled comfortably in the seams of our shirts, breeches, socks and even in our putties. Some grew to be quite a size. The owners were very loath to part with such a prize and detained them for comparison and races with other breeds. Talk about gambling! Did you ever see our men bet on a louse race? Did you ever have a flea? Worse than a million cooties. I had always thought nothing could be in two places at once but I hadn't then met a flea. They bite you fore and aft, bow and stern at one and the same time. Lice always scurry for cover when a flea takes possession.

In ammunition and guns the Hun was far more fortunate than we, equipped as he was with thousands of siege guns, howitzers, naval, lighter artillery, trench mortars, and machine guns of all types and sizes. It was not until nearly six months later—in the Spring of 1916—that munition factories in Great Britain and Canada began to supply shells and guns to the front in any large quantities. The United States added its quota of shells to this supply.

Meanwhile, we conserved our shells, and when we did fire it was always on a target closely spotted. The greatest accuracy was expected of us and the 4th Brigade, C.F.A. soon demonstrated that it could be depended upon.

By constant observation, strong points, machine-gun emplacements, communication trenches, and dug-outs were located and plotted on our fighting maps. These targets were numbered and registered. When movement was reported the guns immediately opened fire. In this way, though we possessed but a limited amount of ammunition, the Hun was led to believe we were well stocked and capable of retaliation whenever necessary. The same policy which was followed all along the line, assisted by nightly raids in "No-Man's Land," greatly neutralized the preponderance in numbers of men, guns and munitions possessed by the enemy.

It was about this time that an old friend, Capt. E. J. Lovelace, original Commander of the Brigade Ammunition Column, arrived amongst us, and was posted to the 15th Battery.

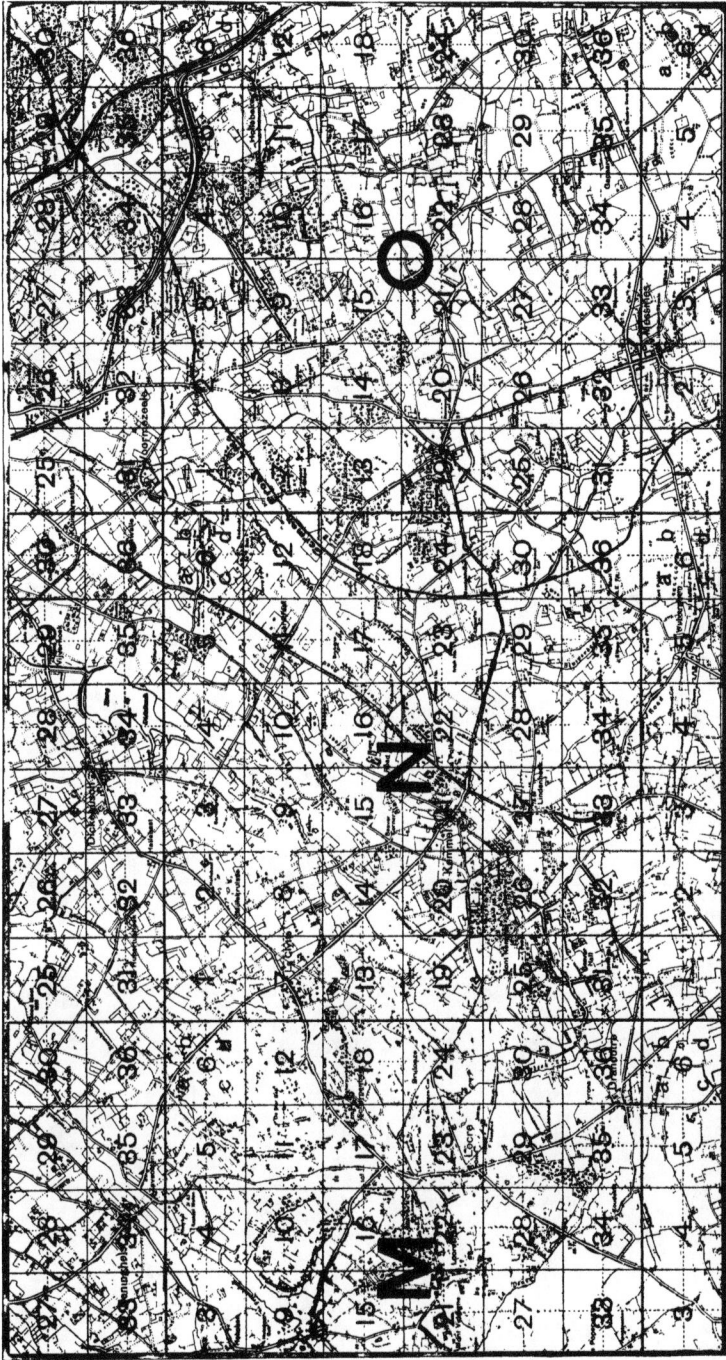

KEMMEL SECTOR, 1915-16

Scale: 1 inch—.63 miles; 1,000 yards to each square

To illustrate to what extent we had the enemy guessing, a Fritz plane was forced to land one afternoon just back of the 15th Battery. The two Heinies were held up by a lineman with a pair of pliers! Such incidents were outstanding because, as yet, we had seen little of real war.

All through the fall of 1915 we covered this sector. The whole country-side seemed flooded and desolate. It had rained incessantly and the mist and dampness made life miserable. The drivers, with their gun limbers and ration wagons, slithered down a road that had become a river bed, fountains of spray rising about their mules and wheels. Buses and supply lorries bucked in the mud beyond the pave, and dispatch-riders with motor cycles side-slipped wildly through boggy tracks.

At the wagon-lines, conditions were even worse. Only with the help of "duck-boards" could one walk about the morass in which huts were built and tents were pitched. Drivers tried in vain to groom their horses and floundered about in their gum boots cursing the mud which clogged bits and chains and bridles.

However, the gun positions were improved and greatly strengthened. Wire nettings, supported by poles and guy ropes, and well camouflaged, were spread over the gun-pits and dug-outs to screen the batteries from aerial observation. In the case of some of the units, elaborate details were followed in order to make their positions the envy of the rest.

The 15th Battery, under the direction of Sgt. Fairbrother, constructed an alternative position off the Kemmel-La Clytte Road. Eight bee-hive irons, bolted together and covered with several layers of sand-bags, sods and netting, formed the gun-pits. The men's quarters, telephone booth and officer's dug-outs were laid out between the pits and built of timbers, sheet iron and sand-bags—all connected together by means of a trench in the rear, and carefully concealed by camouflaged material. Even the gun platforms were of concrete.

This position was known as "Fairy's Dream." Many wondered how he managed it. It was easy when you knew how. Promising his gunners a generous rum ration, Fairy had only to say he wanted certain material, and it would be there in the morning.

On one occasion poles were necessary for the roofs of the dug-outs. The only place these could be obtained was in a field close to a farmhouse, a mile or more away. That night a Belgae wagon was "borrowed." Drawn by one of our teams the fatigue party met at the rendezvous with saws and axes to cut down the farmer's hop poles. An argument arose as to which was the best method to adopt in felling the poles without awakening the inmates of the farmhouse. The saw, although the most silent tool for this job, was voted down, and soon the axemen got busy. Chopping could be heard a mile off. Either Fairy's men were lucky or the farmer was dead to the world on "vin blanc."

The poles were carried across to the road and loaded on the wagon. A start was made for the gun position. Then a pin worked loose and off came a wheel. The wagon had to be unloaded, amid curses. The wheel was put on again, but the pin was nowhere to be found. Not to be beaten after having got thus far, Fairy and his gang determined they would watch the wheel and hold it on. After a long tiring run and numerous mishaps, the hop-poles finally arrived. The rum was served out, and the fatigue party broke up happy.

My mouth waters now as I think of that rum ration! Wasn't it a life-saver on those cold, wet nights?

"S. R. D." was served in gallon jars. No matter how tired the ration party might be, or how many sacks of coke, "bully" or biscuits were left by the way-side, the rum always arrived. To a working party floundering in the mud, slush and rain, it was a god-send. Promise it to them before they set out and these men would work like tigers; deny it to them, and more than half would parade sick in the morning.

Few men took their "tot" in the same fashion, or with the same expression. A "new" man looked at it shyly, hesitatingly raised the cup to his lips, sniffed it, made a desperate resolution, and gulped it down. The old soldiers, however, grasped the cup, looked to see if the issue was a full one, raised it swiftly and drained it without a moment's hesitation.

Do you remember those gas drills we had, and those funny bags we pulled over our heads and tucked inside our tunics? Our sergeants went away to the gas schools and came back and told us all about it. Did you ever sleep all night in a gas mask? No? Neither did anybody else. They's rather take the gas. Everybody had to carry that old gas bag, which later gave way to something more modern. But both types had windows in that you couldn't see through. The earlier ones were handy on cold nights. But I guess they served a useful purpose if only for the moral support they gave a man in having something to resist gas.

I mentioned something about mud. Do you remember your wagon-lines at Westoutre where the horses gradually sank in spirits as well as body? In the morning you might find a corner of a blanket sticking up out of the mud. It had gone down into the "goo."

The horses died from exposure. The incessant rain made quagmires out of the horse lines. The stable picquet was kept busy at night keeping the horses away from the fodder. When he would shout "Halt! Who goes there?" a reply would sometimes come, "Submarine No. 75!" That cursed mud—nothing could equal it except, perhaps, Passchendaele. To one who was through both, it was probably worse at the latter place.

CHAPTER IV

Trench Warfare

CHRISTMAS arrived, but there was no Santa Claus or reindeers visiting the troops. Some large parcels arrived from home. For the majority of us, however, the day passed as any other. And when Christmas came around do you remember how certain N. C. O.'s and men managed to eat fowl, or pork, when the other poor beggars ate bully or "mulligan"? If one was not a noisless chicken scrounger there was one other way of procuring that fowl which proved very effective. You had only to lie in wait behind the barn until you saw your quarry pass unconsciously by, and then with an accurate pitch, heave a tin of jam or rock at the poor chookie's head. It was a more difficult matter to round up a "petit cochon," but if you slept in a pig stye, as some did, and got to understand the weakness of these shiny scavengers, you might stand an equal chance of spearing some pork.

Taking a fellow forager with you, plenty of old bread, and a sack, this feat was easily accomplished. While the old sow was fed by one scrounger and her attention thus diverted, the other made up with the "young 'uns," finally selecting the one he desired. The commotion of squeals was paralyzing, but we generally saw to it that our line of escape was open.

Theft and looting is punishable in the British Army with a death sentence. This fact, and the comparatively few festival occasions which more or less demanded some recognition by change of food, kept the men on "issue diet." Some farmers expected to lose a portion of their stock, and sighed with relief when a unit departed, leaving his property as they found it. Others were hard-crusted, calculating and miserly. This type demanded an inspection of his estate by the departing and relieving officers and an order on His Majesty's Government for any missing articles.

On December 26th Lieut. J. Ivan McSloy became Captain and immediately gave the boys a thrill by announcing that furlough would start shortly. On January 11th, leave began with one officer and five other ranks per week, as a start. It was soon increased to four times this quota.

Although strict orders had been given by the Brigade Commander that there was to be no firing except on "S.O.S.," the 15th Battery, with an officer at the trigger of each gun, celebrated the midnight hour of New Year's Eve with a Battery "Salvo" in perfect unison. Shell cases are still in the possession of those concerned. To this day, the 14th Battery is blamed for their disobedience to orders.

On the last day of January, 1916, a Trench Mortar Group for the 2nd Canadian Division was organized, consisting of three medium batteries, three light and one heavy. The personnel for the light batteries was supplied by the Infantry and for the medium and heavy, the 4th Brigade, C.F.A. and Divisional Ammunition Column. The C. O. for the group and the four sub-officers were supplied by our Brigade. Lt. E. R. Leather was made Act. Capt. The following men from Brigade Headquarters received commissions in the field: Corp W. S. Tuck, Gnr. A. M. Thurston, Cpl. C. M. G. Purchas and Gnr. A. G. Bland.

About this time, the 5th, 6th and 7th Brigades, C.F.A., arrived from England and with the 4th Brigade, C.F.A. formed the 2nd Canadian Divisional Artillery, under Brig.-Gen. Morrison. On the nights of the 3rd and 4th, and 4th and 5th of February, 1916, our Brigade was relieved by the 5th Brigade, C.F.A., and we then took over positions from the 1st Brigade, C.F.A. near "Plug Street." The Lahore Batteries, to whom we had been attached, were then assigned to the newly formed 3rd Canadian Division.

We struggled on through the cold damp days of a Flemish winter in this new sector. Close by was Hill 63, and in front if us the battle scarred village of Messines. Not much firing was done here, and all units enjoyed their "rest." Armentiers, a town of considerable size, though now greatly depleted of its population, was only a few kilometres away. Its renowned estaminets and pretty mademoiselles were a great attraction.

It is humourous, now, to think how we used to visit our favourite haunts to get a peep at Germaine or Julie, although we always claimed we came for "pommes de terre frites" or "des oeufs." Our officers generally had their objectives well planned out too, and a "very" cushy billet arranged for wherever we were located near enough to a village.

On February 15th, under the critical eyes of the G.O.C., R.A. Corps and 2nd Division, a fifteen minute shoot was carriet out on Avenue Farm by all batteries of the Brigade. "O. P." officers were instructed to render their reports to Brigade Headquarters regarding accuracy and noting proportion of rounds that missed the target. Needless to say our shooting was very good on this occasion and the 4th Brigade, C.F.A. was highly complimented on its gunnery by the inspecting General Officers.

About this time a minor action took place at the "Bluff," a small mound overlooking the enemy lines across the Ypres-Comines Canal. This was considered a position of vital importance to both sides, and had been held for a long time by the 3rd British Division. Upon their relief by other British troops, a sudden German attack, after the explosion of a mine, carried the "Bluff." The old "Iron Division" were immediately ordered back to recapture the lost ground from the enemy.

Two weeks later, following a terrific bombardment of the German lines, and assisted by thick fog, British troops of the 3rd British Division advanced and carried their objective. Repeated counter-attacks were made by the enemy, but the "Bluff" was held and our line consolidated.

Preparatory to this action, and, with a view to deceive the Hun as to the real point of attack, the 4th Brigade, C.F.A. were ordered to bombard the enemy lines for two hours. The 13th Battery fired smoke shells, the 14th and 16th engaged in wire cutting, and the 15th shelled hostile batteries, communications, and strong points. During the early morning of March 2nd, the same trench lines were covered and the barrage lifted to the support lines and communication trenches, while the 14th and 16th Batteries enfiladed that section of the enemy front line trench which had been the scene of the wire cutting operation the previous day.

When this little demonstration was over, a highly congratulatory letter was received by Lt.-Col. W. J. Brown from the C.R.A., 3rd British Division, thanking him for the great assistance rendered his troops by this diversion.

A week later, our Batteries were relieved in sections by the 1st Brigade, C.F.A., and marched through Dranoutre and Locre to their old stamping grounds around La Clytte. The gun-positions occupied were as follows:—

Brigade H.Q.—N 7c 6/6	13th Battery—N 15a 9/9
14th Battery —N 3d 6/1	15th Battery—N 4c 1/4
16th Battery—N 4a 5/5	

In this relief all trench maps, aerial photographs, defence schemes, and existing telephone lines were turned over to the incoming batteries.

On March 14th, the 4th Brigade, C.F.A., was known as the "Left Group," 2nd C.D.A., and consisted of the 14th, 15th, 16th, 17th and 23rd Batteries, C.F.A. and the 73rd Battery, R.F.A. The 13th Battery was attached to the 5th Brigade, C.F.A., covering the M to P4 trenches.

Operation Orders issued under this date stated: "All 18-pounder Batteries must be ready at all times to open fire on their own zone within 30 seconds from time call is received, and, after registering their own zone carefully, must fire on all points of value withing the range of their guns." This entailed a considerable amount of extra strain on the observation officers, but the grinding experience they endured here taught them much which serve them well in future operations.

Towards the end of the month more officer reinforcements arrived— Lt. R. H. Massey was posted to the 13th, Lt. E. D. Huycke to the 15th and Lt. N. E. Wallace to the 16th. Changes were also made in Brigade signals—Lt. A. L. Zimmerman being appointed Signalling Officer for the unit.

The weather had been raw and cold for several weeks. Men stamped their feet and blew on their fingers to keep warm. At the guns, the positions were greatly improved and made really comfortable. The horses, which had for the last few months floundered in mud and water, were now under cover and in good standings.

With Spring at hand and troops and munitions pouring into France and Flanders, the future looked bright indeed for the Allies. All along the British front reserve divisions and heavies were concentrated. It appeared as if the Hun was now through, as far as initiative was concerned. The R.F.C., increased by many squadrons, patrolled the enemy lines and back country, daily. Spotting large movements of troops, gun positions, ammunition dumps and camps, they bombed the enemy unmercifully, and for the first time since the commencement of the war neutralized German command of the air.

Time after time our airmen directed shell-fire for the guns, and a special unit was detailed to photograph the enemy trench lines. From the photographs secured, the trench maps were brought up to date, and became a great help to the Artillery.

Observation posts were established and manned day and night. For this duty, each Battery detailed an officer (F.O.O.), two signallers and two linemen. Every twenty-four hours the party were relieved.

In this manner the H.Q. staff of the Battery got to know its section of the front perfectly. 4th Brigade, C.F.A. signallers, under Sgt. F. C. Mayberry, maintained communication with the Batteries, Infantry Brigade H.Q. and Divisional H.Q. and were responsible for these telephone lines. The Batteries, on the other hand, had lateral lines, communicating with each unit, as well as their communications with "O.P." to cover.

The duties of an artillery signaller were highly responsible and dangerous. He was required to send and receive morse code at twelve words per minute by buzzer, flag and lamp, semaphore at the same rate and to thoroughly understand telephones, communication systems, director and range finder. He must also be an expert horseman.

Many of our men had a good understanding of observation duties, and on many occasions were permitted to make corrections for the guns, work out tables, and estimate the "error of the day" from the "meteor."

The front covered by the 4th Brigade, C.F.A., about this time, was from the La Clytte-Vierstraat road to the St. Eloi Craters. Going forward from the guns, one passed through Ridgewood, where a Battalion lay in reserve, up a shell-torn road past Le Brasserie, finally reaching the "P. & O." communication trench, which, wending in and out in haphazard fashion toward the front line, passed through Bois Carré, a strong point in our support-line. On the right was Carré Farm, surrounded with high, uncut wheat and rank grass reaching almost to the shoulder. A good view of the enemy's lines, from Bois Quarante to Grand Bois, could be obtained from this old structure, now merely a skeleton, all battered and torn by shell-fire and machine-gun bullets. One could crawl up on the reverse side of the roof or in the loft, and unless spotted by the Hun, establish an "O.P." and observe fire for the guns.

On the other side of the communication trench—just to the left of Bois Carré, and running parallel with the front—was a long, thick hedge, on fairly high ground. Dug in here, amongst the thick foliage of the hedge, was a fine, elaborately constructed "O.P." and sleeping quarters built of elephant-iron and sand-bags, and so well camouflaged that no one was aware of its existence unless it was pointed out to him. A boxlike slit, two inches high by twelve inches wide at the front and increasing in width to twenty-four inches at the rear, was built into the parapet. A long seat, with desk-like table and fighting-map before him, gave the officer on duty every opportunity of spotting and engaging enemy targets. By swinging the pivoted telescope from side to side, in the slit, a long section of the Hun front was under direct observation. The signallers' booth was below, where a little table and bench gave them plenty of comfort. Double-tiered bunks, enough to accommodate the whole party, completed the establishment of this ideal "O. P."

On arrival, usually after dark, the "F. O. O." and his party relieved those on duty and took over responsibility of observation and maintenance of communication on the sector. For night work, the officer generally arranged shifts among his men, taking the early morning hours himself. When dawn breaks the whole trench garrison "stand-to." Throughout the night our Infantry were on the alert, and never ceased their labours of repairing barbed-wire entanglements, sand-bagged parapets, improving the trenches and dug-outs, and patrolling "No-Man's Land."

As the first light of a new day appeared, we were constantly on the watch for enemy working parties in his trench lines. Nearly every morning some interesting target presented itself. There would come a sharp command, over the 'phone, from the observing officer—"Stand to!"—The gun-crews would spring from their quarters, ready for action. Estimating a switch angle and range from zero-line on the fighting-map, the orders would be quickly transmitted by the signallers to the officer in charge at the Battery. A section would open fire, corrections would be made, and soon the whole Battery joined in the chorus. Presently, when the "F.O.O." considered the target would be sufficiently taken care of, at the order of "Cease firing!" the gunners would lay back on their "S.O.S." lines. Where targets were already registered and numbered it was only a few seconds before the guns switched from their "S.O.S. lines" and opened fire.

Some of our Battery Commanders often checked us up for speed. By pre-arranged plan, if the order "Denmark 1!" was called down to any of the batteries, it was to present a hurried call for one round gun-fire, by the gun designated. At any hour of the day or night this order was likely to be called, and woe to the gun-crew that did not respond.

During the rainy season, doing observation duty was an unpleasant performance, especially if it meant a trip to the front line. The shell-torn fields and roads were bad enough, but the communication trenches were filled with oozy mud and water, in spite of the tireless efforts of the Pioneers and Infantry to keep them drained and clear for the passage of troops. Duck-mats were laid upon stumps or logs, but even these could not be kept in position, due to the inevitable cave-in from heavy shells. Men waded to the firing-line deep in muck, grasping slimy sand-bags to save a headlong plunge into icy water.

The trenches were alive with a multitude of swimming frogs and beetles, and vermin. None but those who actually went through it can begin to understand what our courageous infantryman was up against.

Rats were the worst plague of all. There were thousands of these lean, hungry devils—the dug-outs swarmed with them. They got on your nerves as much as the shell-fire, frisking over the bodies of the living and the dead. When the Canadians first encountered the rats they determined to exterminate them. For months an exciting rat hunt went on. With revolver, rifle, and bayonet the men shot and speared them, throwing the bodies over the trench; but no matter how many were done away with others took their place, and the trench garrison finally had to acknowledge they were beaten—and were forced to put up with them.

Prior to a trench-raid or demonstration, the Artillery Observation Officer was called upon to effect the destruction of barbed-wire entanglements of the enemy. This was a dangerous and exciting pastime. He invariably observed from the front line by periscope, and often by the naked eye—peering over the parapet to watch the effect of the shell-burst, as soon as he heard it whistle overhead.

Later on, at the Somme, this method caused us heavy casualties. If not sniped by machine-gun fire or rifle bullet, the "F.O.O." and signallers were spotted and ranged upon by shell-fire. In some cases "No-Man's Land" was only fifty yards wide, and the least movement in the trenches was immediately noticed.

One great result may be traced to the presence of artillerymen in the front line. This was the whole-hearted respect and thanks of the infantry for the close co-operation given. The battalion or company commander was generally alongside our "F.O.O." when such a shoot was put on, and the liaison thus formed between these two arms of the service did much to create the Canadian Corps spirit—"All for one, and one for all."

Officers, 4th Brigade, C.F.A., Exhibition Camp, Toronto, May, 1915.

CHAPTER V

St. Eloi

A BOUT this time the newly organized 3rd Canadian Division came into the line. Its 7th Infantry Brigade consisted of the Princess Pats, the R.C.R.'s, the 42nd Bn. (R. H. of C.), and the 49th Bn. (Edmonton Regt.); the 8th Brigade 1st C.M.R., 2nd C.M.R., 4th C.M.R., and the 5th C.M.R.; and the 9th Brigade—the 43rd Bn. (Cameron High. of C.), the 52nd Bn. (New Ont. Regt.), the 58th Bn. (Ont. Regt.), and the 60th Bn. (Victoria Rifles of C.). As the Divisional Artillery were still undergoing training in England, the Lahore Batteries, hitherto attached to our 2nd Division, now came under command of the C.R.A., 3rd Canadian Division.

Before handing over its section to the Canadians the V British Corps decided to make one more attempt to better the line. The 2nd Canadian Division was placed in reserve, and the Canadian Batteries allotted zones for the operation.

On April 3rd, amid a tremendous bombardment, six huge mines were blown under the German lines at St. Eloi. The shock was so terrific that window panes trembled and buildings shook as far back as Reninghelst and Poperinghe. When the British Infantry rushed the positions they found huge yawning craters where once had been formidable trenches and redoubts, packed with the mangled bodies of dead and dying foes. Pushing on, a line was established in front of the craters and the troops burrowed out fire-trenches amongst the shell holes and debris of an old support trench.

Next day, into this battered region of mud and slime, the 2nd Canadian Division advanced to relieve the weary Imperial troops. Our 6th Infantry Brigade took over the front lines while the 4th and 5th Infantry Brigades were held in support.

For twelve days our gun crews were constantly answering "S.O.S." calls, day and night. Thousands of shells were poured into this horrible quagmire. Many did not explode, but buried themselves deep in the mud. It was a crucial test for the Hun, but worse for our poor Infantry. A day and a night in the craters was more than the strongest man could stand.

The weather became worse, aeroplane co-operation was impossible, and the position of our forward zone was not at all clear even to the Battalion and Brigade Commanders. Trenches were hip deep in water, parapets had oozed away, and communication trenches were obliterated. To gain access to the craters one had a nerve-racking trip overland through continuous shell and machine-gun fire. Finally the British wounded, who had lain helpless in the open ditches and shell holes, were taken care of. Our losses, too, were appalling, but the men determined to hold on. Large working parties laboured throughout the night bringing up "duck mats," deepening and draining the communication trenches and revetting them. Thousands of gravel-filled sand-bags were brought up from the rear to build parapets that would not ooze away, and heavy pumps cleared out a large amount of water from the trenches. Throughout, we were favored by a thick mist and constant drizzle, which concealed our work from enemy observers. Belts of wire were quietly placed in "No-Man's Land," and it seemed we had won out in this race against time and the enemy.

On the morning of April 6th, however, the real attack came. Following an intense bombardment of our left position the enemy advanced en masse, overrunning our front line trench and finally penetrating into the main craters whose garrisons were overpowered and captured. The Bosches immediately consolidated the ground regained and, in spite of our counter-attacks, held on.

Throughout the days that followed the position was beyond description. The incessant rain had now made the ground impassable —but the 4th Canadian Infantry Brigade was ordered to advance and bomb the Germans out of the craters.

In spite of heavy losses, elements of this Brigade drove wedges in the German front, and all but succeeded in carrying their objectives. Craters 6 and 7 were occupied and held, but the larger craters were now garrisoned by strong forces of the enemy and heavily manned by machine-guns.

To carry on the attack in face of this obstinate resistance would have been suicidal. The 4th Canadian Infantry Brigade was relieved on the 12th by the 5th Canadian Infantry Brigade and reconstruction of the position was begun in earnest. Craters 6 and 7 and other forward posts were linked up with the old front line by new communication trenches, and consolidated. Our position, however, was under constant observation and steady shell fire and daily relief of the forward garrison was necessary.

On the 18th, the 6th Canadian Infantry Brigade again went into the line, after a short "rest" at Voormezeele, relieving the 5th Canadian Infantry Brigade. April 19th witnessed another strong German attack in the evening, following a brief but intense bombardment. The craters that had been won back were again carried by the enemy, and the garrison suffered bitter casualties. Next day we countered-attacked to recapture the lost positions, but when night came the main craters remained in the hands of the Germans.

St. Eloi was a hard struggle for the Infantry. The enemy fought better than ever. The shells, mud, and disfiguration of the ground proved a greater handicap than our men could overcome.

The 4th Brigade, C.F.A. had taken a very active part in this engagement, and having been in the line continuously since Sept 19th, 1915, all of its units, except the 16th Battery, were, on April 8th, withdrawn to the rest area near Godewaersvelde. Three days later they were again back at Dickebusch Lake, having relieved the 23rd Brigade, R.F.A., 3rd British Division. A new group was organized consisting of the 14th, 15th, 16th and 17th Batteries, C.F.A., and 7th Regiment Belgian Artillery—covering the line from Piccadilly Farm to St. Eloi craters. A very agressive policy was followed in dealing with the Hun, and the craters, support lines, redoubts and C. T.'s were "strafed" periodically day and night.

But in remembering these scenes of mud and desolation, we must not forget Bailleul and Poperinghe, which afforded us our earliest acquaintances with French civilization.

About half the time a man was out on rest, and invariably his brief holiday was enhanced by the lure of "Pop," with its ancient crooked streets and grey buildings which seemed to hang over the cobbled pavements. Was there anything in "Pop" that was not for sale?—Lace, wines—white and red—souvenirs de la guerre, even sabots! "Skindles" was reserved for officers, but the men had estaminets.

Who will ever forget these places of merriment of France and Flanders with their low ceiling and ˈscrubbed, tiled floors? Some boasted pianos but all had tables supporting the game of "Crown and Anchor." These places were usually thick with the smoke of Three Witches, Trumpeters and Red Hussars, or issue tobacco. At the back, dark speckled mirrors hung above side-boards lined with bottles. Over all presided a plump matron, assisted by two fair "mam'zelles" who hustled huge jugs of dark, flat beer about the joyous tables.

Here and there was one luckier than the rest of us, who, having received a postal note from home, treated all his friends. Madame, after much gesturing argument, had to accept the Canadian money, then a bottle of "vin blanc," or even a bottle of champagne blossomed forth.

This was followed by "pommes de terre" and "oeufs," and then, as evening wore on, the loud commands of the Military Police sounded at the door, ordering us to depart.

Fond farewells to Madame and her deputies were in order. Perhaps some of us lingered a while, until comrades had departed, to receive special farewells or, shall we say, lessons in French, at the table under the quiet lamp—lessons, which, in the morning, we could not remember.

Then arm in arm, groping our way homeward down the ancient roads of Flanders, the end men of the line feeling for—and often finding —the ditches.

And at the end of the journey an irate Sergeant-Major awaiting us, even though we were gunners, and promising us head chains to burnish in the morning.

On April 26th, the original Battery Commander of the 16th, Maj. W. Simpson, was evacuated sick, and Capt. G. L. Drew assumed command of his unit. A week later, the 14th Battery was ordered to move two guns forward to a position the gunners had previously prepared, and from which the enemy line was visible. Sergeants Briggs and Purdon were in charge of these two gun-crews. "Daddy" Briggs took a bath the night before so that after the slaughter next day, according to his own words, his body would be found clean. This position proved to be untenable. From an "O. P.," in a tree by the guns, Lieut. Harris attempted to register. The Hun immediately retaliated and damaged one of the guns. The next day the enemy allowed the section to register and then retaliated. One gun was completely destroyed, together with the ammunition. That night, May 5th, the section withdrew after a costly experiment, and a few days later the Battery occupied a position at Scottish Wood. Shortly after this episode, Maj. G. E. Vansittart was badly wounded and expired the same day. Capt. G. L. Drew was then recalled and posted to his old Battery, the 13th.

It was rumoured there was soon to be a big re-organization in the Corps Artillery. We hated rumours, especially when, if accurate, they might mean some change in the Brigade. We refused to believe we would be broken up after having served together for so long. However, the "powers that be" decided we could do without a Brigade Ammunition Column, and on the 17th its personnel and horses were transferred to the Divisional Ammunition Column, and Lieuts. Atkin, Greey and Wright, with a number of N.C.O.'s and men, were allotted to the Batteries.

On the 21st. Maj. W. H. Merritt, original commander of the 14th Battery, relinquished his command and was transferred to the C.A.M.C. We were sorry to see him go, for he was loved and respected not only by his own unit, but by the entire Brigade. Capt. S. M. Waldron, formerly Adjutant, 5th Brigade, C.F.A., took over his command.

The following day, a finishing punch was handed the good old 4th Brigade. The 15th and 16th Batteries, who had mobilized with the 13th and 14th, way back in November, 1914, were now to be separated from the unit and transferred to the newly re-organized 6th Brigade, C.F.A. (Brig. Gen. W. M. B. King). Although now segregated the Batteries often re-united, if not in battle, at the estaminets—where toasts were drunk to the "Boys of the Old Brigade!"

Part II

(May 21st, 1916 - March 17th, 1917)

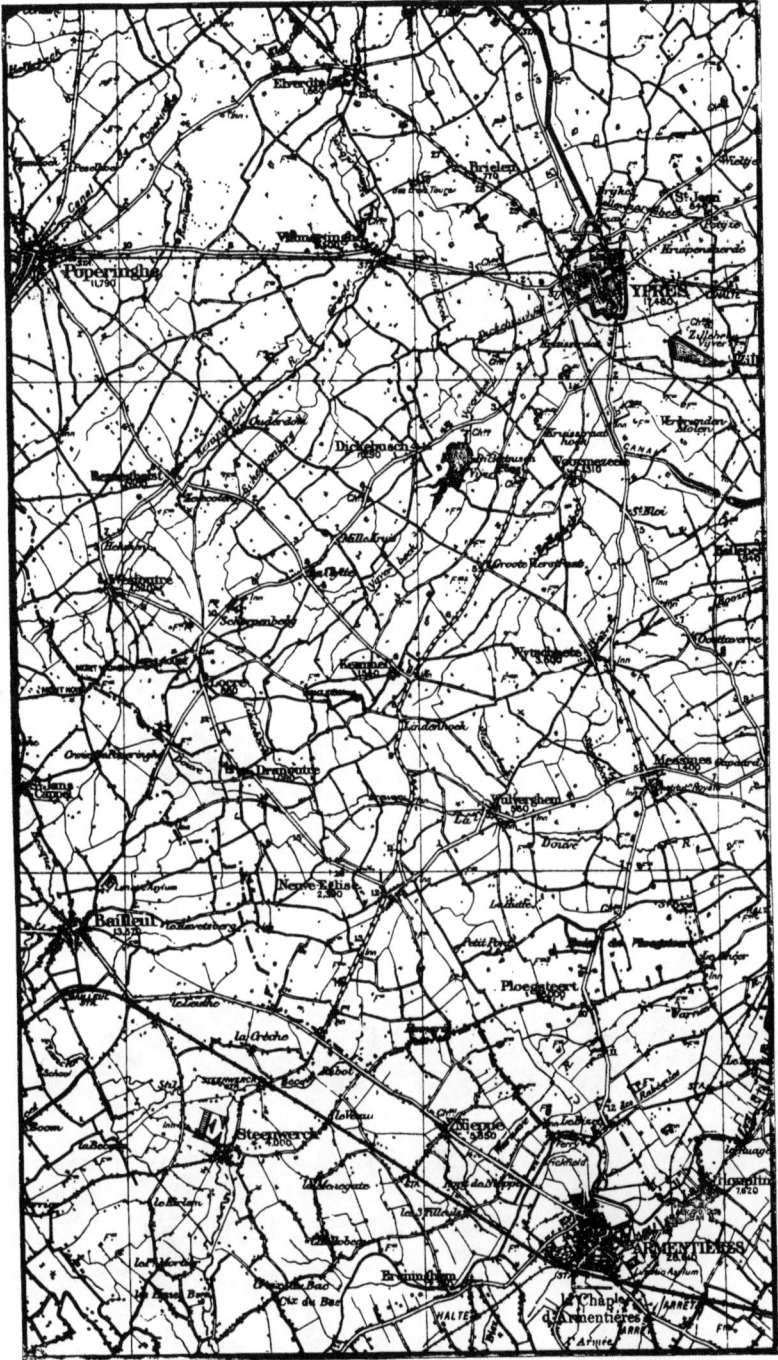

YPRES-ARMENTIERS SECTOR—1915-16

Scale: 1 inch—2.32 miles

CHAPTER I

𝔖anctuary 𝔚ood and 𝔥ooge

FROM May 22nd, 1916, till March 17th, 1917, the 4th Brigade, C.F.A. consisted of the following units:

H.Q. 4th Brigade, C.F.A.—Lt.-Col. W. J. Brown, Lt.-Col. C. H. L. Sharman.

13th Battery—Maj. G. L. Drew.

14th Battery—Maj. S. M. Waldron.

19th Battery—Lt.-Col. J. A. Carruthers, Maj. A. F. Culver.

Following the transfer of the 15th and 16th Batteries to the 6th Brigade, C.F.A., a considerable number of changes were made in the personnel of the officers. Capt. G. L. Drew became acting Major (13th Battery); Capt. S. M. Waldron, formerly Adjutant (7th Brigade, C.F.A.), was transferred and appointed acting O.C. (14th Battery); Lieuts. R. O. G. Bennett and T. H. Atkinson were attached to the Brigade as supernumerary officers and posted to 19th and 13th respectively; Lieut. W. E. Harris (14th) appointed Instructor at Divisional Gas Defence School; Lieut. V. H. de Butts Powell (13th) promoted to Captain; Lieut. O. C. Greey (13th) transferred to 7th Brigade, C.F.A.; Lt. E. B. McLatchey, taken on strength and posted to 13th Battery. For gallantry in the field, May 1st, Lieut. J. C. Auld (16th Battery) was decorated with the Military Cross. This same officer was further honored during 1917 and 1918 with bars to the Military Cross.

After the engagements of St. Eloi, conditions became normal, although our guns were constantly active, sniping at moving targets and retaliating on the enemy lines to silence trench-mortars and whizz-bang batteries which bothered our Infantry. During the sunny month of May the muddy fields dried up. Large working parties began reconstructing our front and support line, while others sited and dug reserve trenches a few miles behind in case the Hun forced his way through the battle positions. Even as far back as our wagon-lines, behind La Clytte, Hallebast Corner, and Dickebusch—strong positions were selected and Corps Troops assigned to their construction.

About this time one of our Battery Commanders had gone to the "O-Pip" near Bus House in the early hours of the morning. Proceeding cautiously, he was very much surprised to hear the roar of a shell and an explosion one hundred yards behind him. This was followed in quick succession by four other bursts, each a little closer. Prudently taking to his heels, he jumped into a nearby trench for shelter. On his return to the Battery he made inquiries as to the cause of this shelling from the rear, but could illicit nothing from his officers regarding the occurrence.

It was not until some time later that the truth came out. It appeared that his "F.O.O.", who was rather new to the game, had observed a German working party behind the enemy lines, had estimated the gun-range and location as well as he could determine it, and reported same back to the officer in charge at the Battery, requesting that the guns open fire immediately.

The first shell was fired, but the "F.O.O." failed to notice the burst, and four times in succession he gave orders to the guns to add one hundred yards. Not having observed any of the shells he concluded that he had not properly "placed" the enemy working party, and, in disgust, abandoned his target. On his return from the "O-Pip", the "F.O.O." checked back the range with the officer in charge of the guns, and found he had miscalculated the range and ordered the guns to fire one thousand yards short.

About the beginning of April, our 3rd Division had taken over the Hill 60—Hooge sector of the Ypres Salient, and the Lahore Batteries were attached until the arrival of the Canadian Divisional Artillery, which was still undergoing training in England. Great activity was noted on this front, and by the constant aerial activity of the enemy and the daily registering and shelling of our forward positions, it looked as though an attack might be expected. Every effort was made to strengthen the trench lines, and the heavies and howitzers ranged on enemy batteries daily. For weeks nothing happened, and it appeared as if the 3rd Canadian Division was undergoing the usual "strafe" handed out to a newly arrived division in the "Salient." The fine weather continued.

Then on June 2nd, at 8.30 a.m., without warning, the Hun began a terrific bombardment of the front. The crash of enemy guns was like a deafening thunder-stroke. The shells came from east, north and south.

Gen. Mercer, General Officer Commanding the 3rd Canadian Division, with Brig.-Gen. Victor Williams of the 8th Infantry Brigade, had gone up to inspect the trenches early in the morning. Occupying the front line, north to south, were the R.C.R.'s, Princess Pats, 1st C.M.R., 4th C.M.R., and the 2nd Brigade of the 1st Canadian Division, with strong supports in the reserve lines and fortified posts behind.

Under the heavy deluge of German gun-fire, the trenches seemed to melt away. Great craters opened gaps in the wire, and machine-gun emplacements and strong points were flattened out. The concentration of fire on the communication trenches and support lines was so thorough and deadly that retreat of forward units was cut off, as was also help from the rear.

In spite of the uproar and destruction, the gallant men of the 3rd Canadian Division held on.

The bombardment continued for five hours without cessation. During this time our front line ceased to exist. The survivors, in battered trenches and shell-holes, worked their rifles and machine-guns like madmen.

Shortly after 1 p.m. the enemy guns lefted, and through the dense smoke-clouds the German infantry, wearing their packs and full field kit, advanced to what they felt would be an easy parade to Ypres. Many of our men left the scant protection of their shell holes and met the oncoming horde, with the bayonet—dying to the last man, fighting. The balance of this gallant body of men, those who were unwounded and able to stand, fell back gradually on our supporting line, disputing each yard with the enemy.

Generals Mercer and Williams with their Staffs were caught in the outbreak of this inferno, the former being stunned, and Gen. Williams wounded. Nevertheless, General Mercer sent back messages for artillery support. He must have been killed while striving to reach our reserve lines, as, later, his body was found in Armagh Wood.

Meanwhile, in spite of shell fire which raged above them, the battalions in support were holding firm. It was against this line that the German infantry came up, and broke. For a time it seemed as if the Huns might break through towards Zillebeke Lake. This critical situation was averted by an officer in charge of one of the C.M.R. battalions in support. Leading his men across country to Maple Copse, under a devastating fire, he awaited the oncoming Bosches with the survivors of another unit. When the German troops came on they did not expect to meet with much resistance. However, they were opposed by such a withering fire that their advancing lines crumpled and the position was held.

Hour after hour our guns were served by frantic crews. The whole front of advance was swept with gunfire, and though our losses were heavy, the Germans suffered terribly. Soon the battlefield was one great shambles.

During the general retirement from Sanctuary Wood, two of our field guns were lost. These had been brought up to within 400 yards of the front line, established in camouflaged gun-pits, and masked. They were to be used only in the case of emergency.

Lt. C. P. Cotton was in command of these "Sacrifice Guns". Although his crews had suffered severely during the bombardment, Lt. Cotton opened fire at 1.45 p.m. and continued in action until the enemy were within a few yards of the pits. A retirement was then ordered, but Cotton and his gallant men all fell, fighting to the last.

A counter attack, planned for 2 a.m. the following morning, did not get under way till 7 a.m., owing to the difficulty experienced in moving up troops from the Corps Reserve. This daylight attack, handicapped by inadequate artillery support, and delivered against a new German trench system not accurately located, failed with heavy loss. Our line, however, was straightened and the gaps to Ypres closed.

A lull now settled down on the field of battle, although artillery bombardments on both sides showed that the fighting was by no means finished. A few days later the front line battalions were relieved by other units of the 1st, 2nd and 3rd Canadian Divisions.

On the 6th, after heavy shelling of our front, four mines were sprung by the enemy under our trenches near Hooge, occupied by the 6th Canadian Infantry Brigade. The explosion was horrible. Nearly one entire company of the 28th perished. Fierce fighting followed. The Bosches advanced in solid formation, but were finally held in check by machine gun fire from our support lines. The loss of Hooge made the situation more critical than ever.

Plans were immediately made to win back our original lines in the Salient, and a great concentration of heavies, field guns, and trench-mortars were brought into action and registered on the enemy lines.

Intensive bursts of gun-fire, to mislead him, kept the Hun continually on the alert for our expected attack. On the evening of June 12th, our Batteries caught him in the middle of a relief and the intense three-quarters of an hour bombardment, prior to the infantry assault at 2 a.m. on the 13th, took a terrible toll of his supports and front line troops. Advancing in four long waves, the men of the 1st and 3rd Divisions carried every obstacle before them, and within half an hour had occupied the original line lost to the Hun, June 2nd, now battered beyond recognition. The cost of life throughout this ten day period was severe, but defeat was turned into victory, and the southern ramparts of Ypres were again consolidated and held.

Throughout this action, the 2nd Canadian Division kept the Hun tied down to his lines in the Hill 60—Wytchaete Sector, and, by constant activity in trench-raids, patrols, trench-mortar and machine-gun fire, forestalled any attempt he might have made to enlarge his advance to our front. The whole Divisional Artillery, while not engaged on enfilade fire to the north, kept up spasmodic fire, day and night, on their own zones—the 4th Brigade, C.F.A., covering the craters and the Damme Strasse.

On the 30th, a detachment from the 19th Battery placed a sniper gun near Moated Grange, within 1,000 yards of the German lines, and, for the next few weeks did very effective shooting, destroying two enemy machine-gun emplacements and scattering a marching body of troops near Hollebeke. Dominion Day was celebrated by firing three salvos on the German front line—then baseball at the wagon-lines.

On this date, the great allied advance on the Somme commenced. Prior to the attack a terrific drum-fire bombardment was placed on the Hun lines from Gommecourt to Bray—a front of twenty miles, and extended a similar distance south of the River Somme, where the French joined in the assault. Mines were sprung, and the whole German trench system shook with the thundering detonations of bursting shells. Except on the left sector, from Gommecourt to Thiepval, all went according to schedule, and thousands of prisoners were captured by the Allies.

During the month of July our battery positions and "O.P.'s" did not suffer greatly, although the Hun shelled our area constantly, concentrating on Scottish Wood, Vijverhock Corner, Dickebusch, Suicide Copse, Bus House, Convent Lane, communication trenches, etc., and searched the main Ypres-Locre road at all times of the day and night.

Just after midnight, on July 12th, a minor operation was carried out against the enemy front line, from Piccadilly Farm to the Ypres-Comines Canal; the Hun being gassed, smoked out, shot up, and raided. The 4th Brigade, C.F.A., guns splashed the craters, communication-trenches, and supports for an hour, while our heavies fired on batteries, roads and depots behind the lines. Two days previously, the 14th Battery and the 19th sniper gun were engaged in wire cuttting. Captured prisoners readily acknowledged the accuracy and deadliness of our shelling, and, if their word could be counted upon, casualties must have been heavy in the trenches, billets, towns and villages behind their front.

N.C.O.'s, 15th Battery, C.F.A., Exhibition Camp (Toronto), 1915.

On July 18th, Lt.-Col. W. J. Brown proceeded to England. We were sorry to see him go, as he was the last of the original senior officers, and the first Brigade Commander of "the good old Forth." Our Batteries were now attached to the 7th Brigade, C.F.A., for tactics and administration, and formed part of "Stewart's Group". A week later Maj. C. H. L. Sharman was transferred from the 7th Brigade, C.F.A., and assumed temporary command of the unit, which consisted of the 13th and 14th, the 19th being attached to "Dodds' Group" since the middle of the month.

On August 2nd word was received that the Brigade would be relieved. For the next ten days we were in the Steenvoorde area on rest—our first breathing spell in nearly a year. Further changes amongst the officers at this time were as follows:

Lt. L. A. Reid transferred from 6th Brigade, C.F.A., and posted to the 14th Battery; Lt. E. B. McLatchey (13th) posted to Trench-Mortars; Lt. J. H. P. Atkins invalided to England; Capt. E. R. Leather transferred to 2nd C.D.A.; Lt.-Col. G. A. Carruthers and Capt. W. L. C. MacBeth struck off strength—proceeded to England. The M.O. was replaced by Capt. M. V. Valiquet.

On return to the "Salient" the Brigade was attached to the 3rd Canadian Divisional Artillery, the 13th and 14th Batteries, to "McNaughton's Centre Group", and the 19th to "Eaton's Right Group", with positions close to the southern outskirts of Ypres. This was indeed a hot spot, the gun crews, reliefs and ration parties having to run the gauntlet of shell fire every time they approached the positions. While located here, Lt. W. A. Townsley reported back for duty to the 14th, and Lt. L. A. Reid was transferred to the 13th Battery.

About this time the 4th Canadian Division arrived from England and was given instruction by the troops of the 2nd Canadian Division, then occupying the front from St. Eloi to Kemmel. Shortly after, Australians appeared in our area and rumors persisted that we were to be sent to take part in the Battle of the Somme.

The "Aussies" were a very fine type—tall, dark-complexioned fellows, sun-tanned from their campaign in the Dardanelles. They wore a different type of uniform to the rest of the British forces,—a loose-fitting jacket, slouch hat with one side pinned up, riding breeches and leggings. At the Battle of the Somme, the Australians not only won the praise of Allied generals, but, like the Canadians, were included in the Hun "bad books".

Finally, on the morning of August 26th, Australian Batteries relieved us—maps, photographs, defence schemes, and existing telephone lines being turned over. The Brigade then set out for wagon-lines at Reninghelst. Next morning, in full marching order, the Brigade started its march to the Somme, and as we topped the last rise at the Franco-Belgian frontier the rumble of gun-fire in the "Salient" sounded faintly, and far away. Capt. V. H. de Butts Powell, riding with Major G. L. Drew (13th Battery), turned his horse and looking back long and earnestly, voiced, I think, the feelings of all ranks, when he said, "Good-bye, Fritz, d—n you! You can

do what you like from now on, but you didn't get me in the Salient!"
Ypres was a nightmare to us in those months. As the long column
marched along the men sang lustily:

> "Far, far from Ypres I want to be,
> Where German snipers can't pot at me;
> Crouching where the worms do creep,
> Awaiting a whizz-bang to send me to sleep."

For several days the whole Division indulged in open warfare training—advancing toward St. Omer. From September 1st to 6th with H.Q.
at Guemy, the Batteries carried on with tactical exercises, signalling and
gun drill—but, due to adverse weather conditions, the expectations of
extensive manoeuvres in conjunction with other units of the Division,
could not be realized. While in this area, Lieut. E. A. Plunkett was taken
on the strength and posted to the 19th Battery; Sgts. S. T. J. Fryer and
N. F. Parkinson (13th) appointed to temporary commissions and posted
to 2nd C.D.A.; and Lieut. E. F. B. Reddy (19th) transferred to 2nd C.D.A.

CHAPTER II

Courcellette

FINALLY, on September 5th, orders were received that the 2nd Canadian Division would proceed immediately to the Somme. At last we were to take part in offensive operations against the enemy.

Next day the Batteries entrained for Candas—the 13th and H.Q. Staff at Ardruicq, the 14th at St. Omer, and the 19th at Arques, arriving at our destination about 1 a.m. that night.

One hour's time was allowed by the Railway Transport Officer for each unit to unload guns, wagons and horses and clear the station yard before the next train came in.

"You've no time to water your teams; just 'Hook in' and 'Walk March'" were his parting injunctions.

Not knowing when our animals would get another drink we located the watering-trough, and, inspite of the "R.T.O.'s" orders, the drivers sneaked their mounts to water. Meanwhile the gunners, under the glare of arc lights, rolled the vehicles off the flat cars down wooden ramps arranged alongside. It was hard and hectic work persuading the horses to vacate the "huit chevaux, 40 hommes" box cars.

Finally, the Batteries hooked in, the teams were fed and the cook had a fire going in a corner with a "dixie" of hot tea for gunners and drivers.

Promptly on the hour feed bags were removed, girths tightened and the orders given "Prepare to mount!—Mount!—Walk march!" Out into the darkness of the French countryside we started on a twenty-mile march to St. Ouen, where we arrived about noon of September 6th. This small manufacturing town was jammed with troops.

After one night's rest we were on our way again, arriving at our billets late in the afternoon. One of the drivers remarked: "Huh! Looks as though we're going to have some dirty weather by the sound of that thunder".

"Thunder be damned!" replied a gunner, "that's the bloody front line."

And as darkness gathered, from our roadside bivouac on high ground above Rubempre, we could see once again the old familiar flicker of the guns along the horizon ahead of us. The air throbbed with the sound of them.

During the last day's march into the Somme, Driver George Wishart, 13th Battery, was leading driver of the leading gun of the leading Battery of the leading Brigade of the 2nd Canadian Divisional Artillery, and mighty proud old George was of that fact.

The Battery was halted in a small village where a certain British Battalion was billeted; and where troops are billeted it is customary to find a Regimental Padre. Down the village street came the British Padre and, with the best of intentions, but nevertheless somewhat too dignified an air, enquired of George, "What Division are you, my man?"

"Second Canadians, sorr!" George answered.

"Ah yes! Where are you going, my man?"

"To the Somme, sorr."

"Ah, indeed!" and glancing along the line of well kept horses, burnished brass, and shining leather, and taking us for new troops, the Padre further remarked:

"I suppose you're going in to your baptism of fire?"

Old George stiffened as he thought of the past twelve months up in the Salient, and with stinging voice replied:

"Baptism is it, sorr? Not by a damn sight! It's our bloody golden wedding!"

This was, of course, hardly the proper manner in which to address a Padre, but could you blame old George? True, some Padres were more man than cleric; our own Capt. Thompson for instance—a big-hearted gentleman, if ever there was one. He would never have wounded an old soldier's pride like that. George Wishart has passed on, going like the gallant old soldier he was, but his memory is ever green with those who knew him.

The end of the second day's march saw the Brigade pull into the "Brickfields" at Albert, with the rest of the 2nd Canadian Divisional Artillery. Batteries and Brigades in a seemingly endless column were marching in, laying out picket lines and settling down till they got their orders to move up through Albert to "the front." The Colonel and the Battery Commanders then went forward to reconnoitre for gun positions.

Long watering-troughs, capable of taking care of 200 horses at a time, were situated under some trees across the main route. It was quite a trick getting across to them, for our Infantry Battalions, at some 200 yards interval, were passing in clouds of dust all day; long columns of tired, dust-coated men, lifted along by their bands and pipers—men who, a few days later, were to make more Canadian history at Courcellette. In this short 200 yards interval, two or three Batteries would, by being all ready in line at the edge of the road, manage to get across to water their horses.

The following day, September 9th, our Batteries began to move forward into action. It is strange, after all these years, to look back to those September days, and yet how vividly they stand out.

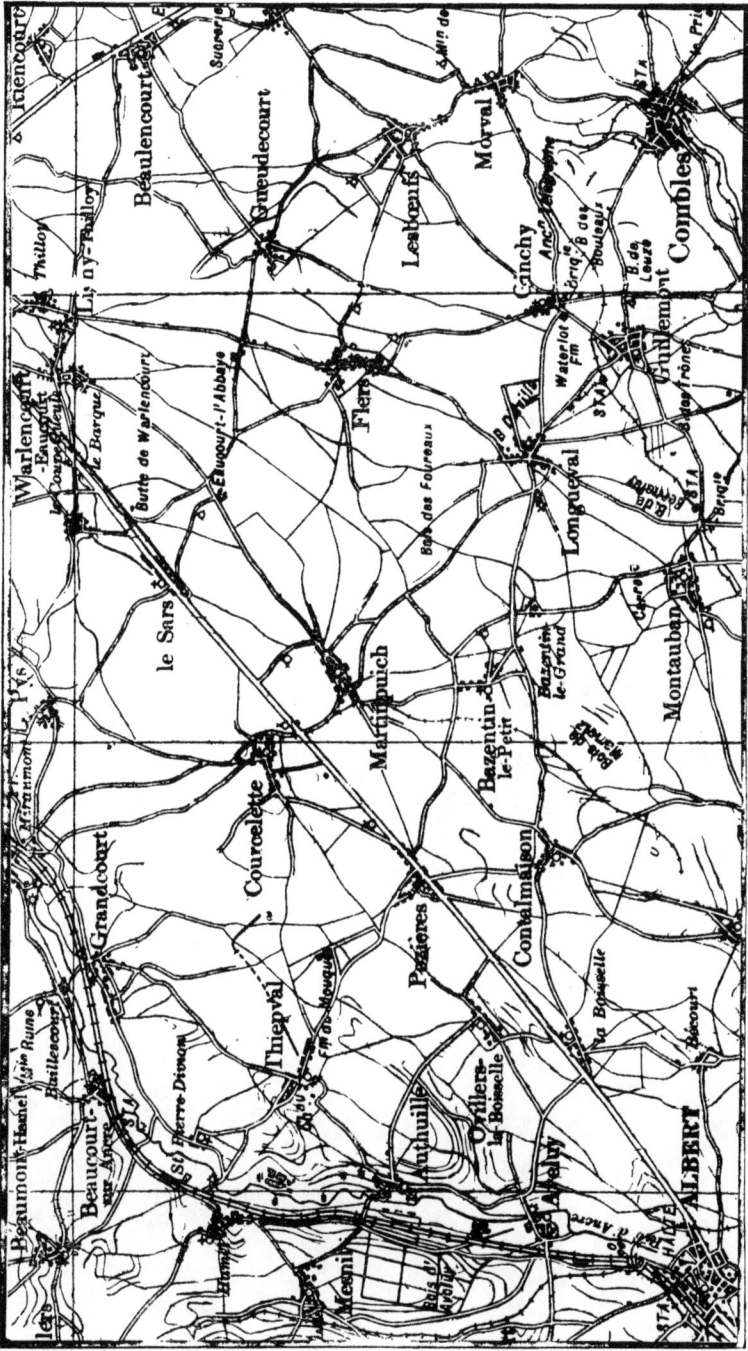

THE SOMME—September-November, 1916

Scale: 1 inch—1.58 miles

The long road dipped down into Albert—passing on our right, some distance down, the cushy billet our Brigade Paymaster had picked out.—How we loved old Mort on pay days! Down under the railway bridge we rumbled and on past the ruins of the Cathedral. I suppose we all craned our necks to look up at the golden Virgin, hanging precariously, head down, from the shell-battered spire. So we came eventually out beyond to Fricourt Woods and La Boiselle and "Action Front" again.

Due to a temporary reorganization from Brigades to Groups, the 4th Brigade, C.F.A., H.Q., remained in Albert, supervising the ammunition supply for 2nd Divisional units, while the 13th Battery was attached to the 6th Brigade, C.F.A. (King's Group), the 14th to the 7th Brigade, C.F.A. (Stewart's Group), and the 19th to the 5th Brigade, C.F.A. (Britten's Group).

With these changes they went into position, some in "Mash Valley", and where space and flash cover permitted, along the Ovillers side road to the left of the Albert-Bapaume Road, others located to the right of La Boiselle and the huge crater nearby.

During the 9th and 10th of September, while the Artillery were going into position, the Infantry of the 2nd and 3rd Canadian Divisions were taking over the line in front of us, the 2nd on the right facing Courcellette, and the 3rd on the left near Mouquet Farm. Immediately the Hun tried to test our morale. After intense bombardments, attack after attack was launched on our forward lines. The gallant Infantry, however, not only defeated these thrusts of "hate," but improved their positions and created strong lines of defence.

By the evening of September 11th, working parties had the gun-pits and dugouts ready for occupation. Sand-bags and elephant-iron sections were drawn from the "R. E. Dump" near Albert, and plenty of timber, piling and planks were available in the captured trenches around Ovillers to make the shelters splinter-proof and comfortable. The guns were then "shot in", large quantities of ammunition "cached" in rear of the pits, and telephone communication established. Next day "O-Pips" were selected, the Batteries registered, enemy trenches located, and destruction of his barbed wire entanglements began.

The German front, though shaken, was still very formidable, and even impregnable in the estimation of its defenders. Line after line of trenches were constructed with long belts of barbed wire, innumerable communication trenches, redoubts, concealed machine-gun emplacements, and strong, deep dugouts (lighted by electricity). The nature of the country admirably adapted it for defensive warfare. The Hun made use of the chalk-pits, quarries and sunken roads, and turned ruined villages into veritable fortresses.

Such were the obstacles that had to be faced and overcome. On every side the fields were pock-marked with shell-holes and craters, and strewn with the debris of war. A mile and a half up the main Bapaume road from Pozières, stood the strongly fortified ruins of the Sugar Refinery, midway between the villages of Courcellette and Martinpuich, and protected by elaborate trench lines in front. Off to the north lay Thiepval Ridge and Mouquet Farm, and in the distance Grandcourt and Miraumont.

Our concentration of guns was tremendous. Looking back towards Albert, and covering the floors of the valleys, were row after row of 18 pounders, 4.5 howitzers, 60 pounders and 9.2's. All was in readiness for the "Big Push".

Watches were synchronized at 10 p.m. and checked a few hours later. At six the next morning, September 15th, in the cool, grey light of dawn the gunners were "standing-to," nervously waiting "zero." The minutes passed slowly with intermittent gun-fire on our flanks and a certain amount of incoming stuff from the Germans. It was 6.20. A heavy gun, far behind, boomed. Almost before the reverberation had died away a crescendo of soud rose and grew to a deafening, rushing roar as the whole front awakened to the sustained tumult of "drum-fire." For miles to north and south, the front was aflame with gun flashes, the ground trembled at the concussions and plunging explosions of the newly devised rolling or creeping barrage.

To the Forward Observing Officers, with the Infantry, it resembled a great curtain of smoke, flickering with light from the shrapnel air-bursts of the field guns, like myriads of giant fire-flies flashing through and through it. Great geysers of earth continually spouted up, as the shells from the heavy guns and howitzers plunged in and lashed out with a roar of explosion.

The gunners back in their rough splinter-proof gun-pits had become temporarily stone deaf, while blood oozed from their ears and noses. Orders were passed in writing, the noise was too terrific for words. Field gun Batteries were firing four rounds per minute, ceasing for a few seconds to lift the range as the barrage crept forward in front of our Infantry.

Thus did the Brigade fight their part of the Battle of Courcellette, work-ing like "Trojans" to support their advancing Infantry.

The enemy, no doubt, was taken unawares; but soon his "S.O.S." rockets were calling frantically for help, and a heavy retaliation fell upon our forward zone. Machine-guns joined in the din of conflict, and 5.9's crumped and slashed into our battery positions with terrifying detonations. In the deafening inferno, it was well-nigh impossible to distinguish between our own and enemy shells.

As the sun shot forth in all its glory, a few hours later, large numbers of prisoners appeared on the horizon, mud-spattered and nerve-shaken, herd-ed down by mounted escort, like a bunch of sheep. Many were badly wounded, and these limped along, supported on the arms of their comrades. As the long lines of Huns passed by the Batteries, another heavy barrage swept the valley. Thus many of these prisoners fell victim to their own gun-fire. The survivors were mighty glad when they reached the barbed wire corral, near Albert. For the first time we saw many dead lying around for days before they could be buried.

Here we saw, too, ingenious engines of war, the Tanks, being used for the first time. These had been secretly devised by the British. "Somme buses" we called them, as they came wallowing across the shell holes and mud. Also in those first weeks of September, as one looked back towards Albert, he would see the sky crowded with flocks of observation balloons. "Sausages" was the Tommies' term for them—30 or 40 up at a time, while Fritz dare not sport more than one or two, far back. During those weeks the Royal Flying Corps had complete mastery of the air, not a German plane coming over to molest our balloons.

On the following day, September 16th, the 7th Canadian Infantry Bri-gade moved on Zollern Trench. The artillery preparation was all that could be desired, but despite the heavy barrage, German garrisons manned the parapets and met the attacking waves with such a withering fire that further advance was impossible. In consequence, the proposed operation against the Redoubt was cancelled. The 8th Canadian Infantry Brigade was more fortunate, and succeeded in capturing Mouquet Farm by an encircling movement. This gain was thoroughly consolidated and held. For the next few days, no further actions took place, but the Infantry and Pioneers were able to link up the forward posts and improve our trenches.

No doubt many will remember that horrible, winding ditch to the west of Pozières, which ran down into the Chalk Pit near Mouquet Farm. Formerly a German Trench, our Infantry now used it as a communication trench to the line in front of Mouquet Farm. Its sides were formed of sandbags and dead bodies. "F.O.O.'s" and signallers will remember grisly nights spent there. One had to smoke cigarettes incessantly to keep the noisome stench from one nostrils, and if lucky, had a bottle of rum to keep away the sickening thought of decaying death about him. Even the rum in time grew to be nauseating, and one longed for tea, for a change, in that ghoulish trench.

More than one sorely wounded infantryman, painfully making his way back from the front line a short hundred yards or so, was given new life by a "shot" of that same rum, passing on with a deep and fervent "Thank God, sir, for that. It's saved my life"—which it actually had, giving strength to reach the Dressing Station, further back.

On the 19th Lt.-Col. W. B. King was evacuated sick, and Lt.-Col. C. H. L. Sharman assumed temporary command of his Group. Three days later, the 4th Brigade, C.F.A., H.Q. relieved 6th Brigade, C.F.A., H.Q. in the line, and the 13th, 15th, 16th, 28th and 22nd Batteries became known as "Sharman's Group." Registration of targets in the enemy lines was carried out daily, and the gunners were constantly called upon to answer "S.O.S." calls, opening up with gun-fire at any time of the day or night. The enemy shelling was very intense on the battery positions, and the Brigade had a large number of casualties during this period, same being very heavy among the "F.O.O.'s" and signallers, as most of the enemy "hate" raked the roads, communication trenches and forward zone. An energetic programme was followed day and night, some Batteries being engaged on aeroplane shoots, while others were employed on wire cutting and harassing fire.

On the 24th new battery positions were built and occupied a mile further forward, about 100 yards west of Pozières. The day after, guns registered on Zollern Trench for a prospective attack the next day.

Advancing on a two-mile front, and preceded by a barrage of exceptional intensity, our Infantry carried the whole length of Zollern Graben trenches, while the British on our left finally ejected the Hun from his impregnable fortress of Thiepval.

The assaulting troops pressed on. North of Courcellette they mounted the crest of the ridge, and gained a foothold in the second objective—Hessian and Kenora Trenches. Some platoons even reached Regina Trench, but no attempt was made to hold this line.

Throughout the night, Courcellette and our new line was heavily bombarded, but in spite of gruelling shelling the positions gained were consolidated. On the 27th a further advance gained Hessian Trench. Until the 1st of October nothing of importance happened, although the shelling on both sides never ceased.

An enemy withdrawal to prepare lines of defense brought our forward posts within striking distance of Regina Trench. About this time enemy artillery fire slackened off considerable, and when retaliatory fire was asked for, the number of shells sent across to the enemy far exceeded those sent back in reply. This was indeed a hopeful sign, especially to the troops in the forward zone.

CHAPTER III

Regina Trench

Not much time was available for censoring outgoing mail. Letters to fathers, mothers and wives had right of way. Those who wrote, as some did, the same letters to six or eight different girls, were not favored by the censor. Such letters had to wait. The poor, misjudged censor was usually some officer who happened to be on rest from "F.O.O." duty.

The men were not very communicative, saying little or nothing of their own discomforts. Drivers often mentioned their cushy little "bivvys" where they were snug and dry, and almost wept as they wrote of their faithful friends—the horses—wishing so much that they could be given more feed and better shelter; then they would be satisfied. The censor, being human, learned to love those chaps through these touches of warm sympathy. Such care and attention they gave these dumb animals! When nothing else was available an old sock was used to rub them down, or to bandage a cracked heel; while breast collar and girth galls were eased by wrapping like articles around the harness to keep it from rubbing against the sore spot. Socks were used for a good many things besides the feet of men.

On September 30th, Lt.-Col. W. B. M. King resumed command of his Group and the 4th Brigade, C.F.A., H.Q. relieved the 7th Brigade, C.F.A., H.Q. (Stewart's Group), which consisted of the 14th, 25th, 26th and 27th and 21st Batteries. Positions were occupied 1,000 yards north of Pozières, with a forward gun near High Trench. Shortly after, Capt. de Butts Powell was wounded in action, Lt. W. H. Gordon (14th Battery) transferred to 7th Brigade, C.F.A., and Capt. M. V. Valiquet (M.O.) relieved by Capt. D. W. McKechnie.

The next big operation took place on the afternoon of October 1st, when the 8th, 5th and 4th Canadian Infantry Brigades advanced over a barren waste of shell holes on Regina Trench. Not only were our men met by a vicious counter-barrage and machine-gun fire, but they encountered a strong network of wire entanglements which the guns had not succeeded in demolishing. In many places the attackers entered into Regina Trench, and, after a desperate bombing and bayonet fight, succeeded in holding their ground.

Long gaps, still occupied by the enemy, separated these parties and prevented consolidation. The Germans immediately counter-attacked in force and, after a long drawn-out battle in the mud, finally ejected the Canadians from most of the ground they had gained. Further operations were interrupted by weather conditions.

For the next week our guns deluged the uncut wire with shells. On the 5th of October the 4th Canadian Division, with the 3rd Canadian Divisional Artillery, arrived on the Somme after a few months trench-warfare training in the Ypres Salient. The Canadian Corps now consisted of over 100,000 fighting men.

Three days later, at 4.50 a.m. another attack was launched on the German lines. Eight Canadian Battalions, supported by British troops on our right and left, advanced gallantly against the Regina-Stuff line. The "Quadrilateral" fell to the 3rd and 4th Brigades, but after a heavy counter-attack in the evening by the Hun, our men were forced out again, as were also the 16th Battalion and R.C.R.'s, who had obtained a footing in Regina Trench. The 13th, 43rd, 49th and 58th were even less fortunate, losing many men in trying to break through heavy belts of uncut wire.

The result of the whole attack was very disappointing, in view of the heavy casualties. Though objectives were not held, our men had no feeling of defeat, attributing the cause of failure to something beyond their control, as they considered themselves far superior to the enemy in battle.

The weather became more inclement, but the artillery duel went on day after day. New trenches were dug close to the enemy and every effort made to improve and consolidate our defences. The artillery raked the German lines and kept up an uninterrupted concentration on his wire. Thousands of shells tore into this formidable obstacle. The Royal Flying Corps finally reported the way clear for a further advance, and our guns kept the Huns from repairing their damaged trenches.

A general attack to break the Regina-Stuff lines, with the II. British Corps on the left above Thiepval, the 4th Canadian Division in the centre north of Courcellette, and the III. British Corps on the right near Le Sars, was planned for October 19th. The rain fell in torrents and the ground became so heavy as to make any movement utterly impossible. Eventually, on the 21st, the guns opened out with the full fury of their massed batteries and the German lines were deluged with shrapnel and heavy shells.

Then the Infantry advanced in open order. The long waves surged forward, their officers in front, as steadily as though on parade. With a deafening "krump!" a 5.9 burst among them. One or two disappeared before our eyes, others on either flank staggered a few paces and pitched forward on their faces, killed or badly wounded. The officers coolly signalled with their arms to incline out of the fire zone. Plunging forward again at a steady pace, and following closely our barrage until it was "lifted" off the German front line, our men on top of the parapet were silhouetted for an instant against the barrage smoke curtain, ere they dropped into the trench to finish off what the artillery had begun.

Nerve-shaken prisoners came staggering out over the top, arms high in the air, running towards our lines and safety, unless, as did often happen, they ran into their own barrage or shell-fire.

King George and Earl Kitchener inspecting
2nd. Canadian Contingent, Beachborough
Park, (England), August, 1915.

Arrival of Batteries at Trawsfynnd, Wales

Most of Regina Trench was taken after hard fighting, and held despite desperate counter-attacks, and very heavy shelling by the enemy. The state of the front line and communication trenches was very bad, mud and water being knee deep and the trenches badly shattered. Working parties toiled for days in an effort to consolidate and build up parapets that would not ooze away.

Two days later, two Battalions of the 10th Canadian Infantry Brigade went over the top against another section of Regina Trench, but meeting with heavy enfilade fire from the "Quadrilateral" were forced to fall back to their original line.

On the 23rd of October, the 4th Brigade, C.F.A., H.Q. was relieved by the 5th Brigade, C.F.A., H.Q., and Captain R. F. Thompson was posted to the Brigade as "Padre." This gallant officer won the M.C. while attached to the 19th Battalion during the Battle of Courcellette.

Bad weather continued for another week, greatly handicapping reliefs and ration parties. Roads, such as they had been, disappeared entirely. At best, they merely consisted of filled-in shell holes and the rough bridging of trenches, so as to make a more or less passable route over the smashed up area that had been fought over as we slowly pushed forward. The Batteries were now far out across that rolling, treeless, grassless, dead and pock-marked battle ground. In pre-war days it had smiled with trees, farms and waving sweeps of ripe grain.

Along the reverse slope of "Corpse Valley", to the left front of Cour-cellette, dead things lay around in hollows and in shell holes full of water. Pack horses, those poor, worn-out, patient brutes, mired in mud to their bellies, had to be shot to put them out of their misery.

It was at this time that we began to get mules as replacements for casualties among the horses. The mule was just as patient and faithful a friend as the horse—a little more particular about his drinking water, but not so fussy about his food.

Gunners, rain-soaked for days and tired to the point of absolute exhaustion, dreamed of a mythical country of cement sidewalks, electric lights, soft beds and white sheets. They found time, however, to crack the odd joke about those mythical sidewalks, and when everyone was feeling particularly miserable, some bright genius would remark: "It's a pity they don't allow cameras here. We might send a picture back home to the folks of happy Canadians digging themselves in on the Somme." Which raised a grin and bucked things up.

Advanced Batteries were up within six hundred yards of the Infantry, without cover and deep in the mud. Cook-house fires were lighted at night only, so that their smoke would not be spotted. The duty of the cooks was to supply hot tea or "mulligan". During the cold, wet days nothing hot was obtainable.

The men wore two or three pairs of socks inside their gum-boots and heavy field service boots, and at frequent intervals managed to affect a change. Dampness had made the socks shrink tightly to our feet. These socks had to be cut away with a knife. Much trouble was experienced with "trench feet", and special treatment had to be administered by the medical authorities to combat it.

Wrapped in ragged blankets, wet through, and crouching for shelter in a hole in the ground, we slept fitfully, often awakening to find ourselves lying in inches of water with rain pouring upon us from a leaden sky. We were weary, lousy, dirty and unshaven, but our morale was high always.

The gunners were working night and day, bringing up ammunition by pack animals. Wheeled vehicles were impossible in the quagmire that was continually being churned up by shell fire.

Men who were teetotallers were taking their rum issue as a medicine. War, under these terrible conditions, had convinced them that there was some good in the warming drink. It has often struck one as curious that, while everybody heard about the rum issue, so little seems to have been mentioned of the lime-juice issued in the summer months to all the troops. A far-sighted War Office, through a few hundred years of fighting experience in many climates and countries, had found rum and lime-juice the two most effective concentrates for troops on active service.

Notwithstanding the wretched weather conditions, our "F.O.O.'s" and infantry patrols reported the enemy occupying Grandcourt Trench in large numbers, working feverishly to strengthen it as well as a new trench, termed by the mapping section, "Desire Trench", which had been constructed along lower ground in front of it.

Although there were no active operations, our patrols continually reconnoitered these new positions and the Corps Artillery maintained a steady harassing fire night and day on the new works, the approaches and hostile batteries.

On October 29th, the 4th Brigade, C.F.A., H.Q. was again called into action to relieve the 7th Brigade, C.F.A., H.Q. Lt.-Col. J. S. Stewart, D.S.O., had been wounded the day before while up forward looking over the situation. He showed much grit in struggling back to the 26th Battery (then in an advanced position) to get help for his orderly, who was too severely wounded for Col. Stewart, in his weakened condition, to bring in without assistance. The Group now became known as Sharman's Group, consisting of the 14th, 21st, 25th, 26th and 27th Batteries.

At last the weather began to improve, and artillery action became more violent. "F.O.O.'s" were called upon to register the guns on uncut wire and machine-gun emplacements, and to harass the enemy trenches and approaches.

Observation posts were established on the high ground around Zollern Trench, further forward in Kenora Trench, and in some cases in that part of Regina Trench already held as our front line. The Forward Observing Officers and Signallers were sitting practically "on top of" their targets. The guns were located in positions varying from 600 yards to 2,000 yards behind, and the "F.O.O." was often 100 yards, or less, from the wire at which he was shooting.

For ten days the guns concentrated on the barbed wire in front of that section of Regina Trench which still held out against us. Finally, on the 11th an intense barrage was laid down on the enemy lines and communication trenches. This bombardment proved so effective that the whole system of the German lines was practically obliterated. Though isolated groups and machine-gunners offered a stout resistance, our three Battalions, the 46th,

47th and 102nd, plunged in and captured it. Within half an hour the whole objective had been gained and a new line consolidated 100 yards beyond Regina Trench.

Throughout the night the enemy counter-attacked strongly, but was unable to bomb the Canadians out of their newly-won position.

The 4th Brigade, C.F.A., H.Q., was then relieved by the 7th Brigade, C.F.A., H.Q.; Lt.-Col. C. H. L. Sharman acting as Liason Officer of the 2nd Canadian Divisional Artillery to the 18th British Division.

Two days later British troops made an attack on the German positions commanding the Ancre Valley, our guns assisting in the barrage. During this operation, Lt. S. T. J. Fryer, 26th Battery (promoted from the 13th Battery, C.F.A.), was wounded on forward duty.

On the 18th of November the Canadians pressed on against Desire Trench, and the 18th British Division continued their advance on Grandcourt. Following a barrage, placed with deadly accuracy and effectiveness on the enemy wire and entrenchments, eight Canadian Battalions ploughed across the quagmire of mud and shell craters, carrying their objective with such ease that they kept on. The "F.O.O.'s" lost touch with the Infantry and, going forward, they found them in Grandcourt Trench, 400 yards beyond Desire Trench.

Several of our observing officers became casualties while on this duty. The Infantry dropped back behind their artillery fire and a new line was eventually established and held, 150 yards beyond Desire Trench. On the left, the British, after a stubborn resistance, cleared the formidable Schwaben and Stuff Redoubts, but failed to win their way into Grandcourt itself. The enemy made no attempt to counter-attack or retaliate.

Finally on the 26th of November, the Canadian Artillery Units were relieved by R.F.A. Batteries, receiving orders to rejoin the 2nd Canadian Divisional Artillery, and proceed to the Arras-Lens front. So, after three months of continuous fighting, in which our guns had been pushed forward some four miles from our first positions of September 9th, the Brigade "handed over" and was withdrawn.

Sir Douglas Haig's tremendous attack had smashed forward, biting deeper and deeper into the great Salient, until the German line was stretched almost to breaking point. We were within an ace of complete success, but the fates decreed otherwise. Rain and mud, in those late October and early November days, pinned us down. Our guns, stuck far forward in the mud, were left there, and the personnel only withdrawn. British gunners took them over on relief.

In those three months the Field Artillery had suffered heavy casualties in both men and horses. The long strain had worn out all ranks. It was with a sigh of deep relief that the sadly depleted Brigade turned its back on the "Blood Bath of the Somme."

On the morning of November 20th, 1916, we moved out from our wagon lines at Bouzincourt, in column-of-route, by Brigades, billeting over night at Amplier, Ligny-sur-Canche, Marquay and Hallecourt, where, after one day's rest, sections of the 13th, 14th and 19th Batteries moved into the line, relieving Imperial Units.

CHAPTER IV

Signal Communication

ON attempting to give a short outline of the duties of the signallers of the Fourth Brigade of Canadian Field Artillery, from the time they enlisted until the Brigade changed its identity in the reorganization of the C.F.A., we have passed over many items of personal interest, feeling that the story of the luck and hardships of the boys, the fun and sorrow have been sufficiently dealt with in other chapters of this book. Please forgive us, then, if this article seems to confine itself to the business end of the signaller's life.

The story of the signalling system of the Fourth Brigade and its operators, forms an important episode in the training and the action of the Canadian Artillery. Through it was developed, between the members of the Battery Commanders parties and the members of the Brigade Headquarters Staff, a firm friendship which had a great deal to do with the preservation of unbroken lines of communication between Brigade and Battery Headquarters under extreme conditions, and a resulting close contact between Division, Brigade and the Batteries.

Upon the formation of the Fourth Brigade, C.F.A., at Exhibition Camp, a number of men were selected by each of the Battery Commanders and Officer Commanding the Brigade Ammunition Column, to act as his special party. The duty of these "B.C." parties was to preserve all battery lines of communication, assist in observation, map reading, range finding, reconnaisance, and other jobs of a technical nature. Signallers of the Brigade Commander's Staff, on the other hand, were required to maintain lines of communication between their Headquarters and all Units of the Brigade, and also to assist in keeping contact with Divisional Artillery and Infantry Brigade Headquarters. Practically the same kind of work had to be carried out, as that expected of the "B.C." parties. Included in the Headquarters Staff were Brigade Officers' servants, orderly room sergeant, cook, and the various N.C.O.'s attached to the Paymaster, Medical Officer, Veterinary, and Dental Officers.

It was fortunate that there were a number of old army signallers serving in these different parties of embryo signallers, for they acted as a nucleus around which it was possible to develop an efficient organization. The names of "Andy" Jackson and "Dodger" Green conjure up fond memories of our first days at Exhibition Park. We had to learn to signal, ride, do gun drill, stables, "P.T.", guards, pickets and all the other thousand and one things every "rookie" in the Artillery had to learn.

Under the efficient guidance and careful coaching of Sergeant Steele and Captain Dunn of the Signal Corps, a few months sufficed to grind in the elements of Morse and semaphore flag, heliograph, lamp and buzzer, Artillery abbreviations and the mysteries of the Message Form. The persuasive crop and tongue of each of our Sergeant-Majors were effective in teaching us not to dismount without orders and to respect "Four feet from nose to croup".

We all have pleasant memories of the spring days when we qualified as signallers, and the long distance signalling tests from the roof of the Royal Bank Building to Pellatt's Castle, Scarboro Bluffs, and Long Branch, when we tested the heliograph, telescope, and flags. Then came the field telephone, which the Brigade was the first to use in Toronto Exhibition camp, and the issue of the Lister sets, telephone wire and ground pins, with which we practiced telephonic communication, and even succeeded once or twice in establishing through lines over which it was possible to hear.

Who will forget the manoeuvres at Leaside, the Humber, Scarboro, and Hanlan's Point; and the setting off of the smoke puffs for the officers to observe; or the target practice in the lake, when we signalled the observations from the tug to the old Chutes with a large Morse flag?

These tests all served to familiarize us with our equipment, and trained us in the proper procedure and the co-operation necessary one with the other. They filled us so full of Morse Code that, during our trip to England, and later, during the first few weeks in France, every flashing light, no matter what its legitimate role, took on the mysterious guise of a spy signal. Many hours have been spent secretly trying to make "acs", "vics" and "dons" out of the flashes caused by some Belgian farmer moving past the lamp in his kitchen.

On our arrival at Westenhanger, training was commenced on the D Mk III phone, the British issue, which we were to use for many months in France. This phone was so simple of operation that Morse signalling was dropped in favor of speech, and the only calls necessary were the call-letters of the different stations. Batteries were supplied with a full complement of D III phones, D I wire, reels and the necessary splicing equipment. A supply of spare "S" cells was carried, and the men trained in the method of filling them with water to make them active.

The equipment of the telephone wagon for the Brigade Headquarters, was completed and they were supplied with D III phones and several miles of D III wire. Although the telephone wagon eventually deteriorated into more of a "G.S." wagon than anything else, the days in England served to develop a crew which would have been hard to beat anywhere.

A short description of the manner in which wire is laid by this wagon crew may be interesting at this point. The primary object is to establish phone-lines between the C.O. and each Battery Commander as soon as possible after going into action. One man sits on a small seat at the rear of the wagon, which is, in reality, an open "chassis" on which six one mile reels of wire are carried, allowing wire to pay out through a thick leather glove, while the N.C.O. in charge, mounted, picks it up in the notch of a crook-stick and lays it in ditches or over hedges, out of harm's way. Should they come to a point at which it is found necessary to cross a road, gate, bridge or other obstacle, the N.C.O. gives orders for the spare men on the wagon-limber to dismount. These men either set up poles, dig a small trench to bury the wire, or tie it up, as they may be commanded.

Signals to stop and start the wagon teams are given by whistle. Speed in completing crossings, under adverse conditions, is a great factor in rapid wire-laying. The paying out and the laying of the wire requires much practice. Reeling in is done in the reverse manner, the reel being turned by gears and a chain driven by a sprocket on the wagon wheel. Experience in running lines to battery positions was obtained during the manoeuvres that were held around Ashford and in the Marshes around Dymchurch. These manoeuvres served to develop a further confidence in ourselves and our equipment, to perfect a smoothly operating inter-battery communication system, and to give us a good knowledge of the personalities and requirements of our respective commanders.

Finally, we were away to Southampton and Le Havre, up to St. Omer, Caestre, Bailleul, Dranoutre, and into action at Lindenhoek, alongside Kemmel Hill. The Fourth Infantry Brigade had gone into action some time ahead of us, and were, of course, experienced in field communication by the time we arrived. Few of us know that the day we took over the Brigade H.Q. from the R.C.H.A., we put into operation a special switchboard which had never been tested in actual practice. It was connected up, tested to all stations and seemed to do the job perfectly. But there were some very faulty connections, and for several hours during the first night we were completely out of touch with the Infantry Headquarters, although we didn't know it. A chance call checked us up, and the next day there was feverish activity in tearing the board to pieces and remodelling it. Either the supply of switch-boards to the Batteries had been completely overlooked, or the "powers" had considered that they were not needed and the R.C.H.A. signallers were, in some cases, kind enough to leave their equipment in place for a day or so, until the N.C.O.'s in charge of signals had time to make simple ones under their instruction.

These boards were constructed as follows: For sockets, or "jacks", as they would be called by the radio fans, the bullet is removed from a cartridge and the latter is emptied of powder. It is then set into a board from the back, so that the open end projects past the surface. The lead is melted from the core of the bullet and the switchboard wire connected into it by means of the molten metal. A number of these cartridges and plugs properly arranged, make a very serviceable connecting-board. The bullet is used as a telephone plug, being inserted in the cartridge upside down.

Such arrangements were numerous and very popular. Special stunts were used, of course, and their number was limited only by the ingenuity of the signallers themselves. A special device was nearly always fitted up to notify the Battery Commander when he was wanted on the phone. It was customary to keep a log of all incoming and outgoing calls, or messages, so that they might be traced later.

Owing to the greater number of lines coming in to Brigade H.Q., a more elaborate switching-system was employed. All battery lines were plugged into a common strip, connected to a loud receiver. Divisional Artillery H.Q. was connected to a receiver, as were also Infantry H.Q. and Report Centre, the grouping being arranged so that little or no noise would be transmitted along the lines from one to another. In case a call for Brigade was heard on one of the receivers, each of which had a distinctive note, the operator listened until the party calling signed, withdrew the plug of the party calling, and plugged it into a strip connected to his station set. This gave him a perfectly clear line to the party who wished to speak to him. Generally it was easy to recognize battery or division calls by the distinctive notes of the different phones.

After we had been initiated into the mysteries of actual warfare, and had become acquainted with the lines, there was little new development in the system throughout our stay at Kemmel, Plugstreet or the first stop at Dickebusch. At "Plugstreet," where we relieved the 1st Brigade, C.F.A., we fell heir to a system of lamp communication which they had installed from the trench stations to the "O.Pips," and from the Batteries back to the haystack alongside Headquarters.

The daylight electric signalling lamps were used exclusively in this work. It was here that their worth was first noted and our boys trained in their use. Although it was never necessary to call the lamp into service through the failure of the phone lines, the system was kept in repair. Here, also, we came into contact for the first time with the Pigeon Service of the Royal Engineers. The loft of the house in which Brigade H.Q. was located was partly given over to the housing of a great number of homing pigeons. We were never given much information as to their use, but they were sent away in hampers, and after being released in the field or the trenches, came back to the loft, carrying their messages in small metal tubes attached to their legs. Many stories have been written and told of the endurance of these carrier birds in the war, and we could not fail to notice the wonderful care they received at the hands of the N.C.O. of the R.E.'s who had charge of them.

As has been remarked, there were few new developments in the method of signalling during this period, but there was certainly plenty of trouble for the linemen. There was only one line, as a rule, from Brigade H. Q. to each Battery, to the Ammunition Column, Infantry H. Q., Division, etc. There was also but one line to each of the stations with which each Battery kept up communication. Every one of these single lines had to be kept in perfect repair, day and night, and linemen were detailed for this particular duty. Brigade signallers acted as linemen during their period off duty at the board and it was in this work that the goodwill of the Batteries toward Brigade signallers was of such importance. Although they were not obliged to pay any attention to the lines to Headquarters, the signallers were one and all ready at all times to go over their end of a broken line.

Each lineman carried a D III telephone set, a reel of wire, splicing equipment, pliers and knife. The earth terminal of the phone was grounded to a steel plate on the bottom of the leather case, and a flexible lead, fitted with a large safety-pin for attaching to the line, was fitted to the line-terminal. The line was gone over for a distance and a test taken. If the lineman got his own operator, he knew he had not reached the break. If he got the operator at the other end of the line from that at which he started, he knew he had passed the break. In this way he localized the trouble. The plate on the bottom of the phone case gave him a simple ground and obviated removing the phone and getting it covered with mud. The boys who did the line work have many stirring tales to tell of trips overland to "O Pips" and in exposed areas and many well-deserved decorations have been awarded for their work.

As we became more and more accustomed to the duties and a regular routine was established, the question of more and better lines came up. The result was that when we were settled at LaClytte, permanent steel lines were run between the batteries and Brigade H. Q., and tie-lines run between the batteries, while duplicate ground lines were still maintained to all these locations. Contact was established with the Balloon section attached to the Lahore Artillery, and several balloon shoots were held, the observer in the "sausage" sending corrections to the battery firing.

The importance of the battery signaller and lineman cannot be stressed too strongly; above all else each was a "Jack-of-all-trades". Battery signallers were divided up as follows: Three men at battery; three at "O-Pip", with the observing officer; three in the trenches. The tour of duty at each point was three days, with three days rest; but the rest period consisted of acting as emergency lineman or assisting with any other odd job that might turn up. In addition to the signallers' regular duty at the battery, keeping "logs" of all messages, they had also to record all ammunition expended and keep stock of what was received, fired, or found defective. They had, too, the responsibility of keeping map records of all lines, of bringing same neatly into the signalling dugout, and properly labelled at all times. Spare gunners were instructed in the layout and maintenance of telephone lines so that they might act in an emergency as linemen. This was a very important duty and was carried out as soon as a new position was occupied.

The duties of the signallers in the trenches consisted of keeping in touch with the Infantry H. Q., transmitting calls for assistance or retaliation given by the C.O., to the battery. Sometimes wire-cutting shoots were carried out and then the observations were sent direct to the battery from the trenches instead of from the "O-Pip", so that a close-up view of the condition of the wire might be reported. Every artillery signaller can remember sending or receiving a call in the middle of the night: "Denmark One", or "Salvo—all Guns" and the resulting row.

Early in 1916, the simplification of lines caused the establishment of the Report Centre, or forward collecting station for lines between Infantry, Artillery and other units in the forward area, in order to do away with long exposed lines back to each Divisional Headquarters, before getting contact with each other. "Emma Vic," the report centre at Martha's Vineyard, will be remembered by most of the signallers who were with us at that time. The "Walled Garden," at Dickebusch, of such unpleasant memories, was a Report Centre. From each of these centres, buried cables connected with Division.

On our arrival at Dickebusch, Ridgewood, Suicide Copse, Bedford House and the surrounding area, the action became much more brisk. It was then it was discovered that the old system of earth return telephone lines was a very easy and certain method of giving away information to the enemy, whose powerful amplifiers, using the principles of the present-day radio valve, enabled them to pick up all the earth currents sent out by our phones and to read all messages with perfect ease.

Two methods were adopted to overcome this trouble, the first and simplest being the introduction of the Fullerphone. This new instrument used a new system in signalling in that it sent out impulses of direct current instead of the high frequency, alternating currents of the D III set, which were so easy to detect. The direct current impulses of the Fullerphone could only be detected by another Fullerphone fitted with special equipment and attached to the telephone wire.

The other method, and the one which solved many difficulties at the same time overcoming the ground current trouble, was the armoured cable. Under supervision of the Engineers, trunk lines were laid out so as to furnish accessible lines to all batteries, and other units and working parties were furnished by the infantry of labor battalions to dig deep trenches along these pre-arranged routes.

As soon as the trenches were dug, the cables were laid and the trenches refilled, the whole operation, in no case, taking longer than from dusk to daybreak. Test boxes were installed at convenient intervals along these trunk lines, so that in case of trouble it would not be necessary to dig down to get at any cable. Then the required number of cables was allotted to each unit and the whole system maintained by the Engineers, except for the ordinary line-trouble, due to shells tearing them up.

All armored cables furnished metallic return circuits, or two wires, instead of the old system of one wire and an earth return. This, of course, eliminated effectively the possibility of the enemy overhearing conversations or buzzer signals. It is worthy of note that some development had been done during our stay at "Plugstreet" along these lines, and it had been recommended that all telephone lines should be made two wire, back from the enemy front line at least one thousand yards.

Early in 1916, also, it was found that wireless communication from aeroplane was possible, and, with the idea in mind of using aeroplanes for artillery observation, a number of signallers were sent to the wireless school, Sid Williams being sent by the Fourth Brigade and trained in wireless procedure and aeroplane contact methods. On his return, some work was done with aeroplane contact with very satisfactory results, messages to the aeroplanes being sent by means of laying out strips of cloth twelve feet long and one foot wide, on the ground in the shapes of various code letters. Observations from the planes were received on regular wireless receivers and transmitted to the firing battery by phone.

It might have been mentioned that, early in the war, not only was 18-pounder ammunition scarce, but also telephone wire. We used to go out on foraging parties and collect every scrap of spare wire we could find, having regard, of course, for the fact that some of the wire we found was in service. Such wire as we collected served not only as emergency stock, but was known to find its way even into very comfortable home-made bed springs.

Following out the general improvement in the telephonic communication the summer of 1916, about the time of our departure for the Somme, brought the new switchboard, the four plus three, which was simply a small type of commercial board, using, instead of lamp signals, receivers. The idea, while much in advance of what most Brigades had been using, was but a commercially-made product of the same design and idea as we had been using ever since the night the board didn't work. Its adoption brought a general improvement in all army phone communication.

Arrival at the Somme brought trouble in plenty, not only for gunners and drivers, but for signallers and linemen. There were no trees, ditches or reasonably safe places to conceal wires, so they were run open across the shell-holes as quickly as possible and we had to take a chance on them lasting a few hours before being blown up. As soon as a line went out of commission, a lineman had to be sent out on it at once. It seemed like a superhuman task to try to keep lines in order in such a place, but it was surprising to find lines lasting several hours at a stretch, although others often lasted only a few minutes. Runners were pressed into service when urgent messages were to be delivered, as the Batteries were grouped fairly close together.

At the Somme was developed, as a fine art, the "Zero" hour, the "synchronizing" of watches, and the use of the "twenty-four hour dial". All officers concerned, in case of a proposed attack, would be advised that a certain minute, for instance 4.20, would be called zero hour, at which the action would commence. All operations for that particular action would be timed to take place at a certain number of minutes past that zero hour and would be timed as plus 0.1 or minus 0.5, etc., rather than at the actual minute as shown by the watch. It was found here also that as Artillery Signallers had to go forward a great deal to the front line, they should have distinguishing badges of some kind and they were given blue half covers for their tunic lapels, of the same color as the Signal Corps of the Engineers. The necessity of uniformity in signalling procedure brought the attachment of a Signal Corps Officer to Brigade Headquarters to supervise all the communication of the Batteries and Brigade.

From the Somme onward, one prominent change in the method of signalling which seems to have developed, was the use of the daylight lamp, as it could be relied upon to get its message through when wire phone lines had been blow to bits. It was used at Vimy and to much greater advantage at Passchendaele, when no phone lines could be kept intact at all, and Battery-to-Brigade service was maintained entirely by runners. "S.O.S." calls from the front line were sent to the Batteries by means of the lemp and in at least one case we know of, the alertness of a battery signaller was responsible for picking up an "S.O.S." which, although not directed to his Battery, had not been seen by the station to which it was intended. The result was that he reported to his Battery Commander, the guns were let loose and a very serious situation for the Infantry averted. From this time on, the greatest change in the signalling system or conditions, were the greater hazards to be faced by the man on the lines, owing to the more intense artillery fire rather than any important change in the equipment for sending and receiving.

In addition to the members of the "B.C." parties who distinguished themselves in this way, a great many were recommended to commissions and, after passing through the Artillery Training Depot and the Canadian School of Gunnery in England, returned as commissioed officers to take up more advanced duties with various Batteries throught the Canadian Corps.

CHAPTER V

In Front of Vimy

A S the last vehicle of the column passed through Bouzincourt, and the long line of guns and ammunition wagons headed north, we all sighed with relief to be at last rid of the mud and misery of the Somme. No more would we crouch in chalky muck and shell-holes to dodge 5.9's, no more would we lead frightened pack-animals through to Pozières, or curse like mad when we became lost on a rainy night in the maze of battered trenches— trying to find the "O.P." Those trying days were over, but only for a time, others even more terrible were yet to come. Many critics claim that for pure unadulterated misery the Somme could not be equalled, but what of Vimy and Passchendaele?

On arrival at Hallicourt, the 4th Bde. C.F.A., was again split up, H.Q. remaining in rest, the 13th Battery attached to the 6th Bde., C.F.A. (King's Group), the 14th Battery to the 7th Bde., C.F.A. (McKay's Group), and the 19th to the 5th Bde., C.F.A. (Britton's Group). Two days later, 4th Bde. C.F.A. H.Q. (Col. Sharman) relieved the latter H.Q. in the line near Aix-Noulette Wood, and remained in action there for two weeks, after which they went into billets at Hersin.

To the left lay Bully-Grenay, with its battered houses, broken engines and mine cars. Day and night the Germans pounded it with phosgene gas shells. Further south and just in front of us was the strongly fortified village of Cité Calonne, surrounded by monster slag heaps, broken power stations and pit heads.

Angres and Liévin, bristling with hostile machine-guns, barred the approach to Lens from the Souchez Valley, which ran east from Carency. This section of the line had seen considerable fighting in the early days of the war, but for the past year was considered the quietest sector on the British front.

Gun positions were in the vicinity of Bully-Grenay, and "O-Pips" on Lorette Ridge.

After the mud, misery, devastating shell-fire and all-round unpleasantness of the Somme where as the rain-sodden days and nights wore on and every one wondered how much longer must we suffer, the march north was a pleasant realization. Steel was rusty, harness and kit mud-encrusted and yet, as the march progressed, and even for a few days after our arrival at Hersin, not a word was said about cleaning harness. The town was not placed "out of bounds"; it was like a new era, and all ranks made the most of the welcome respite. French beer and "cognac" never tasted better, and never was it consumed in such quantities. This little reaction after many days of strain a nddiscipline were appreciated by all, and to make this reaction complete, leave re-opened on a liberal scale.

Throughout December a great improvement was noticed in the condition of the horses. Covered standings, a well-earned rest, and good clear water brought health and vigor to the sorely-tried animals, and made them fit and ready for the strenuous days to come. At the guns, the men were quite comfortable and enjoyed a long period of comparative inactivity. On January 1st Lt.-Col. C. H. L. Sharman assumed command of the Centre Group from Maj. G. L. Drew, who returned to duty with the 13th Battery, 4th Bde., C.F.A., H.Q., remaining at Hersin.

Lt.-Gen. Sir Julian Byng determined to make a raid in the vicinity of Cité Calonne, near the Double Crassier. This raid was entrusted to the 4th Canadian Infantry Brigade, commanded by Brig.-Gen. Robert Rennie. The Artillery preparations were assigned to Lt.-Col. J. K. MacKay, whose command was enlarged to twenty-four Batteries, and assisted on the right flank by the 4th Brigade, C.F.A., also the Stokes Guns and Trench Mortar Batteries.

Wire in front of the German trenches was tremendously strong and neither the French nor the British had taken a prisoner in that vicinity.

Two weeks were spent in cutting the enemy barbed wire entanglements and preparing for the attack, during which time intermittent bursts of fire were ordered. This was before the advent of "106 Fuze".

On the morning of January 21st the 20th and 21st Battalions sprang from their trenches and assaulted the enemy's front line. A snow storm, with a following wind, aided our attack. An artillery officer accompanied the advancing troops and installed a telephone in the German trenches. The success of the attack was unique. The wire proved to be no impediment, so thoroughly had the Gunners done their work. One German officer and ninety-nine other ranks were captured, a great many of the enemy killed and our casualties comparatively small.

Congratulatory messages were received by Gen. Rennie and Col. Mac-Kay from the Commander-in-Chief, the Army Commander, and Sir Julian Byng.

Needless to say, while the careful preparations and thorough organization contributed to the success, the success itself was really due to the invincible valor and determination of the platoon commanders, N.C..O.'s and other ranks. This was admittedly the most successful raid carried out by the British Army up to that time.

On the 24th, the 2nd C.D.A. was relieved by the 1st C.D.A. for open warfare training, and marched to Pernes area, via Barlin, Houdain, Ourton and Dieval. The 4th Bde., C.F.A., H.Q. and the 13th Battery were billeted at Marest, and the 14th and 19th Batteries located at Bours. The weather had become cold and as there was much work to be done on the horse standings, gun parks, and billets, little training could be followed. On the 31st the Brigade marched to Nédon via Pernes, and Aumeral, where it remained until Feb. 15th. Conditions here were much better.

After thorough instruction in section and battery gun drill, foot drill, manoeuvres, lectures, and riding, the unit returned to action via Pernes, Camblain-Chatelain, Division, Houdain, Estree Cauchie, and Les Quatre Vents. A relief of the 38th, 30th, 39th and 43rd Batteries (3rd C.D.A.) was carried out, and six-gun battery positions taken over a mile or so in front of Maroeuil. The 4th Bde., C.F.A. became known as Sharman's (Centre) Group, consisting of the 13th Battery plus one section of the 27th, 14th Battery plus one section of the 27th, 19th Battery, plus one section of the 26th, and the 21st Howitzer Battery plus the X/2/C Trench Mortar Battery. On the 22nd Lt.-Col. Sharman proceeded on leave to England, Lt.-Col. J. S. Stewart assuming command of the Centre Group.

The Vimy region had seen no action of importance since the spring of 1916. Both the Germans and British had been satisfied to sit tight in their positions, and use this sector as a recuperative spot for battle-wearied divisions. When the Canadians came into the line, however, the perpetual quietude and inactivity changed rapidly to a systematic wearing down of the Hun "morale". This unexpected attitude made the enemy feel panicky and peevish. He posted notices in front of his trenches reading, "CUT OUT YOUR DAMNED ARTILLRY. WE, TOO, ARE FROM THE SOMME". Our replies were not in words, but with shells, and more shells.

Trench raids followed in rapid succession. These excursions must have been very trying to German nerves. Prisoners were secured on nearly every occasion, heavy casualties inflicted on the enemy, and his dug-outs and strong points bombed and destroyed. Our guns registered on prominent targets, engaged hostile batteries, trench-mortars, and machine-gun emplacements, and carried out an extensive programme of harassing fire day and night. No longer was it necessary to conserve our ammunition. By the New Year, the munition factories of Britain, Canada and the U.S.A. had hit their stride. Guns and shells poured into France by the thousands and the great army of British Territorials formed a large reserve for future operations. At last the tide had turned!

During the summer and fall of 1915, the French had forced the Germans back from their almost impregnable positions at Notre Dame de Lorette, Ablain Ste. Nazaire, Souchez, Carency, La Targette, and the famous Labyrinth near Neuville Ste. Vaast, but Vimy Ridge itself still remained to the enemy. These villages, once beautiful and prosperous with their clean brick cottages and churches, now presented a scene of desolation and ruin. Graves of those who had fallen in battle numbered into the thousands, while here and there bodies and bones still lay exposed to the mercy of the elements. The whole countryside was strewn with the kit of war and abandoned trenches.

Vimy Ridge was one of the most formidable buttresses in the German defence line in France. Since then the enemy had made his position into a veritable fortress. To our observers at Mont St. Eloi, no sign of life was visible on the long bare ridge. The gradual slope of its western face was seamed with line after line of deep, well-constructed trenches, protected by wide belts of barbed wire. From the eastern slope, dropping off suddenly to the Douai plain below, underground communication trenches led through to the front line. Lateral underground passages connected these long tunnels. They formed a perfect screen to movement, and a sure means of communication with the flanks, front, and rear. Large bodies of troops utilized these tunnels for reliefs and refuge from heavy shell-fire. Another perfect concentration point was the caves of Vimy, constructed many years before by the Huguenots, and capable of accommodating several thousand men These were used by the enemy for assembly stations and first aid hospitals.

Wide, deep dug-outs, 30 feet below ground level, lined with heavy planks, well-furnished with stolen goods, and lighted by electricity, provided the greatest comfort to Regimental H.Q. and enemy trench garrisons. Field-gun batteries were located just beyond the crest, and among the ruins of battered villages and shell-torn woods. Many of these positions consisted of reinforced concrete gun pits, two to three feet thick. At the foot of the ridge, on the Douai plane, howitzer batteries lay in perfect security and were only visible by aeroplanes.

In the trenches taken over by the Canadians, parapets had to be rebuilt, duck-walks raised, and communication trenches, due to the incessant rains of the preceding months, drained and improved. As the weather changed, and winter approached frost helped to make the ground more passable, but even with the light blanket of snow covering the mud and desolation, the cold dampness and driving storms of sleet gave the men added misery.

The winter of 1916-17 was a very severe one on horse transports. The animals shivered in their scant shelters and many died from exposure and overwork. Roads and wagon-lines became a regular quagmire of thick, slimy mud. Horses and vehicles, becoming mired, had to be dug out. Others sank so deep in the sludge they had to be abandoned. On such terrible days, the issue of "S.R.D." was a God-send. To facilitate the passage of troops and munitions to the forward zone, a complete system of narrow-gauge railway, 20 miles in all, was installed by the Engineers, existing roads improved, and construction of corduroy roads commenced. The most important of these was the one from Mont St. Eloi across the shell-torn fields, past Berthonval Farm, to the Arras-Bethune Road. Its rapid construction was due in no small measure to the untiring efforts of the Forestry Corps, who toiled for months behind the lines, cutting logs into planks, and hauling them forward during the frosty days of February to the waiting gangs of men near Mont St. Eloi. Fortunately, the enemy failed to discover this project until the work was almost completed. His area shoots on the back country caused considerable disruption of traffic, but the immunity of the plank roads, from concentrated shell fire, permitted a constant flow of ammunition and supplies to pour forward to the guns and trench depots.

As the rainy season ended and cold weather approached, the horse lines needed considerable attention. For those who passed through those terrible days of Vimy, the experience of an artillery driver and his team will ever be remembered. From "Reveille" to "Lights-Out" he was constantly at work, and quite often during the hours of darkness, hauling up ammunition to the guns by pack-mule. And the mud! Who will ever forget the horror of it? Mud on our clothes—all over our persons, in our blankets and even iu our food!

The standings, once considered clean and comfortable, had vanished out of sight into the mire. In many cases overhead cover was not available. Try and imagine the state of the ground after two months of incessant rain and the passing to and fro of one hundred and fifty horses. Wagon-lines were shifted from place to place, but the same conditions existed everywhere. Finally the Engineers, equipped us with piling, sheet iron and a large supply of brushwood. The latter was pressed into the morass of mud and water. To our great surprise the huge bundles vanished in the "goo", but as more and more were laid down, a good foundation was secured. A layer of broken brick and rubble made the standings perfect. Trench mats were laid across the mud, comfortable huts erected, and soon permanent camps were created out of the desolation. Hitherto, through lack of fuel, we had stood and shivered in cold shacks. Now coke was available and home-made heaters or "braziers" blazed brightly while the men off duty gathered around a game of "crown and anchor".

To-day as we sit around the table enjoying roast turkey and plum pudding one compares his luxurious fare with the issued rations at Vimy. Do you remember the little twister of bacon, a slice or two of bread (if you were a friend of the cook, you might have them "gypoed") and the mess tin of tea with a shot of klim to color it? And those noon and supper snacks of mulligan, bully, McConachie, hard tack, bread, cheese, margarine, Tickler's jam, not to mention "buckshee fags"—Woodbines, Arf a mo's, Three Witches, Ruby Queens, etc.!

But when the mail arrived! This was one parade the "sick and dying" always attended. The lucky boys who received parcels were highly in favor with the gang and it wasn't always the owner of a parcel who opened it. A cake from home, no matter how stale it was, or who made it, was the luxury of the hour. "Share and share alike," was the rule of the army. Seldom, if ever, was a man allowed to guzzle down the "works" in sight of the rest of the boys, unless he was the Sergeant. N.C.O.'s had the Indian sign on the common herd.

It was about this time that French leave opened to the Canadians. About a dozen passes were sent to the 4th Brigade H.Q. and the units drew lots for them. Soon after, however, it was much easier to secure continental furlough than the regular English leave, and a great number of us visited Paris, Lyons and Marseilles.

A trip to Paris, after the mud and misery of Vimy, was a revelation, with its gay life and all-night parties—the scandals of Montmartre—the cafes whose tables jut out into the street, crowded with allied soldiers, statesmen and midinettes; the Folies Bergère—and the merry throng parading the boulevardes. And only ten days to do it in! Many, not satisfied, begged for another visit, and, on the next occasion, found their paradise usurped by the newly-arrived Americans.

Alighting from the Boulogne Express, some of us passed through the Gare Ste. Nazaire, and laden down with our kits of war, proceeded by one cylinder taxi to the Grande Hotel or some such palace in the heart of the city. Others of us picked rooms on the Champs Elysées, or near L'Etoile and the Arc de Triomphe. After a good turkish bath and thorough clean-up our steps inevitably led us to the fashionable Boulevard des Italiens, and on to the Place de L'Opéra.

A Canadian was easily spotted—the Maple Leaf was known far and wide—and if one were able to steel himself to resist the many offers of a female escort, he turned them down with smiling thanks. Who will forget the beautiful blondes and brunettes? Stopping at the Cafe de la Paix for "une verre de cognac, un liqueur", or a rare bottle of champagne, it was sure a wonderful sight to scan the faces at the tables. A dark-haired, faultlessly dressed cuirassier with his smiling partner; a tall, tanned, blue-eyed Britisher; a gaily kilted Scot; and maybe a husky Australian mingled with the many races of civilians and scantily garbed damsels. Many lingered on, but as there were similar places to visit, a soldier on leave usually "made the rounds".

Day after day we got to know Paris better and better. It was to some like a trip to Fairyland, and a wonderful tonic to make them forget the miseries of the battle zone. After an inspection of the historic Louvre, the Palace Gardens, the Place de la Concorde, les Invalides, the Bourse, the Eiffel Tower, the Trocadero, the Bastile, the beautiful cathedral of Notre Dame, the Bois de Boulogne, Ste. Cloud, and Versailles, one investigated further the life of the Parisiennes themselves. These people, though gay and bright, had all suffered terribly from the horrors of the Great War. Some had lost a father, a brother or a sister. Others were in constant fear lest their last offering to France would fall before the dawn of Peace. The heroic spirit of the French is unequalled. The singing of "La Marseillaise" sends them into a frenzy of enthusiasm.

When you made friends among these gay people, it was not merely an acquaintanceship—it was an "entente cordiale". And, on the last day of your leave, did not your conscience bother you, and did you not say—"Well, why not stay over another day? I'll never live to see it again." The M.P.'s and Transport Officer at the station were only too glad to see the delinquents arrive, and though our passes were a day or two late, we were ushered aboard for a return to the trenches and a soldier's life once more.

By the first of March, the weather had become mild and rainy; the frost had come out of the ground, and the whole battle area was again a sea of mud. Motor lorry and vehicular traffic was not permitted beyond rail-head, and all ammunition had to be taken to the gun positions by narrow-gauge railway or pack-mule. Due to the heavy work expected of them, the animals suffered terribly, especially the horses, and all units were far below strength. The mule then came into his own, and earned the admiration and respect of the army by his untiring perseverance and faithfulness. In the early days of the war, batteries were equipped with horse transport only, but as time went on, and casualties increased, mules were sent to us as replacements. The Battle of the Somme took a heavy toll of the battle-wearied horses, and by the end of the terrible winter of 1916-17, nearly half the animal strength of the Artillery was composed of mules.

On delivery from the remount depots, we found these mules wild, suspicious, and hard to handle. Their large, floppy ears, lean, hungry-looking bodies, and long black tails were objects of interest. Their extraordinary eating capacity amazed us. Like men from a foreign country, they herded together, and would not mingle with the horses. The driver delegated to

Major G. L. Drew, D.S.O.
13th Battery

Battery
Commanders

Major W. H. Merritt
14th Battery

4th

Bde.

Lt.-Col. W. J. Brown

Maj. F. F. Arnoldi, D.S.O.,Bar
15th Battery

C.F.A.
—
1916

Lt.-Col. W. Simpson
16th Battery

break in a team of mules had a big job on his hands. In turn, we taught them to accept the bridle, bit, and saddle; act like a docile statue at "Stables"; draw the water cart or "G.S." wagon; and finally, after a homeric battle in which not a few of us came out second best, managed to "break" them in as teams for the ammunition wagons. As a pack mule, however, the "moke" could not be equalled. Ignorant and fearless of danger, he went through the thickest of shell-fire, mud and water. If his master became lost, he could always be counted upon to find the way home.

Since the summer of 1916, British miners had been working on the construction of three parallel tunnels from our reserve trenches to the front line. These were half a mile apart and equipped with exits to convenient points in the trench system. By the spring of 1917, a few weeks before the famous Battle of Vimy Ridge, these tunnels were extended through to the Hun lines in preparation for the laying of mines. The narrow-gauge tramways took away the excavated chalk in sand-bags.

Due to the inadequate and unsafe means of signal communication with the Batteries and forward zone, the Engineers began to lay underground cable connecting Divisional, Brigade, and Battalion H.Q. Considerable labor was expected of the artillery units in tieing in to this trunk system. Hostile shelling became heavier as time went on, and the cable lines were so badly damaged by shells, and so difficult to repair, that most units reverted to the former overland routing of their telephone wires. The artillery signaller deserves much credit for his splendid work and devotion to duty during this trying period. His lines were always in jeopardy, and though not always broken by enemy shell-fire, were constantly at the mercy of careless drivers and working parties. At any time of the day or night such breaks were liable to occur, and no one envies a lineman his task of repairing a telephone wire under such conditions as existed at Vimy.

Despite the discomfort of occasional snow flurries and sleet storms, the energetic programme of trench raids and harassing fire continued. No large raids were attempted, but forays were made by small groups of men at all hours of the day and night. These raids, scattered along the front, were very trying to German nerves. The frequent taking of prisoners kept up to date the identification of enemy troops. The Artillery was mostly occupied on target registrations of enemy barbed wire, front-line trenches, support lines, machine-gun nests, "O.P.'s" snipers' posts, trench mortars, assembly areas, communication trenches and cross-roads. These points were covered periodically day and night.

The "F.O.O.'s" observed from the "O.P.'s" and kite balloons, noting magnetic bearings of gun flashes to locate hostile batteries, while the R.A.F. signalled corrections to the guns by wireless, lights, and Claxton horns. German retaliation was very weak, clearly indicating an inferiority in gun power and munitions. Meanwhile the Hun strengthened his already well-nigh impregnable positions. Between Souchez, and Arras, at least 12 lines of defence lined the Ridge, and construction of an even stronger line, known as the Drocourt-Quèant Switch, had been commenced covering the city of Douai. The Hun was quite aware of the impending attack on Vimy, but did not know just when the blow would fall.

By the middle of March, the condition of the roads became so acute that great concern was felt as to whether preparations for the offensive would be completed in time. The rain and sleet continued, and the whole countryside resembled a huge quagmire of pools and impassable fields. The trenches streamed with running floods, and the encampments and wagon-lines were no better. In spite of such handicaps, however, the supply of ammunition was maintained at 1,000 rounds per gun. This necessitated nightly trips for the drivers—who toiled uncomplainingly from Camblain L'Abbé to La Targette with their precious stores of water, rations and shells. The gunners, too, were kept very busy, while one detachment manned the guns, another was occupied on the construction of the battle-positions to be used by extra Batteries in the Vimy barrage. These were carefully camouflaged, and stocked with ammunition. Material had to be brought forward by narrow-gauge, and hauled by pack-mule to the positions, but by the end of the month all was in readiness for occupation.

For the past six weeks the Brigade had been in constant action, and had suffered many casualties. According to rumour, we were in for another re-organization, but hardly felt "the powers-that-be" would make any further changes in the old Brigade. However, we were doomed to disappointment. In operation orders, dated March 17th, the 4th Brigade, C.F.A. lost its original identity—Lt.-Col. Sharman returning to England, H.Q., and the 14th Battery were absorbed by other units—and the 7th Brigade, H.Q. with Lt.-Col. J. S. Stewart assuming command, transferred "en bloc," to relieve the old 4th Brigade H.Q. of its duties. On re-organization, the composition of the new unit was as follows:

4th Brigade, C.F.A.—Lt.-Col. J. S. Stewart, C.O.

13th Battery from 4th Brigade—Maj. G. L. Drew, D.S.O.

19th Battery from 4th Brigade—Maj. A. F. Culver

21st Battery from 7th Brigade—Maj. M. N. Ross

27th Battery from 7th Brigade—Maj. J. C. Stewart

Part III

(March 17th, 1917 - June 21st, 1917)

CHAPTER I

Battle of Vimp Ridge

O N reorganization of the Corps Artillery, March 17th, 1917, Batteries were increased from four to six gun strength, many units losing their identity and former associations. The 14th Battery, which was the first of the Second Divisional Batteries to be mobilized at Toronto, in 1914, became broken up, one of its sections going to the 19th Battery and the other to the 27th Battery. Major Waldron, its popular O.C., assumed command of the 15th Battery, 6th Brigade, C.F.A., and members of the H.Q. Staff were absorbed by various units of the 2nd C.D.A. In order to bring the 13th and 21st Batteries up to the new establishment, drafts were required from England.

The Canadian Field Artillery now consisted of nine Brigades of six gun Batteries, or in all, 216 guns, the Lahore Divisional Artillery, covering the 4th Division, adding another 72 guns. The formations were as follows:

1st C.D.A.—1st, 2nd and 3rd Brigades.

2nd C.D.A.—4th, 5th and 6th Brigades.

3rd C.D.A.—8th 9th and 10th Brigades.

Lt.-Col. J. S. Stewart was made Commanding Officer of the 4th Brigade, C.F.A., with Capt. H. M. Savage as Ajutant; Lieut. H. O'Hallor-an, (Orderly Officer); Capt. A. M. McCausland, (M.O.): Capt. C. Gilson, (Paymaster); Capt. A. M. Lee, (V.O.); Capt. R. B. Day, (Chaplain), and Capt. W. E. Shaw, Lieuts. A. B. Dewberry and V. H. Sutherland were taken on the strength as supernumerary officers and assigned to the construction of "G" group gun positions.

During the latter part of March most of the guns had been sent to the "I.O.M." for overhauling and, at times, only nine guns were available in action. The Brigade covered 1,000 yards of front from the south edge of Neuville St., Vaast, with the 4th and 6th Infantry Brigades alternating in the line. For weeks, wire cutting and destructive shoots were carried out along this sector and, every night, Batteries were engaged in harassing fire—sweeping the roads, communication trenches, villages, and area back of the Hun lines. Behind us, innumerable heavy guns and large howitzers were engaging the enemy batteries and rail-heads. Our intense bombardments clearly indicated to the Hun that an attack might come at any day or any hour. Frequent raids, feint attacks and rumours spread along the front, misled the enemy; and the few Canadian prisoners secured by them could give nothing definite as to our real plans. Only the Divisional Generals and those in high command knew of the exact date of the big offensive. The enemy "stood to" for eleven days prior to our attack and must have suffered terribly. This intense strain was enough to ruin the strongest nerves.

The question of ammunition became serious, as 1,000 rounds per Battery had to be expended daily to carry out the program of harassing fire set forth in the Operation Orders. The roads became jammed with traffic. An unbroken stream of vehicles extended from Camblain l'Abbé all the way up to La Targette. Horses became totally exhausted; the hauling of ammunition was indeed a heavy task. Animals and vehicles sank two feet or more in the mire and it became necessary to call upon the narrow-gauge tramways to bring up the shells by rail. Capt. Savage superintended this work and the horses were thus relieved of a great portion of their heavy work.

The watering of horses also gave much trouble as the drivers did not get back from the guns till late and had to leave early again the next afternoon. As days passed, the situation became more acute and large numbers of remounts had to be secured from the 5th (British) Division to bring us up to horse strength.

During the last ten days of March, a series of very successful raids on our sector were carried out by the 4th and 6th Canadian Infantry Brigades, our unit supplying the barrage to cover these demonstrations. The Brigade was highly complimented on its work by Brig-Gen. H. D. B. Ketchen of the 6th Canadian Infantry Brigade, who stated, "I have received reports from the O.C. 31st Battalion and O.C. 27th Battalion that the Artillery of the covering groups in the two raids run off on the nights of the 23rd and 29th of March was excellent and the results most marked. I wish to express the appreciation of myself and all ranks to you and your Brigades for the most efficient manner in which the Artillery preparation and support was carried out."

About this time the extra sections from England arrived to bring the 13th and 21st Batteries up to strength and the following officers were posted: Lieut. A. A. Gillis to D/21; Lieut W. G. Humphries to the 27th: Lieut L. M. Larkin to the 13th Battery.

Hostile artillery fire became more severe and, on the 31st of March we were subjected to a heavy strafing. Our retaliation, however, completely silenced the enemy. For the next week or more ammunition expenditure increased and the Brigade had to fire, daily, 2,500 shrapnel, 2,500 high-explosive and 1,000 gas shells. The task of harassing fire and destructive shoots was further augmented by practice and demonstrative

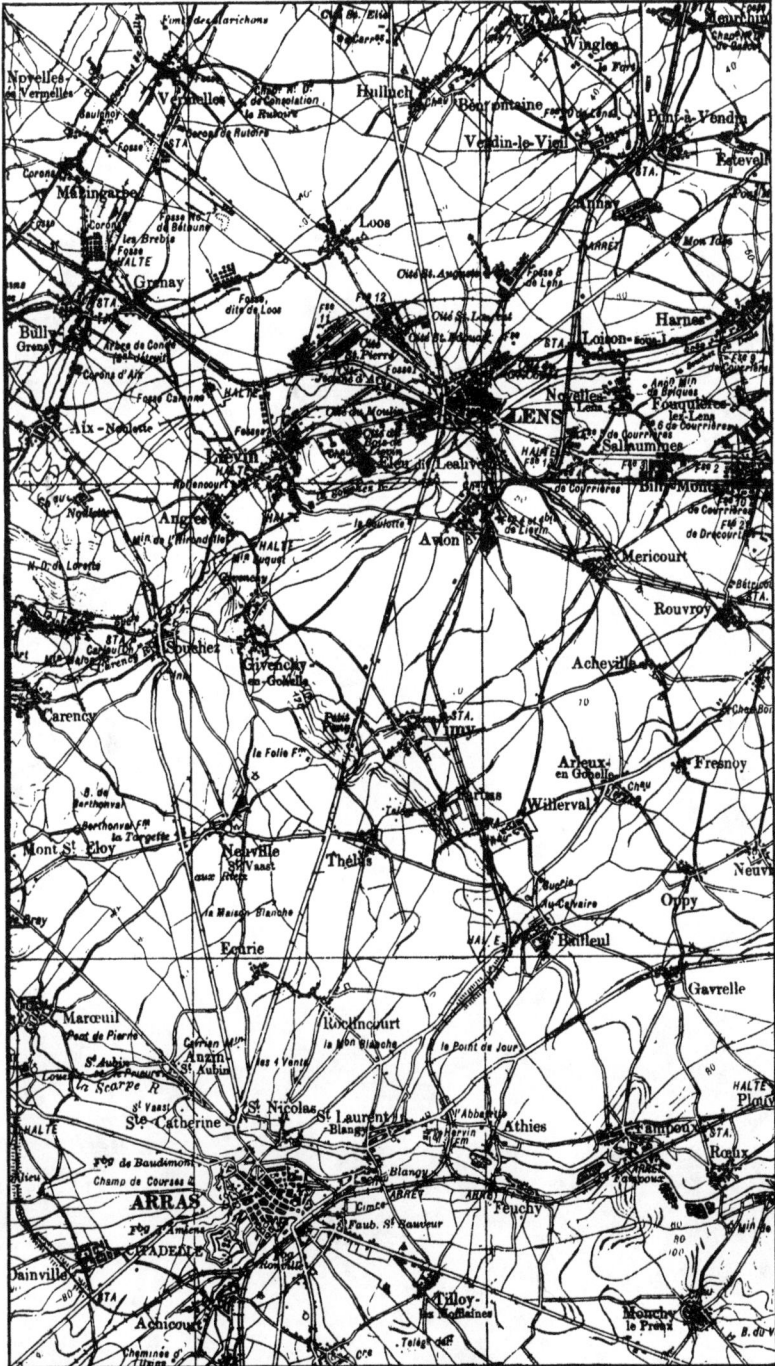

LENS—ARRAS SECTOR, 1917-18

Scale: 1 inch—2.35 miles

barrages on the enemy front lines, support trenches and Thélus Village. Wire cutting continued in spite of the rain and sleet.

On April 4th, Operation Orders were received from the Corps Commander, as follows; "On 'Z' day, which has been communicated verbally to all concerned, the Canadian Corps will undertake the capture of Vimy Ridge from Commandant's House to Kennedy Crater, in conjunction with the operations of the XVII Corps, whose objective is the southern end of the Vimy Ridge from Commandant's House (exclusive) through Maison de la Cote and Point du Jour to the River Scarpe at Athies."

These orders also gave detailed instructions as to the time, points of assembly and routes to be followed by each of the units on "Y" day and on the night of "Y-Z," which prevented congestion of traffic and general confusion on the roads and assembly areas, not only prior to and during the attack, but also when the whole line began to move forward on the afternoon of Easter Monday.

The week preceding was occupied in adding finishing touches to preparations for the show. We all knew the attack was drawing very near and every one worked with great tenseness. When news reached us that the United States had declared war on Germany, we felt sure the end would soon be in sight. German airmen made daring excursions over the lines in an effort to destroy our observation balloons, but the heavy anti-aircraft fire drove them back. It seemed as if the enemy had nullified our air supremacy, as several British machines were seen to fall in aerial combat over Vimy. These fast German machines, painted a bright red and cleverly handled by intrepid aviators, were finally beaten when the new type of British machine came into action a few days before the battle of Vimy Ridge.

On April 5th, the Brigade received a visit from Brig.-Gen. Panet and Maj.-Gen. E. W. B. Morrison, who inspected the Batteries in action. Two days later, Canadian Corps Operation Orders announced, "Zero hour is fixed for 5.30 a.m., April 9th, 1917." For the opening attack, each Brigade was advised to detail an "F.O.O." and party to go farward with the Infantry, at zero. All units and H.Q. drew lots for this honor but, as the same policy was to be followed on each succeeding day, Lieut. O'Halloran of H. Q. volunteered for duty on the 9th and each of the Batteries, commencing with the 27th, 13th, 21st and 19th carried on in turn.

On the evening of Easter Sunday, attacking troops took up their allotted posts in the forward assembly areas, many advancing through the long tunnels prepared by the Engineers. Throughout the long hours of the wet and stormy night that followed, these tunnels provided many men refuge and comfort. Many others huddled against the parapets in the drizzling rain and sleet and blew on their fingers to keep warm. At the same time the eight tanks allotted to the 2nd Canadian Division left their hiding places in Moreuil Woods and proceeded toward the front.

The Brigade was in readiness, with spare parts, springs, and barrels of water to keep the guns cooled, and ammunition polished. The gunners were fully rested. During the night artillery fire decreased very perceptibly, which served the double purpose of puzzling the Germans and giving the gunners a chance to get their shells carefully sorted and the fuzes set so there would be no break in the barrage the next morning.

Sundays at the front were much like other days of the week. Easter Sunday, 1917, will always stand out in the memories of those who served in the Canadian Corps. For them, it was one of the soul-stirring days of the war. Outwardly, it was the nearest approach to Sabbath quiet that the men had known in many weeks. Underneath this superficial calm was a multitude of human emotions which were too deep to find utterance. All watches had been synchronized twice during the afternoon and evening of April 8th. A mistake of a single second in the lifting of the barrage or in the advance of the Infantry might have resulted in serious casualties to the attackers. After day began to break, it became evident that observation would be very difficult. Four seconds before zero, all the guns except the trench mortars ceased abruptly. The silence was blood-chilling. Then, exactly at 5.30, every gun on the twelve mile front opened up. In the morning light the scene was awe-inspiring. The whole countryside was lighted up with sharp stabs of flame and the earth trembled with the shock. At the opening of the barrage, the rattle of machine-gun fire, and the thundering of the trench-mortars added their quotas to the deafening inferno.

A great number of these trench-mortar batteries were engaged in placing a heavy smoke screen along the German lines. The barrage moved on with the smoothness and precision of clock work. Each gun was allotted its particular zone and, after firing on the German front line for four minutes, lifted its fire in perfect unison with other batteries in a rolling barrage of steel. The high explosives tore into the earth and threw up great columns of debris, and the sharp, wicked flashes of shrapnel spread their bullets over the intervening ground. It was a wonder that the whole German garrison was not exterminated.

The enemy sent up signals of distress all along the front but his batteries responded weakly. Our counter battery work must have been perfect. As the day broke, snow flurries and sleet swept the fields and made the scene even more terrible. The Infantry advanced steadily, in extended order, with bayonets fixed, and rifles at the trail. While the first wave captured and consolidated the German front line, another "leap-frogged" through them and proceeded to the next objective. Behind them, line after line of reserve troops pushed forward with supplies of ammunition, while others, detailed as "moppers-up," ousted the enemy, after stubborn fighting, from points of refuge in cellars, dug-outs and tunnels.

Some of the Germans fought tenaciously while others surrendered as soon as our men came up to them. By six in the morning large groups of German prisoners could be seen making their way back to the Arras-Bethune Road, unattended, where they were taken in charge by pickets who piloted them to barbed-wire cages in the rear. At the same time streams of wounded began to flow back, and stretcher bearers, assisted by German prisoners, moved over the newly captured ground, gathering in the wounded.

Shortly after zero hour, the 4th Brigade, C.F.A. patrol of nine men, under Lieut. O'Halloran, advanced with the Infantry and established communication with the guns by 8.45 a.m., from the "Red objective." This was the first official word sent back that the position had been carried. Our Infantry went on and captured all objectives by noon. Lieut. O'Halloran established a good "O.P." on the top of the Ridge, from which a splendid view of the Douai plain could be obtained. From here he spotted enemy guns, teams and infantry all day long and signalled these targets to the gunners. In the afternoon, the 27th Battery moved up to Pulpit Crater in the German front line, 13th Battery to A9b 31/35 and the 19th Battery to A9b 66/31. The ammunition wagons were called upon to haul up ammunition and all the Batteries were in action again by evening. In going forward, we noted the terrible execution of our gun-fire. The artillery preparation had been marvellous and the German front line was practically obliterated.

Throughout the whole day the Brigade had only one casualty, Gunner Drummond of the 21st Battery being wounded.

German resistance became stronger as our Infantry advanced, but, by evening all objectives on the 1st, 2nd, and 3rd Divisional fronts had been carried, with much smaller losses than had been anticipated.

On the left, the 4th Canadian Division, where the Germans were strongly entrenched, met with terrific resistance and did not make the headway expected. During the night, however, Hill 145, above Batter Trench, was stormed and taken after heavy bayonet fighting. Large enemy concentrations were noted coming up from Lens and Douai, by our aviators, who bombed and dispersed them. On the following day, our left flank cleared the Germans from the "Pimple" and forced their retirement to the flats below.

During the stormy night of Easter Monday, the task of bringing up guns, ammunition, and supplies went on. The snow had melted, and the muddy, shell-torn battlefield became practically impassable. Horse transport suffered terribly, the animals being absolutely exhausted from their strenous toil of the past two months. Brig.-Gen. Panet, noting a long column of artillery wallowing in the mire, immediately ordered their withdrawal to the wagon-lines until the roads had been rebuilt and the weather had moderated. At the same time the Light Railway Troops began an extension of the narrow-gauge system across "No-Man's Land" to the crest of the ridge. Within a few days they were able to haul large quantities of ammunition and material to the forward zone. Engineers and Pioneers worked like "Trojans" on the roads, filling up the yawning craters, trenches and shell-holes with brick and rubble from the nearest ruins, and laying brushwood fascines on the old road-bed to give a proper bearing surface for the heavy vehicular traffic that was bound to follow. For nearly a week supplies to the gun positions were only possible by pack-mule.

On the 12th, Maj. J. C. Stewart, O.C. 27th Battery, was slightly wounded by a bomb bursting near his dug-out and Capt. H. M. Savage the Adjutant, assumed command of his unit, while Lieut. M. O'Halloran (Orderly Officer) became Acting Adjutant. All Batteries worked hard on their quarters at the gun positions. For some time they remained "in the open," and the gunners took refuge in shell holes round about. Owing to the heavy loss in horses, only four guns per battery were available for offensive operations. The situation had indeed become critical. To bring the gun strength up to establishment, the 13th and 21st Batteries salvaged German guns and large quantities of ammunition. A section of 7.7's were set up in Goulot Wood by the 13th, and two 4.2 Howitzers placed in position by the 21st. For several days enemy shells were fired into Acheville, Méricourt and the trench lines below.

On the left front of the Canadian attack, the Hun retired to Givenchy-en-Gohelle. The 46th British Division captured Bois-en-Hache and the whole defensive system in that region collapsed. In the Vimy attack 4,000 prisoners, 63 guns, scores of machine-guns, trench-mortars, and great quantities of war materials had been captured. The success of 4th Canadian Division threatened Lens. The Germans seemed panic-stricken and considered abandoning the city. Liévin, a suburb to the south-west of Lens, and Avion were evacuated, and, on the 12th, civilians were forced to leave the district.

Lens had not been shelled by us, and the coal-mines were still in operation. If the weather had been at all favourable, after the battle, the Canadian and Imperial troops might easily have forced its evacuation. The capture of Lens or Douai would have been of great moral and strategical value. The impossible conditions of the battle-field, however, slowed up the advance to such an extent that the Germans had plenty of time to readjust their defences and turn the mining district into a veritable fortress.

Following the retreating enemy, Liévin, Vimy and Bailleul were occupied with little fighting, and strong defences were erected on the newly-won ground, while the Artillery toiled to get into new locations beyond the Ridge. In the meantime, the enemy worked feverishly to complete the Avion-Méricourt-Acheville-Oppy Line, and large numbers of Huns were observed in strength in the Drocourt-Quéant defences barring our approach to Douai.

CHAPTER II

Minor Operations

BATTERIES of the Brigade were now almost out of action, due to the long range, but enemy guns, captured in the sweeping advance over Vimy Ridge, were trained on the Bosches, the 13th Battery having one section of 7.7's at Goulot Wood, the 27th a sniper gun in T 21 c, and the 21st, two 4.2 howitzers in the brickfield at T 26 d 3.5/1.0.

The condition of the roads beggars description. None of our 18-pounders could be moved forward, so we remained where we were, and the 6th Brigade, C.F.A. came into action north-west of Thélus. On our right, however, the 5th (British) Divisional Artillery managed to haul their guns through the mire of the old battlefield and were the first Batteries to struggle into position on the plain below. For the next few days it snowed heavily, the roads became impassable, and hundreds of horses dropped by the wayside, totally exhausted.

Meanwhile enemy gunfire increased, thousands of gas-shells, shrapnel, and high-explosive being directed on our advanced posts and lines of communication. To push forward supplies over the Ridge, or carry out reliefs during the hours of daylight was found to be impossible, as German observers were on the alert for every movement. Consequently roads and communication-trenches down the face of the slope had to be camouflaged, and all supply columns were obliged to move up after dusk —by pack-mule.

By April 20th the weather changed, and it became warm and sunny. The ground dried up rapidly and at last the roads across the old battlefield were passable to heavy traffic. Positions near the Avion-Farbus railway embankment were now selected and occupied, and wagon-lines were also moved forward. These new locations were as follows:—

UNIT	GUN POSITION	WAGON-LINE POSITION
13th Battery	T 21c 4/4	At old battery position.
19th Battery	T 21c 3/4	In field near Mt. St. Eloi.
27th Battery	T 21c 5/3	Near Aux Rietz Corner.
21st (How.)Battery	T 26d 4/3	Near Aux Rietz Corner.

Then commenced a long series of disasters for the Brigade, with a direct hit on one of the 19th Battery gun-pits, and severe losses among the horses due to heavy shelling of the 21st and 27th Battery wagon-lines, back of Neuville St. Vaast. Day and night, enemy artillery "plastered" our forward area with 5.9's and gas, gun after gun being put out of action. The gun-crews suffered terribly.

On the 24th, Major J. C. Stewart, O.C. of the 27th Battery, returned from hospital, Capt. H. M. Savage going back to Brigade H.Q. as Adjutant. The weather gradually improved. The rain ceased. Early summer was at hand. Artillery duels increased in intensity, clearly indicating a renewal of the offensive.

At 4.25 a.m. of the 28th, the tumult broke forth on an eight mile front, with a heavy bombardment of the German lines. Advancing steadily with our barrage, the 1st Canadian Division stormed and captured Arleux, and after stubborn hand-to-hand fighting consolidated a strong position beyond the village. On their right, however, the adjoining Division failed to carry Oppy, and another opportunity of piercing the enemy front was lost. A few days later, while Batteries were registering, German observers spotted our guns near the railway embankment, and ranged on us perfectly.

On May 3rd, the offensive continued, with an attack by the 1st and 2nd Canadian Divisions. All day the battle raged, and by evening, in spite of another failure on the right at Oppy, the strongly entrenched village of Fresnoy was taken by the 1st Canadian Division, and held against many fierce counter thrusts by the enemy. At dusk, only eight out of eighteen field guns of the 4th Brigade, C.F.A. remained in action. Three had been blown to bits. Over 7,000 rounds of ammunition was destroyed, and two men had been killed and seven others wounded. Neighbouring Batteries received retaliation too, but our Brigade certainly got its worst dose of shelling since the Battles of the Somme.

As there was better "flash-cover" available further to the south, the guns were moved in behind Willerval, and placed in the following positions: 13th Battery—B 3c 9/1, 19th Battery—B 9a 5/3, 27th Battery —B 9a 7/5, and the 21st (How.) Battery—same location in the "Brickfields."

For the next week, hostile artillery was very active over the whole forward area, Fresnoy, Arleux, the railway embankment, Bailleul, Farbus and Vimy being heavily shelled with phosgene and lachrymatory gas-shells.

On the 8th, a German surprise attack was directed against Fresnoy, now held by a Brigade of the 5th (British) Division, resulting in its recovery by the enemy. For a time it seemed as if the Bosches would broaden the breach of their advance, but Canadian Battalions in the line, assisted by our heavy concentration of gun-fire, held up the enemy and prevented the loss of further territory. A forward sniping howitzer of the 21st Battery, at T 29c 3/8 remained in action all day, and by its telephone line to the Ridge, a clear, concise report on the situation was available. That night, while our gun-crews were being relieved, the battery positions were "strafed," resulting in another large number of killed and wounded.

Unveiling Monument to the Fallen of the Canadian Field Artillery—Vimy Ridge, 1918.

Canadian Official Photograph.

Since April 1st, the 4th Brigade, C.F.A. had lost:—

| | Officers | | Other Ranks | |
Unit	Killed	Wounded	Killed	Wounded
13th Battery	1	1	2	16
19th Battery		1	8	20
27th Battery			2	4
21st (How) Battery			1	4
	1	2	13	44

For months the condition of the horses and mules had caused great concern. The weather, mud, and shell-fire took heavy toll of them. Most of the Batteries were down to half strength. But, as the warm days of summer approached and the country dried up, the animals took on a new lease of life, and showed great improvement under the watchful care of the N.C.O.'s and drivers. On May 15th, remounts started to arrive, but as we were still far below strength it became necessary to utilize "outriders" for the purpose of packing up ammunition to the guns. The Padre's mount, of which he was very proud, was pressed into service. Being without means of transport for two or three days, this "Honoured Gentleman" made a journey on foot to the gun position and laid a complaint to the O.C. of the Battery, to which he was attached, stating that he would be unable to cover his rounds without his "four-legged friend." The Battery Commander assured him the matter would be adjusted as soon as possible, and on the next visit of the wagon-line officer to the guns, instructions were given to find a horse for the Padre.

Next day remounts arrived and among them was a little cream coloured "Jenny-mule," which was much too small for artillery purposes.

The following Sunday the full complement of the Battery was ordered out for church parade, under command of the O.C. The newly arrived "Jenny" was saddled up and the Padre was informed a mount had been found for him. On seeing the mule being led to him, the Padre's dignity was touched and he complained bitterly to the Battery Commander. After listening with much patience, this harassed officer replied, "Now, Padre, there was a much better man than you rode into Jerusalem on a similar mount, and I am afraid you will have to be satisfied with what we have offered you."

The situation on the front now became normal, the "heavies" and Reserve Artillery Brigades were gradually withdrawn, and the Infantry began to dig an extensive trench system.

On May 17th, the 19th Battery relieved the 16th at B9b 9/5 and the 6th Brigade, C.F.A. were grouped in positions on top of the Ridge in support. Three days later, Major G. L. Drew, O.C. of the 13th Battery, was evacuated sick, and shortly after returned to Canada to recuperate. Every night Batteries kept up harassing fire, searching and sweeping the roads, communication trenches, and assembly areas. The 21st Battery still had its two 4.2 German howitzers in action, and a large supply of ammunition available. Forward guns were placed in good positions, the 13th section at T 27d 9/1, and the 19th at T28d 0.1, carrying out harassing fire in conjunction with the 21st Battery.

Off to the left, on the 4th Canadian Division front, a very successful raid was carried out on the night of June 2nd-3rd, when a large party of our Infantry advanced on the Brewery and Power Station of La Coulotte. In this brilliantly executed engagement our men captured the village and 100 prisoners. Enemy machine-gunners who fought valiantly were overcome only after severe hand-to-hand fighting. Shortly after dawn, the ruins of the Brewery and Power Station were deluged by the German guns, and the place becoming untenable the Canadians withdrew to their original lines.

For gallantry in action, during the Vimy operations, the following officers were decorated: Major M. N. Ross (21st), D.S.O.; Lt. W. A. Townsley (27th), M.C.; Lt. M. O'Halloran, (H.Q.), M.C.; Sgt. Purdon (19th), M.M.; Gnr. Armstrong (21st), M.M.; Gnr. Thom (21st), M.M.; Bdr. Brown (H.Q.), M.M.

On June 4th, the Batteries withdrew to the wagon-lines, and the 4th Brigade, C.F.A. became attached to the Reserve Divisional Artillery, the 6th Brigade, C.F.A. covering our old zone.

Next day, we marched to Carency, establishing new wagon-lines on the banks of the river, and occupied gun positions in support of the 4th Canadian Division. H.Q. (M26d), 13th (S2b 9/2), 19th (M33b2/9), 21st (M32b 5/1), 27th (M32b 8/2). Guns were immediately calibrated, "O.-Pips" and signal communication established, and 600 rounds per gun delivered to the Batteries.

Raiding activity continued along the front. At 3.30 a.m. on the 5th, a party of the 102nd (British Columbia Battalion) attacked the Electric Generating Station outside of Lens, a strongly fortified post protecting the city, and after heavy fighting, drove out the enemy garrison and consolidated the position in our lines.

Another party of the 102nd Battalion (4th Canadian Division) carried out a minor operation at 8.30 p.m. on June the 8th against Callous, Cancel, and other trenches north of the Souchez River to the junction with the 46th (British) Division who raided Hill 65. This attack was a complete success, 12 prisoners being taken and the enemy trench garrisons along the front badly rattled. The captured trenches were then handed over to the 46th (British) Division, operating on our left. The 4th Brigade, C.F.A. took an active part in this barrage.

At 11.45 p.m., the same evening, another raid was carried out by the 3rd and 4th Canadian Divisions, our troops entering the German positions on a wide front, causing many casualties, and destroying dug-outs and defences before returning to our lines. Slowly but surely we were closing in on Lens.

On June the 11th, the Brigade withdrew to the wagon-lines, at Carency, for a few days rest and training, its zone being taken over by a British A.F.A. Brigade. During this period, the Batteries engaged in harness cleaning, mounted drill and sports. Many took advantage of the cool waters of the river, and bathed daily. "Doc" McCausland inoculated the men against typhoid, and "Tim" O'Halloran, acting Paymaster in the absence of Capt. Gilson, gave everybody the odd few francs.

In the mounted sports, Capt. C. Sifton won the officers' prize in jumping, with Capt. J. I. McSloy second, while the 19th Battery cleaned up in the six-horse team competition. After a good rest, and issue of new uniforms, the Brigade were again ready for another spell in action, and on the 15th occupied their old positions, vacated a few days before.

This sector of the line was quiet, but very interesting, especially from the observation posts. Lens and its suburbs, enemy trench lines, and activity behind the city were clearly distinguishable. Much sniping was done and soon the enemy began to realize that Canadian artillerymen were no mean marksmen.

Lens was literally deluged by concentrated shoots of high explosive and gas shells.

The 5th Lincolns carried out a very successful operation on the 19th, capturing and consolidating a large portion of the enemy trench system. Each Battery fired over 1,000 rounds during the evening and night, following the attack—in answer to "S.O.S." calls from the British infantry on our left. Next day, the Brigade again pulled out for another period of training, being relieved by the 18th A.F.A. Brigade.

For some time it had been rumoured that the Canadian Corps was soon to have a new Commander, and we all hoped a Canadian would be chosen to succeed Sir Julian Byng. General Turner, V.C. and General Currie were the favorites among the men of the fighting forces. On the 9th of June they were each gazetted Lt.-Generals, the latter receiving command of the field forces in France, and the former being placed in charge of the organizations in England. In bidding the Corps farewell, Sir Julian Byng's message to the troops was as follows:—

"In saying good-bye to the Corps, I find it very difficult to give expression to the feelings of pride and affection which dominate all other sentiments. During the year of my command, the unvarying success in battle, the progress in training and discipline, and the unswerving devotion and loyalty of all ranks are features which stand pre-eminent in the history of the Corps; that history will last forever, and my association with you, in the making of it, is a joy that can never be impaired."

On his appointment as commander of the Canadian Corps, Lt.-Gen. Currie received the following congratulatory message from Sir Robert Borden, Prime Minister of Canada.

"To General Sir Arthur Currie, the new Canadian Commander of the Canadian Army Corps at the front, my colleagues and I send hearty congratulations on your appointment to the command of the Canadian Army Corps. We are confident that the gallant Canadians who already have brought such splendid distinction to their Country, and such magnificent support to the Allied Cause, will have an equally glorious record under your command. We bid all God-speed in the great work which lies before you, and send the firm assurance that Canada will, without fail, give to you and the officers under your command all needed aid and support to maintain your efforts, and to ensure success."

On the 20th of June, the 4th Brigade, C.F.A. ceased to be part of the 2nd Canadian Division. Mobilized at Toronto, in November 1914, the

13th, 14th, 15th and 16th Batteries were the first units of Field Artillery to be embodied in the 2nd Contingent, and the only Brigade ready for the front when the Division embarked for France, Sept. 14th, 1915. Since that time, though separated by reorganization in May 1916, the personnel of these units wore the "navy blue patch."

In Operation Orders from 2nd Canadian Divisional Artillery, June 21st, 1917, the following instructions were received:—

(a) The 4th Canadian Divisional Artillery is constituted from this date.

(b) Lt. Col. C. H. MacLaren, D.S.O., now commanding 1st Brigade, C.F.A., will assume command with the rank of Temporary Brig.-General, and will report forthwith to G.O.C., 4th Canadian Division.

(c) The 3rd Brigade, C.F.A., of the 1st C.D.A., will be transferred forthwith to the 4th Canadian Division, and will report to Brig.-General MacLaren.

(d) The 4th Brigade, C.F.A., of the 2nd C.D.A., at present attached to the Reserve Divisional Artillery will be transferred to the 4th C.D.A. and will report to Brig.-General MacLaren as soon as it is relieved by the 18th A.F.A. Brigade, R.F.A.

(e) No. 2 Section 1st C.D.A.C. and No. 2 Section 2nd C.D.A.C. will be transferred to the 4th Canadian Division to form part of the 4th C.D.A.C., and will be transferred to the 4th Divisional Area.
The new reorganization was a great surprise to all units concerned.

For months previous we had heard "rumours" of further changes, but as it was generally believed the 5th Canadian Divisional Artillery, still in training at Witley Camp, England, were to be attached to the 4th Division on its arrival in France, the few "originals" left of the Old Brigade did not think it possible that they would ever become separated from the 2nd Division. The 3rd Brigade, C.F.A. undoubtedly felt the change very badly too, but both units realized the switch was made for a purpose, and from June, 1917, till demobilization members of the 4th C.D.A. considered themselves inferior to none. From this date on, a green patch replaced the "navy blue."

The Lahore Divisional Artillery, was at last detached from the Canadian Corps. For five months Lahore Batteries covered the 2nd Canadian Division until February, 1916, when the 5th, 6th and 7th Brigades, C.F.A., came into the line. From then till October, 1916, these R.F.A. units acted as Divisional Artillery for the 3rd Canadian Division, and upon relief by the 8th, 9th and 10th Brigades, C.F.A., assumed the "rôle" for the 4th Canadian Division until June 20th, 1917, when the 4th C.D.A. was organized. Their long association with the Corps was deeply appreciated by all ranks, and many glowing tributes were tendered them as they marched out of the line.

As part of the Indian Expeditionary Force "A," under General Sir James Wilcox, the Lahore Division arrived in France on the 22nd of October, 1914, at Marseilles, and was immediately rushed up the line to take part in the First Battle of Ypres.

Their record was, from the first, as might have been expected from a Regular Division, a splendid one, but perhaps they are best remembered for their unexcelled Divisional Artillery, whose C.R.A. was General Maxwell.

They supported Canadian Infantry so often and were so intimately associated with them, that in the famous "Battle Book of Ypres," by Beatrix Brice, they are listed in the Index of Formations and Units under "Canadian Divisions!"

Canadian Troops will particularly remember the splendid help they received from the Lahore Divisional Artillery on the 26th of April, 1915, during the Gas Attacks of the Second Battle of Ypres, when the Infantry of the Division "charged up an open slope in the face of overwhelming shell, rifle and machine-gun fire and clouds of poison gas, and with the Canadians, prevented a German advance, thus ensuring the safety of Ypres.

The Lahore Division was later transferred to Mesopotamia—a climate which was more congenial to its brown-skinned warriors, who had suffered terribly from the mud, rain and cold of Flanders.

Memories of its good-natured, dark-skinned men still remain in France, of tall, turbaned, bearded Pathans, of tiny clean-shaven Gurkas, of "Sweepers" and "Havildars," of goats and gee, of bravery, of kindliness, and above all, of good humour.

It has been aptly said of them, "though many died and there was much glory," few died with greater courage, and no pathos could be more poignant than the fate of these soldiers from the rolling plains of the Five Rivers and the hills beneath the Safêd Koh, who of their own free will, crossed the ocean to die for the British Raj in the mists of a strange land.

Part IV

(June 21st, 1917 - May 28th, 1919)

CHAPTER I

𝕾iege of 𝕷ens

THE country about Lens, once a thriving centre of the colleries of Northern France, was now a barren waste of charred woods, ruined houses, flooded mine shafts, and battered enemy trench lines. Hilly and undulating, this area, prior to the War, had boasted of prosperity, beautiful villas, and numerous suburban municipalities, centred about a region of intense industrial activity.

In 1914, Lens was the most important centre of the community, and large numbers of workman were employed at the coal mines, and iron and steel foundries. Close by, in well-kept cottages, these men resided. To the north lay Cité St. Auguste, Cité St. Emile, Cité St. Laurent, Cité St. Edouard and Cité St. Elizabeth. On the west were Cité St. Theodore, Cité St. Jeanne d'Arc, Cité du Bois du Liévin, Cité du Moulin, and the towns of Cité St. Pierre and Liévin; while on the southern outskirts of the city were Cité St. Antoine, Cité du Nord, and the village of Avion.

As early as 1906, the population of Lens was officially reported to have been over 27,000. Liévin, some two miles westward, contained, with its suburbs, a population almost as great. As the advancing enemy neared the district to occupy positions at Lens and Vimy, in the fall of 1914, most of the population fled—leaving behind them homes it had taken them half a life-time to build and which in due time, became the wreckage of the battlefield.

After four days rest at Carency, the 4th Canadian Divisional Artillery, of which the 4th Brigade, C.F.A. was now a part, was suddenly called into action on the evening of June 25th, to take part in the operations against Avion. Within an hour and a half after receiving the message to move forward, our guns were in their old positions near Liévin. Information having been received from the 46th (British) Division "that it appeared as of the enemy were retiring," patrols of the 10th Canadian Infantry Brigade were immediately sent out, Canada Trench was gained, and posts established leading to Ontario Trench.

On the following morning the 38th, 72nd, and 85th Canadian Infantry Battalions, under an artillery barrage, took part in a general advance, resulting in the capture of La Coulotte. While but little opposition was encountered on our right, on our left, where the 85th were operating, there was plenty. June 27th proved fairly quiet, the troops being occupied chiefly with the consolidation of the line gained the previous day.

At 2.30 on the morning of the 28th, amid rumbling thunder and lightning flashes, the 12th Canadian Infantry Brigade, supported by the usual artillery barrage and 200 drums of flame projectors, attacked with the same Battalions. Avion Trench was soon captured, but the village of Eleu dit Leauvette did not fall into our hands until considerable opposition had been overcome. During this operation, 27 prisoners and 7 machine-guns were captured. Troops of the 3rd Canadian Division attacked simultaneously on the right and greatly improved their positions. Throughout the day, consolidation proceeded and preparations for exploitation of our success were gotten under way.

At 7.10 p.m., Battalions responsible for the early morning gains were launched against the enemy positions, and our line was advanced to the western outskirts of Avion; the Horse Shoe Trenches east of Eleu dit Leauvette were also captured. Owing to the flooded state of the ground, caused by inundations made by the enemy from the Souchez River, our troops found it impossible to attain some positions included in the final objective. However, the line gained was made good and touch established with flanking Divisions. The attack had powerful artillery support and was made in conjunction with similtaneous advances by the 3rd Canadian Division on the right, and the 46th (British) Division on the left.

Meanwhile, our Batteries had been firing at extreme range and it became necessary to move the guns further forward, in front of Liévin. Detached sections were then used for sniping purposes, while the main positions were being prepared. On June 30th the 4th Brigade, C.F.A. occupied their new gun-pits, the 13th Battery being located at M28 d 6/5, the 19th at M 34d 4/4, the 27th at M35a 2/4, and the 21st in a perfectly-sheltered position on the western edge of Riaumont Hill, at M29c 1/8.

All units of the Canadian Corps Artillery celebrated Dominion Day with a special shoot on the Bosche trenches, by salvos. The enemy evidently thought we were about to launch another attack, and he immediately retaliated with 5.9's along our forward lines. Those who were not on duty at the gun-positions indulged in baseball and football games, races, and other sports. The weather had become ideal, and as the warm summer days passed, we all felt very happy in our new surroundings—very unlike the weeks we experienced following the Battle of Vimy, when our guns were planted in the open plain near Willerval and under constant shelling by the enemy.

O July 2nd, the 2nd Canadian Division began relief of the 46th (British) Division on our left, and next day the 1st Canadian Division relieved a portion of the 3rd Canadian Division on our right. Though our outposts were close to the city, the price of its immediate capture was considered far too high, and the Corps settled down to a systematic series of raids and harassing fire in an effort to wear down the enemy "morale," and deplete his trench garrisons.

Batteries of the Reserve Artillery Brigades were now withdrawn, and the 3rd C.D.A., the 4th C.D.A., the 179th Brigade, R.F.A., and the D5 and D11 Howitzer Batteries covered the 3rd Canadian Division front.

For the next few weeks our Group indulged in sniping, registering suspected trench-mortar emplacements, "O-Pips," and strong points, and harassing the German back areas and communications day and night. Hostile trench-mortars worried our Infantry continually, and not until we had "strafed" their front line with several bursts of gun-fire, did these "Minenwerfers" cease fire.

On one occasion the 21st Battery had spotted and registered a section of the Round House, near Avion, where the enemy had machine-guns concealed. When fifty howitzer shells had failed to demolish this troublesome "nest," the "heavies" were called upon to engage it. We afterwards found out that the walls of this place were bolstered with reinforced concrete, several feet thick, and impervious to all but a direct hit by naval shells.

Meanwhile our gunners strengthened their positions by utilizing material from the battered houses of Liévin. In many cases foraging parties succeeded in locating stoves, carpets, and furniture, which articles added a touch of luxury to our already comfortable dug-outs. All along the new sector, light-gauge railway lines had been laid to bring up shells, engineering materials, food and water to the gun positions. This afforded the drivers and horses a much needed rest.

During this period, Capt. A. McCausland (Brigade M.O.) was awarded the M.C. for gallantry in action, under heavy shell-fire. Extricating a number of badly wounded men, who had become buried in a dug-out and in danger of suffocation, this officer, regardless of risk to himself, dressed their wounds, and by devotion to duty won the respect and admiration of all ranks.

A few days later, Rev. Capt. Robt. Thompson (Brigade Padre) was recalled by the 2nd Division; Lieut Dent became Signalling Officer; Brig.-Gen. C. H. MacLaren went on leave and Lt. Col. J. S. Stewart became Acting C.R.A. 4th C.D.A.; Major M. N. Ross assumed command of the 4th Brigade, C.F.A.; Capt. H. M. Savage and Lieut. W. A. Townsley were transferred to the 24th Battery (8th Army Brigade) and Lieut. M. O'Halloran became Adjutant of the Brigade. Major J. C. Stewart (27th Battery) also left the unit at this time, being appointed to command the newly organized 8th Army Brigade, C.F.A., with rank of Lieut.-Colonel.   ....

On July 11th, King George V, Sir Henry Horne and Staff of the 1st Army visited the Vimy-Lens sector. No special review was arranged for the distinguished visitors. His Majesty viewed the men at their ordinary tasks, shook hands with several, and inquired as to whether they had any complaints to offer as to food, clothing, etc. Thousands of soldiers lined the roads when news spread of the King's arrival, and as His Majesty passed by in an open car with no guard of honour, the men cheered him madly. Ascending the crest of Vimy, King George earnestly surveyed the German defence lines, and paid glowing tribute to the Canadian Corps Commander for the part our citizen army had taken in the great spring offensive. Later that day, on Vimy Ridge, Lt.-Gen. Currie was dubbed a Knight by the King, and on return to the waiting car, His Majesty passed through the Canadian cemetaries, paying respect to our fallen heroes.

On the 16th of July, 125 gas cylinders were projected into the German lines on the right, near Avion. Later in the day, by the aid of observation balloons, the enemy directed a heavy "strafing" of over 3,000 shells on the area occupied by our Batteries, Lieut. Plunkett of the 19th being killed and four other ranks wounded. On any other occasion the Brigade would undoubtedly have retaliated immediately, but as we were under direct observation of enemy ballons, our officers reluctantly ordered the gun-crews to take cover.

At noon of July 16th, the 1st Canadian Division took over the Loos sector from the 6th (British) Division. Lens was now besieged by Canadians on the north, west, and south.

A week later, on the 23rd, the long spell of inactivity was broken by a very successful raid by the 116th Battalion (3rd Canadian Division), which penetrated the enemy lines, near Avion, on a 600 yard front, taking 50 prisoners. This attack was supported by the 4th Brigade, C.F.A. in conjunction with other Brigades covering the front, the barrage blasting everything in its path, from the "Brickfields" south-east of Avion to the railroad embankment from Méricourt to Lens. Enemy counter-attacks were beaten off with heavy loss, and the raiders returned to our lines with few casualties.

Major M. N. Ross, Acting C.O. of the Brigade, and Lieut. Cowan were in Avion consulting the infantry officers regarding further support of the guns, when the Germans made their counter-attack. The C.O.'s orderly was wounded, but the Batteries responded to the "S.O.S." call immediately, saving a critical situation. During the day we fired over 5,000 rounds of ammunition and at times our gun-positions were heavily shelled, the 27th Battery having two of its guns put out of action. Lt.Col. J. S. Stewart returned to duty that evening, and Major M. N. Ross reassumed command of the 21st Howitzer Battery.

Again the sector seethed with activity. An avalanche of gas-shells poured into Lens. The Germans were getting a dose of their own medicine, and in good quantity. Both sides were eager for identification. Nightly raids, seeming to be attacks in force, continued in rapid succession.

Each day our Infantry made small gains of ground, seeking advantageous positions in preparation for a further offensive on Lens. This type of warfare had a very wearing and depressing effect on the enemy. Becoming greatly concerned at the aggressive attitude of our troops, the Bosches doubled his gun-power. Not only did he strafe our forward zone, but at dawn each day he bombarded and searched our roads, communications, villages and battery positions.

On the 26th, our Brigade was given a new zone to cover, necessitating considerable work in enlarging the embrasures of the gun-pits.

Guns were then registered, and all Batteries joined in a 19 minute rolling barrage on the enemy trenches and strong-points, as a feint to draw his attention from our perparations for battle further north. The Hun artillery replied heavily. The same procedure was followed at 5.30 p.m. the next day, and again on the 29th, enemy gunners retaliating on Liévin.

A gas attack, planned for the 28th, had to be posponed on account of contrary winds and adverse weather conditions. At 2.30 a.m. of the 30th, however, a large quantity of gas was discharged on the German lines, our Batteries laying down a harassing fire on Lens and its suburbs for forty minutes. At the same time the 3rd C.D.A. carried out a feint barrage on their front. The enemy, expecting an attack in force, replied furiously. This diversion certainely achieved the object desired.

During the next week it rained incessantly, and the misty weather afforded us every opportunity to make final preparations for the offensive against Hill 70. On August 2nd, at 4.45 a.m., another rolling barrage was fired on the Hun lines, drawing considerable retaliation. By these demonstrations of the Artillery and the resultant reprisals by hostile batteries and trench-mortars, a numbered list of active German positions was compiled for our use on "zero" day.

Since the middle of June, at which time Sir Herbert Plumer's Second Army had stormed and captured the heavily fortified Wytschaete-Messines Ridge, the Battle of Flanders had raged on. British and Australian troops were now pushing the enemy towards Roulers and Menin. The battle line had reached a point four miles east of Ypres. It seemed as if our armies were at last to realize the fruits of a big triumph, but bad weather again set in, the enemy resistance increased, and the struggle became a deadlock.

Making the most of his temporary advantage, the Bosche completed the construction of a large number of concrete forts, called "pill-boxes," which he sited along the front in carefully concealed positions. On the occasion of the next British offensive in Flanders, our gallant infantrymen carried the enemy forward zone with ease, but the advancing waves broke down when they came upon the line of "pill-boxes."

Such was the situation in the early part of August. On the Lens sector, the German command was quite aware that the Canadians would make some kind of a demonstration, but did not realize the proposed operations would be on such a big scale. Von Armin, hard-pressed by the British in Flanders, called upon the German army opposed to us for reinforcements. For days, our observers noted train-movement from Douai and back of Lens, and the gradual reduction in gun-power along the front.

On the 4th of August, the Corps Artillery and "heavies" carried out a concentrated shoot on the enemy lines, strong-points, machine-gun and trench-mortar emplacements and houses in Lens and its suburbs. The retaliation was very weak. In the meantime our Infantry continued to push out out-posts, which necessitated a change in the artillery "S.O.S." lines. Two days later the weather cleared, and the Royal Air Force co-operated with the "heavies" in destructive shoots, while the 21st Battery engaged hostile trench-mortar and machine-gun emplacements and the fortified crater in the German lines. Three new officers were taken on the strength of the Brigade at this time, viz.: Lieut. Avery, Lieut. Watson and Lieut. Doheny, the first named being posted to the 27th Battery, and the other two to the 13th Battery.

On the 9th, at 4.15 a.m., the 4th Brigade, C.F.A. co-operated in a barrage covering a raid of the 2nd Canadian Division, and about the same time the 11th Canadian Infantry Brigade (4th Canadian Division) made an excursion into the German lines opposite, bringing back two prisoners, and killing twelve of the enemy.

For the next few days we continued our programme of harassing the Hun with short intense bursts of fire on registered targets and shelling the canal bank, Aloof trench, and Alpaca trench to cover the activities of our working parties in the front line. The German artillery also became more active, firing a barrage on our front each morning, and, through the continual use of his observation ballons, causing considerable havoc in the villages and back areas during the day.

On the 13th, further changes were made in the officer personell of the Brigade, Capt. Dowding becoming Paymaster, Capt. R. A. Thomas attached in the absence of Capt. McClausland, and Capt. J. E. Read, Lieut. A. L. Zimmerman and Lieut. W. R. West transferred and struck off the strength.

The following day, Brigade H.Q. and the 27th Battery were heavily shelled with high-explosive and phosgene gas-shells, causing considerable inconvenience to these units.

All was in readiness for the offensive against Hill 70. Operation orders stated the attack would commence on the 1st and 2nd Canadian Division fronts (north of Lens) August 15th at 4.25 a.m. In co-operation with this assault, the 11th Canadian Infantry Brigade (4th Division) was to push forward offensive patrols a few hours after the troops of the 2nd Divisions had attained their objective, on a front from the Souchez to their junction with the 2nd Division. The zone to be covered by the 4th Brigade, C.F.A. was the enemy lines between Cotton and Amalgam communication trenches.

CHAPTER II

𝕳ill 70

The Canadian Corps was never in better fighting trim. Each Division had taken its turn of rest and open warfare training behind the lines for the Hill 70 operation. The Infantry units practiced the show on dummy trenches. Their objectives had been taped out, and each platoon knew just what trenches and ground they had to take in the big fight of the 15th. That the enemy undoubtedly expected an attack was demonstrated by his unusual daring in patrols and aerial observation. The wire entanglements in front of his lines were very formidable indeed, rising from four to six feet in height and in belts twenty feet wide along the whole sector.

During the night of August 14th-15th, our Batteries poured a steady stream of "high explosive" into the German lines, but, as zero approached, the guns ceased firing, and an oppressive stillness reigned along the front. In line for the operation were the 1st Canadian Division to the north of the St. Laurent-Hulloch-La Bassee Line, the 2nd Canadian Division from this boundary to a line immediately south of Cité St. Laurent and Cité St. Emile, and the 4th Canadian Division from this point to the Souchez River. The 3rd Canadian Division was held in reserve.

Promptly at 4.25 a.m. on August 15th, every gun in the area opened fire, while oil drums containing burning liquid were directed into the Hun trenches, causing great demoralization to the enemy. Under a deadly accurate rolling barrage, the Infantry slowly advanced. The earth shook with the terrific detonations; the very contours of the ground were blasted beyond recognition, and counter-battery work of the "heavies" was so thorough that enemy guns did not respond at full strength.

Within sixteen minutes, the "first objective" had been gained along the whole front, and eight minutes later the second wave passed through this line to its "final objective"—Hugo Trench (on the left), Norman Trench (in the centre), and Nun's Alley (on the right)—reached fifty minutes after—a total gain of one mile in depth, on a front of two miles.

Hill 70 had fallen at last. Made famous and historic by the dashing attack of the Highland Battalions in the Battle of Loos (Sept. 25th, 1915), and their subsequent defence of the "mound" against great odds and final ejection by the Germans, this northern bulwark of Lens was now in our hands, as was also Cité St. Laurent, Cite St. Auguste, Cité St. Elizabeth and Cité St. Emile. The enemy had made all preparations to meet the thrust and hold his positions, but the thorough artillery barrage and the speedy advance of our impetuous Infantry swept away all opposition.

During the operation, perfect co-operation with the Infantry was afforded by the Royal Air Force, our troops, by the use of ground flares, enabling the aviators to keep the Artillery and reserves thoroughly informed as to the progress of the advance.

At 6.05 a.m., on the front of the 4th Canadian Division, the guns fired smoke shells to screen the operation against Hill 70, and from 8.25 a.m. laid down a shrapnel and high-explosive barrage to cover the advancing patrols of the 11th Canadian Infantry Brigade on the western outskirts of Lens. For hours the situation was unsettled. At first our men had been successful in reaching the objective assigned to them, but finally, after heavy counter-attacks by the enemy, our outposts were forced to withdraw to their original lines.

Throughout the day our advance troops toiled to consolidate the positions gained. Time after time the Germans counter-attacked. The pick of the Guards Regiments were thrown into the battle, and after five furious, futile thrusts to regain their lost ground, the enemy were forced to accept defeat. Our "S.O.S." barrages played havoc with the Bosches, and not once did their attacking troops reach our trench lines.

On the 16th, the bitter fighting continued, Battalions of the 1st Canadian Division occupying the Quarries, while along the remainder of the front our men were kept busy beating off repeated counter-attacks.

On the 17th, at 4.35 a.m., the 102nd Battalion (4th Canadian Division), and the 18th Battalion (2nd Canadian Division) launched an attack upon the enemy salient formed by Amulet, Aloof, Amalgam and Cotton Trenches. The Germans fought with great courage, and put up such a strong resistance that only partial success was attained. The western bulwarks of Lens were held in force, and could not be taken without greater preparation.

On the right, near the banks of the Souchez, lay another strong point of Lens, called the Green Crassier—a heap of mine refuse, heavily sown with machine-guns and connected with the caves and cellars of the city by long tunnels. At zero hour, our barrage tore into this formidable obstacle, battering in the machine-gun emplacements which had been previously spotted and registered. The resistance of the enemy was long and stubborn, and only after terrific hand-to-hand fighting was the Green Crassier cleared of the enemy. Our men then returned to their original lines, as this attack was only intended as a raid.

Apparently the Germans profited by their defeat at Hill 70 in more ways than one. From the middle of August onwards, they held their front lines very lightly, instead of in force as had been the case since trench warfare had set in nearly three years before. Enemy outposts were now ordered to retire to their battle zone or "line of resistance"— in the old support trenches—when heavy pressure was brought to bear upon them in local attacks or trench raids. The German front line, therefore, became a series of posts only, and in most cases consisted of machine-gun or trench-mortar (minenwerfer) crews located in camou- flaged shell-holes, connected with the "line of resistance" by means of tunnels. It then became very difficult to spot the enemy defences, and absolutely impossible to photograph them from the air—hitherto our most reliable means of correcting trench-maps for the use of the Artil- lery and raiding parties.

Hostile artillery became more active, causing our consolidating troops much worry and many casualties. Liévin was now a mass of broken brick and rubble, and the roads leading up to the battery posi- tions were continually under fire, day and night. Enemy observation balloons watched our every movement. The Canadians, too, were fol- lowing a vigorous programme of wearing down the Bosches, and by short advances here and there to improve the line, a feint barrage every morning, and continual harassing fire by gas and high-explosive on Lens, Cité du Nord, and the assembly areas around Sallaumines, kept the enemy ever on the alert.

For the next week the Germans made desperate efforts to retake some of the lost ground. On the 18th, preceded by liquid-fire and gas, the enemy advanced in force against the lines of the 1st Canadian Div- ision, in the vicinity of Hugo Wood, and at the same time stormed the trenches of the 2nd Canadian Division near St. Laurent. Both of these attacks were beaten off by the Artillery and machine-gunners, the ad- vancing waves of the enemy being literally wiped out by the withering "S.O.S." barrage that fell upon them.

During these operations the 4th Brigade, C.F.A. were engaged in sniping enemy movement in Aloof, Cotton, and Amalgam Trenches. Our guns were continually in action, either harassing the Bosches or answering "S.O.S." cales. On the 19th, our Artillery Group was rein- forced by the addition of Batteries of the R.C.H.A., R.H.A., and the 463rd Battery (179th Army Brigade, R.F.A.), and became known as "Spencer-Smith's Group."

Two days later, forward positions and assembly areas on the 2nd Canadian Division front were subjected to intense trench-mortar and artillery fire. When the Canadians leaped over their parapets, they found that the Germans were already assembled in "No-Man's Land." Here a desparate fight took place. The capture of over 60 prisoners, mostly men from a Prussian Guards Division, proved the superiority of our men in close fighting. An attack was also delivered on the front of the 4th Canadian Division, but it was not successful. Aloof Trench still held out, and at nightfall we occupied our original line.

On the 23rd of August another operation by the 4th Canadian Div- ision was directed against the Green Crassier. At 3 a.m., supported by a heavy barrage, our Infantry advanced to the assault. The enemy garrison was apparently exhausted and caught unawares, for it was easily overcome and the majority of the surprised Huns either killed or captured. At 10 a.m. our observers reported that they could see our men being pushed back by large forces of the enemy from the Crassier and Fosse 4. Our guns immediately responded to the aid of the sore-pressed Infantry, and kept in action nearly all day. By evening, how-ever, the Germans were firmly entrenched in their old positions, and full of fight. The operation, though costly indeed to our forces, had to be called off.

Till the end of the month our Brigade continued to "strafe" the enemy positions on the Crassier and surrounding trenches, many fine targets being engaged by the 21st (Howitzer) Battery and much sniping being done by the "eighteen-pounders" on movement in the vicinity of Lens. Meanwhile the 11th Canadian Infantry Brigade had finally over-come the German resistance in Aloof Trench. This strong position was consolidated in our lines.

A further reinforcement for the Canadian Corps Artillery arrived in France on August 21st. The 5th C.D.A. took up positions near the village of Liévin, and was attached to Batteries of the 2nd and 4th C.D.A. for training—the 13th Brigade personell to the 2nd C.D.A. ad the 14th Brigade personell to the 4th C.D.A.

Appreciation for the good work done by the Canadians at Hill 70 was received in the form of a congratulatory message from Sir Douglas Haig to Sir Arthur Currie:—

"I desire to congratulate you, personally, on the complete and im-portant success with which your command of the Canadian Corps has been inaugurated. The two Divisions employed by you on the 15th in-stant defeated four German Divisions, whose losses are reliably estimated at more than double those suffered by the Canadian troops. The skill, bravery and determination shown in this attack in maintaining the positions won against repeated counter-attacks were, in all respects, admirable."

Prisoners, captured in the recent operations, stated: "Your gas-shells descend on us by the ton, and life in the underground defences of Lens is simply Hell."

The Germans used large quantities of "mustard-gas," but our retali-ation by "phosgene" was far more effective, and much more demoral-izing. Night after night the enemy continued "gassing" the area. Our reprisals with "phosgene" had a very good effect. Most of the shelling for the next few weeks was by shrapnel or high-explosive.

In the meantime Sir Arthur Currie had made preparations for an attack on the strongly fortified area back of Lens, known as Sallaumines. All units of the Corps became actively engaged in rehearsing the oper-ation, and perfecting details. New battery positions had to be selected and built, and the roads and tram-way systems of the district improved. Though the German Infantry seemed content to "sit tight" in their positions and bother us no further, they were undoubtedly aware that something unusual was going on behind our lines as their aircraft be-came very active all along the front. Nearly every day we were spec-tators of most thrilling "dog-fights" in the air, and yelled ourselves hoarse when a "Heinie" plane would fall in flames, brought down by the R.A.F.

On the night of September 5th, the 61st Battery, (5th C.D.A.) took over the 27th Battery gun position, the 19th Battery its two detached guns, and the 13th Battery, relieved by the personnel of the 27th Battery, went to the wagon-lines for a well earned rest. The following morning, from 1.45 till 3.20, the battery positions were heavily shelled with gas and "H.E.". Our men, rudely awakened by the night-guard, donned their masks immediately, and took shelter in deep gas-proof dug-outs and cellars nearby.

The 21st (Howitzer) Battery now moved forward to M 23c 35.15. New Brigade wagon-lines were selected at Ablain St. Nazaire, and a forward gun was located at S4b 00.90, from which considerable day and night firing was directed on selected targets. Each Battery manned it in turn, the crews' tours of duty being 24 hours.

On the 8th of September, the 4th Brigade, C.F.A. came under the tactical control of the 2nd C.D.A., and preparations were made for an operation against Sallaumines. Battery Commanders visited the various observation posts along the front, scanning the forward zones for possible positions, in the event of the Artillery having to move ahead after the original barrage and render further support if necessary.

Three days later the Brigade was switched to cover the sector held by the 1st Canadian Division, the artillery support being as follows:—

Right Group—Lt.-Col. J. S. Stewart, D.S.O.—4th Brigade, C.F.A., 14th Brigade, C.F.A. with 463rd Battery, R.F.A. (attached).

Centre Group—Lt.-Col S. B. Anderson, D.S.O.—1st Brigade, C.F.A., 2nd Brigade, C.F.A.

Left Group—Brig.-Gen. W. O. M. Dodds, C.M.G.—13th Brigade, C.F.A., 8th Army Brigade, C.F.A.

The gun positions at this time were: 19th Battery, M34d 44/47; 66th Battery, M27b 80/86; the 60th Battery, M22a 50/80; 21st Battery M23c 35/15; the 27th Battery, S4b 90/26; 61st Battery, M35a 60/40; 463rd Battery, M10a 80/18; and the Brigade "O.P." was located in a quarry on Hirondelle Ridge. The 13th Battery relieved the 27th on the night of the 12th, the latter going back to the wagon-lines at Ablain St. Nazaire for a rest, while the 4th Battery took over the position of the 60th Battery and established a forward gun to carry out night harassing fire.

At the wagon-lines all units were getting ready for the winter. Brick standings, with crushed-stone as foundations, were laid in the muddy, chalky soil. This material was procured from the ruins of the village. Each Battery "idented" for a "Nissen" hut, and within a short time had not only made comfortable quarters for the men, but had constructed an elaborate system of horse stables from timber, piles, and corrugated iron secured from the Engineers.

Along the front, the situation continued normal, although now and then the enemy artillery carried out an area "strafe" on our forward zone or gun positions.

On one occasion a German bombing party attempted to rush one of our posts in Alpaca Trench. No "S.O.S." had been given, but the Brigade, on request of our "F.O.O.," took precautionary steps and dispersed the attackers with heavy loss.

Day after day the 21st Battery engaged hostile trench-mortar batteries and became so proficient in silencing them that our Infantry continually complimented Major M. N. Ross and the Colonel on the wonderful co-operation of the Brigade. The "eighteen-pounders" carried out a systematic harassing fire every night on Lens, and during the hours of daylight sniped at any target they could reach. Thus "O. Pip" work became very interesting, and the enemy, kept under cover, became more exasperated than ever, and prayed that the Canadians would be relieved by a more considerate unit.

On the 20th, the 19th Battery relieved the 27th in action, the latter taking its turn of rest at the wagon-lines. The 21st, now in its own positions, boasted of a real "home." This was situated along the side of a road, with its gun embrasures cut into a huge retaining wall, and equipped with deep, strongly-constructed dug-outs under the pavé of the road. The pits were very strong. Nothing but a heavy naval shell could demolish them. Though all Batteries were heavily shelled during the month, the Brigade suffered few casualties. On the 21st, the C.R.A., 4th C.D.A., Brig.-Gen. MacLaren, inspected the units in action. Lt.-Col. J. S. Stewart went on leave, and Major M. N. Ross assumed command of the Brigade. Five days later the 4th Battery was relieved by the 66th Battery, C.F.A.

Till the end of the month nothing of consequence occured, although preparations went on for the operation against Sallaumines. The weather continued fine, with clear, cool days, and moonlight nights, and a thick haze shutting out the panorama of the trench-lines till nearly noon.

On the 30th, Lieut. Cowan of the 27th Battery, and Lieut. Watson of the 13th Battery, with twenty-six other ranks, went out to Nedon to take part in a demonstration on the first Army Ranges for an enfilade barrage. A large gathering of Infantry and Staff Officers attended, and were invited to offer criticisms on the effect of the firing.

For the impending offensive Major M. N. Ross was appointed Brigade Liasson Officer to the two attacking Brigades, and Lieuts. Maunder and Lorimer as L. O's. Major A. J. Culver, O. C., 19th Battery, then assumed command of the 4th Brigade, C.F.A. and Major M. N. Ross went to the wagon-lines. For the next day or so the L. O.'s reconnoitred the forward zones with Infantry officers of the 12th C.I.B. and took part in a dress rehearsal in order to become thoroughly familiar with their duties.

On October 3rd, Lieut. Cumming reported and was posted to the 13th Battery. The same day this unit relieved the 27th Battery, the 27th relieved the 19th, and the latter went out on rest to Ablain St. Nazaire.

Lt.-Col. Stewart returned from leave on the 5th, and the 5th and 7th Batteries, 1st C.D.A., took over the positions of the 61st and 66th, 5th C.D.A.

Rumours of a march to Flanders now passed through the Canadian Corps, and there certainly seemed to be some ground for such news, as on the night of the 7th we were relieved by the 2nd Brigade, C.F.A. and all units were withdrawn to the wagon-lines.

For days it had been wet and miserable, and even our comfortable quarters at Ablain St. Nazaire appeared chilly and desolate, until news arrived on October 9th that our Division was to proceed to the Haze-brouck area immediately. All Batteries drew guns at Villers au Bois, the equipment was checked up and cleaned, and everything made ready for the long march. We were sorry to hand over such wonderful horse-lines, prepared at much labour for the cold, hard days of winter, but all ranks craved action.

On the 12th, the Divisional Artillery left the Lens district, our column passing through Grand Servins at 9 a.m., and on to Gonnehem via Hersin, Bethune and Chocques. As we passed through St. Venant, on the second day's march, President Poincaré of France, and other notables, were being entertained by the Portuguese staff. Here, billets were very poor, and the guns and horses had to be placed in an open field, while the gunners and drivers slept in barns nearby. By 3 p.m. the next day we pulled into Steenvoorde, the men being allotted to large farms in the district. Bombing could be heard at night, and we realized we were not far from the "Bloody Salient."

CHAPTER III

Passchendaele

THE Canadian Corps was now to take an important part in concluding for the year, British operations begun in June with the storming of the Wytschaete-Messines Ridge. By the capture of Passchendaele, Ypres would be relieved, the door to Calais closed and a good jumping-off line secured for the 1918 campaign.

In their attack of October 12th, Australian and New Zealand troops, impeded by the mud, marsh, and slime, and swept by bitter machine-gun fire from the high ground at Bellevue, Crest Farm, and Passchendaele, had met with misfortune.

The German positions were most imposing. Consisting of a series of ridges, hog-backs, and spurs, interspersed with valleys and copses, these natural defences bristled with machine-guns, and were further strengthened by concrete forts known as "dreadnaughts" and "pill-boxes," built into the ruins of farms and villages. It was against these formidable obstacles that the "Anzac" attack broke down.

Our front line was by no means a clearly marked line of trenches. In the appalling state of the ground no such definite work could be carried out. The low ground about Ypres had always been a bog, and the constant concussion of heavy shells had pitted the whole surface, so that crater lapped crater, and foetid water—foul with every abomination—filled deep pools of unexplored depth. Nowhere was there any solid ground, except the roads, or what remained of them.

These approaches to the "Salient" were under constant fire. Every yard was registered, and the dead bodies which lay unburied along the way, swelled in numbers as day succeeded day. To avoid the "death-walk" by striking across country meant a plunge into the death-trap mud and the shell-pits of deep water. The best defence possible under these conditions was made of shell-holes, fortified and garrisoned, irregularly sited and linked to each other. A "tour" in the trenches meant 48 hours spent in a drain of mire and water, where, quite apart from the fact that death or mutilation threatened at any moment, mere existance was wretchedness.

Back to this, land of horror and destruction, truly termed the grave-yard of the Empire, came the Canadian Corps. How many British dead lie there may never be known! Following the Battles of 2nd Ypres, Sanctuary Wood, Hooge, and the long tour of trench warfare fighting, Canada's buried sons number into the thousands.

On October 15th, the 4th Brigade, C.F.A. crossed the Franco-Belgian Frontier near Abeele, passed through Poperinghe, and finally reached its allotted wagon-line area in the vicinity of Vlamertinghe, before dark.

A bare, open, shell-torn field was to be our future "home." Not a shelter of any type was available. Thousands of troops and mounted units were concentrated on every side, camped in the open. All ranks "set-to" with a will. Vehicles were parked, horse-lines laid out, and within a few hours improvised shelters had sprung up here and there, as if by magic. As evening wore on and the trumpeters sounded "Lights Out," the faint drone of enemy "Gothas" could be heard, followed soon after by the crashing of bombs in the villages and camps around us. Such was our welcome back to the "Salient."

Next day the Batteries of the 4th Canadian Divisional Artillery went into the line; the 4th Brigade, C.F.A. taking over guns in action from the 42nd Brigade, R.F.A., near Zonnebeke; the 21st (Howitzer) Battery being located at Zonnebeke Church; the 19th a little further back, and the 13th and 27th just in front of the famous "pill-box" at "Kink Corner." Nearby were Batteries of the 2nd Canadian Divisional Artillery, and in the front line, troops of the 3rd Australian Division.

Going forward from Vlamertinghe, we passed the "Asylum" and wended our way through Ypres. The city had suffered cruelly since our departure for the Somme, in August, 1916. No longer could one trace location of streets, buildings, shops, and gardens. German "hate" had made a shambles of the place. The Cloth Hall and Cathedral were now a total ruin, and the streets were piled with broken brick and twisted wreckage. Great craters and shell-holes, partly filled with gas-infected water, added a further touch of desolation to the scene. No one lingered in Ypres. The enemy still shelled it unmercifully. Hardly a day passed without heavy casualties to troops marching through. Dead horses, broken limbers, lorries and Red Cross trucks lay by the wayside, battered and torn by enemy shell-fire.

As we left Ypres, feeling we had passed through the "Gates of Death," we immediately had to break column, due to the heavy road shelling by German long range guns, and approached the assigned posi-tions near Zonnebeke with great caution. The British artillerymen were pleased indeed to see us, and did not waste much time in moving off, once relief was completed.

We now began to realize the difference between our "cushy" gun-pits at Liévin and the bleak, cold dreariness of these open positions at

Zonnebeke. Elephant-iron, pit-props, and timber were nowhere to be had. Only trench-mats and sand-bags were available. So, in the morass of mud and water, the Batteries toiled to improve their accommodations, building sand-bag platforms for the guns, salvaging ammunition from the mire, laying "duck-mats" and planks across the shell-torn ground to afford solid footing, and, with bags of mucky earth, erecting hovels in which to sleep. These flimsy "bivvies" gave no protection whatever against enemy shell-fire, but served the useful purpose of keeping the gun-crews dry and sheltered from the elements.

After checking "S.O.S." lines, communications, and registering the guns on permanent points in the enemy lines, Batteries were engaged on harassing fire night and day. Before we had been in action 48 hours, casualties began, and till relieved twenty-eight days later, the gun positions were under constant fire from the German Artillery.

Meanwhile, Engineers and working parties strove to facilitate the movement of men and materials to the forward areas. East of "Kansas Cross," the ground was utterly impassable—without roads and "trench mats." After hours of labour, foundations were established on the mud, and planks laid upon them. Though shelled and bombed daily, these were kept in constant repair. From the end of the plank roadways, "duck-walks" were extended toward the trenches. Supply lorries and ambulances were now enabled to drive up withi two miles of the front line, greatly relieving the impossible situation that had hitherto existed.

The nervous strain on these motor truck drivers was intense and the personal danger great. They drove without lights, feeling their way as best they could in the darkness, never knowing where the road had been broken by a great shell hole, shrewn with debris, or blocked by fallen trees. They were so utterly exausted that sometimes they fell asleep while driving; and yet, shaken and exhausted as they were, they never failed to respond to the demands made upon them.

Every night long lines of pack-mules negotiated the shell-swept roadways, delivering ammunition, water, and rations to the gun crews. The devotion to duty of our splendid drivers deserves special commendation. Required to groom and care for their mounts daily, these men were nightly engaged carrying supplies and ammunition, or replacing disabled guns. They worked 18 hours a day, without relief, and always had to dodge a barrage on the road both coming and going from Vlamertinghe.

Nearly every day shell-splinters tore into the oil buffers, smashed a wheel, or injured the breech mechanism or sights. Guns that were disabled had to be drawn to the Ordinance Depot near Poperinghe, and if possible, replaced. The number of guns blown up or put out of action was incredible. The 13th and 21st Batteries each lost eighteen in this way during its stay in the "Salient."

Shortly after our arrival, a squadron of Gothas bombed the forward area, roads, and city of Ypres, causing heavy casualties. The weather, though cloudy, cold and damp, showed no sign of clearing and the fields remained an impassable quagmire of mud, making it necessary for the gunners to clean and polish each shell before inserting it in the gun.

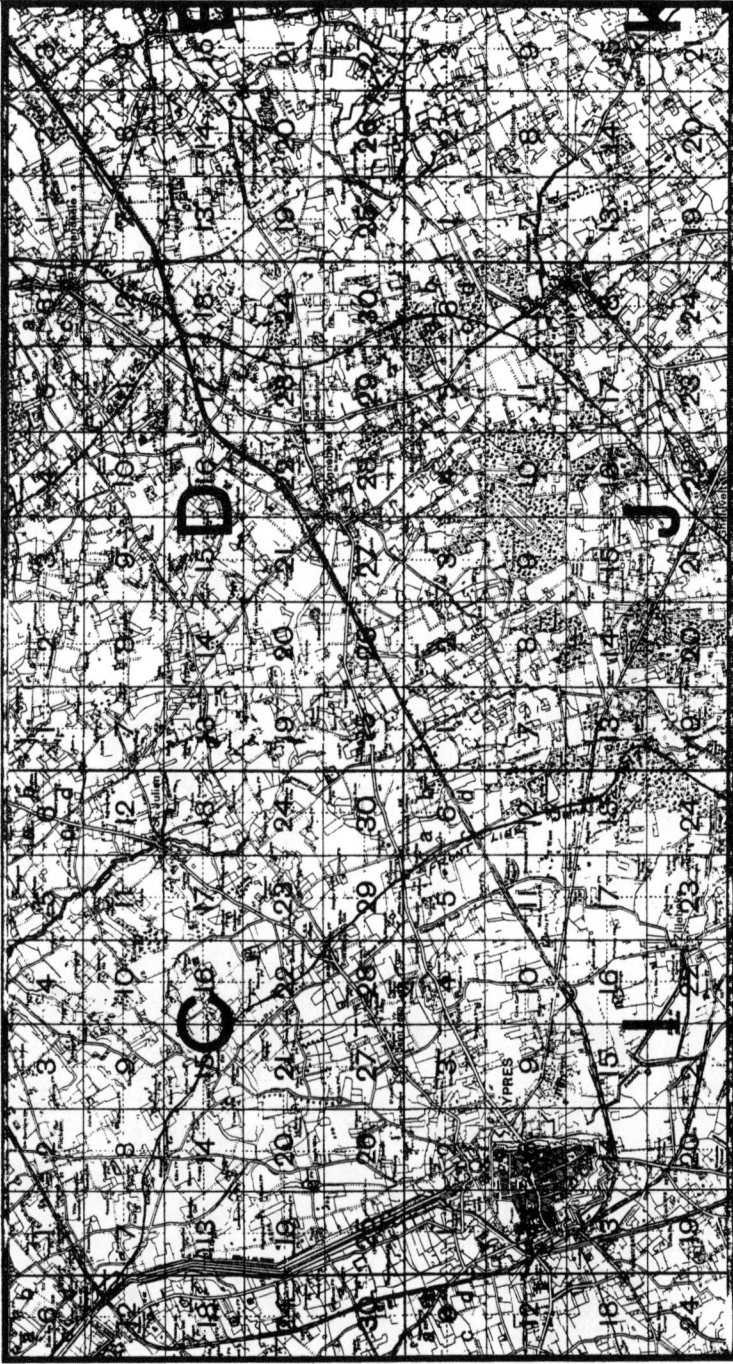

YPRES SALIENT—October-November, 1917

Scale: 1 inch—.63 miles; 1,000 yards to each square

The Brigade was unfortunate in losing three of the most efficient officers at this time, Major Hyde, Lieut. Haywood, and Lieut. Hyndman. Six men had been killed, one missing, and 12 wounded. Lieut. Haywood, while being taken to the rear, was struck by another fragment of shell and killed.

On the 19th, the 49th (British) Division relieved the 3rd (Australian) Division and occupied the trenches in front of us till our Infantry came into the line.

The packing up of ammunition went on, and soon 800 rounds per gun were available at the positions. On the 22nd, preparatory barrages and bursts of fire began. Early each morning and every evening we "strafed" the enemy trenches and communications, while our "60-pounders" and heavy howitzers engaged hostile batteries and carried out destructive "shoots" on the back areas.

About this time a new position in the ruins of Zonnebeke Church was occupied by the 21st (Howitzer) Battery. Though somewhat sheltered, this spot was soon registered by the enemy and heavily shelled. When the church was rebuilt in 1924, members of this unit had a bronze memorial tablet placed on one of the buttresses of the new structure bearing these words:—

IN MEMORY OF THE FALLEN

OF

D 21 BATTERY

CANADIAN FIELD ARTILLERY

Les ruines sur lesquelles cette église a été reconstruite

étaient l'emplacement de la D 21 Batterie, pendant

La Bataille de Passchendaele, Oct.-Nov., 1917.

ERIGE PAR LEURS CAMARADES

All Batteries found it impossible to obtain engineering material. Guns lay in the open, between shell-holes, and often sank to the hubs in the mire due to insufficient means having been provided to construct proper platforms. In most cases all that was possible was done, but the only solid base, and the one that proved the most efficient under the circumstances, was a few layers of sand-bags in the mud.

All was in readiness for the big attack. The Canadian front, 3,000 yards in width, extended across the mud flats of the "Salient," from the Ypres-Roulers Railway to Wallemolen. Adjoining us on the north was the 63rd (British) Division, and on the south the 1st Australian Corps. In line for the operation were the 8th and 9th Infantry Brigades (3rd Canadian Division) and the 10th Infantry Brigade (4th Canadian Division) with the 7th and 12th Infantry Brigades in reserve.

Before us was the formidable Bellevue Spur, bog and swamp, and the fortified line of "pill-boxes" representing the outer defences of Passchendaele. Only supreme effort could win success from the ordeal which lay ahead. The enemy believed his position to be impregnable, and the Bavarian garrison was ordered to hold their ground at all costs. For several days artillery preparatory barrages had been fired on the enemy lines, communications had been improved, and the Canadians were prepared for every eventuality.

At 5.40 a.m. of Oct. 26th, the front awoke to the thundering roar of thousands of guns. Brom Abraham Heights, the spectacle was clearly discernable. The condition of the battlefield was worse than ever. A steady, all night drizzle had turned the already muddy ground into a bog of small pools and lakes. It was to be a battle against the elements, as well as the enemy.

Wallowing waist deep through the mud, and facing a withering machine-gun barrage our troops advanced. The 10th Canadian Infantry Brigade, operating on the right, carried the spur along the Zonnebeke-Passchendaele Road overlooking Passchendaele village and Decline Copse, a strategic position further on. In the centre and on the left of the advance, Battalions of the 8th and 9th Canadian Infantry Brigades encountered desperate enemy resistance and stubborn hand-to-hand fighting before the heavily fortified redoubts and "pill-boxes" at Laamkeek and Bellevue were overcome. The initial attack failed but a final advance later on in the day, made without artillery support over 1,000 yards of open ground which was swept with shell-fire and machine-guns from the front and the flanks, won the whole objective. This brilliant operation was one of the outstandings feats of the War. Bellevue Spur had fallen. Late in the afternoon two German battalions counter-attacked in an effort to dislodge our tired troops, but "S.O.S." rockets brought the Artillery into action at once and the enemy thrust was broken. At Decline Copse and along the Spur overlooking Passchendaele Village, also at Laamkeek and Bellevue, the enemy made many attempts to regain lost ground during the evening and night. When dawn broke, however, the Canadians were still in possession, and successful all along the line. The first phase of the battle was over.

Mr. Phillip Gibbs said, in the "Daily Chronicle," The most important position in the attack was given to the Canadians to carry, and the story of their capture of Bellevue Spur, is a fine and thrilling act of personal courage by bodies of men struggling against great hardships and under heavy fire. Nothing that they did at Courcelette and Vimy and round about Lens was finer than the manner in which they fought their way up the Bellevue Spur, where, beaten back by an intensive, destructive fire, they reorganized, scaled the slope again, and drove the German machine-gunners out of their block-houses."

Throughout the day our Batteries were constantly in action. The gunners had no rest, neither had the drivers. The 4th Canadian Divisional Artillery fired over 12,000 shells during the action. Ammunition had to be replenished, cleaned and fuzed, and the guns cooled when not firing. We snatched a bite to eat when able, but could not leave the positions, even though the enemy shell-fire threatened our very existance.

Shortly after "zero" the German Artillery switched its fire on the back areas, approaches and communications, endeavouring to cut off the supplies and supports from Ypres. Long lines of traffic struggled along the plank roads—marching infantry, artillery wagons, Red Cross ambulances, and lorries. Here and there a huge shell fell amongst them, tearing an ugly gap in the column and wrecking the road. Comrades immediately cleared the debris, made the necessary repairs, and the line came on.

About noon, walking wounded were painfully making their way through the gun positions to dressing stations in the rear, covered with mud and slime, exhausted, and rudely bandaged by first aid men; they presented a pitiful appearance, but all wore the expression of having accomplished something worth while.

Evacuating the serious cases was a heavy task for the stretcher bearers, who had thousands of yards to cover before they could reach a medical officer. German prisoners, under escort, were pressed into service to help them.

One of the terrible features of the battle was that the wounded were never safe from bursting shells. Even as far back as the main dressing stations or the casualty clearing stations they were not out of danger. As one refuge after another was shelled, the wounded had to be hastily removed, sometimes to the open shell-torn fields.

Signal communication in the forward areas were very bad, and it became almost impossible to keep the cable and overland lines in operation, due to incessant shelling by the enemy. The signallers were therefore obliged to establish constant patrol of the telephone wires. This entailed very dangerous work and resulted in a considerable number of casualties. The fearlessness and bravery shown by the signallers at Passchendaele stands out as one of the bright spots of the battle.

On the 27th, the rain continued. It was a very trying experience for the men in the trenches. Artillery duels continued unabated, and hostile batteries carried out area "shoots," in an effort to destroy our guns. Meanwhile German airmen showed great daring, flying low, in broad daylight, over crowded roads—bombing and machine-gunning the endless stream of traffic. Our pilots undoubtedly did likewise behind the enemy lines. Aerial battles and "dog fights" over the Salient were daily occurences, many planes, both enemy and British, being brought down.

Late in the afternoon of the 28th, during a terrific bombardment of the 13th Battery gun position, an "S.O.S." rocket was observed by the lookout-man. The gun crews responded on the double, and maintained an intense barrage for 25 minutes. Meanwhile, enemy shells continued, all signal communication was broken, and it was impossible to arrage for another battery to take over the zone. Three caches of ammunition, in the actual gun lines, were exploded by direct hits and every gunner was covered with flying mud from the concussions of the big shells which fell amongst them. Only the extreme softness of the ground, which allowed the shells to sink before exploding, permitted the men to live through this terrible ordeal.

At midnight, October 28th, German shock troops carried out a surprise attack at Decline Copse and ejected our men from the position. Reinforced, the Canadians returned and after heavy fighting regained the position. By morning they had advanced their line along the high ground overlooking Passchendaele Village. We were now within a thousand yards of the inner defences. In the centre, the battlefield consisted of swamps and deep shell-craters filled with water. The enemy was strongly entrenched at Crest Farm and Meetcheele—the keys to Passchendaele.

At 5.50 a.m. on October 30th, the front blazed forth again on a ten mile front, from Houlthoust Forest to Gheluvelt. In line for the assault were the 63rd British Division on our left, the 7th and 8th Canadian Infantry Brigades against Meetcheele, and the 12th Canadian Infantry Brigade against Crest Farm; while the 1st Australian Corps co-operated on the right. Conditions for the attack were terrible. A drizzling rain all evening had made the countryside almost impassable. All night the Infantrymen lay waiting for the battle to commence, cold and shivering from the dreary elements.

Skirting the quagmire of the Ravebeeke, the attackers struggled up to the higher ground levels. Crest Farm was captured at 6.35 a.m. after a brilliant action, the advancing troops being obliged to pass through a shell-swept defile, with a swamp on one side and a fortified wood on the other. The Bosches were undoubtedly dazed by our concentrated gun-fire, as they did not put up the resistance expected.

On the left front of the attack, after wading through treacherous swamps, the 5th C.M.R.'s gained Source and Vapour Farms, and fought all day with flanks exposed and bog around them, on every side. The ground was so bad on their left that the 63rd British Division did not come up. Though heavily bombarded, these gallant men of the C.M.R. hung on till reinforced at night. Meetcheele, the northern gate of Passchendaele, was taken by the Princess Patricias after bomb and bayonet fighting. The "Pats" had to advance over 1,000 yards of open country, pitted with deep shell-holes, and marsh, in the face of withering machine-gun fire before they could come to grips with the enemy. Less than 100 yards down the road was the strongly held "pill-box" near Mosselmarkt, guarding entrance in to Passchendaele village from the north. Further artillery preparation was necessary before the advance could be resumed, and the Canadians began consolidation of the positions they had gained.

Throughout the day one counter-attack after another was made to dislodge our Infantry, but machine-gun and artillery fire dispersed every attempt against our lines, and the Bosches retired in disorder, losing many men. Between Meetcheele and Mosselmarkt, Canadians and Germans arranged a temporary truce, buried the dead, and evacuated the wounded. Time after time, in the next five days, the enemy fought desperately to retrieve their losses, making fierce thrusts along the front. In spite of the continual pressure, and terrific shelling, the Canadian Infantry held on.

On the afternoon of October 30th, Brig-Gen. MacLaren, our C.R.A., was evacuated, broken down with incessant stress and strain, and Lt.-Col. J. S. Stewart assumed command of the 4th Canadian Divisional Artillery. During the initial barrage the 27th Battery suffered heavy loss, sustaining two direct hits on its guns and two gun-crews wiped out. In two weeks fighting the 4th Brigade, C.F.A. had lost eleven killed and forty-one wounded.

October 31st and November 1st passed rather quietly, and our Infantry improved their positions without much opposition—patrols of the 3rd Canadian Division occupying Furst Farm, and the 4th Canadian Division pushing advanced parties into Passchendaele itself. At 1.15 a.m. the following morning, platoons of the 1st C.M.R.'s carried out a surprise attack on Vanity House and Vine Cottage, both these "pill-boxes" being taken. The enemy counter-attacked strongly and our Infantry were forced to withdraw from Vine Cottage, but Vanity House was held and the position consolidated. At 5 a.m. the Germans attacked along our whole front, from the Ypres-Roulers railway to north of Meetcheele, in a desperate effort to retrieve themselves. "S.O.S." rockets had been fired as soon as the enemy concentrations were noted, and before the Bosches had completed preparations for an advance, an intensive gun-fire barrage of all calibres fell upon them and the attack broke down with heavy loss. No further attempts were made against our positions, and at 10 p.m. that night the Canadian Artillery opened up a five hour bombardment of the enemy lines, while relief of the 3rd and 4th Canadian Divisions by the 1st and 2nd Canadian Divisions began.

Although our battered Infantry had completed its task, and marched to a well-earned rest, the Batteries of the 3rd and 4th Divisions remained in action to the end of the Corps Operations. Mosselmarkt and the inner defences of Passchendaele still held out, the German forces were in great strength, and additional guns had been brought into position against us. Forward areas, communications, plank roads, and Batteries were continually gassed and "strafed" by the enemy. Dead men, horses, broken vehicles, and "derilect" guns dotted the old battlefield from Weiltje to Zonnebeke and Abraham Heights. And to add to the horror of it all, German airmen bombed our gun positions, transport and wagon-lines at every opportunity.

Casualties steadily mounted and many were overcome with gas and trench-fever, among whom were Lieut. Aitkens and Capt. R. F. Thompson. Both these officers received a bad dose of gas—the former had to be evacuated, but the latter, though very sick, refused to leave.

The stage was now set for the final phase of the battle, and to facilitate the storming of the Ridge, the Canadian front was narrowed on both flanks to afford greater concentration. The 1st British Division, with the "pill-boxes" around Goudberg as their objectives; the 1st Canadian Infantry Brigade facing Vine Cottage, Valour Farm, Vegetable Farm, Mosselmarkt, and Graf; and the 6th Canadian Infantry Brigade against Graf Wood, Passchendaele village and Grun, formed the attacking force for the operation set for November 6th, at 6.20 a.m. Vine Cottage, on the left of the Canadian front, was considered a peril to the advance, and the troops of the 1st Brigade carried the position during the night, after desperate resistance.

For three days our guns had carried out a constant bombardment of the enemy positions. Plank roads and "duck-walks" had been extended, and many Batteries had moved forward to Abraham Heights.

At "zero," favored by good weather, the Canadians, closely following the artillery barrage, advanced to their objectives, and, in spite of terrific machine-gun and enemy shell-fire, succeeded in overcoming all opposition. Passchendaele village was a mass of battered brick and masonry, but hundreds of Bosches still remained hidden in the cellars and dug-outs and had to be bombed out.

On the left, at Mosselmarkt, the enemy resisted stoutly and the line of "pill-boxes" in this sector was not captured without close and grim hand-to-hand fighting. British troops on the northern flank made partial progress only, but as evening came on the gains were held and consolidated in spite of heavy counter-attacks by the German forces.   .

For the next three days no further infantry actions were attempted, but the artillery duel continued fiercer than ever. Since the battle had commenced, on October 26th, our Batteries had fired at least three barrages every twenty-four hours. On November 7th, the 4th Brigade, C.F.A. received a further reinforcement of officers—Lieuts. Penno, Redmond, Whitehead, Millard, Burrage, Odell, Wilson and Grier, while Capt. Shaw was transferred to the 4th C.D.A. Enemy shelling had greatly decreased since the capture of the Ridge, and it was quite apparent that the Germans had moved their artillery further to the rear.

On November 10th, another assault was made on the enemy positions, with a view to broaden the Salient, and drive the Bosches into the Roulers Plain. Attacking on a 600 yard front, the 8th and 7th Battalions (2nd Canadian Infantry Brigade), the 20th Battalion (4th Canadian Infantry Brigade), and troops of the 1st British Division, pushed forward in drizzling rain. The German Artillery shelled our forward lines, supports, battery areas, and communications very heavily, but within half an hour after "zero" all objectives had been gained on the Canadian front. Due to the impassable condition of the terrain in front of them, British troops were unable to conform with the movement, but later in the day a defensive flank had been set up, and the whole front consolidated, despite deadly enemy shelling from the north, east, and south, and determined counter-attacks.

Fierce German onslaughts were launched against our newly won positions, but concentrated artillery fire smashed every attempt and the enemy retired with heavy loss. In the Passchendaele operations nearly twelve hundred prisoners had been taken, the whole system of defence on the Ridge captured, and below us—to the east—was a beautiful rolling country of green fields, good roads, orderly farms, villages, and towns; while behind us lay the morass and desolation of the "Salient," with its thousands of crosses and unburied dead.

Again it rained and the countryside became dotted with miniature lakes and ponds. We sighed with relief when, on November 11th and 12th, units of the 33rd Brigade, R.F.A. arrived and took over our positions. The personnel of the 4th C.D.A. then proceeded to Vlamertinghe by motor-lorry, and as we passed on down the line the rumbling of the guns became fainter and fainter.

On November 13th we bade a final good-bye to Flanders, passing through Poperinghe and Abeele to Caestre. En route, the Brigade was inspected by Lt.-Col. J. S. Stewart, A/C.R.A. of the 4th Canadian Division. That night we parked our horses and vehicles on the road near

Caestre, and slept in barns nearby. Next day the column marched through to Thiennes.

On the 15th, we continued on, by daily marches, to Ham-en-Artois, Houdain, and Olhain. Here two of the Batteries went into wagon-lines, while the 19th billeted at Gauchin-Légal, and the 13th at Fresnicourt. Orders were then received that we were to relieve the 48th Divisional Artillery, with wagon-lines on the Mont-St. Eloi road. On the 18th, advance parties proceeded by bus from Estree-Cauchie to the new locations. This sector was now very quiet and much changed since we left it in May, and when the Brigade "took over," we moved into comfortable quarters—our first for many weeks.

CHAPTER IV

Return to Vimy

THE grim fighting of 1917 was now over, and the Canadian Corps, returning to the Lens-Arras front, enjoyed a long period of comparative inactivity. Canadians had made this area their own before they went to Passchendaele. The fact that winter was coming on, with all its ordeals of cold and exposure, did not matter. They slipped into their old positions, happy and dejoicing.

From Hill 70 our front line, following the higher levels, skirted the west edge of Cité St. Auguste, half-circled Lens, the Green Crassier, and Cité St. Antoine, passed in front of Avion, and ran in irregular fashion toward the south, facing Méricourt, Acheville, Fresnoy and Oppy. The front was familiar to all units of the Corps, and we settled down to a comfortable rest in the line.

On November 18th, the 4th Brigade, C.F.A., completed relief of the 48th (British) Divisional Artillery, taking over guns "in situ," and became known as the Right Group—covering the 6th Canadian Infantry Brigade, on the Méricourt sector. Weather conditions were of the best, with clear, cold days and nights. The gun positions, built by our predecessors, afforded every comfort, and at the wagon-lines the horses began to show a gradual improvement in health, due to careful grooming and daily exercise.

A few days later, Major J. Ivan McSloy and Capt. C. Sifton proceeded to England on a four weeks' Battery Commanders' course. Shortly after, the Brigade took over the Acheville zone, covering the 4th Canadian Infantry Brigade, with the 1st Canadian Division on our left, and the 31st (British) Division on the right.

A rest in the back country was not far off. On the 27th, Lt. Reid proceeded to Marles-les-Mines to look over billets, and on the following day the 5th Brigade, C.F.A., (Lt.-Col. Constantine) commenced relief of our units in action, guns being handed over "in situ."

On the 30th, the Brigade marched from its wagon-lines to Marles-les-Mines via Mont St. Eloi, Camblain l'Abbé, Estrée-Cauchie, Olhain,

Lt.-Col. J. S. Stewart, C.M.G.,
D.S.O., Croix de Guerre

Major C. Sifton, D.S.O.
13th Battery

A /Lt.-Col. A. F. Culver, M.C.
19th Battery

Battery
Commanders

4th Bde. C,F.A.
1917 - 1918

Major J. I. McSloy, D.S.O.
21st Battery

Major J. C. Stewart, D.S.O.
27th Battery

Lt.-Col. M. N. Ross, D.S.O., Bar

Houdain, Divon and Calonne-Ricouart, and were comfortably settled in billets before dark. On relief, command of the 4th Brigade, C.F.A., was assumed by Lt.-Col. J. S. Stewart, who had returned to duty, Lt.-Col. W. B. M. King having been sent from England to fill the vacancy left by Brig.-Gen. C. H. MacLaren as C.R.A., 4th C.D.A.

For all ranks our stay at Marles-les-Mines was long and enjoyable. Parades were few, but daily physical exercises, rides, lectures, bathing, route marches, grooming, and an occasional inspection whipped the units into fine shape. Each man drew fifty francs Christmas money, and cast his vote in the Canadian elections. Seven candidates for commissions left to attend Artillery Courses in England, and many more filed applications for transfer to the "R.A.F."

Shortly after our arrival, Lt.-Col. J. S. Stewart left to attend a Senior Officers' course, and Major M. N. Ross again took over command of the Brigade. Among other changes in the personnel of the officers, Lt. L. J. B. Aitkens returned from hospital, Lt. M. O'Halloran went on leave, and Lt. H. W. Larkin became Acting Adjutant. Many awards came through at this time, twenty-one Military Medals being published in Brigade Orders.

For some time the Y.M.C.A. had fostered the idea of furthering the introduction of concert parties to entertain the troops when they were out of the line, on rest. Shortly after the Battle of Vimy Ridge, every Division had its own entertainers including the famous "Maple Leaves" (4th Division), the "Y Emmas" (Y.M.C.A.), the "See Toos" (2nd Division), and the "Dumb-Bells" (3rd Division), who still play to audiences throughout Canada and the U.S.A.

While at Marles-les-Mines, our Batteries had the privilege of attending one of these performances, and marched in body to Auchel to see the fun. The theatre, where the show was staged, was a ramshackle old building, unheated and with holes in the roof. The audience sat on rough wooden benches and planks facing a stage that contrasted strikingly with the rest of the interior. It was draped with the flags of the Allies, and rendered more or less brilliant by the liberal use of footlights and a glaring spot-light operated by one of the company from the rear of the building. A dilapidated old piano stood in one corner. Every one was happy, not least the French mothers and fathers and children of the village who had come as the honoured guests of the players.

The show commenced with an opening chorus by the troupe, gaily decked out in pierrot costumes, the slouchy garb of "coons," and above all—a "lady" in all the latest finery from "gay Paree." A novelty quartette followed, then amid great applause, solos, nigger dialogues, and skits from a soldier's life in France. All were fine singers, and gave clever renderings of popular war-time plays from "Zig-Zag," "Chu Chin Chow," and "Maid of the Mountains" which plays were the rage in old London at this time. The boys of the Brigade greatly enjoyed the show, and marched back to Marles-les-Mines singing lustily—"Take me back to dear old Blighty," Pack all your troubles in your old kit-bag," "It's a long, long trail," and other tunes, fond to the ears of the Canadian soldier.

As Christmas approached, we all looked forward to a big celebration. This was the first occasion during the war that all 4th C.F.A. Brigade units had been concentrated in one camp at this season of the year. In 1915, and 1916, the gunners had had their Christmas dinners served to them at the guns, and at the wagon-lines the drivers had been given everything from "soup to nuts."

Alas! We were doomed to disappointment. Orders were received on the 18th of December that we were to relieve the 1st Brigade, C.F.A. in the line, and our C.O. and Battery Commanders went forward to look over the positions. The next day a special dinner was served, and the boys sat down to a wonderful spread, in their billets. In the evening, one section per Battery marched for the new area, and on the morning of the 20th the gunners departed in lorries to take over from the Batteries of the 1st Brigade, C.F.A., while the remaining sections proceeded to the new wagon-lines at Ablain St. Nazaire.

The weather became colder, and a light blanket of snow covered the ground. Christmas Day passed quietly, the C.O. and Battery Commanders of the 19th and 21st reconnoitring for new positions, while the gunners carried on, playing poker and "Crown and Anchor." A few days later, the Brigade settled down in earnest, strengthening the gun pits, while the 19th and 21st moved into their new positions in the valley south of Riaumont Hill. For the first time proper shelters were built for the horses, standings being laid with brick and soft stone from the ruins nearby, while iron sheeting and other materials were procured from the Engineers to serve as roofing and walls. Our horses soon showed the benefit of these precautions, and, by constant care, losses and disease throughout the winter were practically nil.

The duty of "stable picquets" was an unenviable one, especially at night, when horse-lines were being bombed or shelled. Quite apart from the danger of the explosions, there was always the chance of the picket-ropes breaking, and the horses stampeding, a most dangerous occurrence for any one in the neighbourhood. Horses frequently fought and kicked, becoming entangled in the ropes, and had to be followed and caught, in the darkness. Some Batteries acquired steel cables from the mines roundabout and substituted these for the regular issue picket-ropes. It was impossible to break, or wear them out. They would not stretch or become loossened, but as they could not be coiled in the regulation manner and strapped on the vehicles, we had to leave them in place when our wagon-lines were taken over by another unit. The stables and officers' huts at Ablain St. Nazaire were so well constructed they still remained standing in 1922, being used by returned civilians until the village was rebuilt.

Throughout the month of January nothing of importance took place to relieve the monotony of trench warfare, although our Batteries were engaged in barraging the German lines to cover raids of the 10th and 11th Canadian Infantry Brigades on the 9th and the 13th. Shortly after, on the nights of January 19th, 20th and 21st, the 5th Brigade, C.F.A. (Lt.-Col. Constantine) relieved the 4th Brigade, C.F.A. by sections, and we then took over positions from the 14th Brigade, C.F.A. (5th C.D.A.) close to the northern slopes of Riaumont Hill and near adjoining houses, where the detachments could avail themselves of comfort and protection in the cellars. Brigade H.Q. located in an old ruin in Liévin, the sig-nallers occupying the basement of the Bishop's residence, as command centre.

The enemy soon began to strafe our area more systematically, and thousands of 5.9's and gas shells poured into the forward zone, and searched the roads leading up to Liévin and the Ridge. The Brigade "O. Pip." on Riaumont Hill was smashed in, and Lieut. F. P. Vokes, officer on duty, was wounded, while Lieut. Doheney and Driver Wishart became casualties at the gun positions. Wishart was one of the few 13th Battery originals still with his unit at the time, and his death, a few days later, was greatly felt by his comrades.

Since we left, a slight advance had been made on the front, and our outpost line was now quite close to the Lens-Arras road, among the houses. The miners' cottages, mostly built in pairs and fifteen or twenty yards apart, afforded good observation for our "F.O.O.'s" and fine protection for our trench-mortar batteries. From here, good photo-graphs were taken of the Lens district, enabling us to obtain much use-ful information as to wire, trenches, targets, etc. Had these been taken at an earlier date, such disappointments as the failure of the Green Crassier attack might not have occured. Our observers at Hirondelle, Riaumont, Cité du Moulin, and Cité St. Emile kept constant watch for movement in the enemy lines, and throughout the long months of winter made a systematic study of the entire front, and kept the Bosches under cover by liberal use of our sniper guns.

During the first week in February, aerial activity increased on both sides, and our Batteries were heavily shelled. Many raids on the German lines kept up indentification of regiments opposed to us, and caused great worry to enemy units. Hostile excursions on our trenches failed miserably, not a trench, machine-gun or prisoner being taken. The Germans then became sullen and peevish and dosed our trenches, back areas and villages with gas shells.

On the 9th, promotions were posted in Brigade Orders as follows:

Major M. N. Ross, D.S.O., to be Lt.-Col.
Capt. C. Sifton to be Major.
Lieuts. O'Halloran, Maunder, Morse and Reid to be Captains.

All units toiled on to make their gun-pits and dug-outs shell-proof, and by the end of the month only a direct hit in the mouth of the gun embrasure itself would prove effective. It was well that these pre-cautions were taken, as Liévin was systematically "strafed" soon after with 5.9's. Though we had no serious casualties among the men, several guns were put out of action.

From the middle of February activity increased all along the Can-adian front from Acheville to Loos, a distance of 13,000 yards. The enemy grew more aggressive each day. Large German forces were now avail-able for the Western front, owing to the Russian debâcle, the overthrow of Serbia and Roumania, and the disastrous defeat of the Italians. The "morale" of the enemy was at its highest. A big offensive was expected any day, and the French and British made extensive preparations to meet it.

From Ypres to St. Quentin, the front line was heavily wired, and a battle zone, with redoubts and strong-points well-garrisoned by machine-gunners, laid out in our old support lines a mile in rear. The defensive was to be one of elasticity. Anti-tank and sniper guns were located in well-screened positions close to the battle zone, and masked for use in the event of a surprise attack.

While these preparations were being made to receive the enemy, the United States continued to pour its fighting forces into France. On arrival at Le Havre the "Yanks" were given further training by capable French and British instructors, and on completion of this rigourous course were assigned to army reserve. Paris was crowded with troops, and the "Yankies" were wildly acclaimed by the nation. Germany decided to strike before they were ready, and Belgium and France resounded to the rush of marching men. The enemy commenced a series of raids all along the line, endeavouring to feel out the strength of our trench garrisons. No one knew where the blow would fall, but every Division was on the alert. Throughout this whole period the Canadian Corps pursued an aggressive policy, keeping the Bosches continually on edge.

On the 12th and 19th of February the 4th Brigade, C.F.A. were called upon to take part in a barrage covering raids on the enemy lines, on the first occasion co-operating with the Division on our left to create a diversion from the front of the attacking troops, and a week later engaging the enemy's attention while gas was being projected on the St. Emile front. At the wagon-lines all units commenced agricultural work in an effort to procure vegetables for the coming season. For this purpose foray parties scoured the surrounding countryside for suitable equipment, and in a very short time were in possession of an almost complete set of farming implements.

In the meantime, working parties carried forward large quantities of gas projector cylinders and buried them behind the support lines, in readiness for a demonstration against the enemy, near Lens. For the next few weeks no further "shoots" were directed on the German battle zone as no one wished to draw retaliatory fire under such circumstances. It was decided to release the gas as soon as a favourable opportunity presented itself.

On February 26th another new officer came to us, Lt. A. R. Gordon, who was posted to the 19th Battery. To better engage enemy movement behind the lines, and mask our main positions as far as possible, forward sections were called upon to do all the firing for the Brigade. Unfortunately, their gun flashes were immediately spotted, and the positions registered by the enemy, resulting in a few casualties.

On March 4th, after a heavy artillery preparation, the Bosches attempted to raid our lines near Lens, but were driven off with heavy loss. During this bombardment our forward "O. Pip." was blown in, the N.C.O. on duty being killed, and four of the party wounded. The following night four of our 18-pounders were hauled over to Cité St. Pierre to cover a surprise attack on the enemy opposite St. Emile. These guns were able to fire at very short range across the front, and proved of great assistance to the attacking Infantry.

About this time Majors Sam Robson and J. S. McPherson reported for duty and were assigned command of the 19th and 21st Batteries respectively, and the Brigade participated in barrages covering a successful raid of the 4th Canadian Infantry Brigade, and the repulse of an enemy attack on our trenches to the left. On March 19th, the 18th Battery (5th Brigade, C.F.A.) relieved the 19th Battery, which unit became transferred to the C.O. No. 4 Group for tactics. Another hostile raid, March 21st, was driven off with severe loss to the enemy; and in the evening, at 11 p.m., "M" Special Co., R.E., fired 450 gas bombs from the 1st Canadian Divisional sector on to the enemy defences in Bois de Quatorze and Bois Dixhuit. It had been intended to project 2,000 bombs and to include Cité St. Auguste, but owing to unfavourable wind conditions the remainder of the projectors were not fired.

The poisonous gas seeped into enemy dug-outs, supports and reserve areas. His whole front was lit up with "S.O.S." rockets. A few minutes later our guns, supported by the "heavies" and trench-mortars, opened a slow bombardment, increasing in intensity for nearly three-quarters of an hour, when the German positions were swept with a short, intensive creeping barrage which raked his trenches and rear areas with high explosive.

The enemy was caught without warning, and lost heavily by our gun-fire as he emerged from the dug-outs and cellars of Lens. This was certainly the most awe-inspiring sight we had witnessed in the war, and the Germans must have been demoralized by the unexpected deluge of gas and shells. Five hours later the enemy retaliated on the Hill 70 Sector, raiding our trenches after a heavy trench-mortar and artillery bombardment, but was beaten off, leaving the dead behind him, and no prisoners to show for the demonstration.

Just before 5. a.m. on the 21st of March, a bombardment of great intensity opened against practically the whole fronts of the Fifth and Third British Armies, from the Oise to the Scarpe River. Portions of the front between the Scarpe and Lens, and also our positions from south of the La Bassee Canal to the River Lys were also heavily shelled. By 9.45 a.m. a general attack had been launched on a battle front of fifty-four miles between the Oise and the Sensée Rivers.

The method of "infiltration," so successfully used by the enemy against the Italians at Caporetto, again proved effective, and large gaps were opened up along the front. British Divisions and isolated posts fought with the greatest courage and resource, but all their efforts were unavailing. All day the battle raged, and by evening most of our forward zone had been overrun. General Gough, commanding the Fifth Army, did everything possible to stem the tide, but as the front was broken in places, and several Divisions were liable to be outflanked, a retreat was ordered to the old Somme battlefield.

This retirement made it necessary for the Third Army (General Byng) to withdraw from strong positions further north.

For the next few days the situation became very critical. Even Arras and Vimy were threatened by this sweeping advance of the

Bosches, and it became necessary for General Currie to take immediate steps to strengthen the front held by the Canadian Corps.

On the 21st, three of our Divisions were in the line, the 1st in the Hill 70 sector, the 4th from St. Emile to Avion, and the 3rd from Avion to Méricourt, while the 2nd was in rest in the Auchel area. Three days later the 3rd Canadian Division was in line from Avion to Hill 70; while the 1st went into Army reserve at Chateau de la Haie, and the 2nd into G.H.Q. reserve. Two Divisions were now holding a frontage of 17,000 yards, normally covered by at least four Divisions.

On March 22nd the zone of the 4th Brigade, C.F.A. was switched to the St. Emile sector and the 10th Battery (3rd Brigade, C.F.A.) was attached to us for tactics. The aggressive attitude of the Canadians continued and gas was projected on the enemy lines from Hill 70 to Lens.

The area of the German offensive spread northwards on the 28th of March, until from La Fére to beyond Gavrelle some sixty-three miles of our former line were involved. Prisoners stated emphatically that it was the intention of the German command to envelop Vimy Ridge from the south, piercing our front north of Arras, in the vicinity of Roclincourt. In view of such a possibility, every precaution was taken by Lt.-Gen. Sir Arthur Currie to meet it.

On the night of March 29th-30th the 4th Canadian Division which had been holding the Lens-Hill 70 sector, was withdrawn from the line and rushed to relieve the battle-wearied men of the 56th British Division holding the threatened gap between the Scarpe and Willerval. The 3rd Canadian Division remained in position from Avion to the line occupied by the 4th Canadian Division. A few days previously the 2nd Canadian Division had been detached from the Corps and despatched to aid the hard-pressed British troops at Neuville-Vitasse, south of Arras. It came into line on the 29th-30th, holding a front of 6,000 yards from the Cojeul River to Telegraph Hill, and the 1st Canadian Division filled in the remainder of the Arras sector from there to the River Scarpe.

The 4th C.D.A. was relieved by British Batteries the night of March 28th-29th and the following day proceeded from wagon-lines at Ablain St. Nazaire to Acq. Enroute, the C.O. and Battery Commanders were called upon to reconnoitre positions to the north of Arras, and the battery captains led the units on to Acq. On arrival we found the village so crowded with troops and transport that new wagon-lines had to be established in another part of the neighbourhood, while the guns were taken forward to Roclincourt to assist in holding that front against the threatened attack of the enemy.

CHAPTER V

Holding the Ridge

RECONNAISSANCE for positions near Roclincourt all but resulted in casualties to our senior officers. On March 29th, Lt.-Col. M. N. Ross, D.S.O., had received orders to relieve the 230th Brigade, R.F.A., H.Q., on the Gavrelle-Oppy front, considered a very peaceful area since the fighting of the previous summer. Leaving their horses at the top of the ridge, the C.O. and Battery Commanders proceeded on foot toward their destination. As they neared the reserve trenches and the village of Bailleul, no one was to be seen except occasional infantrymen, scurrying from shell-hole to shell-hole, a short distance ahead. The spot where the Colonel and officers dismounted on the crest of Vimy was immediately shelled, and the horses had to be led to cover in old trenches, nearby.

The whole countryside showed signs of the previous day's battle. Not a field gun could be seen along the front. Obviously some mistake had been made in the map location given to the Colonel, so he and his reconnaissance party returned and finally located the H.Q., which they were seeking, about a mile south-west of Bailleul. The R.F.A. Batteries had been withdrawn from the original positions and were now on the Ridge not far from the Arras-Bailleul Road, considerably further south. Roclincourt was therefore chosen as Brigade H.Q. as the location taken over was too far removed from the gun positions.

Our guns were close to the crest and within easy range of all parts of the front. The 56th (British) Division had held up the German attack on this flank. The counter battery work of the enemy had been well-nigh perfect. Many of the gun emplacements and shelters were utterly destroyed, ammunition scattered, and bodies of gunners and horses lay amongst the debris. Detachments from the wagon-lines toiled long into the night and following day salvaging what remained that was of any value.

From the "O. Pip." on the forward slope of the ridge, Germans could be seen moving about in every direction, a great number wearing red cross brassards, and there were many stretcher parties covering the plain. A substantial advance had been made, almost to the railway embankment in front of us. For the first few days these parties were not fired upon, but after watching them carefully, our observation officers became satisfied they were not looking for wounded, but salvaging kits and rifles and carrying these articles in their stretchers to the rear. Our Batteries were therefore ordered to clear the plain below, and keep the enemy to his trenches.

When matters looked darkest for the Allies, Sir Arthur Currie issued a Special Order to the Canadian Corps, an order which should rank among the great documents of Canadian history:—

"In an endeavour to reach an immediate decision the enemy has gathered all his forces and struck a mighty blow at the British Army. Overwhelmed by sheer weight of numbers the British Divisions in the line between the SCARPE and the OISE have fallen back, fighting hard, steady and undismayed.

"Measures have been taken to successfully meet this German onslaught. The French have gathered a powerful Army, commanded by a most able and trusted leader, and this Army is now moving swiftly to our help. Fresh British Divisions are being thrown in. The Canadians are soon to be engaged. Our Motor Machine-Gun Brigade has already played a most gallant part and once again covered itself with glory.

"Looking back with pride on the unbroken record of your glorious achievements, asking you to realize that to-day the fate of the British Empire hangs in the balance, I place my trust in the Canadian Corps, knowing that where Canadians are engaged there can be no giving way.

"Under the orders of your devoted Officers, in the coming battle you will advance or fall where you stand, facing the enemy.

"To those who will fall, I say: 'You will not die, but step into immortality. Your mothers will not lament your fate, but will be proud to have borne such sons. Your names will be revered forever and ever by your grateful country and God will take you unto Himself.'

"Canadians, in this fateful hour, I command you and I trust you to fight as you have ever fought, with all your strength, with all your determination, with all your tranquil courage. On many a hard-fought field of battle you have overcome this enemy. With God's help you shall achieve victory once more."

The threatened German attack on our immediate front never developed. Enemy preparations to renew the offensive on the morning of March 30th were effectually overcome by the massed fire of our Artillery which was continued throughout the night, and which was increased at 3.45, 4.30 and 5 a.m. to a drum barrage on the front line, communication trenches and assembly areas.

On April 1st an enemy airman flew over our lines and in spite of intense machine-gun and anti-aircraft fire, brought down four observation balloons, one after another, and flew back in safety to his own lines. It is recorded this bold aviator was decorated with the Iron Cross for his exploit. He was killed shortly afterwards in an aerial battle.

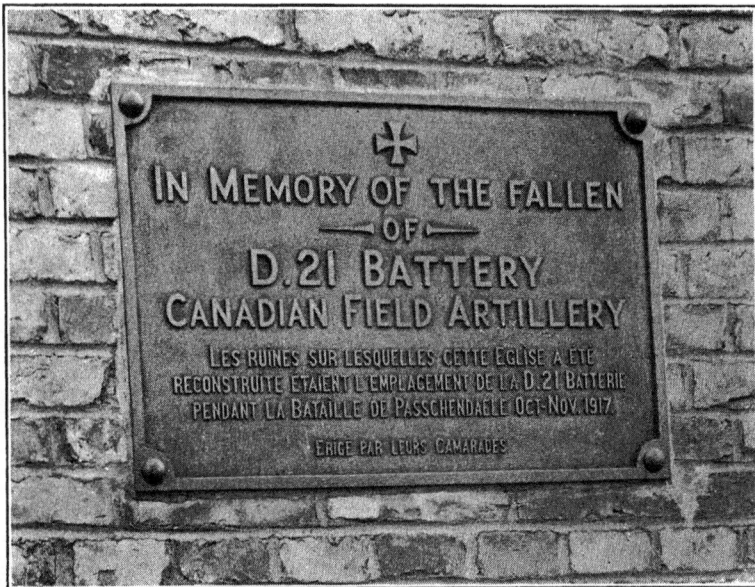

IN MEMORY OF THE FALLEN
—OF—
D.21 BATTERY
CANADIAN FIELD ARTILLERY

LES RUINES SUR LESQUELLES CETTE EGLISE A ETE
RECONSTRUITE ETAIENT L'EMPLACEMENT DE LA D.21 BATTERIE
PENDANT LA BATAILLE DE PASSCHENDAELE OCT-NOV. 1917.

ERIGE PAR LEURS CAMARADES

The above tablet to commemorate our fallen comrades was erected on the rebuilt church at Zonnebeke to mark the battery positions of D.21 in the battle of Passchendaele Ridge.

In Flanders' Fields

"In Flanders' fields the poppies grow
   Between the crosses, row on row
   That mark our place; and in the sky
   The larks, still bravely singing, fly
Scarce heard amid the guns below.
We are the Dead. Short days ago
We lived, felt dawn, saw sunset glow,
Loved and were loved, and now we lie
     In Flanders' fields."

—Col. John McCrae.

By this time the positions occupied by our Batteries had been registered and shelled by the Bosches, and as they were considered too exposed in case of a massed attack, alternative locations were selected further back, forward sections only being kept within short range of the enemy.

During the following week the whole 4th Canadian Division was engaged in strengthening their positions, and reserve trenches and gun-pits were prepared along the Lens-Arras road, in the event of further retirements. From what we had seen, however, it appeared that to retire under such conditions was impossible, and the Batteries would have to fight where they were.

On April 9th, the enemy, foiled in his efforts to break through at Arras, attacked on the Lys front, from La Bassée to Armentieres. This thrust was a direct threat to Bethune and the envelopment of Vimy Ridge from the north. Hostile Artillery became very active along our front from the Scarpe to the Souchez. For days our guns thundered in reply, and, on the 9th and 10th of April, raids were made on the enemy lines by units of the 10th and 11th Infantry Brigades (4th Canadian Division), the 4th Brigade, C.F.A. taking part in the barrages.

Vimy was again the centre of German hate. Cities, towns and villages far behind the lines, the main roads, camps and wagon-lines were shelled by high velocity guns. The constant stream of "evacués" from Bethune and Arras added to the panic of the civilians. It was now seen that the German onslaught on the Portuguese, holding the Lys sector, was not merely local, but intended as a major operation.

On April 12th, the 46th (British) Division was ordered north to take part in the battle and the 3rd Canadian Division front was extended to take over their section of the line in the Lens-St. Emile-Hill 70 sector. At the same time the 4th Canadian Division extended its front northward to include the Acheville sector. The Corps was now in occupation of no less than 29,000 yards of trenches held by three Divisions, and extending from the Scarpe to Hill 70. The task was a highly responsible one. By capturing the colleries of the north, the Germans could still greatly paralyze France, even though they had failed to separate the French from the British forces.

The tremendous length of line assigned to the Corps made it impossible to hold it in any strength or depth, and as a result of the enemy advances to the north and south, Vimy Ridge became the point of a deep salient, open to attacks from the flanks. To deceive the German command, our Battalions in the line adopted a very aggressive attitude, raiding the enemy on some section of the front nearly every night, carrying out an extensive programme of harassing fire on his forward and rear area, and on many occasions employing lethal gas. Though the situation was highly critical, Sir Arthur Currie made use of all Corps Troops to strengthen the line and show a bold front to the Germans opposite us.

During the latter part of April, the 4th Brigade, C.F.A., now part of the Right Group (Lt.-Col. J. A. McDonald), was engaged daily, harassing the enemy and, co-operated with other units, covering raids of the 11th

Canadian Infantry Brigade. On one occasion the 13th Battery set up a field gun on a narrow-gauge truck and shelled the Hun from a spur near Bailleul. Our Infantry complained against the demonstration, stating such action was liable to bring heavy retaliation on their trenches. We, therefore, had to be content to remain immobile, and do all our firing from the gun-pits.

On May the 3rd the 4th Brigade, C.F.A., was finally relieved and went to Acq, the 70th Brigade, R.F.A. taking over our positions near Roclincourt. On the same day Major Sifton, Major McPherson, and Lieut. Johnston were sent to hospital with influenza, which epidemic had spread throughout the Corps.

We were now booked for open warfare training, and proceeded to Agny in the Aubigny area to join the rest of the 4th Canadian Division. Shortly after, Major Sifton returned for duty, and though many more were stricken with "flu" the cases were not serious. The change of scenery and long period of rest worked wonders with the Batteries. Though the usual ritual of stable duties, gun drill, signalling practice, riding and manoeuvres were followed, plenty of time was found for sports. The Batteries formed a baseball league, and football teams as well.

The area round about Agny was not adaptable to Brigade man-oeuvres, but the Headquarters Party of each Battery practiced Field Artillery Training, daily, with the Observation and Reconnaissance Offi-cers, and became highly proficient with morse flags, semaphore, helio and lamp. Due to the continual routine of trench warfare in the past, the signallers had done all of their work on foot, having used their mounts only when the Brigade was on the march to a new front. Now, however, with open fighting planned for the summer and fall, they became obliged to undergo a vigourous course in riding. Within a short time Headquarters Parties had "learned their stuff," and in the "Last Hundred Days" showed the benefit of this training under the able direction of Sgt. Hancocks, an old British Regular who had gleaned valuable experience as a signaller in India.

On the 22nd we moved to Magnicourt, which place afforded much better facilities for open warfare manoeuvres than that previously occupied, the ground being diversified in character and well adapted for all conditions likely to be encountered in battle with the enemy.

By this time the various units had perfected themselves in their duties, the battery officers and gun crews having practiced gun drill daily, battery manoeuvres with the drivers, and series after series by signalled corrections from "O.P.'s." Brigade tactics and co-ordination of all units was then followed, and soon the old 4th Brigade, C.F.A. was working like a well-oiled machine.

As time went on the training was broadened by combined schemes with the Infantry, Tanks, and Air Force. In addition to the regular routine, preparations were made for a counter attack on the Bethune front, in the event of a further enemy advance there. This area was carefully covered by the Colonel and Battery Commanders, forward and reserve positions selected and plans made for a number of guns, crews and ammunition to be hauled up by the Tanks. Orders had been issued by the Canadian Corps for 18 gunners to be detailed from the C.F.A. for duty with the Tanks, and a number of our gunners left to join this unit. Some of us availed ourselves of the opportunity of travelling inside these monsters on trial demonstrations against dummy trenches.

One such experience was enough. The interior of a Tank was like a fiery furnace and when travelling over rough ground we not only got sick and dizzy, but received many bad bumps as these iron-clad monsters lurched and dipped unexpectedly over an unseen obstacle in our path.

Two Lewis guns were now allotted to each Battery, and the gunners soon became proficient in their use.

Throughout the summer many German air raids were made on London, but the most inhumane atrocity yet perpetrated by the enemy was the bombing of the Canadian and British Hospitals in the Etaples District during the latter part of May. A great number of badly wounded men lay recuperating in tents and hutments in this quiet town by the sea, when, without any warning, huge "Gotha" planes hovered overhead and released their death-dealing missiles on the area, killing a great many of the helpless patients.

Casualties connected with the Canadian Hospitals were as follows :—

	KILLED	WOUNDED	TOTAL
Patients	15	67	82
Personnel	54	94	148
	69	161	230

Of the killed, 3 were Nursing Sisters, and of the wounded, 7. There were other casualties in the area, especially on the 19th of May, when 124 other ranks were killed. 89 of the British wounded died of their wounds later.

During the month of June, training continued. Nightly manoeuvres were in order, the Batteries bivouacing for days at a time in the open. The Brigade M.O. inoculated all ranks.

In the evenings we played baseball and football and made good use of a swimming pool in the neighbourhood of La Comte. On the the 15th, all units gathered at Pernes for Divisional Sports, and three days later the 4th C.D.A. had a horse show. About the same time, the "flu" epidemic broke out again and many of our men went to rest camp to recuperate. Major S. Robson was transferred to the 5th C.D.A., Capt. W. E. Steacy assumed command of the 19th Battery, and all units marched to Amettes, where the guns were calibrated. On the 27th, further awards were posted in Brigade orders, Sgt. W. F. James and Corporal F. H. Dowton being awarded the M.S.M.

On Dominion Day, July 1st, the Canadian Corps held a big field day at Tinques, and a whole holiday was extended to those units out of the line. Approximately 50,000 attended, including the Duke of Connaught, Sir Robert Borden and other Cabinet Ministers, Marshal Pétain, Sir

Douglas Haig and leading British Army Commanders, and many of all ranks from the Canadian Divisions.

Three days later the 4th Brigade, C.F.A. and other units of the 4th Canadian Division were inspected by the Canadian Cabinet Ministers at the sports field and marched past in column of batteries. Another inspection followed on July 10th in a drizzling rain. The Canadian Corps Commander, Sir Arthur Currie, took the salute and congratulated our Colonel on the fine appearance of horses, personnel and equipment.

Our open warfare training was now about completed, and after further inspections by the M.O., dental officers and the C.O., we marched on July 11th to Mt. St. Eloi, where we bivouacked in the open. Relief of the 256th Brigade, R.F.A., by sections, followed on the nights of the 12th and 13th, near Willerval. Lt.-Col. Ross then proceeded on leave to England. Maj. G. L. Drew (13th Battery) assumed command of the 4th Brigade, C.F.A. and was relieved a week or so later by Major A. A. Durkee.

The Vimy front had quieted down after the hectic days of March and April, but the enemy became very nervous when they discovered the Canadian Corps was again in the line and likely to be used in an offensive against the Douai defences and the Drocourt-Quéant Line.

In the summer of 1918, the Corps was considered the most powerful fighting machine on the Western Front, with its 107,370 storm troops. Political parties in Canada endeavoured to split the Canadian army organization in France, suggesting that two Army Corps of three Divisions (modelled on the new British Army establishments) replace the existing formation of four Divisions, over strength, and the leadership be divided between Sir Arthur Currie and Sir Richard Turner, V.C.

This meant that a British General would again direct the destines of our forces, and the Corps spirit, the essential that had won us success in recent battles, would be broken.

As an alternative, Sir Arthur Currie recommended that the 5th Canadian Division be retained in England as available reinforcements to replace the heavy casualties during the remainder of the war, and that conscripted men be rushed to England to take their place in reserve. This brilliant soldier had his way in the end, and his judgment was more than recognized when the Canadian Corps had proven by its splendid fighting qualities during "The Last Hundred Days" that no enemy or Allied Corps was equal to it in striking force, initiative, or "morale."

Plans had previously been made that, in the event of an allied offensive being made from Arras, Orange Hill, Monchy-le-Preux, and the heavily-fortified enemy positions along the Scarpe would be stormed by the Canadians. The Divisions were now in line from Neuville-Vitasse to Willerval. Immediately they began to show a bold front to the Germans, harassing their communications, sweeping the back areas, and raiding their trenches night after night. This led the enemy to believe an attack was impending, and large reserves, slated for further operations against the French, were diverted at the last moment and sent to oppose the Canadian Corps.

However, a much more enterprising scheme was planned for another part of the front, and on July 20th Sir Arthur Currie was informed that the Corps would take part in an offensive near Amiens.

Quoting Sir Douglas Haig:—

"Preliminary instructions to prepare to attack east of Amiens at an early date had been given to the Fourth Army Commander, General Sir Henry Rawlinson, on July 13th, and on July 28th the French First Army, under General Debeney, was placed by Marshal Foch under my orders for the operation. Further, to strengthen my attack, I decided to reinforce the British Fourth Army with the Canadian Corps, and also with the two British Divisions which were then held in readiness astride the Somme.

"In order to deceive the enemy and ensure the maximum effect of a surprise attack, elaborate precautions were taken to mislead him as to our intentions and to conceal our real purpose. Instructions of a detailed character were issued to the formations concerned, calculated to make it appear that a British attack in Flanders was imminent. Canadian Battalions were put into line on the Kemmel front, where they were identified by the enemy. Corps Headquarters were prepared and Casualty Clearing Stations were erected in conspicuous positions in this area."

Battalions and Batteries in the forward zone were secretly withdrawn, and immediately began their march to the new area. On July 31st-August 1st, the 4th Brigade, C.F.A. was relieved by the 311th A.F.A. Brigade, R.F.A., and proceeded with the 4th Canadian Division towards Amiens.

CHAPTER VI

Battle of Amiens

PROSPECTS of open warfare at last, after nearly three years of trench warfare, made the Canadians enthusiastic and confident of the outcome. Most of the units were despatched to the new area by train or bus. Those who were not fortunate enough to have transportation, marched at night and rested by day. In this way the great movement of troops was screened from enemy airmen, and secrecy maintained.

On completion of relief by the 311th A.F.A. Brigade, on August 1st, the 4th Brigade, C.F.A., under cover of darkness, moved from its wagon-lines at Mont St. Eloi on its long "trek" to the south. Proceeding by forced marches each night, and resting during the day, we finally reached Boves Wood in the early morning of August 5th, stopping at Savy, Amplier and Forêt de Vignacourt. At last we had reached our destination, and found we were a few miles south of the big city of Amiens.

The concentration of guns and troops was tremendous. The whole Canadian Corps had moved to this area in preparation for an immediate offensive. The long village street of Boves led to the River Avre. On the opposite side lay the hamlet of St. Nicolas, and above, on the crest of a gradual slope from the river, Gentelles Wood. There was little movement during the daylight hours, but at night the whole countryside teemed with traffic. It was very fortunate that at this critical time the weather was misty and detrimental to enemy observation, for the watering facilities necessary for such a large number of horses were absolutely non-existent; in most cases the animals had to be taken for miles across the open to be watered. More troops were arriving every hour, and Australian and French Battalions, the guardians of Amiens, passed our camp at intervals on their way to and from the trenches.

All the impedimenta of war was gathered for this offensive. Our great fighting machine surged silently toward the front; marching men,

Battery after Battery of field guns, long lines of supply lorries, heavy trucks and traction engines towing great howitzers.

The weather was perfect. Occasionally enemy aeroplanes appeared, but the Bosches failed to discover the great concentration against them, although heavy area and harassing fire made us wonder if they were suspicious.

On arrival at Boves Wood the Brigade immediately made preparations for the "show" and on the night of August 5th-6th and 6th-7th occupied battle positions, to the right of the Amiens-Roye Road, back of Domart.

Each night was spent in packing up ammunition and caching it under camouflage material at the gun positions, until 600 rounds per 18-pounder and 500 rounds per howitzer had been delivered. Owing to the short time allowed before the launching of the attack, all units had to get their supplies forward, with the result that the road was jammed with traffic from dusk to dawn. It sometimes took us an hour to move even half a mile, and only through the rigid enforcement of traffic regulations and the skill in handling our vehicles were we able to move at all.

None of the guns had been registered on the enemy lines, but as they had all been calibrated, angles and ranges were worked out from the map and corrected for wind, barometer, temperature, and muzzle velocity. The Brigade was never in better condition. The rigourous open warfare training of the summer months had made the horses and personnel fit and ready for the long marches and fighting ahead of them.

The front of the attack extended from Morlancourt on the Somme to Breches, on the Avre, a distance of fifteen miles; the III British Corps operating between Albert and the Somme, the Australian Corps from the Somme to the Amiens-Chaulnes Railway Line, the Canadian Corps, from the railway line to the Thennes-Roye Road, and the First French Army carrying out an offensive against the huge Montdidier salient on our right.

On the Canadian sector, to keep up the veil of secrecy, Australian units still occupied the front line trenches. Attacking Battalions of the 2nd Canadian Division on the left, the 1st Canadian Division in the centre, and the 3rd Canadian Division on the right proceeded to their jumping off line a few hours after midnight on the 7th-8th of August. The 4th Division was in reserve behind the 3rd, ready to pass through as soon as the prearranged line was reached.

With the exception of those Batteries engaged on harassing fire, the night was still. As zero approached it was seen that our advance would be clouded in mist. A deep fog hung over the battlefield.

Close to us, and to the left in Hangard Wood, great, lumbering Tanks crept toward the enemy. Watches had been synchronized a few hours before.

Two minutes to go!

4.20 a.m.!

Promptly on the second, 644 guns belched forth in a thunderous roar on the German lines, communications, assembly areas and hostile batteries.

Enemy "S.O.S." rockets called wildly on their Artillery for help. The German gunners, however, were having their troubles, too, and in many cases took refuge in their dug-outs against the heavy blast of our 6-inch, 8-inch and "9.2's." Some of their big howitzers replied to our fire and caused our Batteries several casualties, a heavy retaliatory barrage being laid on the area around Gentelles Wood, Domart and the approaches to the battle zone.

Great credit is due Brig.-Gen. A. G. L. McNaughton, in charge of Canadian Corps counter battery work, for his thorough development and effective use of the "heavies" in neutralizing the activity of enemy Artillery at Amiens. But for the wonderful work of the big guns the lighter Field Batteries and Infantry would undoubtedly have suffered terribly in the opening barrage, August 8th.

As the bursting screen of "H.E." and shrapnel rolled on at the rate of 100 yards every few minutes, the Infantry and Tanks surged forward. These heavy engines of war crushed and destroyed every obstacle in their path, flattening out enemy defences like matchwood. Hun machine-gunners, the pride of the German Army, fought to the last, and the Tanks rolled them down.

Quoting Sir Arthur Currie :—

"At 4.20 a.m. August 8th, the initial assault was delivered on the entire Army front of attack, and the First French Army opened their bombardment. The attackers made satisfactory progress from the out-set, on the whole front. East of Hourges, opposite the 3rd (Canadian) Division, the high ground which dominated our front and a portion of the French front had been seized quickly by the 9th Canadian Infantry Bri-gade, and the way was opened for the Canadian Independent Force and the 4th (Canadian) Division. The very complete arrangements made by the 3rd (Canadian) Division to keep the bridge open and to repair the road quickly, allowed the reserves to go forward without delay. The heavy task of the Engineers was remarkably well carried out.

"By afternoon the Canadian Corps had gained all its objectives, with the exception of a few hundred yards on the right in the vicinity of le Quesnel, where stiff resistance was offered by unexpected reserves, but this was made good the following morning. The day's operations, in which the four Canadian Divisions took part, represented a maximum penetration of the enemy's defences of over eight miles, and included the capture of the following villages : Hangard, Demuin, Beaucourt, Auber-court, Courcelles, Ignaucourt, Cayeux, Caix, Marcelcave, Wiencourt, L'Equipée and Guillaucourt. In addition to these, the Canadian Independ-ent Force assisted the French in the capture of Mezières, which was holding up their advance.

"The surprise had been complete and overwhelming. Prisoners stated that they had no idea that an attack was impending, and captured documents did not indicate that any of our preparations had been detec-ted. An officer stated that the Canadians were believed to be on the Kemmel front."

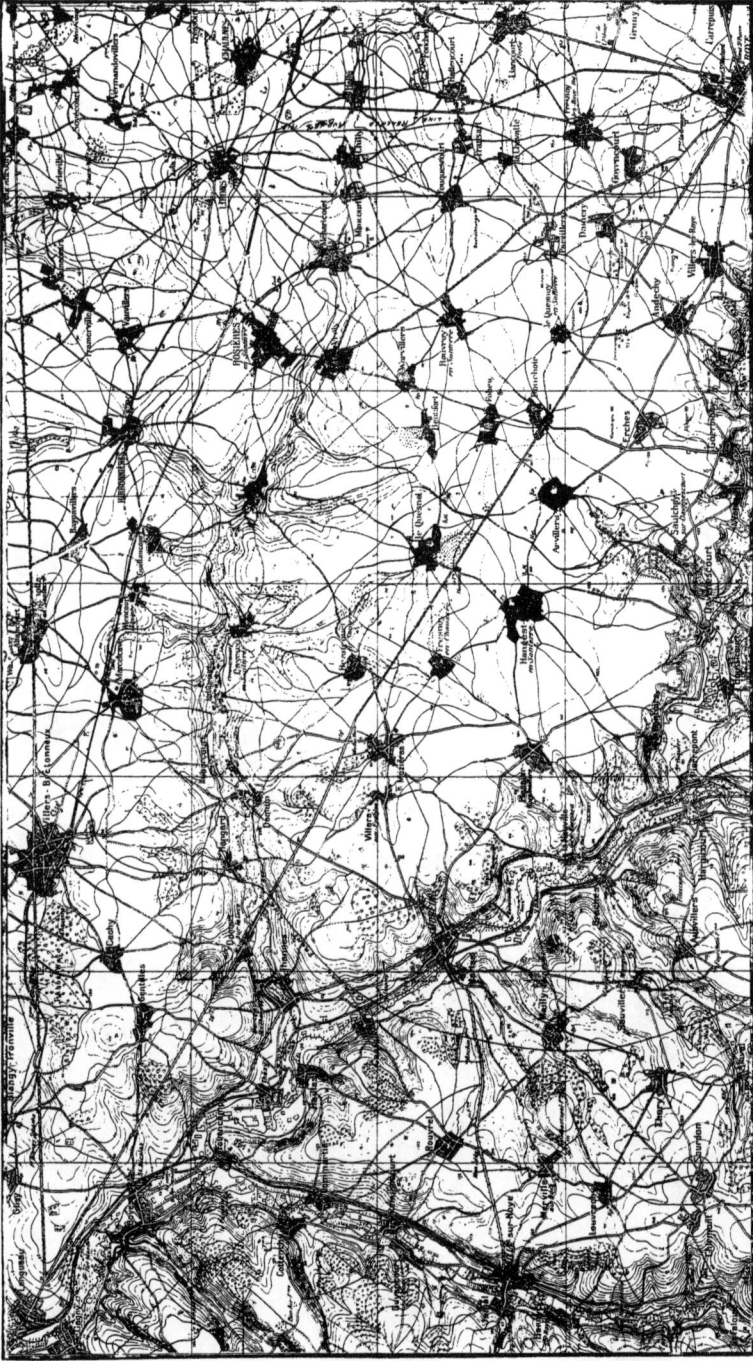

AMIENS——AUGUST, 1918

Scale: 5,000 metres—1 inch—3.1 miles

At 8.30 a.m. the Batteries finished their appointed task, and the snap of the field guns ceased. Gun teams were then called up and the Artillery prepared to move forward.

It was on this occasion that the first experiment was made in the use of "Contact Batteries"—an experiment that was so dramatic and so satisfactory in the results achieved that special notice was given in the London daily papers describing the daring exploits of Major Clifford Sifton's command.

Two months previously the Canadian Artillery had been undergoing a rigourous course of training in open warfare. Past experience had led those in high command to believe that field guns could be effectively employed in close support of the Infantry for the purpose of engaging "opportunity targets" at close range, once the enemy line of resistance had been broken. A more dangerous task for artillery could be scarcely imagined, but all ranks were eager for open action.

As soon as the initial barrage had ended, a section from each of the 13th, 19th, and 27th Batteries assembled under the command of Major Sifton. For the day's operations each section was to function as a separate unit, with an "F.O.O." in close contact with the Infantry, an officer at the guns, and an n.c.o. in charge of the horses and wagons. Following up the advance of the 12th Canadian Infantry Brigade(Brig.-Gen. MacBrien), the "Composite Battery" crossed "No-Man's Land," and each section, covering a third of the Infantry Brigade front, prepared to take on any targets in its zone.

While on reconnaisance a mile north of Beaucourt, Major Sifton was suddenly attracted by the sound of heavy machine-gun fire not far ahead. Proceeding around a wood, to investigate, he was met by a sharp burst-of-fire, and retired, wounded in the wrist. While the Infantry, supported by Tanks, commenced a flanking movement to the left, one of the sections of the "Composite Battery" opened fire from a semi-covered position—only the tips of the "dial-sights" showing above the crest.

The 19th Battery section, not to be out-done, decided to risk a dash into the open. Led by Lieut. Pilgrim, one gun, with horses straining low against their breast-collars, galloped 300 yards in front of the spot where Major Sifton had been wounded, and came into action with lightning speed. Spotting an enemy machine-gun in a quarry to the south-east, three rounds of "high-explosive" were fired, and so accurate was the range computed that all three bursts landed on the target. Meanwhile, Lieut. Grier rushed the other gun forward in full view of the enemy and joined in the miniature battle. Both guns then used shrapnel, and poured a deadly fire into the German "nest." As the enemy retired, the range was lengthened, and with each shell the gunners were urged by surrounding infantrymen to "Soak 'em again!" "A little more right!" etc. The way was then cleared for the attacking forces. Many lives had undoubtedly been saved by the quick and thorough manner in which the situation had been handled. "Contact Batteries" had proven their worth.

The remaining units of the Brigade moved forward in the late afternoon, taking up positions in Claude Wood, between Cayeux and Beaucourt. By evening the Canadian Corps had taken approximately 5,000 prisoners and many guns, and had reached the old Amiens defence line.

Ludendorff, in his book on the War, clearly admits that the confidence of the German General Staff was shattered by this unexpected reverse:

"The defeat of our armies on August 8th in the Franco-British offensive near Albert and north of Montdidier, finally resulted in our losing hope for a military victory."

On both flanks of the Canadians, the advance was almost as rapid, the First French Army, attacking through hilly country, with the assistance of the Canadian Independent Force, captured Moreuil and Mezières after hard fighting, taking 4,000 prisoners; while the Australians went forward with a rush and swept all before them. The penetration of the "Anzacs" was almost as great as our own. Further north, where the III British Corps was operating, German resistance was so severe that British troops became held up, and were unable to conform with the movement further south.

When the advance stopped at night, the usual precautions were taken, "S.O.S." lines arranged for, and preparations made to continue the attack the next day. In the centre, on the 1st and 4th Division fronts the enemy put up a strong resistance, and fought all night to prevent the Canadians from breaking through. In the end, however, the German Brigades were either routed or captured, and, as dawn broke, fresh troops continued the advance eastward.

Large numbers of enemy guns were now organized into Pan-Germanic groups, and with the big stock of ammunition available, the enemy was dosed with his own shrapnel during the following week.

The task assigned the attacking Battalions on August 9th was not so formidable as that on the previous day, but meant an advance to an average depth of 4 miles on a 5-mile front, the primary objective being the Bouchoir-Rouvroy-Meharicourt road. The country was almost flat and very open, with only a few villages and small woods upon it.

Advancing steadily, in face of heavy machine-gun fire, our long lines pushed forward. Where the Infantry became held up, Tanks and Cavalry broke down the enemy resistance. By evening, the 2nd Division, on the left, had carried Rosières, Meharicourt, and Vrély; in the centre, the 1st Division captured Warvillers, Beaufort, and Rouvroy; and, on the right, the 3rd Division, advancing down the Roye Road, secured Folies and Bouchoir, and then went out of the Corps area to assist the French in taking Arvillers. It was another day of triumph for the Canadian Corps.

Throughout the fighting on the 9th, the 4th Brigade, C.F.A. remained in reserve, but in the evening moved forward to positions along the edge of the wood, near Cayeux. Enemy planes became more active and bombed the area heavily, causing several casualties in the wagon-lines.

On the 10th, at 4.30 a.m., we moved ahead, going into action just west of Vrèly to support an attack on Chilly. A few hours later we took up positions in a valley west of Meharicourt, with Brigade Headquarters in a tree-lined road, 1,000 yards in front of Vrèly. The weather was perfect, the sun shone forth in all its glory, and at night the stars flickered clearly above us.

Enemy bombing planes, though checked in the day-time by our gallant aviators and anti-aircraft guns, came over in large squadrons every evening and wrought havoc in our horse-lines and back areas. On one occasion, near Meharicourt, enemy planes flew low over the Batteries of the Brigade, and threatened to put us out of action. Our "Lewis gunners" immediately engaged them with bursts of machine-gun fire, and one of the German machines was seen to fall, brought down by men of the 19th Battery.

No doubt the gun positions were spotted, as next day the German Artillery shelled us heavily, the 13th Battery losing Lieut. C. H. Watson (killed), Lieut. . J. MacKenzie (wounded) and a number of the gunners, while Lieut. D. H. Cole of the 27th Battery also received a "Blighty."

On the 11th, Brigade Headquarters moved forward to the village of Meharicourt to be close to the Infantry Brigade Headquarters, in preparation for a renewal of the offensive against the Roye-Chaulnes Defence Line.

Covering the operations, Sir Arthur Currie states:—

"The attack was continued on the morning of the 10th, with the 3rd Canadian Division on the right and the 4th Canadian Division on the left, the 1st and 2nd Canadian Divisions being held in Corps Reserve. After the 3rd Canadian Division had taken the village of Le Quesnoy-en-Santerre, the 32nd Division. which had come under the Canadian Corps on the night of the 9th-10th, passed through it and advanced the line somewhat further through the old British trenches west of Parvillers and Damery.

"During the day, the 4th Canadian Division succeeded, after very hard fighting, in occupying Fouquescourt, Maucourt, Chilly, and Hallu. During the night of August 10th, a strong enemy counter-attack developed against a part of the front of the 4th Canadian Division east of Hallu. This counter-attack was beaten off, but owing to general conditions the line at that point was slightly withdrawn to the railway embankment immediately to the west of Hallu. Subsequent upon this slight withdrawal, and with a view of reducing the existing salient forward of Chilly, the line was further withdrawn to the eastern outskirts of that village.

"On the 11th, at 9.30 a.m., the 32nd Division launched an attack against Damery, but was not successful. The 4th Canadian Division improved their line by advancing it locally to reduce the Chilly salient, which was still very pronounced. During the night of the 11th, the 32nd Division and the 4th Canadian Division were relieved by the 3rd and 2nd Canadian Divisions respectively."

For the next few days the 4th Brigade, C.F.A. remained in position near Meharicourt, carrying out harassing fire day and night on the German lines and communications. Due to the long range we could not indulge in our favourite pastime—"sniping"; but, on the return of Lt.-

Col. Ross from leave, August 12th, forward positions were reconnoitred near Fouquescourt, and ammunition dumps established in preparation for further activities against the enemy.

One day, at noon, we were surprised to note the appearance of a large number of Australian gun-teams and limbers, trotting up towards Fouquescourt. As fas as we could see they were unaccompanied by an officer. On demanding their reason of approach to such a dangerous shell-swept area, the "Aussies" announced they had come to take out their guns. It did not take long to convince them they had become lost and were in danger of complete annihilation. The "Aussies" scattered, some driving right through our gun positions, while others made for the open field. German Batteries then opened fire and we became the unwilling spectators of our gallant Anzac comrades being shelled as they galloped through Rosières, followed by enemy whizz-bangs. Had it not been for the long range, and the inaccurate shooting of the Bosches, undoubtedly the "Aussies" would have suffered many casualties.

The first stage of the Amiens offensive was now over, and all units prepared for another period of trench warfare. About this time a number of changes were made in the personnel of the officers: Capt. R. Forsyth, Lieut. C. O. Scott, Lieut. J. P. Atkins, and Lieut. G. R. L. Hill reported for duty, the first three being posted to the 27th Battery and the latter to the 13th Battery, while Major G. L. Drew, (13th Battery) left to take command of the 1st Battery, C.F.A., and Capt. E. B. P. Armour became Major of the 60th Battery, C.F.A.

Again quoting Sir Arthur Currie :—

"On the nights of August 15th-16th and the 16th-17th, the 1st Canadian Division relieved the 3rd Canadian Division, the latter being withdrawn to Corps Reserve. Progress was made during the 16th-17th, the enemy being driven out of Fransart by the 4th Canadian Infantry Brigade (2nd Canadian Division), and out of la Chavette by the 1st Canadian Division, our line on the right being advanced in co-operation with the French.

"The relief of the 2nd Canadian Division by the 4th Canadian Division was carried out on the nights of the 15th-16th and the 16th-17th, the former being withdrawn to Corps Reserve on the 17th. The operation, which had been projected for August 16th, had been postponed and it had been decided to transfer the Canadian Corps back to the First Army, the move to begin by strategic trains on the 19th.

"The 18th was quiet along the front, but, on the 19th, the 4th Canadian Division carried out a minor operation near Chilly, which greatly improved our line in that neighbourhood. Four hostile counter-attacks to recover the newly-won ground were beaten off during the night.

"On the 19th, the 2nd and 3rd Canadian Divisions started their move to First Army, and on the night of the 19th-20th, the relief of the 1st Canadian Division, by the French, commenced. This relief was completed on the 22nd and the 1st Canadian Division was placed in Corps Reserve. On August 22nd I handed over command of the Canadian Corps front to the G.O.C., Australian Corps, and my Headquarters moved north to Hautecloque, opening there at 10 a.m. of the same day.

"Between August 8th and 22nd, the Canadian Corps fought against 15 German Divisions; of these 10 were directly engaged and thoroughly defeated, prisoners being captured from almost every one of their Battalions; the 5 other Divisions, fighting astride our flanks, were only partially engaged by us.

"In the same period the Canadian Corps captured 9,131 prisoners, 190 guns of all calibres, and more than 1,000 machine-guns and trench-mortars. The greatest depth penetrated approximated to 14 miles, and an area of over 67 square miles, containing 27 towns and villages, had been liberated.

"The casualties suffered by the Canadian Corps in the 14 days' heavy fighting amounted to:—

	OFFICERS	OTHER RANKS
Killed	126	1688
Wounded	444	8659
Missing	9	436
	579	10783

"Considering the number of German Divisions engaged, and the results achieved, the casualties were very light."

On the 22nd, warning orders were received by Lt.-Col. Ross that the Brigade was to be relieved by French Artillery units, and on the following day a rendezvous was arranged with their officers to take over the positions and "O.P.'s." All units, except the 13th Battery, moved out after dark on the 24th. A clear moonlight night gave enemy airmen every opportunity to follow the relief.

It was interesting to see French poilus coming into action. They marched along swiftly, in long overcoats and with full equipment. The transport was a real curiosity, with its many types of vehicle loaded down with odd looking articles; the queer rope harness; and the crates containing chickens, rabbits and pigs.

All night enemy planes roared back and forth, bombing the horse-lines, camps and roads. We finally halted in a small valley near Ignau-court, now a total ruin after the shelling of August 8th. Next day the 13th Battery rejoined the Brigade, and on the 26th, the "trek" was continued northward to Agny, passing through Villers-Bretonneux, Corbie, Toutencourt, Saulty, and Lattre St. Quentin, covering most of the distance in forced marches by night.

By the night of August 29th-30th the 4th Brigade, C.F.A. was back at its old "hunting-grounds" near Arras.

CHAPTER VII

Breaking the Hindenburg Line

AS the 4th Brigade, C.F.A. marched north from Amiens, news reached us that the 2nd and 3rd Canadian Divisions had won another wonderful victory near Arras. There were some who thought we would be too late to join in the battle, but the 4th Division arrived when it was needed most and gave the deciding "punch" in the operations that followed.

On August 26th, Sir Arthur Currie had struck hard on the Neuville-Vitasse sector with our 2nd and 3rd Divisions and by the end of the day had captured Orange Hill, Monchy-le-Preux, Chapel Hill, Guémappe and Wancourt; while the 51st Highland Division, operating on our left, carried Gavrelle. Over 2,000 prisoners were taken, and a penetration made of 6,000 yards into the enemy lines. Two days later, the attack continued against the Fresnes-Rouvroy Line, the 2nd Division capturing Chérisy and forcing the crossing of the Sensée River, while the 3rd Division took Bois du Vert and Bois du Sart.

Ludendorff became very worried as he saw first one front broken in and then another. Marshall Foch had started the "ball a-rolling" in his counter offensive near Paris, July 18th. The Canadian advance on the Amiens front had followed just three weeks later, and now the whole Third and Fourth British Armies were moving ahead in conjunction with the French on a front from Roye to Albert to Arras. Even in the north, on the Kemmel-Bailleul-Merville sector, the enemy was about to retire. At last we were to see a great war of movement, and everyone hoped for an allied advance to the Rhine.

The fighting was hard and our losses very heavy, as the enemy had received orders to hold the line at all costs. The 22nd Battalion covered itself with glory that day. When relieved, not an officer was left. Only a handful of men held an important position, in charge of a junior n.c.o.

The next objective of the Canadians was to be the Drocourt-Quéant Line, a switch of the Hindenburg Line.

Reaching Agny, on the night of August 29th, the 4th Brigade, C.F.A. turned in for a well-earned rest, and next evening established wagon-lines east of Wancourt. Due to the shelling of the roads, much difficulty was experienced in hauling up ammunition. A great battle had been in progress for some days and the area south-east of Arras was clear of the enemy. Our gun positions were completely concealed by the Vis-en-Artois ridge and it was not considered necessary to dig pits or afford special protection, beyond opening out shell holes for shelter in case of bombing.

There were a great number of horses concentrated in the Wancourt Valley, and the wagon-lines became a favourite target for enemy airmen and long range guns, resulting in a heavy loss of animals to the Brigade.

The ridges afforded excellent observation of the enemy lines. His elaborate barbed wire defences were clearly discernable on the distant slopes, and appeared as solid black lines disappearing for to the north. Our guns had been pounding away daily in an effort to destroy formidable obstacles in front of the Infantry.

The Artillery in support of the 4th Canadian Division Infantry on this date consisted of the 70th and 71st Brigades, R.F.A. (on the right), the 3rd and 4th Brigades, C.F.A. (in the centre), and the 52nd and 126th A.F.A. Brigades, R.F.A. on the left.

The attack on the Drocourt-Quéant Line had been planned for September 1st, but on account of additional wire cutting, it was necessary to pospone it until September 2nd. The day was utilized in improving our positions by local encounters to secure a good "jumping-off line."

In line, from left to right, were the 4th (British) Division, 4th Canadian Division, and 1st Canadian Division. A week before, the battle had opened. For the first few days all had gone well, a deep penetration being driven into the heart of the enemy defences. But since then the task had grown harder, until the whole line became involved in a furious battle to secure ground necessary for further offensive action.

The enemy was fully on the alert. His defences swarmed with men, the pick of his reserves. They were determined to fight till the last. Another defeat here would mean their certain retirement further south, and in all probability, a retirement far to the rear.

The dark, stormy night wore on. Towards morning the sky cleared, but mist still hung low over the valley. On our left a furious bombardment was in progress. There was none of that tense stillness preceding a surprise attack. At 5 a.m. on the 2nd, the barrage opened in support of the attack and pandemonium let loose. Far to the north and south were British troops ready to co-operate if this great effort to break the Hindenburg system were successful. The concentration of guns was tremendous (800 guns were in action); the front was narrower; the targets more limited.

The enemy retaliatory barrage was instantaneous and the rush of shells and detonations were terrific as high velocity guns searched our battery positions, the sunken roads, trench lines and assembly areas in the rear.

As the mist lifted, our Tanks could be seen making their way on the far slope among enemy wire and machine-gun posts. Many fell victim to anti-tank fire, but a few lurched on to their objectives, flattening out what remained of the heavy belts of barbed wire, machine-gun emplacements and dug-outs.

Our barrage had been deadly, and very thorough. The Drocourt-Quéant Switch, with its trench lines, supports, and strong points had fallen at last. The position was not only captured, but destroyed. Armoured cars and mounted machine-gun sections drove into the open to gain the Marquion Bridge over the Canal du Nord. These gallant fighters got within sight of their objective, but the German defence was so strong that they were forced to retire.

Then commenced a retreat to the eastern banks of the canal, leaving the Canadians in undisputed possession of the newly-conquered ground.

As Sir Arthur Currie reported: "Although the crossings of the Canal du Nord had not been captured, the result of the day's fighting was most gratifying.

"The Canadian Corps had pierced the Drocourt-Quéant line on its whole front of attack, and the exploitation of our success by the XVII Corps on the right had further widened the breach and made possible the capture of a large stretch of territory to the south.

"To stem our advance, and hold the Drocourt-Quéant line, the enemy had concentrated eight fresh Divisions directly opposite the Canadian Corps; but the unparalleled striking power of our Battalions and the individual bravery of our men had smashed all resistance.

"The number of unwounded prisoners captured exceeded 5,000, and we had identified every unit of the seven Infantry Divisions and the one Cavalry Division engaged. Our Infantry had penetrated the enemy's defences to a depth exceeding 6,000 yards.

"In prevision of the attack on the Canal du Nord taking place the same day, the Engineers had rapidly prepared the bridges and roads, advanced the light railways and pushed forward the personnel and all material necessary for future construction."

During the advance Composite Batteries from the 3rd and 4th Briades, C.F.A. kept in close touch with the assaulting troops. These units were commanded by Major McTaggart and Major McSloy. Sections were drawn from each Battery of the 4th C.D.A. and put under command of these officers. A few hours after zero they were in position and firing on the retiring enemy. Major McTaggart, while observing from a knoll near Mont Dury, was killed by machine-gun fire.

Throughout the day both of the Composite Batteries had many excellent targets to fire upon; in many cases German guns being shelled at 1,000 yards range, or even less. The enemy put up a stubborn resistance during his retirement, and on many occasions rushed machine-gunners by motor-lorry to strategic points along the line. These came under heavy fire from the Composite Batteries.

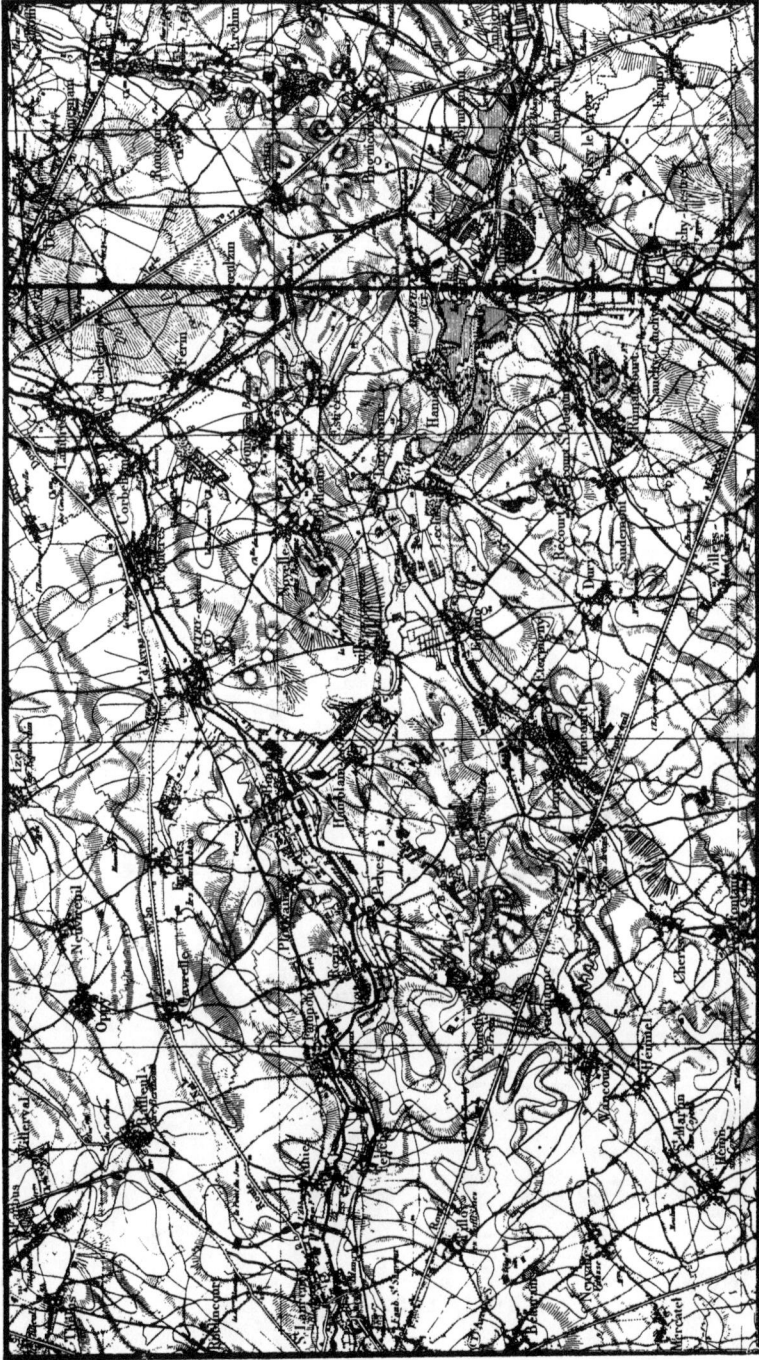

DROCOURT-QUEANT LINE (August-September, 1918)

Scale: 1 inch—2.5 miles

A further detail in charge of Lt. F. C. Whitehead, M.C., was sent forward with the Infantry to take over and bring into action any advanced German guns that might be found. This party was fortunate in securing a field gun located near the crest of the ridge from which a view could be obtained far to the east. A hostile Battery was engaged at close range, over open sights. Soon after, the enemy discovered this position and directed a heavy fire upon it, Whitehead's gun being ultimately destroyed and his party forced to seek other enemy weapons. At the end of the fighting the Infantry Commanders sent in very complimentary reports on the excellent support given them by the Composite Batteries.

By 12.15 p.m. the remainder of the 13th and 19th, and one section of the 21st (Howitzer) Battery were moving forward, and at 1.00 p.m., information having been received that our Infantry was checked along the line north and south through P28 central, it was decided that in all probability a barrage would be necessary. Four guns of the 27th and 21st Batteries were therefore ordered to remain in their positions to concentrate where required.

By 3.00 p.m. the situation was still obscure, and as nothing further could be accomplished without artillery preparation, a barrage was planned for the morning of the 3rd. The 8th and 282nd Army Brigades were then attached to the 4th C.D.A. and ordered to take up positions in P13 and 19 and P24 and 30. Our own Batteries were situated behind Mont Dury Ridge in the vicinity of the Drocourt-Quéant Line.

Our fighting planes had gone back, after assisting in the attack, and a few observation planes appeared. These were attacked and dispersed by a heavy German formation, four of our airmen being brought down near the Dury cross-roads. Thereafter, the enemy had complete control of the sector from the air, flying low and machine-gunning the roads and forward areas.

Brigade Headquarters advanced with the Batteries and located near the positions occupied by Whitehead's detachment earlier in the day. Although many linemen had been detailed to lay and maintain the Brigade Forward Observation Officer's line, due to enemy shell-fire much difficulty was experienced keeping it repaired.

About 10 p.m., Lt.-Col. Ross visited the Infantry Brigade Headquarters, and plans for the following day were discussed. Our troops were to continue the assault and the Artillery was to support them as circumstances required. The British on our flanks had finally moved forward and it was evident that the enemy would be obliged to withdraw during the night.

At dawn, September 3rd, two Batteries advanced to positions beyond the cross-roads, from which point direct fire could be brought to bear on the country overlooking the canal. On this occasion a sufficient number of linemen went forward with the Brigade Forward Observation Officer, accompanied by Lt. Penno (Brigade Orderly Officer) who was wounded soon after. An observation post was selected in a sand pit, affording a clear, unobstructed view for miles to the east. Our Infantry continued to advance, apparently with no opposition.

Meanwhile, our heavy guns were bombarding Ecourt St. Quentin. Dense clouds of orange-red dust could be seen rising from the crumbling brick buildings. A number of civilians were advancing slowly towards our lines from the village, so our linemen promptly sent a message through to Divisional Headquarters, requesting that the fire of the "heavies" be stopped at once. As the civilians arrived, they began to congregate about our observation post, drawing heavy artillery fire from the enemy.

It was evident that the only thing to do was to establish a relay station in a dug-out, and the observing party pushed forward. On orders from Col. Ross, the Batteries were ordered to advance again, two of the units taking up positions near the Cambrai Road and the other two lying in wait behind Rumaucourt for further orders. Large numbers of enemy troops in transports could be seen retiring towards the Cambrai-Lille Road, but they were beyond the range of our guns.

The large ammunition dump upon which we had been firing during the night, was seen to be burning fiercely. Our Infantry had now reached the low-lying ground on the western banks of the Canal du Nord; the enemy were in great strength at Bourlon Wood and the high ground to the north. A further advance was impossible, and our troops were instructed to consolidate the positions gained and push forward outposts to keep in touch with the enemy.

The Brigade now took up positions sheltered from observation and Headquarters was established in a very large farmhouse in Rumaucourt which had been looted by the enemy. Much of the furniture remained, and the kitchen was well equipped, even to an enormous joint of horse flesh, already prepared for roasting. Communications were then established to the Batteries and Infantry Battalions in the line. Due to the low ground that we now occupied, all precautions had to be taken against gas shelling.

As the guns were located close to shattered villages, and as there were plenty of cellars and dug-outs available, the men had excellent refuge during the heavy shelling and gas bombardment that followed. Our advance had carried us forward a considerable distance, and all units experienced much difficulty in bringing forward ammunition and food supplies. However, the work was done and a great deal of credit is due the D.A.C. and supply units who made this possible.

Apparently the enemy had had enough of our whirlwind attack. They contented themselves in strengthening the positions east of the Canal du Nord. For the next few days large supplies of engineering material poured forward and everything possible was done to give our men protection at the gun positions.

It was imperative that a good observation post be selected for the use of the Brigade in order to engage and disperse enemy movement. Nearby at Ecourt-St. Quentin, a church with a tall and intact spire seemed to offer great possibilities to our "C.O." A short distance away was a huge enemy supply depot, which also appeared to afford a good view of the country we were covering. After much debating the latter was decided upon as the "O-Pip." and in a few hours the church tower was no more. The enemy apparently thought it would be used for this purpose. Their heavy fire changed it into a useless wreck.

The villages of Ecourt-St. Quentin and Rumaucourt, through which a broad gauge railroad passed on the shore of a chain of small lakes, had evidently been utilized by the Germans as large supply depots. Close by, was an attractive casino. This place had been used as an officers' club. Numerous notices were posted around the ponds that it was "verboten" to destroy the fish with hand bombs.

It was here that we found, in a large store, many tons of horse shoes and farrier's rasps, of which we were much in need at the time. Although the villages were heavily shelled from time to time, we were very comfortable. Hostile naval guns frequently searched the roads behind the trees where our two advanced Batteries were located, but no casualties resulted.

When it became evident that the enemy was not likely to make an attempt to attack across the river, the two Batteries beyond the Cambrai Road were brought to positions at the south end of Rumaucourt. The detachments secured good shelter in the buildings. Owing to the open state of the country and the poor watering facilities, our wagon-lines had to remain far to the rear, entailing long nights of toil for the gunners on ammunition supply. Fortunately the weather was fine and the ground dry and hard.

During these operations the Batteries suffered heavily in personnel and horses, and were very pleased to be relieved by the 10th Brigade, C.F.A. On the night of September 6th we marched back to Etrun where all units were in rest until the 10th, when we proceeded to Habarcq.

Many inspections followed. Equipment was checked and everyone had a change of underwear and a good bath. It seems funny when we speak now of a bath. At that time we were lucky to see enough water to bathe in once a month.

Most of the enemy guns hauled out from the battle area were drawn to the Canadian Corps "Captured Gun Park," but four 7.7 field pieces were retained by the Brigade for instruction, in the event of our having to use German guns on another occasion.

The weather then became rainy, chilly and disagreeable, but we all enjoyed our stay at Habarcq. For sports we played baseball, the 21st Battery beating all opposition in many closely contested games.

Officers of the Brigade celebrated their brief holiday by a dinner at Avésnes-le-Comte.

CHAPTER VIII

𝕮𝖆𝖓𝖆𝖑 𝖉𝖚 𝕹𝖔𝖗𝖉

A T two a.m., September 22nd, the Brigade pulled out of Habarq, halting at Agny for breakfast, and proceeded to the Croisilles area, establishing wagon-lines north of the Quéant Road and east of the village of Quéant. While the Battery Commanders carried out their reconnaissance, the remainder of the unit was engaged in hauling ammunition to battery positions occupied by the 286th Brigade, R.F.A.

Three days later we moved our horse-lines to the neighbourhood of Quéant and took over the gun positions of the 286th Brigade, R.F.A. The Canadian Corps, as part of the Third Army, was to carry out one of its most brilliant advances of the War. The line of the Canal du Nord had been heavily fortified by the Germans, and with their extensive forces located along the slopes of Bourlon, the position was considered well-nigh impregnable.

Quoting Sir Arthur Currie :—

"The Canal du Nord was in itself a serious obstacle. It was under construction at the outbreak of the war and had not been completed. Generally speaking, it followed the valley of the river Agache, but not the actual bed of the river. The average width was about 100 feet and it was flooded as far south as the lock, 800 yards south-west of Sains-lez-Marquion, just north of the Corps' southern boundary. South of this and to the right of the Corps' front, the canal was dry, its bottom being at the natural ground level; its banks had been constructed with earth and bricks."

At the most vulnerable sections of their defence, on the left of our front, German Engineers had flooded a large area from the waters of the Sensée River, thus making it impossible for our attacking forces to out-flank the position from the north. From the high ground at Oisy-le-Verger, opposite Ecourt-St-Quentin, the enemy commanded a clear view of our operations. The 2nd and 3rd Canadian Divisions had relieved the 1st and 4th Canadian Divisions on September 5th and were holding our sector of the front. The two latter Divisions then went out to refit and reorganize. The XVII Corps, south of Moeuvres, on our right, had failed to drive the Germans across the unflooded end of the canal and there was a possibility of a counter-attack from this direction. Sir Arthur Currie was given the task of assaulting the canal from the line of the Sensée River to Sains-lez-Marquion. It was the boldest, most daring and amazing tactical scheme the Canadian Staff had ever worked out.

For the initial attack on the Canal du Nord, the 4th and 1st Canadian Divisions were to capture Bourlon and Marquion, respectively. The 3rd Canadian Division had orders to pass through the right of the 4th Canadian Division and advance in an easterly direction towards Neuville-St. Remy. The 11th (British) Division was to come up on the left of the 1st Canadian Division and advance north-easterly towards Oisy-le-Verger and Epinoy; while the 2nd Canadian Division was held in reserve. After crossing the canal on a 2,600 yards front, the Canadian Corps had to expand fanwise to a front exceeding 15,000 yards.

The enemy were apparently unsuspicious of the impending attack. At 5.20 a.m., on September 27th, our barrage commenced. The concentration of guns was tremendous. The German losses were very great. But few escaped. The enemy defences were practically wiped out of existance.

Advancing across the canal from Inchy, the 10th Infantry Brigade (4th Canadian Division) established themselves firmly in the enemy trenches. The 12th and 11th Infantry Brigades passed through them to carry out the assault of Bourlon Wood. As day broke, this grim, natural fortress stood out strong and imposing. Some of the Batteries had been detailed to lay a smoke barrage across the intervening ground and to cover the right flank. This undoubtedly saved many lives.

To our right, British troops of the XVII Corps again failed to carry their objectives and the preliminary plan, to surround Bourlon Wood from the north and south, had to be changed. Maj.-Gen. Sir David Watson, the gallant Commander of the 4th Canadian Division, made a quick decision and altered his original plans to suit the situation. By noon, Bourlon Wood and the village to the north of it had been taken. Our 4th Division had reached its objective and had advanced to the trench line covering Fontaine-Notre-Dame.

Meanwhile, on the left flank of the attack, the fanwise operation was finally carried through to a successful conclusion, after terrific resistance by the enemy at Marquion, Sauchy-Lestrée and Oisy-le-Verger.

Fifteen minutes before zero, the 4th Brigade, C.F.A., H.Q., had moved to its battle position in a dug-out in the western embankment of the canal, south-east of Inchy. Shortly after the barrage started, Batteries of the 3rd and 4th C.D.A.'s moved forward. Hundreds of guns were located close behind the crest near Inchy, firing at short range on the enemy lines. The artillery plan consisted of two barrages, the first to be fired by all units except the 3rd and 4th C.D.A.'s, whose Brigades were to be harnessed up and in readiness to take up pre-arranged positions on the west bank of the canal, a few hours later. These Batteries were to fire a barrage to cover the second plase of the battle.

An unusual circumstance in this attack was the comparative absence of enemy shell fire along some portions of the front. This was undoubtedly due to the excellent counter-battery work of the "heavies," directed by Brig.-Gen. McNaughton, who had located almost all of the German Batteries by photographs and sound-ranging. The effect of their shell fire was devastating that several of the enemy Batteries did not take part in the battle. Hostile trench-mortars of all sizes and enemy machine-guns had been spread along the front. These gave our Infantry much trouble.

As the mist began to rise from the valley, a few hours after "zero," the leading gun-teams of the Brigade trotted down the long slope towards the canal, followed by the rest of the Batteries. Each unit wheeled right and left to their positions, parallel with the canal bank and as close to it as the angle of fire permitted. These positions were 200 yards beyond the line previously occupied by the Infantry and within a few yards of the locations chosen by reconnaissance officers the previous day. Undoubtedly the Artillery going into action in this manner was one of the most spectacular sights of the day.

Behind us, machine-guns and field guns were firing steadily. The noise was almost deafening. A few enemy Batteries splattered the area, making it desirable to take cover. Several of our gun-teams became casualties while rushing through the hostile shell-fire. Dense clouds of steam rose from the horses as the gunners halted and unlimbered the guns. A stratum of smoke from bursting shells hung close to the ground, and when, a little later, the sun shone forth, the scene of activities stood out in cameo clearness, making a wonderfully effective picture.

Bustle, surrounding the positions, seemed more intense than ever. Officers ran about with directors, and men with aiming posts, while linemen laid their telephone wires to Batteries on the flanks. Gunners unloaded and piled the shrapnel and high-explosive shells in neat rows on the ground; the wagon teams moved off to the rear as rapidly as the rough going would permit. Occasionally the smoke of a bursting shell obscured them from view. As horses became injured the drivers detached them, rapidly mounted other horses and moved off again.

Meanwhile, the Forward Observation Officer and his party began to establish connection with the forward zone. Cooks had brought up the rations with the guns, and in a few minutes the thin smoke from the "cook-house" fire ascended to blend with that left by vomiting guns; the smell of cordite and bursting shrapnel was replaced by the aroma of frying bacon. By 8.20 a.m. the guns were ready for action and breakfast was rapidly eaten between intervals of work.

As the Infantry and Tanks advanced, the atmosphere having cleared somewhat, they could be seen approaching the top of the ridge, meeting with heavy opposition. The second phase of the barrage commenced at the appointed time, but could not be observed from the gun positions. After firing for an interval, it became evident that there had been a check to our advance on the right, and we received orders to switch and fire across our front to points far in the rear of the line attained by the 4th Canadian Division.

No information had come through from the "F.O.O." and "L.O.'s" so Col. Ross decided to reconnoitre in person. Quoting his remarks: "My horse having been brought up, I rode forward, meeting Brig.-Gen. Mac-Brien, who was also on his way to the forward area, at the canal crossing. As he was unable to give any news of conditions in front, I followed the direction taken by the "F.O.O.," accompanied by Lieut. Haldiman of the 13th Battery and my groom. Presently we came under a few bursts of enemy shell-fire, intended to destroy one of our returning Tanks which was lumbering past us towards the rear. One of the shells burst under Lieut. Haldiman's horse, momentarily obscuring it. I continued on a short distance to clear the Tank, and on looking round, saw Haldiman running after me, and the horse galloping back towards the Batteries, uninjured. Though the results might have been serious, it was impossible to overlook the comical side of the incident. We then moved on at a slow rate, leaving the horses with the groom in a quarry behind the crest. Soon we found two of the linemen and followed the wire until we reached the "F.O.O."

"From the "O-Pip" the ground towards Bourlon and to the north of it was visible for miles. Scattered parties of our men could be seen gradually approaching the lower ground toward Bourlon village and the railroad embankment behind which the Huns were evidently establishing themselves in great strength. The view to the right rear was cut off by a ridge higher than the one we were on, but intense firing could be heard from that direction, and enemy Batteries continued to shell our vicinity. Clearly distinguishable, large bodies of German Infantry could be seen retiring toward the east, but as our guns were still engaged in firing the second phase of the barrage, these troops could not be ranged on."

The 4th Brigade, C.F.A. telephone line was one of the first to be established along the front, and for some time was used by the Infantry to send important messages to the rear. A report of the situation, as far as it could be obtained, was sent to Lieut. Larkin, who had remained with the Batteries, and he in turn relayed the information on to Divisional H.Q. As infantry supports moved up, great difficulty was experienced in maintaining the line, so the heliograph was set up, conditions being ideal for its use. It was used by the Infantry and ourselves till their signallers arrived and set up another.

During the afternoon, our Batteries moved up to positions chosen by the Colonel, north of Quarry Wood. A short distance away lay a German field gun, which had not been fired that morning. Even the camouflage net remained upon it, as well as the breech and muzzle covers. Further off lay a complete Battery of enemy guns. The position had been abandoned. Gun-teams had made an effort to reach it, but they had been caught in our counter-battery fire and destroyed.

The cause of the check on the British front to the south of us was now easily explained. A large sugar-refinery, strongly defended by machine-guns, lay in the centre of a shallow basin, close to the Cambrai-Bapaume Road. The ground gradually sloping up from it to the encircling ridges, afforded a clear field of fire in all directions. Any attempt to advance beyond the sky-line was suicidal. It was some time before heavy guns, already engaged on pre-arranged targets, could be brought to bear on the refiinery, thus enabling the Infantry to carry out its task.

During the night of September 27th-28th, our Infantry continued to push out posts and keep in touch with the enemy, while the guns and ammunition poured forward to new positions north of Bourlon.

The offensive was resumed at 6.00 a.m. on the 28th, after another intense artillery preparation. On the right, the 3rd Canadian Division cleared Fontaine-Notre-Dame, which had held up a British Division operating on our flank, broke the Marcoing Line, and reached the western outskirts of Ste. Olle, a suburb of Cambrai. Meanwhile, the 4th Canadian Division, in spite of terrific resistance at Raillencourt, conformed with the movement, and on their left, the 1st Canadian Division advanced beyond Haynecourt, which had fallen the previous day. To protect the northern flank, the 11th (British) Division attempted to carry the high ground north-east of Epinoy.

Gun limbers were ordered up and the Brigade moved forward at 9.00 a.m. Meanwhile, Lt.-Col Ross and the Battery Commanders proceeded ahead on a reconnaissance toward Haynecourt.

Arriving at the Arras-Cambrai Road, heavy machine-gun and shell fire was heard a short distance away. The Battery Commanders then returned to lead up their Batteries and the Colonel selected positions for the guns in a valley south of Haynecourt. While waiting for the Batteries, he explored the vicinity, finding a very useful series of German maps in an abandoned field-gun position, nearby. Besides showing active gun positions, strong points, "H.Q.'s" and ammunition dumps, these maps clearly designated the natural features of the ground, especially sunken roads, light tramway lines and valleys. On the British issue the contours determined the general lay-out of the land, but gave no such minute detail as this. These documents were deemed so valuable that the Colonel despatched one of them to Divisional Headquarters.

A deep cutting in the hill to the left of our positions undoubtedly accounted for the heavy fire that came from that direction. When crossing the Arras-Cambrai road, the Batteries had to pass through a scattered barrage fire, but suffered no casualties. As soon as they got into position, fire was opened on various points where movement could be seen, and on the ridge to our left. A second "F.O.O." went forward with linemen and succeeded in keeping in touch with the Infantry.

Word reached us that enemy machine-gunners were firing on our Infantry from a church tower a short distance away. The 21st Battery immediately ranged upon this target and after a few rounds, managed to bring the tower down. Lieut. Larkin, on his way forward, had found a fine pair of periscopic observation glasses mounted on a stand. These proved of estimable value in subsequent operations.

Toward evening two enemy observation balloons appeared, directly in front of us. Lieut. Whitehead, M.C., who had had previous experience with 4.2 cm German howitzers, asked the Colonel if he might turn the abandoned section of enemy guns and fire upon the balloons. Our C.O. saw the possibilities of the situation and granted Whitehead's request.

The third round burst close to one of the "sausages," and both of them were immediately hauled down.

Soon afterwards, German Batteries opened fire upon our area and some of the guns had to be moved slightly to obtain more cover. Earlier in the day, a troop of Cavalry had come up and halted near our positions. Their commander was warned to move off to the flank, but for some reason would not act. A few minutes later they were dispersed by hostile shell-fire, and galloped to the rear.

That night, harassing fire was directed on the railroad embankment, sunken roads, and points on the German map indicating routes that might be used by the enemy for reliefs or counter-attacks. As a result, our drivers, busy all day, secured no rest during the night, as they had to bring forward large quantities of ammunition from the dumps as far back as Inchy. Luckily, hostile shelling was very light, and the night too dark for bombing.

At 8.00 a.m. of the 29th, the advance was resumed, the 3rd Canadian Division pushing forward to the junction of the Arras and Bapaume Road, the western outskirts of Neuville-St. Remy, and the Douai-Cambrai Road southwards towards the Canal de l'Escaut. The 4th Canadian Division, after carrying Sancourt, crossed the Douai-Cambrai Railway and entered Blécourt, but later, attacked by large enemy forces, was forced to withdraw to the line of the railway. On the left, both the 1st Canadian Division and the 11th (British) Division made progress in the face of stiff opposition, although they were unable to occupy the high ground north-east of Epinoy.

Shortly after the barrage, each Battery of the Brigade sent forward a section of guns to assist the Infantry in overcoming resistance of enemy machine-guns. Owing to the obstinate fighting that characterized this day, many targets were fired upon and the Infantry given good protection by the sniping activities of these guns. Later in the day, the remaining sections of the Brigade moved up, and far into the night answered "S.O.S." calls and laid down sharp bursts of fire along the German front. Enemy resistance had stiffened considerably, and a large number of heavy howitzers had come into action, shelling our battery positions, villages, and forward areas, while long-range naval guns kept the Arras-Cambrai Road under constant fire, and bombing planes wrought havoc in the back country.

During these operations the 13th Battery (Major C. Sifton) experienced a very heavy loss from night bombing. The unit had just established wagon-lines a few miles west of Raillencourt, and were in the act of "feeding-up" when a German plane swooped down from the clouds and dropped its load of bombs amidst the men and horses. One driver was killed, nine others were wounded, and a large number of animals destroyed. The affair was over in less than 30 seconds; but the bursting charges, the shouts of men and the agonized shrieks of injured and terrified horses made a scene of indescribable chaos. The enemy achieved this dreadful effect through the barbarous use of the newly-invented and deadly efficient "Daisy-Clipper" or "Stick-Bomb," which exploded a few inches from the ground, its splinters flying in all directions instead of upward and outward as had been the case with former types used by the Germans. Our only effective defence against bursting bombs had been to lie flat on the ground, allowing the flying fragments to pass over us. Now, however, the "Daisy-Clipper" minimized our chances of escape, and greatly increased our casualties.

The Canadian Corps had now reached the fringe of the large plateau which extended from the Scheldt to the Sensée. The enemy was fighting tenaciously to hold the crests. Ludendorff, the celebrated German Chief of Staff, was now with his back to the wall. The huge Reserve transferred from the Eastern Theatre of War was practically exhausted, but he still hoped to carry out an orderly retreat to the line of the Woevre and hold on there till a satisfactory armistice could be arranged. Marshal Foch, however, determined to cut the communications of the enemy forces in France, and a general advance of the American and British was arranged to conform with the operations of the French armies. In a series of brilliantly executed movements, the German front was pierced in many places and the enemy rolled back toward the Belgian frontier; thousands of prisoners had been captured, and large quantities of trench-mortars, machine-guns, and war material fell into the hands of the Allies. The Germans finally realized they were beaten, but though their main lines of defence had fallen, they fought on with the courage of despair. Picked troops were thrown in to hold the Canadians, as a deep advance on our front would seriously jeopardize the successful withdrawal of enemy forces further south.

At 6.00 a.m., the 3rd and 4th Canadian Divisions continued the pressure. Advancing towards the bridge-heads at Pont d'Aire and Ramillies, troops of the 4th pushed through Blécourt, but owing to the smoke screen covering the attack becoming blown away, our men were forced to withdraw to their lines in front of Sancourt.

The 3rd fared somewhat better, carrying the villages of Tilloy, Morenchies and Ramillies. Massed German counter-attacks, forced the Canadians back to Tilloy. The enemy still held the plateau.

Quoting Sir Arthur Currie:—

"The tremendous exertions and considerable casualties consequent upon the four days' almost continuous fighting had made heavy inroads on the freshness and efficiency of all arms, and it was questionable whether an immediate decision could be forced in face of the heavy concentration of troops which our successful and, from the enemy's standpoint, dangerous advance had drawn against us.

"On the other hand, it was known that the enemy had suffered severely, and it was quite possible that matters had reached a stage where he no longer considered the retention of this position worth the severe losses both in men and morale consequent upon a continuance of the defence. It was therefore decided that the assault would be continued on October 1st, the four Divisions in line attacking simultaneously under a heavy barrage, co-ordinated by the G.O.C., R.A."

At 5.00 a.m. on October 1st, the Canadian Artillery laid down a beautiful barrage on the Hun lines, and the Infantry advanced. Excellent progress was made in the early stages, our troops reaching a line from the Scheldt, east of Neuville-St. Remy to Morenchies Wood,

Cuvillers and Bantigny. Five hours later, heavy enemy counter-attacks developed up the Bantigny Ravine, supported by enfilading fire from the high ground near Abancourt and Cuvillers, and Bantigny, and Blécourt had to be evacuated.

Again quoting Sir Arthur Currie :—

"To continue to throw tired troops against such opposition, without giving them an opportunity to refit and recuperate, was obviously inviting a serious failure. Accordingly I decided to break off the engagement. The five days' fighting had yielded practical gains of a very valuable nature, as well as 7,059 prisoners and 205 guns.

"We had gone through the last organized system of defences on our front, and our advance constituted a direct threat on the rear of the troops immediately to the north of our left flank, and their withdrawal had now begun.

"Although the ground gained on the 1st was not extensive, the effects of the battle and of the previous four days' fighting were far-reaching, and made possible the subsequent advance in October and November, in so far as the Divisions engaged against the Canadian Corps drew heavily on the enemy's Reserves which had now been greatly reduced.

"It is worthy of note that the enemy employed six Divisions to reinforce the four Divisions already in the line, making a total of ten Divisions engaged since September 27th by the Canadian Corps."

During the operations of October 1st, the 4th Brigade, C.F.A. expended 8,000 rounds of 18-pounder ammunition and 1,800 rounds of howitzer shells. On the night of October 1st-2nd, the 2nd C.D.A. relieved the 4th C.D.A., the 4th becoming superimposed over the 2nd C.D.A. and available only for "S.O.S." purposes, or any special support required.

For the next few days the front became very quiet, but all Batteries had plenty of opportunities to fire on enemy movement. Finally, on October 4th, we were relieved, the 5th Brigade, C.F.A. (Lt.-Col. Constantine, D.S.O.) taking over our zone.

That night the 4th Brigade, C.F.A. moved out to its wagon-lines north-east of Bourlon, where a great number of artillery units were concentrated due to the scarcity of water elsewhere. The supply here was very bad, consisting of the usual village reservoir of surface rain water. Ie seemed nothing more than liquid mud. Next evening our Batteries marched by the Arras road to Vis-en-Artois and camped in the open, on the battered battlefield of September 2nd, to rest and refit.

CHAPTER IX

Cambrai to Valenciennes

DURING the night of October 1st-2nd, the 2nd Canadian Division came into the line, from the railway, south of Tilloy to Blécourt, and relieved the 4th and portions of the 1st and 3rd Canadian Divisions, the 4th Canadian Division going into Corps Reserve in the Inchy-Quéant Area.

South of Tilloy, from the Canal de l'Escaut, the line was held by the 8th Brigade, Canadian Mounted Rifles (Brig.-Gen. D. C. Draper), and to the north of the 2nd Division sector, the 11th (British) Division, after completing relief of the 1st Canadian Division on the 2nd-3rd, maintained well-fortified positions to the Sensée River, south of Cambrai. The XVII Corps were now close to the city.

Commanded from three sides, there was nothing left for the Germans to do but evacuate Cambrai, their boasted impregnable citadel and railway centre.

On October 5th and 6th, incendiary fires were observed in the big square of the city. A steady stream of supply columns and lorries could be seen moving materials toward the rear. There was no great change in the general situation along the front until October 8th, but our troops harassed the enemy in many ways— the "heavies" bombarding his Batteries with gas, the motor machine-guns and armoured cars driving into the German lines and disorganizing his defences, while the Infantry battered their way forward in minor operations.

Meanwhile, the Third British Army had crossed the Scheldt, and threatened the complete downfall of the Bosche south of Cambrai. It was now determined that the XVII Corps should assault the high ground to the south-east at Awoignt and if this operation proved successful, the 8th Brigade, Canadian Mounted Rifles would attack across the canal and join up with the British troops north-east of the city.

In preparation for this movement, the 2nd Canadian Division was ordered to make a night attack against the bridge-heads along the

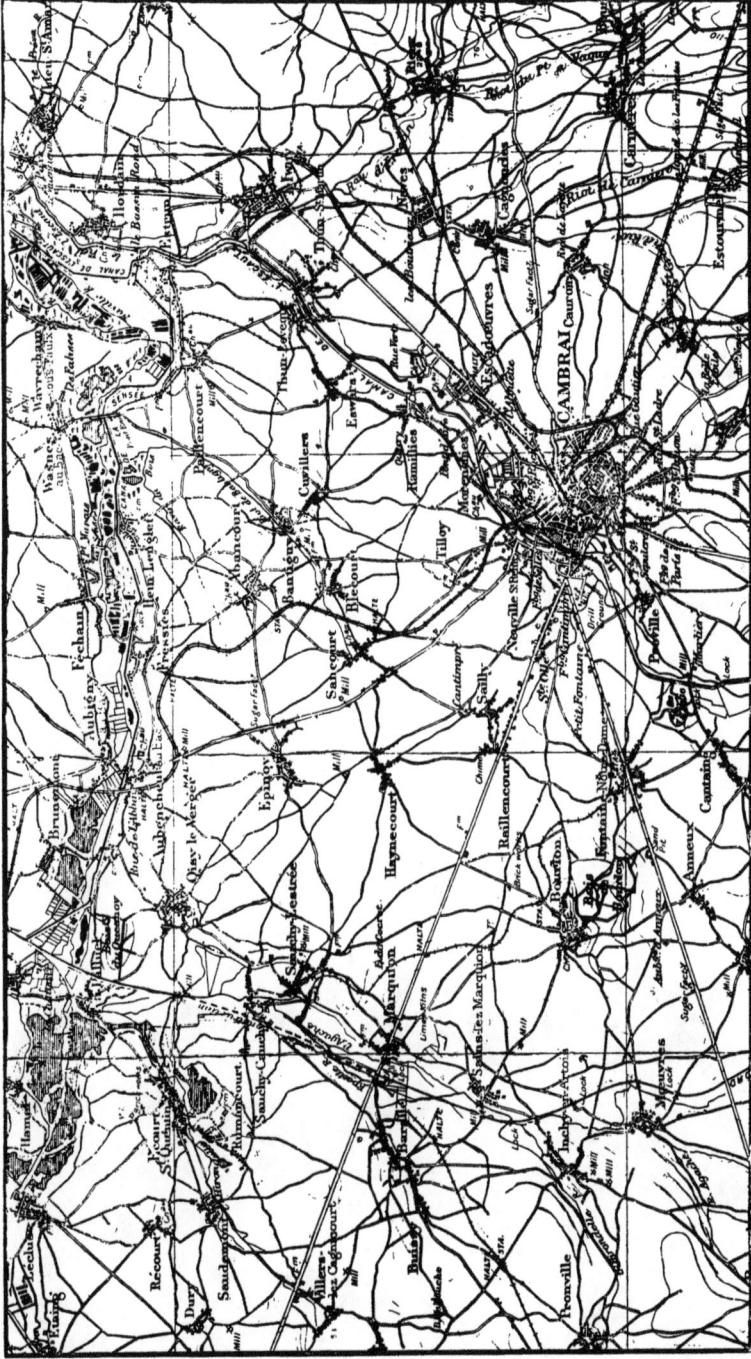

CAMBRAI—September-October, 1918

Scale: 1 inch—2.35 miles

Scheldt, and the Canadian Independent Force (Brig.-Gen. Brutinel) was to push through and capture the high ground beyond. Preceded by a shattering artillery barrage, the Canadians carried out this difficult manoeuvre, resulting in the fall of Cambrai and a further retirement of the enemy. Sir Arthur Currie's despatch covering this operation was as follows:—

"At 4.30 a.m. October 8th, the Third Army attacked, and at the same hour an artillery demonstration was carried out on the Canadian Corps front. The XVII Corps on the right did not reach Awoignt, but in the evening they were ordered to continue their advance on the morning of October 9th to capture this town; concurrently with this advance the Canadian Corps was to secure the crossings of the Canal de l'Escaut.

"In spite of the darkness of a rainy night the assembly was completed, and the attack was launched successfully at 1.30 a.m., October 9th. Rapid progress was made, and at 2.25 a.m. the 2nd Canadian Division had captured Ramillies and established posts on the Canal there, and patrols were pushing out to the north-east. On the right, the Infantry, assisted by a party of Engineers, rushed the crossings at Pont d'Aire, and, after sharp fighting, captured the bridge intact, with the exception of the western spillway, which had been partially destroyed. Two cork bridges were then thrown across, and by 3.35 a.m. our Infantry were well established on the eastern side of the Canal. The 3rd Canadian Division had cleared the railway, and their patrols were pushing into Cambrai, while the Engineers were commencing work on the bridges.

"By 8.00 a.m., the 2nd Canadian Division had captured Escaud-oeuvres, and had established a line on the high ground immediately to the north and east. Detachments of the 3rd Canadian Division had by this time completely cleared Cambrai of the enemy, and troops of the Third Army could be seen coming up towards it from the south.

"Cambrai was to be deliberately set on fire by the enemy. Huge fires were burning in the Square when our patrols went through, and many others broke out in all parts of the city. Piles of inflammable material were found ready for the torch, but the enemy was unable to carry out his intention owing to our unexpected attack and rapid progress. A party of one officer and a few men, which had been left with instructions to set fire to Cambrai, was discovered and dealt with before it could do any further damage. The fire were successfully checked by a large detachment of Canadian Engineers who entered the city with the patrols. A considerable number of road mines, "booby-traps," etc. were also located and removed.

"An air reconnaissance at dawn indicated that the enemy had withdrawn from the area between the Canal de l'Escaut and the Canal de la Sensée, and that all bridges over the latter had been destroyed. Brutinel's Brigade, passing through the Infantry of the 2nd Canadian Division, seized the high ground at Croix St. Hubert and pushed Cavalry patrols into Thun Leveque.

"The 2nd Canadian Division east of the Canal progressed towards the north and occupied Thun Leveque. Thun St. Martin, Blécourt, Cuvillers and Bantigny, and the 11th Division occupied Abancourt and reached the outskirts of Paillencourt.

"The 3rd Canadian Division was withdrawn at 7.10 p.m. when the 24th Division (XVII Corps) passed through and joined up with the 2nd Canadian Division, and Cambrai and our positions to the east were taken over or occupied by the XVII Corps.

"The 3rd Canadian Division was moved on the following day to bivouacs in the Inchy-Quéant Area, to rest and refit after twelve days of battle."

Meanwhile, patrols (3 platoons, 13th Brigade) of the 1st Canadian Division, holding the line of the Trinquis from the Scarpe to the Canal du Nord during a Chinese attack, pushed forward and enlarged a bridge-head which had been handed over at Sailly-en-Ostrevent, October 8th. The Germans were expected to withdraw at any time, and test barrages were fired at dawn, daily, to harass the enemy and ascertain his strength. Two days later, patrols of the 3rd Infantry Brigade captured the village of Sailly, and entered the Drocourt-Quéant Line to the north-east. A heavy counter-attack, however, overcame these advanced posts and our troops fell back to the bridge-head.

The 4th Brigade, C.F.A., in rest at Vis-en-Artois, received orders to relieve the 189th Brigade, R.F.A., in the Dury-Récourt area, covering the front of the 1st Canadian Division. Positions were taken over, and all units became comfortably situated near Lécluse. As both the Trinquis and a canal, with numerous ponds and marshes, lay between us and the enemy, there was no reason to expect an attack. Observation posts were established on the high ground north of Lécluse, and the front carefully watched. Though the enemy were very quiet, and showed no undue activity, any movement close to the canal was promptly fired upon. Our stay here was very much in the form of a rest. Fishing-nets had been found by some of the gunners, and our favourite occupation was to sit by the ponds and secure fresh fish for the cooks.

On the 11th, in conjunction with an attack of the 8th (British) Division on the left, patrols of the 1st Canadian Division forced their way over the narrow crossings of the Sensée and Trinquis, in face of heavy machine-gun fire. By evening our Infantry had reached a line from Hamel to Estrees to Noyelles. The enemy continued to withdraw the next day. Arleux was cleared by the 2nd Infantry Brigade but not without heavy fighting, and the 1st Canadian Division reached the west bank of the Canal from Palleul to Corbehem after strong resistance from German howitzers and machine-guns.

During this advance, a section of the 19th Battery, C.F.A. kept in close support of the Infantry. Further operations were out of the question. We were up against a very serious obstacle, in that the canal was flooded, and defended in great force by the enemy. All bridges had been blown away. It was impossible to push on without further preparation. The Batteries then moved up to new positions, and wagon-lines were established at Lécluse.

To the right of the 1st Canadian Division, the line remained stationary from Palleul to the Scheldt Canal.

Meanwhile, the 2nd Canadian Division were heavily engaged in an attempt to carry the strongly fortified town of Iwuy. Here, the German garrison fought with great fury, launching a heavy counter-attack, supported by Tanks, to stay our advance. The 2nd were not to be denied and although our line was forced back slightly, Iwuy was finally captured, the 49th British Division gaining the high ground east of this village. The enemy then fell back rapidly. Assisted by the 49th, (British) Division, our troops pushed on, captured Hordain and reached Bouchain, where the flooded area of inundations and marshes prevented a further advance in this direction; while on their left, the 11th (British) Division cleared the enemy from the area between the Scheldt Canal and the Sensée, taking Paillencourt, Estrun and Hem-Lenglet.

During the night of October 11th-12th, the 2nd Canadian Division was relieved in the line east of the Iwuy-Denain Railway by the 51st (Highland) Division and on completion of this relief, the command of the remainder of the 2nd Canadian Divisional front, from the Iwuy-Denain railway to Canal de l'Escaut, was assumed by the Canadian Corps.

At 1.45 p.m., on the 12th, the 2nd Canadian Division took over the 11th (British) Division front to Aubencheul-au-Bac. The 56th (British) Division, relieved by the 4th Canadian Division on the 14th-15th and 15th-16th, improved the line by establishing, on the 13th, a bridge-head at Aubigny-au-Bac. In this little operation two hundred prisoners were taken. As the 4th came into the line, on the 16th, three Divisions of the Canadian Corps were once more fighting side by side—the 2nd from Bouchain to Aubencheul-au-Bac, the 4th from Aubencheul-au-Bac to Palleul, and the 1st facing the canal from there to Corbehem.

Prisoners reported that Douai had been cleared of its population and that all the towns and villages through which the enemy had passed in their retreat, were being sacked, military stores destroyed, and the roads, bridges and railways prepared for demolition. These rumours were confirmed by our observers, who noted many explosions and fires behind the German lines.

This interesting period of the operations has been summed up by Sir Arthur Currie as follows:—

"Test barrages were carried out on the Corps front each morning to ascertain the enemy's strength and attitude, and on October 17th he was found to be extremely quiet and did not retaliate to our Artillery fire on the front of the 1st Canadian Division. Patrols were, therefore, sent out on that front and succeeded in crossing the Canal in several places, meeting only slight opposition. Stronger patrols followed and made good progress.

"On the front of the 4th Canadian Division, however, all attempts to cross the canal were still met by machine-gun fire. After the 1st Canadian Division had secured crossings, a Battalion of the 4th Canadian Division was sent up to take advantage of these crossings and, working down the east side of the canal, cleared the enemy on the 4th Canadian Division front, and enabled the advance to commence there.

"Further to the right, at Hem-Lenglet, the 2nd Canadian Division succeeded in crossing the canal later in the day, and patrols were pushed on in the direction of Wasnes-au-Bac.

"Only enemy rear guards were encountered during the day, and the opposition was nowhere heavy, although more organized and stubborn on the right, opposite the 2nd Canadian Division.

"By 6.00 a.m., October 18th, practically all the Infantry of the 1st and 4th Canadian Divisions and several Battalions of the 2nd Canadian Division were across the Canal, and the following towns had been liberated: Ferin, Courchelettes, Goeulzin, le Raquet, Villers-au-Tertre, Cantin, Roucourt, Brunenmont, Aubigny-au-Bac, Fechain, Fressain, Bugnicourt, and Hem Lenglet.

"During the day, two armoured cars, one squadron of the Canadian Light Horse, and one Company of Canadian Corps Cyclists from Brutinel's Brigade, were attached to each of the 1st and 4th Canadian Divisions to assist in the pursuit of the enemy. These troops rendered valuable service to the Divisions to which they were attached, although the enemy's very complete road destruction prevented the armoured cars from operating to their full extent.

"Throughout the advance now begun, a great amount of work was thrown upon the Engineers, and their resources in men and material were taxed to the utmost. The enemy's demolition had been very well planned and thoroughly carried out, all bridges over the canals and streams being destroyed, every cross-road and road junction rendered impassable by the blowing of large mines, and the railways, light and standard, blown up at frequent intervals. The enemy also considerably impeded our progress by his clever manipulations of the water levels in the canals which he controlled.

"Foot-bridges were first thrown across the Canal, and these were quickly followed by heavier types of bridges to carry Battalion Transport and Artillery. In addition, eight heavy traffic bridges, ranging in length from 90 to 160 feet, were at once put under way. On the front of the 1st Canadian Division on the left, the enemy drained the canal and it was found impossible to complete and use the pontoon bridges first commenced.

"The Engineers in the forward area concentrated their efforts on road repair, craters being quickly filled in, for the most part with material gathered on the spot and found in enemy dumps. In addition, the whole areas were searched immediately after their occupation, many 'booby traps' and delayed action mines being discovered and rendered harmless, and all water supply sources being tested.

"It was clear from the wholesale destruction of roads and railways that the reconstruction of communications would be very slow and that it would be difficult to keep our troops supplied. Canadian Railway Troops were brought up, and, as soon as the enemy had been cleared away from the canal, work was commenced on the repairing of the standard gauge railway forward from the Sauchy Lestree. The construction of a railway bridge over the canal at Aubencheul-au-Bac was immediately commenced.

"The enemy retirement now extended considerably north of our front, and the VIII Corps on our left began to move forward. During October 18th, rapid and fairly easy progress was made, and the following towns and villages were liberated from the enemy: Dechy, Sin-le-Noble, Guesnain, Montigny, Pecquencourt, Loffre, Lewarde, Erchin, Masny, Ecaillon, Marquette, Wasnes-au-Bac, and the western portions of Auberchicourt and Monchecourt.

"During the day, the advance had carried us into a large industrial area, and well-built towns became more frequent. It also liberated the first of a host of civilians, 2,000 being found in Pecquencourt and a few in Auberchicourt. These people had been left by the retiring enemy without food, and faced as we were by an ever lengthening line of communication, and with only one bridge yet available for anything but horse transport, the work of the supply services was greatly increased. This additional burden was, however, cheerfully accepted, and the liberated civilians, whose numbers exceeded 70,000 before Valenciennes was reached, as well as our rapidly advancing troops, were at no time without a regular supply of food."

During these operations the 4th Brigade, C.F.A. fired test barrages on the 1st Division front, and on the 18th, when the German forces began their general retirement, our Batteries crossed the canal to Roucourt, one section of the 13th Battery keeping in close support of the Infantry.

Early the next morning we pushed on from Roucourt, passing through many towns and villages filled with cheering civilians. Everywhere the "Tricolour" was in evidence, and the people could not do enough for us. Every time the column halted, cups of steaming hot coffee and biscuits were handed to the men, and our horses were garlanded with flowers. Finally we reached West-Nornaing, a small town a few miles north-west of Denain, and on the 20th the Brigade was relieved by the 8th Army Brigade, C.F.A.

Up until this time we had been covering the advance of the 1st Canadian Division. Orders were now received to move into the 4th Divisional area at Bellevue. The German forces continued to retire, after the fall of Denain, which had just been captured on the 19th by the 10th Canadian Infantry Brigade. Next day, the 4th Brigade, C.F.A. advanced to Haveluy and the Batteries went into action near Oisy and Herin, while a detached section of the 27th Battery kept in close touch with the Infantry.

On the 22nd the Infantry slowly advanced towards Valenciennes, the 19th and 27th Batteries taking up positions in the vicinity of Aubry. The following day the rest of the Brigade moved forward, and Lt.-Col. M. N. Ross established his Headquarters in the beautiful chateau at Beuvrages, near the Canal de l'Escaut and a short distance north of the city of Valenciennes. This place had been previously occupied by the German Area Commandant, and although a considerable distance in front of the Batteries, it was close to Battalion H.Q. and in a good location to keep in close touch with the situation along the canal. We had now reached the main enemy line of resistane and soon came under heavy fire from his Artillery. Hostile gun-fire swept the roads and villages, but the civilians still remained in occupation of their houses.

Continuing Sir Arthur Currie's despatch:—

"The XXII Corps, advancing on our right from the south, gained touch with the 4th Canadian Division just east of Denain, on the evening of October 19th, pinching out the 2nd Canadian Division, which was then concentrated in the Auberchicourt area where good billets were available.

"In spite of bad weather and increased resistance, more ground was gained on the 20th, and the villages of Hasnon, Les Faux, Wallers and Haveluy, with a large population, were freed.

"During the day resistance had stiffened all along the line. The ground over which we were advancing was very flat, and there was no tactical advantage to be gained by pushing forward; a further advance would also increase the difficulties of supply. In addition, on our left, the VIII Corps had not been able to cope with the supply question and had not advanced in conformity with our progress. In view of these considerations, orders were issued that Divisions were to maintain touch with the enemy without becoming involved in heavy fighting.

"For a time, on the 20th, the 4th Canadian Division was held up just east of Denain by machine-gun and artillery fire. It was not until late in the afternoon that our troops could make progress there.

"Continuing the advance on the 21st, a footing was gained in the Forêt-de-Vicoigne, and the following villages were captured: Aremberg, Oisy, Herin, Rouvignè, Aubry, Petite Forêt, Anzin, Prouvy, Bellaing and Wavrechain. As on the previous day, all these villages contained civilians who subsequently suffered considerably from deliberate hostile shelling.

"The 1st Canadian Division had now been in the line for two weeks without having an opportunity to rest and refit since the hard-fought battle of the Canal du Nord, and orders were issued for its relief by the 3rd Canadian Division. At dawn on the 22nd, in order that touch with the enemy be maintained, the 1st Canadian Division pushed forward. Following closely, the 3rd Canadian Division passed through the 1st Canadian Division during the forenoon, on the left Brigade front, about 9.00 a.m., on the line of the St. Amand-Raismes railway, the Forêt-de-Vicoigne having been cleared of the enemy. On relief, the 1st Canadian Division came into rest, with billets in the Somain-Pecquencourt-Masny area.

"The 3rd and 4th Canadian Divisions pushed on during the 22nd. By nightfall Trith St. Leger, La Vignoble, La Sentinelle, Waast-le-Haut, Beuvrages, Bruay, and practically the whole of the large forest of Raismes, were in our hands. On the left Brigade front of the 4th Canadian Division, the Canal de l'Escaut had been reached in places. A very large area north-east of Valenciennes and a smaller area to the south-west had been flooded. To the west of the city, the canal itself provided a serious obstacle. To the south-west, beyond the flooded area, Mont Houy and the Famars Ridge made a natural line of defence.

"The XXII Corps on our right had been held up along the Ecaillon River, and the VIII Corps on our left had not been able to make any considerable advance, chiefly owing to supply difficulties, and were still some distance behind us.

VALENCIENNES—October-November, 1918

Scale: 1 inch—2.37 miles

"The Divisions continued to push forward in the face of steadily increasing opposition, and by the 25th had reached the canal and the western edge of the inundated area along the whole Corps front.

"Our troops had had a very arduous pursuit, and the rail-head for supplies and ammunition was still very far to the rear. It was therefore decided that we should make good the west bank of the canal and stand fast until the flanking Corps had made progress.

"Attempts to cross the canal proved that the enemy was holding in strength a naturally strong position, and it was ordered that no crossing in force would be attempted without reference to Corps Headquarters. The Engineers established dumps of material, well forward on selected sites, so that the bridges necessary to cross the canal on the resumption of our advance could be constructed without delay.

"It now became apparent that, unless the enemy withdrew, Valenciennes could only be taken from the south. The XXII Corps, on the right, had meanwhile succeeded in crossing the Ecaillon River, after a hard fight, and had captured the Famars Ridge. They had, however, been unable to take Mont Houy, which commanded Valenciennes from the south."

The country round about us was unusually interesting. On the left was the great forest of Raismes, on the edge of which was a very large factory where railroad wagons were manufactured. Most of the buildings and large piles of lumber had been set on fire by the enemy as they retired. On the right was Anzin, a suburb of Valenciennes. Though it stood on high ground, no clear view could be obtained of the city on account of the numerous intervening buildings. Scattered about were many substantial and comfortable houses, the owners evidently being people of considerable wealth.

An enormous store of hay and straw was found and, for once, the horses had more than they could eat. Vegetables and fruit were abundant and these were a welcome addition to the rations. All buildings, especially mines and factories, had to be explored cautiously, as "booby traps" and trip-wires had been laid across the approaches to them."

Hostile firing became more active with each succeeding night and our Batteries retaliated strongly, harassing the enemy communications, roads and assembly areas.

Owing to the difficulty experienced by runners and despatch riders in finding Brigade H.Q., orders were received to display a distinguishing flag outside these places. Lt Whitehead, the Orderly Officer, always ingenious and ready to turn his hand to anything, acquired a linen towel of suitable size. A silhouette of a howitzer in action was cut out of green cloth and sewn in the centre. Thus came into being the Brigade flag, which was then displayed over the gates of the chateau and used to mark future Headquarters.

For the Colonel and his staff, life in the chateau was by no means peaceful. Situated as it was near a road junction, the locality was frequently shelled by the enemy. The large conservatory, at one end of the building, which had been filled with plants and pools of goldfish, on our arrival, was now demolished. Meals had to be served in the cellars. Orderlies and linemen, coming up at night, had many rough experiences and narrow escapes.

On one occasion, while the chateau grounds were being heavily shelled, Brig.-Gen. King phoned Col. Ross and tried to persuade him to evacuate such an exposed position. Between the detonations and crashing of shells outside, the Colonel tried to carry on a conversation, keeping the mouthpiece covered as much as possible so the General could not hear the shell-fire. In the end he convinced the General that he was in a safe and advantageous position, on account of its close proximity to Infantry Headquarters, and ended by inviting the General and his Brigade Major to lunch the next day.

The tables were decorated with flowers from the gardens and nothing occurred to mar the occasion. The General enjoyed himself and Brigade H.Q. remained in peaceful occupation until we withdrew to another sector.

On the 26th of October, a section of the 19th Battery was sent up to a position under the railroad embankment near the canal, to enfilade the enemy lines during a minor operation by the Infantry, further south. The approach was easily visible to the enemy, but for once their observers could not have been on the lookout. Both guns were registered before before dark and the operation was carried out successfully during the night. Immediately afterwards, the section was withdrawn and the following day the Hun splattered its former vicinity very heavily.

Two days later, on the 28th, units of the 3rd Canadian Divisional Artillery relieved our Batteries and we withdrew to wagon-lines at Prouvy. The following night, the guns were put into position near Trith, west of the Canal de l'Escaut, and shortly afterwards hostile Batteries fired a heavy barrage along our whole front in an effort to dislodge our Infantry.

It was planned to capture Valenciennes by an enveloping attack from the south, in conjunction with operations of the Third and Fourth British Armies. As part of this operation the 51st Highland Division of the XXII Corps was to assault Mont Houy, and two days later, probably, the 4th Canadian Division was to follow up the advance by taking the high ground east of Valenciennes.

On October 28th, the Highlanders advanced to their objective and carried it, but, later in the day, heavy enemy forces counter-attacked and the position was lost. It then became necessary to change the original plans and the Canadians were called upon to extend their front further south. The task of storming Mont Houy fell upon the 10th Canadian Infantry Brigade. Relief of the British troops in this sector was completed the night of October 29th-30th and the operation set for the morning of November 1st. In conjunction with the attack, the 3rd Canadian Division was ordered to cross the canal and the inundated area on its front and establish a bridge-head to enable the Engineers to reconstruct the bridges leading into the city.

Brig.-Gen. King and Brig.-Gen. McNaughton made good use of the guns at their disposal. The position was eminently suitable for the use of enfilade as well as frontal fire, the general direction of the attack being parallel to our front. Full advantage of this was taken in so arranging the artillery and machine-gun barrages.

As many civilians in Valenciennes and surrounding villages still occupied their homes, strict orders were issued that the city was not to be bombarded. Shelling, however, was directed on a row of houses on the eastern side of the canal, strong points, and trenches occupied by a large number of enemy machine-guns. Elaborate arrangements were made to place heavy smoke screens along certain areas, in order to hinder German observation of our operations. Before dawn, on November 1st, all preparations had been completed and the time for the assault was fixed at 5.15 a.m.

Promptly at "zero hour" the 10th Canadian Infantry Brigade left its positions south-east of the canal and following our barrage in a northerly direction, captured Mont Houy, Aulnoy and the high ground south of Valenciennes. At the same time, the left Brigade of the 4th Canadian Division and troops of the 3rd Canadian Division forced a crossing north of the city and the German garrison was obliged to withdraw to the north-east.

At 8.50 a.m. the barrage ceased and the Batteries moved forward, the 13th, 19th and 27th going into position in the southern outskirts of Valenciennes. Aeroplanes reported that the enemy was concentrating for a counter-attack and the necessary precautions were taken to meet it. Nothing developed, however.

On the night of the 3rd, following a further withdrawal of the German forces, the 4th Brigade, C.F.A. took up positions east of the city and on the following morning moved on to the vicinity of Estreux, with the 13th Battery in close support of the Infantry. During the day, Lt. Pilgrim was wounded while on observation duty. That night we moved on to Rombies. A barrage was fired at dawn the next morning and the Infantry slowly followed the retreating enemy.

Finally we were relieved by the 2nd Canadian Divisional Artillery at 10 p.m. on the night of November 6th.

Our guns had fired their last barrage in the war and we marched back to billets in the vicinity of Valenciennes, with Headquarters at No. 2 Boulevard Carpeaux.

CHAPTER X

Armistice

SINCE the middle of August, Ludendorff's mighty armies had suffered blow after blow, first from the staggering thrusts of Field Marshal Earl Haig, then in turn by the French, Americans, and Belgians. With each successive blow, the enemy losses became greater and greater, until, by the first of November, the German "morale" was shattered.

The huge salient bulging towards Paris was finally broken. Marshal Foch's enveloping and pincer movements had brought about the downfall of the enemy. At last their confident and arrogant mien was changed to one of submission. A "rot" set in in the German ranks, and a hurried withdrawal on limited lines of communication brought the battle-line to the Franco-Belgian frontier. Thousands of German prisoners had been captured, and hundreds of guns, large quantities of war material, and rolling stock. The end was not far off.

Valenciennes was now freed, and wagon-lines were established on the garrison parade ground just outside the city. With the exception of a small portion of the outskirts, very little damage had been done to Valenciennes, as neither the British or German Artillery had shelled it. Aeroplane bombs had, however, demolished certain sections in the neighbourhood of the station and the canal locks. Practically all machinery had been removed by the enemy and sent to Germany, especially electrical equipment.

A few civilians had remained during the recent operations, and here and there a shop was opened and the owner prepared to carry on business, though there was little offered for sale.

On relief by the 2nd Canadian Divisional Artillery, on the night of November 6th, our gunners returned to Valenciennes, and all Batteries settled down to a well-earned rest in comfortable billets near the garrison parade ground.

A day or so later, an inspection of our horses was made by the Chief Veterinary Officer of the Third British Army. In his report, the

ADVANCE TO MONS—NOVEMBER, 1918

Scale: 1 inch—1.58 miles

4th Brigade, C.F.A. was highly complimented on the condition of its animals, the 13th Battery received special commendation, which was highly appreciated by the officers, n.c.o.'s and drivers. The heavy strain of the last hundred days of marching and fighting had undoubtedly had its effect on the stamina of the horses, but this handicap was greatly minimized by the careful attention given by the men in grooming, grazing and exercising their teams at every opportunity.

New uniforms were issued, bathing and pay parades held, and all ranks settled down to check over equipment, clean and grease the vehicles, and "smarten up."

On the 10th, President Poincare of France, accompanied by other notables, visited Valenciennes and made a speech in the Place d'Armes, complimenting the Canadians on their wonderful achievements in relieving the city.

Meanwhile, the 3rd and 2nd Canadian Divisions continued the advance, the 3rd operating on the north, from the Valenciennes-Mons Road to the Condé Canal, and the 2nd assuming the other half of the Corps zone to the south. Although stubborn resistance was offered here and there, our troops pushed on rapidly, and the German retreat gained more momentum each day.

By November 9th, the troops of the 3rd Canadian Division passed Jemappes, and were close to Mons, but German machine-guns, placed in advantageous points along the railway embankment east of Cuesmes, and a sweeping fire from hostile artillery, on Jemappes and other approaches in the neighbouring district, prevented immediate capture of this city. Throughout their advance the 2nd Canadian Division met with strong opposition in the densely populated mining district through which they passed; however, on the evening of the 10th, they succeeded in reaching the Mons-Givry Road, outflanking the city from the south.

During the night of the 10th-11th, the 7th Canadian Infantry Brigade (Brig.-Gen. J. A. Clark) closed in and, capturing Nimy, effected an entry into Mons by way of the railroad station. By 6.00 a.m. the next morning, the stubborn machine-gun resistance had been broken and the city cleared of the enemy.

Co-operating on their right, the 4th Canadian Infantry Brigade carried out a successful night attack against the Bois-la-Haut, thus securing the right flank of our 3rd Division, and pressed on towards the Mons-Symphorien Road where a satisfactory line was established for the defence of Mons.

In the meantime, word had been received, through First British Army, that an Armistice had been signed in acceptance of the Allied terms:—

"Hostilities will cease at 11.00 a.m., November 11th. Troops will stand fast on the line reached at that time, which will be reported to Divisional Headquarters immediately. Defensive precautions will be maintained. There will be no intercourse with the enemy of any description."

Everything went on as usual until official word confirming this message came over the wire. At first there was no cheering, no outward manifestation of that joy and relief each of those grim fighting units must have experienced at being granted the reprieve of peace, for the iron of warfare was still in the soul of each—the flash of guns and thunder of battle, the sight of crumpled and broken comrades—the whole a stark panel of hell itself lay still etched in cameo clearness upon the canvas of bloody conflict. Their minds were numb, incapable of grasping the news in all its significance. Only in eyes where dull apathy had dwelt for so long, there shone a great and wonderful light. No more would they be obliged to suffer torments through exercising a splendid duty. The great war was over.

How was the news taken throughout the British Empire? Perhaps it is best described in the words of "Mr. Punch." In the main, soberly, and in a spirit of infinite thankfulness, though in too many thousands of homes the loss of our splendid, noble, and gallant sons—alas!—so often only sons—who made victory possible by the gift of their lives, had made rejoicing impossible for those who were left to mourn them. Yet there was consolation in the knowledge that if they had lived to extreme old age they could never have made a nobler thing of their lives.

*   *   *   *

"At last the dawn creeps in with golden fingers
    Seeking my eyes to bid them open wide
Upon a world at peace, where Sweetness lingers,
    Where Terror is at rest and Hate has died.
Gone are the days when sleep alone could break
    War's grim and tyrannous spells;
Now it is rest and joy to lie awake
    And listen to the bells."

*   *   *   *

Only the healing hand of time could allay the grief of those for whom there could be no reunion on earth with their nearest and dearest.

"They shall grow not old, as we that are left grow old:
Age shall not weary them, nor the years condemn.
At the going down of the sun and in the morning
We will remember them."

—BINYON.

*   *   *   *

At eleven o'clock at the Grande Place of Mons the Mayor presented to Brig.-Gen. J. A. Clark the keys of the city in honour of its capture by his Brigade that morning. Bands played "La Brabanconne" and "O Canada" while a review of the troops was held by Gen. Sir Arthur Currie.

Such was the dramatic end to the work of the Canadian Corps in the last hundred days—from Amiens along the Roye road; then from Arras through the Drocourt-Quéant Line to the Canal du Nord; across the Canal du Nord, over the hard field of Cambrai, and so through Denain and Valenciennes, to Mons.

Most of the soldiers, however, could not realize that for them the horror of war was over, and it was not until late in the afternoon they began to fully understand that their task was done. The civilians went wild with joy and enthusiasm, opening wide their doors to their deliverers.

At Valenciennes, the rejoicing was not so pronounced, which was probably accounted for by the fact that our men had been in the city since the first day of the month. As the days passed, the novelty had worn off and all units of the 4th Canadian Division, in rest, in this neighbourhood, fulfilled their daily duties as they had during other periods of the War.

On November 15th, orders were received that the Canadian Corps would advance into Germany, and to prepare for the march to the Rhine, Gen. Sir Arthur Currie ordered the 1st and 4th Divisions to the Mons area. Since the Armistice, all units had spent several hours each day checking over equipment. Steel had been thoroughly burnished, harness cleaned. The horses were in fine trim. Never had our men looked better.

Leaving Valenciennes, on November 16th, we passed through village after village of cheering civilians until we reached Elouges. On our way forward we crossed the Franco-Belgian frontier at Quiévrain, passing from ruin into prosperity, from dire want into relative plenty. Thousands of refugees trudged westward to their homes. These people had been evacuated by the enemy from towns as far away as Lille, Douai, Lens, and Cambrai. Many had no shoes. The clothing they wore was of all sorts and shades. Some carried huge bundles, others pushed along little dog carts and baby carriages to carry their meagre belongings, while still others dragged wagons in which had been placed their bedding and other necessaries.

There were no horses. The Germans had confiscated every horse in the country. Such a pitiful sight will never be forgotten. These people had been fed by the advancing troops and in many cases had been helped to the rear by our motor lorries. However, the stream of refugees was so great, the majority of them had to go on foot.

The vicinal railroad, running along one side of the paved road, had been destroyed by the enemy, as well as the standard gauge line, paralleling the highway. At many rail joints, dynamite charges had blown away the steel and wrecked the embankments. Highways were rendered impassable by exploding mines at the cross-roads and other places where it was thought the greatest damage could be done.

Four days later the 4th Brigade, C.F.A. moved on to Cuesmes, a mining town a mile south of Mons, and established wagon-lines and billets in the area. Since passing the Franco-Belgian frontier, the country seemed more densely populated and the civilians appeared to be living in comfort and carrying on their usual vocations. Though covered standings could not be secured for all the horses, separate stables were found, while the personnel of the unit were comfortably housed in the village. No longer did our men have to live in battered houses and cellars, with no windows, doors or roofs to protect them from the elements.

The weather now became colder. Rain fell more frequently but we did not dread the coming winter as we had dreaded the three previous ones. We were now far in advance of railhead and due to the rapid advance, great difficulty was experienced in transporting food supplies to the units near Mons. The surrounding country being more or less industrial, we had no opportunity to graze the horses; daily exercise, however, kept the animals in good condition. Some Batteries were fortunate enough to secure hay from the manager of the mines, who kept a large supply on hand for his mine ponies.

The people of Cuesmes were very kind and courteous to our men, doing their best to make them comfortable. In return, the units staged occasional entertainments and dances, the whole population being invited to attend.

On Saturday, November 23rd, it became known that only the 1st and 2nd Divisions of the Canadian Corps would proceed to the Rhine. The 3rd and 4th were then transferred to the 4th British Army.

On Sunday, the 24th of November, Hon. Capt. R. F. Thompson, held a farewell church service and three days later the King of the Belgians visited Mons, where he was given a great ovation. Leave to Brussels now opened for all ranks, the men proceeding by motor lorry to this "Second Paris" as they termed it.

An inspection of the Brigade by Gen. Sir David Watson followed on December 2nd, the Batteries and Divisional Ammunition Column marching past the saluting base in Cuesmes Square. Meanwhile, educational classes and concert parties were organized, and with the continuous stream of leave warrants, all ranks enjoyed their prolonged stay in the area.

Finally, orders were received that the 4th Canadian Division was to move into the Brussels area. On December 12th we proceeded through the city of Mons to Hain St. Paul, continuing on by daily marches through Courcelles, Lambricourt and Spy to Aische-en-Refail, where wagon-lines were established. Brigade Headquarters was located at the Chateau in the village, the 13th, 21st, and 27th Batteries billeting on the civilians, while the 19th Battery located comfortable quarters at Liernu.

We had finally left the mining district and were now in a farming country. The fields showed evidence of occupation and care, many of them having been under crop, but as practically all horses had been commandeered, the work of cultivating had been carried on chiefly with cows, this being the common practice in parts of Belgium even in peace times.

The condition of the people was in strong contrast to that of those residing in Denain, Valenciennes and other places in France, as the Germans had allowed all those who wished to work for them at the mines and other places a fair rate of pay and a special ration supply. As a rule, these people looked healthy and strong. Clothing was evidently their most urgent need.

Our Batteries passed through the outskirts of Charleroi, where many of the mines were being worked, but, owing to the general unsettled conditions and communist propaganda, many of the miners were on strike.

After leaving the Charleroi area our columns moved in a northeasterly direction, over higher ground. In several of the villages at which we stopped, there was a general air of unfriendliness towards us, but as we reached our destination at Aische-en-Refail—a small and odoriferous village, in which each house had its own manure pile at the front door, and where pools of liquid filth lined the roads on either side—we found the people more kindly disposed towards us.

Directly after our arrival, December 17th, the Colonel was called to attend a conference at Divisional Headquarters, situated in a very magnificent Chateau an hour's ride away. On his return the Battery Commanders were advised that all units would remain where they were for the present.

The first consideration at Aische-en-Refail was to enable everyone to be as comfortable as possible and for the Brigade to cultivate good relations with civilians. There was practically no fuel in the village and no means of obtaining it, due to a scarcity of horses. Volunteers were called for from the various units to haul coal from the mines and deliver their loads to needy homes.

In a very short time all Batteries settled down. Leave could be obtained to visit Brussels and other places and although the distance from the railroad to our lines seemed a little too far, many men took advantage of the opportunity.

We were now about to leave Aische-en-Refail and the villagers were certainly sorry to see us go. This had been their first experience in four years of being treated as human beings and being able to have free intercourse with neighbouring villages. Our men had generously shared their rations and nearly everyone had close friends among the populace.

On January 3rd, 1919, the 4th Brigade, C.F.A. marched to Nil St. Vincent, halting for one night and continuing on to Ottignies, a fair-sized village twenty-five kilometres from Brussels, and on the main railroad. Good billets were available here for everyone and most of the horses were under shelter. The people were mostly of the working class, a far superior class to those we had met so far, and went back and forth to Brussels on business.

Leave warrants continued in large numbers and our men were given every opportunity of paying farewell visits to Paris, only a sufficient number being retained at the wagon-lines to carry on the necessary duties. Some travelled by rail to Bonn and Cologne in Germany, visiting points of interest there. In our own neighbourhood, Waterloo was not far distant and many of the men journeyed to the battlefield by motor lorry.

Shortly after our arrival at Ottignies some of the Batteries gave entertainments, but their first attempt to organize dances was promptly squashed by the Curé, who, when interviewed, explained that his action was taken as a result of some regrettable incidents which had occured at a dance in a neighbouring village, shortly before. The Curé was assured that the men of our Brigade were a far superior crowd and not at all like those referred to. He was promised that if he would allow his flock to attend, they would be suitably chaperoned by an officer of the Battery concerned, and that any parents, who wished, might accompany them. Finally he agreed, and no complaints were heard either in connection with the dances or our relations with the civilians.

In many ways, this period of occupation had its difficulties. The war was over. The impossibility of arranging for the immediate return of Canadian troops was not obvious to everyone. Many felt that their time was being wasted and golden opportunities lost. Some felt that slackers were gobbling up all the good jobs and as leave to London was finally cut off, and only visits to Brussels allowed, the men became dissatisfied.

The weather got colder and colder and snow lay on the ground for long periods of time.

Demobilization then began and the 3rd Canadian Division was despatched to England, prior to its departure for Canada. Shortly after, word came that the 4th Division was to follow next, and we were instructed to prepare our equipment and animals for delivery to the Ordnance Depôt at Wavre. Several of the animals were led down to the loading platforms and sold to the civilians by auction and the remainder turned over to the Belgian Government.

On March 8th, 1919, the 3rd and 4th Brigades, C.F.A. marched to Mousty and were reviewed by Brig.-Gen. W. B. M. King. The weather cleared. The snow had disappeared and all units prepared for sports. Ten days later, Lt.-Col. Ross, who had gone to England on leave the month previous, returned to duty.

From the 1st to the 15th of April, the Batteries were principally engaged in routine work in connection with Demobilization, the scheme for which was issued by the 4th Canadian Division on April 6th.

Married men with dependents were despatched to England on the 9th, in order to make arrangements for the return of their families to Canada.

In accordance with Divisional instructions, Batteries were reorganized into Groups, for dispersal purposes as follows:—

UNIT	GROUP NO.	DISPERSAL AREA
13th Battery	17	Toronto
19th Battery	18	Toronto
21st Battery	19	Toronto
27th Battery	20	Montreal

Sufficient personnel was retained at Unit Headquarters for purpose of administration, the remainder being posted to Groups in accordance with Dispersal Areas.

Entraining at Wavre on the 15th of April, the Brigade arrived at Le Havre early on the morning of the 17th. Eight days were spent in the

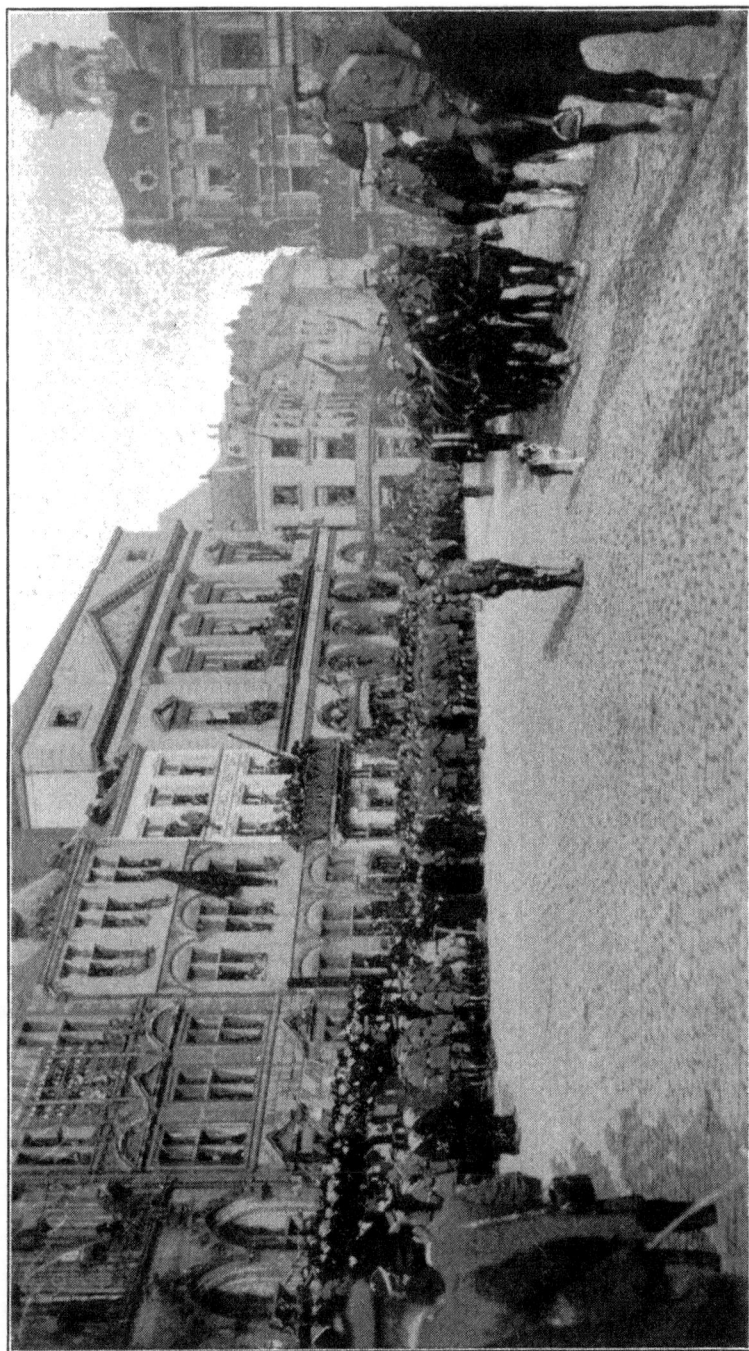

Armistice Day (Mons), November 11th, 1918.

Canadian Official Photograph.

Concentration Camp where splendid arrangements had been made for the reception of the troops. We then embarked for Southampton, which was reached at 8.00 a.m. on the 26th. Waiting specials convoyed us to Liphoek Station for Bramshott Camp.

On arrival, units of the 4th C.D.A. were allocated to "B" wing, C.C.C. Documentation and medical inspections occupied most of the time at Bramshott. Each man was allowed "Sailing leave."

The Triumphal March of Dominion Troops in London, on May 3rd, 1919, was a great success. Personnel from the Batteries of the 4th Brigade, C.F.A. took part. In a congratulatory letter, the Corps Commander expressed his pleasure at the marching and bearing of the troops.

Groups 17, 18, 19 and 20 (which included personnel of the 13th, 19th, 21st and 27th Batteries) entrained at Liphoek at 10.10 a.m. on the 18th of May, for Southampton. This port was reached about noon, when the units immediately embarked on the "Aquitania." Owing to a strike of dock and other hands, the ship did not set sail until the 19th, when she left her moorings without the aid of tugs.

The "Aquitania" also had on board personnel from the 9th, 10th, 11th and 12th Batteries, sections from the 4th C.D.A., and the 11th Canadian Field Ambulance. After a glorious though uneventful voyage, we arrived at Halifax on May 25th.

Troop trains then carried us through to Montreal where the 27th Battery were demobilized. The balance of the Brigade "mustered out" at Toronto, May 28th, 1919.

Book II

(The 15th and 16th Batteries, 6th Brigade, C.F.A.)

C̄

2nd Cdn. Div.

Operations, 1916

CHAPTER I

ON reorganization of the 2nd Canadian Divisional Artillery, May 22nd, 1916, the 6th (Howitzer) Brigade, C.F.A. was broken up— the 21st Battery being allotted to the 5th Brigade, C.F.A., the 23rd Battery to the 7th Brigade, C.F.A., and the 22nd Battery, along with the 15th and 16th from the 4th Brigade, C.F.A., and the 28th, from the 7th Brigade, C.F.A. being formed into the 6th Brigade, C.F.A.

Lt.-Col. W. B. M. King assumed command of the new unit, with Capt. Rawlinson as Adjutant. The Battery Commanders at this time were as follows :—

15th Battery, C.F.A.—Major F. F. Arnoldi.
16th Battery, C.F.A.—Capt. A. M. Brown.
28th Battery, C.F.A.—Major R. Crocker.
22nd (How.) Battery—Major J. K. McKay.

With Headquarters at Dickebusch, and Batteries located back of Scottish Wood, the Brigade took over the zone covering our trenches from the St. Eloi Craters to Piccadilly Farm.

Hostile artillery showed more activity than usual, and carried out a systematic shelling of the villages and roads between Ypres and Locre, pounded our forward zone, and harassed our communications night and day. One of these "strafes" landed amongst the battery positions, the 15th suffering two wounded. A week later, on the 31st of May, while firing on the enemy lines, the gun flashes of the 15th Battery were spotted by a German balloon, resulting in heavy shelling of the position and the loss of two men killed (Sig. Plato and Gnr. MacDonald), and seven wounded, including Lieut. E. D. Huycke. The bodies of those killed in action were laid to rest—side by side—in Dickebusch cemetary.

The Canadians continued their aggressive policy against the enemy. Infantry patrols toured "No-Man's Land" at night, inspecting the wire entanglements and carrying out surprise raids on the German lines, while the Artillery used its limited supply of ammunition to good advantage in demolishing hostile trench-mortar and machine-gun emplacements, firing on movement, and destroying his front line and communication-trenches. A German offensive had been expected for some time in this sector, and all units were on the alert to meet it. On May 28th, the following "Special Defence Scheme" was sent out to the Batteries of the 6th Brigade, C.F.A. :—

"When an attack on the front of the 2nd Canadian Division appears probable, the message "Stand by" will be sent to all units concerned.

On receipt of this message, which will be acknowledged immediately by telegram, in writing, by an Officer, all Batteries will "Stand to." Ammunition wagons at Battery Wagon-Lines will immediately be sent to the dump and filled. Orderlies will be at once sent to Brigade H.Q. to carry messages in case telephone communications fail. Special communications by lamp, or other visual methods, will be at once established.

"In the event of an action such as foreshadowed by the above, each Battery must be prepared, to act strictly on its own initiative, doing its best, always, to maintain touch, by any means, with the Infantry it is supporting, and supporting them to the fullest extent. Battery Commanders must make preparations beforehand to keep in touch with the Infantry by visual signalling.

"All guns will remain in present positions for defence of the Voormezeele Switch, with the exception of forward guns which should be brought back to the Battery at the first opportunity.

"G.H.Q., 2nd Line, 2nd Canadian Division, will run from Bellegoed Farm to La Brasserie Farm, covering Kruisstraathoek and Elzinwalle.

"In the event of this line being occupied, the 15th and 28th Batteries will withdraw to positions back of Hallebast Corner, the 16th remain in action, and the 22nd cross country to a position behind the Ypres Road north-east of Dickebusch. H.Q. will remain in its present position.

"All Batteries must be prepared to cover any portion of the Divisional zone, also 1,000 yords to the right of same. Battery Commanders will lay out lines-of-fire from G.H.Q. positions, and make book registrations, covering all principal points on their G.H.Q. front.

"Every officer and n.c.o. should know the routes to G.H.Q. positions, "O-Pip's" should be selected, and lines from Batteries to "O-Pip's" scouted so that there will be no delay in bringing fire to bear from the new positions."

Early on the morning of June 2nd, a heavy bombardment of enemy guns fell upon the front of the 3rd Canadian Division, from Hooge to Hill 60. Until noon the deafening inferno continued, and all Batteries of Corps were called upon for retaliation. In spite of most gallant resistance, the C.M.R. Brigade (Brig.-Gen. Williams) lost heavily, and their trenches were over-run by the advancing Bosches. The situation then became very critical and Ypres was in grave danger, due to a gap in the line near Zillebeke. Reserves from the 1st Canadian Division were rushed forward from their rest billets near Vlamertinghe, and by evening had consolidated a strong defence line protecting the City. Counter-attacks failed to dislodge the Germans from the high ground they had gained. For days the battle swayed. All along the line, from Hooge to "Plug Street," the enemy shelling continued. It appeared as if this minor action might become generalized, so all units of the Brigade were advised as follows:—

"In the event of an attack on our front, or that of the 56th British Division on our right, all Batteries will immediately open fire on the enemy's front line on the zones already allotted, switching, and, where necessary, searching, so as to cover every portion of the front. If the enemy gain our front-line trenches and drive out its garrison, a barrage known as "British Front-Line Barrage" will be established on our front-line trenches."

From June 6th till mid-night of the 11th, British and Canadian Batteries kept up a steady harassing fire on the German lines from Hill 60 to north-east of Sanctuary Wood—in an effort to prevent consolidation. Just after mid-night of the 11th-12th, our Infantry advanced to the assault, following our barrage closely, and by dawn all objectives had been gained and the original trench-lines of the 3rd Canadian Division re-established.

During the period the battery positions at Dickebusch Lake had been heavily "strafed," and it became necessary to move into alternative locations—the 15th Battery placing three of its guns in enfilade pits near Vierstraat, and retaining a forward gun in Scottish Wood. Considerable firing was done from these positions, and so well were they concealed that no further casualties were suffered. Shortly after, Lieut. G. A. Drew (16th Battery) was so badly wounded in the arm, that he did not return to France.

Though artillery duels continued for some time after the Battles of Sanctuary Wood and Hooge, no further infantry actions took place, and the situation became normal again. To relieve the monotony of trench-warfare, the 27th Battalion (6th Infantry Brigade), and the 22nd Battalion (5th Infantry Brigade) raided the enemy lines near Piccadilly Farm the nights of June 27th and June 30th. The 6th Brigade, C.F.A. provided the necessary artillery preparation.

Dominion Day was celebrated by all units of the 2nd C.D.A., who fired three battery salvos, at noon, on the German front line. No retaliation resulted. On the nights of July 4th-5th and 11th-12th, further raids were made by our Infantry, in the vicinity of Piccadilly Farm and Canada Trench.

As Imperial officers of the 56th Division claimed the 15th Battery were in their area, a new position had to be selected, and we moved from our comfortable spot at Vierstraat to gun-pits prepared by Sgt. Fairbrother back of Ridgewood, and nearer to the other units of the Brigade. The 16th Battery was now commanded by Major Jos. Dixon, Major G. L. Drew, in temporary command since the retirement of Capt. A. M. Brown, (about the middle of June) being transferred back to his old Battery—the 13th.

On August 10th, the 15th, 16th, and 28th Batteries put on a demonstration drum-fire barrage on the enemy front-line trenches and craters, the guns averaging 16 rounds per minute. King George and his Staff, Brig.-Gen. Morrison, C.R.A., (2nd C.D.A.) and Lt.-Col. W. B. M. King witnessed the spectacle from Mont Kemmel. Infantry patrols and raids continued throughout the month, and the Bosches retaliated heavily, with an intensive bombardment of our forward zone, supports, and back areas. It was the heaviest shelling we had experienced to date, and all units of the 2nd C.D.A. were called into action, even the heavies, to carry out the necessary counter-barrage.

The 4th Canadian Division arrived in the Salient about this time, and also the Batteries of the 3rd C.D.A., who were given training by the various units of the 2nd Canadian Division. It was now rumoured that the Corps would move south to take part in the Battle of the Somme, and on the nights of 25th-26th and 26th-27th we were relieved by Batteries of the 4th Australian Division. Next day the 2nd C.D.A. marched from Reninghelst to the Cassel area, where we indulged in open warfare training—advancing each day towards St. Omer.

On September 5th we entrained for the Somme, reached Candas, and "trekked" to St. Ouen. After a day's rest here, the 6th Brigade, C.F.A. went on to Bouzincourt Plain, just west of Albert, where temporary wagon-lines were established. Gun positions were then selected, and working parties sent forward to prepare them for occupation. Ammunition wagons poured through Aveluy to the gun pits, night after night, until nearly 3,000 rounds of ammunition per battery were available. Meanwhile,, horse-lines were secured along the Ancre Canal close to Albert, the guns were "shot" into position, "S.O.S." lines registered, and communications established. All was in readiness for the "Big Push."

The 6th Brigade, C.F.A., now known as "King's Group," consisted of the 15th Battery (Major Arnoldi), the 16th Battery (Major Dixon), the 28th Battery (Major Crocker), the 22nd (How.) Battery (Major McKay) and the 13th Battery (Major Drew). The first day in action, the 22nd Battery had 1 killed and 2 wounded, and from then till relieved, November 27th, the Brigade suffered terribly in men and horses.

At 6.20 a.m. of September 15th, the 2nd and 3rd Canadian Divisions attacked in conjunction with British Troops, and aided by armoured Tanks. By the end of the day the Sugar Refinery and Courcellette had been captured, with many prisoners. Throughout the day and in subsequent operations units of the 2nd C.D.A. were covering the front of the 3rd Canadian Division at Mouquet Farm and Zollern Graben Trenches. Lieut. Bond and two O.R.'s of the 16th Battery were wounded on the 16th, and their wagon-lines were heavily shelled a few days later, several men and horses becoming casualties. The 15th also suffered heavily, Sedgewick, McDermott, MacDonald, Wright, Glennon, and Bird being wounded.

On September 24th, new positions (previously prepared) were occupied—half way between Ovillers and Pozières, and the following day a heavy barrage was laid along the Zollern Graben trenches in preparation for an advance of the Infantry. Mouquet Farm and Thiepval fell at last, and the enemy were gradually thrown back toward Regina and Hessian Trenches.

For the next week the German lines were swept fore and aft by our guns. Aeroplane "shoots" were carried out, and enemy strong points, communication trenches, and approaches from Bapaume and Miraumont were continually harassed night and day. Intelligence Officers gained valuable information from prisoners, and learned of the shaken condition of the German "morale." The "Blood Bath of the Somme" took its toll of German reliefs when they were within twenty miles of the fighting zone. Our airmen bombed their stations, trains, depots and roads constantly, and our field guns combed the forward area to perfection. No wonder the Bosches called this battle a "Blood Bath."

On October 1st the offensive was resumed with an operation designed to capture Regina Trench. For hours the guns thundered in a concentrated shoot on the enemy lines, and the Infantry fought doggedly to break through. By the end of the day, however, the Germans were still in possession, due, no doubt, to our inability to thoroughly destroy the barbed wire entanglements, machine-gun nests, and strong points—which had held up the advance. Throughout the operation, Lieut. Hammond (15th), and Capt. Poole (16th) served as "F.O.O.'s" with the Infantry, and were recommended by General Lipsett for their gallantry in action. Three of their telephonists were buried by the explosion of a big shell and had to be dug out. A great number of our casualties occured in a similar manner, the observation parties of the 15th Battery in particular suffering heavily in nearly every tour in the forward zone.

New positions were selected on the 2nd of October, to the north of Pozières, and while preparing the gun pits for occupation, Sgt. Parnell and Gnrs. McKay, Cooper, Green and Trays (15th Battery) were wounded by a "premature" from guns firing in rear. A few days later Cpl. Mac-Cormack (15th) was killed while patrolling the telephone line to the "O.P."

Weather conditions became worse each day, and the state of the ground was almost impassable. Vehicular traffic was no longer possible, and all ammunition and supplies for the guns had to be sent up by pack-mule. Before a further advance could be attempted, the wire had to be thoroughly cut and destroyed; so the Batteries of the Brigade worked night and day on this task.

On the 8th, another barrage was fired to cover an operation of the 7th and 9th Canadian Infantry Brigades against Regina Trench, but though some ground was gained the main position still held out against us. Following this attack it rained incessantly for several days, and the countryside became a quagmire of mud and water. Observation was impossible for further wire cutting, so all Batteries were engaged on harassing fire to prevent the enemy from repairing his damaged defences.

Casualties mounted fast. On the 16th, Major Crocker of the 28th Battery was wounded, and next day the 15th lost Gnr Challicom (killed) and Sgt. Fairbrother (wounded), while the 16th also suffered heavily.

The attack on Regina Trench was resumed on the 25th, in conjunction with operations of the British troops on our left against the Stuff Line and the enemy defences in the Ancre valley. After severe hand-to-hand fighting the objective was gained, and our Infantry were then in commanding positions close to Grandcourt and Miraumont. Though many minor engagements followed in the course of the next month, no further advances were made, and we settled down to wear down the enemy "morale."

November was wet, cold, and miserable, and our horses and mules suffered terribly from exposure and mud; while many of the men contracted trench-fever and had to be evacuated. During this period, Capt.

G. V. Taylor (2nd C.D.A.C.) was killed by a "premature," and Lieut. Hammond and his "O.P." party of Signallers Coutts and MacCormack were wounded.

The following doggerel, composed by one of the 22nd Battery gunners, expressed the feelings of many :—

> We'll never leave the Somme this Fall,
> That's the fear in the heart of us all;
> We're ready to leave by train or boat,
> For sure the Somme has got our goat.
>
> Every day you'll hear us shout
> "Come on, for G— sake, take us out!"
> Every night you'll hear us call;
> "We'll never leave the Somme at all!"

Finally, on the night of the 23rd-24th of November, the Batteries were relieved by units of the 51st British Division, and on the 28th began its march from Bouzincourt to the Bully Grenay sector. Major F. F. Arnoldi limped to the wagon-lines. The terrific strain and mud of the Somme had done its work, and this gallant officer was forced, against his wishes, to hospital with acute rheumatism. Capt. C. J. Swift then assumed command of the 15th Battery.

On arrival at Bruay, wagon-lines were established, and we relieved the 18th (Lahore) Division in action, December 2nd. The positions taken over were first class, and the covered stables and billets proved a comfort to our battle-wearied units. From the Lorette Ridge a wonderful view could be obtained of the enemy lines. To the left lay "The Double Crassier;" in front, Angres and Liévin; and to the right, the long, sloping ridge of Vimy. The front was indeed interesting, and though not much firing was done, all Batteries carried out a programme of "sniping" and harassing fire.

©perations, 1917

CHAPTER II

The 1st Brigade, C.F.A. (Lt.-Col. C. M. MacLaren) relieved us on January 23rd, and the 6th Brigade, C.F.A. marched out of action to the Pernes Area. No covered standings or billets were available here, and we reverted to open wagon-lines and shacks till our return to the line, February 15th. At this time our Brigade was known as the Left Group, and consisted of the 15th, 16th, 22nd, 25th, and a section of the 26th Battery, occupying positions near Neuville St. Vaast.

Preparations were now in full swing for the spring offensive. The Canadian Corps was to take Vimy, and all units of the Artillery commenced the construction of battle possible for the "Big Show." An aggressive attitude was followed by the Infantry, raid after raid carried out along the front, and every effort made to secure identification and worry the enemy. Meanwhile, we harassed the German lines, communications, and back areas, and the "heavies" ranged on hostile Batteries all along the front.

On March 7th, wagon-lines were transferred from Camblain l'Abbe to Grand and Petit Servins, and ten days later a re-organization of the 2nd C.D.A. converted the 15th and 16th into six gun Batteries, each of these units absorbing a section from the 28th Battery. The 6th Brigade, C.F.A. then consisted of the following :—

15th Battery, C.F.A.—Major S. M. Waldron
16th Battery, C.F.A.—Major Jos. Dixon
25th Battery, C.F.A.—Major J. F. McParland
22nd (How.) Battery—J. K. McKay

When the 14th Battery became split up in this re-organization, one section went to the 19th, and the other to the 27th, while its popular O.C., Major S. M. Waldron, was given command of the 15th Battery.

Relieved by Batteries of the 3rd C.D.A., on March 24th, the 6th Brigade, C.F.A. moved into "battle positions" at La Targette Cross Roads. It was here Lt. G. R. Gouinlock joined the 15th Battery. Constructed of "bee-hive' 'sections, deep dug-outs, and well strengthened by layers of chalk, brick, and sand-bags, the pits gave every protection to our men.

Behind the ruins of the soap factory, where the 15th were located, was a battered chimney, several feet high, undoubtedly used by the enemy as an "aiming point." To confuse German observers a camouflaged substitute was set up off to the flank of the battery positions, and the old chimney dismantled.

Day after day, and night after night preparations went on in connection with the forthcoming Vimy operations, and all units of the Brigade were engaged on wire cutting, trench destruction, practice barrages, and destructive shoots on Thélus.

At 5.30 a.m. on the 9th of April, the assault was launched on Vimy Ridge, the barrage opened promptly and without a hitch. Valuable information was sent back to our "F.O.O.'s"—Lieut. B. B. McConkey (15th Battery), and Lieut. F. G. Bond (16th Battery)—who succeeded in laying telephone lines through Volkner Tunnel and thence to the crest of the Ridge at Goulot Wood. Both of these Officers received the M.C. Lieut. W. G. Wright (16th) and Lieut. J. D. Hickman (15th) as Liaison Officers with the 24th Battalion and 2nd K.O.S.B. also distinguished themselves that day.

Throughout the day and night of April 9th-10th we fired at intervals, and again next morning. The 15th Battery engaged two 7.7's in T26 and had several direct hits on the gun-pits. Between 3 and 4 p.m. all Batteries took part in a bombardment of Vimy village, and by evening our guns were out of range.

Throughout the 11th, all units struggled to move their guns forward through the morass of the battlefield, the 15th managing to get two 18-pounders into position. The other guns of the 15th and 16th Batteries (except two of the 16th still at La Targette) were stuck and blocked on the road. Everywhere was mud and desolation. The recent rains had turned the countryside into an impassable bog. The original road-beds had vanished, due to the incessant shelling of the past two years of trench warfare, and it became necessary to rebuild these highways and lay temporary cordoroy roads before the heavy impedimenta of war could move ahead.

Our Batteries, however, made every effort to cross the shell-pitted ground, and with the help of 150 men of the 22nd Battalion, 3 guns of the 15th Battery got into action from where they were stuck on the Neuville-St. Vaast-Thélus Road, and the 16th located behind Pulpit Crater at A4d 1.1. Numerous horses dropped by the wayside and died from fatigue.

All Batteries were in action, registering, by the 13th, except one gun of the 16th still stuck on the road, and the Brigade was covering the right of the 2nd Canadian Division.

For the next two weeks positions were being prepared for occupation on the Vimy Plain, to the north of New Brunswick Road, and about a half mile in front of the Avion-Farbus railroad embankment. While pack-mule trains carried up ammunition at night, a detail section of the 15th Battery manned German 7.7's and carried out harassing fire on Méricourt, Acheville, and Rouvroy. On the 20th an attempt was made to get the guns up to the new positions but the roads were so badly congested the project had to be called off. Shortly after, a shelling of the 15th and 16th Battery wagon-lines necessitated a hasty move, and an alternative location was selected near Aux Rietz corner.

On the night of April 30th-May 1st, the 15th and 16th occupied the gun-pits prepared for them at T20c 05.55, and T21c 4.7 respectively, and in the morning began to register. Though located in a shallow basin of the ground, with a slight crest in front of them, all Batteries in the neighbourhood were in direct view of enemy observers on the high ele-elevations back of Méricourt, and movement during the day was consequently forbidden. Hostile artillery was not long in spotting our gun flashes, and by noon of May 1st, the 15th had one gun put out of action; a terrific area "strafe" continued throughout the night, and as the valley was congested with field guns, the enemy was highly successful in his destructive shoot.

Night firing was carried out by the Brigade on the 2nd-3rd, and at 3.45 a.m., the barrage to cover the operation against Fresnoy commenced. All day the enemy shelled the Batteries, and our casualties numbered twenty-three, including Major Jos. Dixon, Capt. C. J. Swift, Lieut. A. Kerr, Lieut. N. F. Parkinson, and Lieut. Hersey (wounded). The 15th Battery suffered heavily during the German bombardment, and though the crews were ordered to take shelter in neighbouring shell-holes, Sgt. Jackson was killed, and Strong, Fairbrother, and Bird wounded.

Sgt. Whall then assumed command of the Battery, no officers being left, and called for volunteers to return to the gun-pits (still under heavy shelling) and carry out the specified programme of harassing fire. For his devotion to duty, this gallant n.c.o. was decorated with the Military Medal. Major Lancaster replaced Major Dixon, and was given temporary command of the 16th Battery; while Major S. M. Waldron Lieut. H. R. Hammond and Lieut. G. R. Gouinlock went up from the wagon-lines to the gun position of the 15th Battery.

Shelter trenches and "funk-holes" were then laid out and dug in rear and to the flanks of the gun-pits. At 3.15 a.m. on the 4th, the Batteries again opened fire in support of an operation to the south. Shortly after the barrage had ended and the crews had taken shelter, the enemy laid down another heavy bombardment on our area, a "5.9" crashing through the officers' dug-out of the 15th Battery, causing the death of Major Waldron and his telephonist, and wounding Lieut. Hammond.

Capt. A. H. Bick, of the 25th Battery, was then transferred to the 15th and assumed temporary command. At 1 p.m. orders were received that the Batteries were to remain silent, and to fire only on special orders or on "S.O.S." Other officer additions to the 15th Battery at this time were Capt. Baker, Lieut. Thompson and Lieut. Jacobs; while on May 12th Major Lancaster (16th) was evacuated "shell shock," and Capt. E. Flexman came from the 22nd Battery to take command of that unit.

During the night of May 6th-7th, the 15th Battery moved to T20d 2.6, and the personnel at the guns were relieved every 48 hours. The following day, May 7th, the 16th received a heavy shelling. In one week the Brigade had lost 8 killed and 34 wounded. On the 8th, a German attack on Fresnoy was successful, and all units fired on "S.O.S." during the day. For a time it appeared as if the enemy might try and exploit his success, but the heavy barrages of the Canadian Artillery prevented this possibility.

The 15th Battery received another heavy loss on the 11th, when one gun crew was wiped out—Cpl. Staples, and Gunners Johnson and Catchpole being killed, and on the following day A/Sgt. Wingfield and our cook were killed and eight other men wounded. Until the night of the 16th-17th the whole area was shot up, gassed, and harassed by the German artillery. Then we were relieved by the 26th A.F.A. Brigade and went back to reserve positions on the Ridge, with Brigade H.Q. at Mill Cave near Thélus. While here, every opportunity was taken to rest the personnel.

On the 29th we relieved the 5th Brigade, C.F.A., the 15th taking over from the 18th Battery at T20d 6.3, and the 16th and 17th Battery at T20d 8.4. For the next few weeks practice barrages were periodically laid down on the "S.O.S." lines, and all units worked on and strengthened their positions. Forward guns were placed in Willerval for opportunity targets and night firing.

A further reorganization of the Corps Artillery took place on June 20th, and our old comrades of the 4th Brigade, C.F.A. were switched from the 2nd Canadian Division to constitute the 4th C.D.A. with the 3rd Brigade, C.F.A. of the 1st Canadian Division. The 2nd Divisional Artillery from this time on consisted of the 5th ad 6th Brigades, C.F.A.

About the beginning of July the 6th Brigade, C.F.A. moved to the new Divisional area near Lens, taking over positions in front of Maroc, with wagon-lines near the mining villages of Fosse 10 and Sains-en-Gohelle. Battle positions were then selected in the vicinity of Liévin, and working parties toiled night and day to prepare them for the coming operations against Lens and Hill 70.

Sgt. Fairbrother, who had only recently returned to his unit, took charge of the construction of the 15th Battery gun-pits, and converted a row of battered miners' cottages into a "bomb-proof" network of dug-outs and shelters for the guns, all connected by underground tunnels, gas-proof, comfortable, and spacious. The position was also equipped with a light-gauge spur, carefully camouflaged, and all ammunition and supplies were delivered by tramways. Each dug-out boasted double-tiered bunks, a table, chairs, and even pictures and mirrors "rescued" from the ruined village of Liévin.

Shortly after, the Batteries occupied their battle positions, and till the middle of August, they kept up a steady harassing and sniping fire on the enemy lines. As the subsequent operations have already been dealt with in previous chapters of this book, no further details are necessary, but it must be said that the 15th and 16th Batteries took a very active part in the Hill 70 show. Lieut. J. C. Auld of the 16th Battery became Adjutant for the big operation.

It is generally conceded that the barrage on August 15th was as near perfection as possible. The terrible gruelling of Vimy Plain, instead of making the officers and men nervous and erratic in their gunnery, had the opposite effect, the "F.O.O.'s" (both drawn from the 15th and 16th), claiming that the synchronization of our guns was so perfect that at zero hour the opening rounds sounded like "the crack of a drum." On August 20th, Lieut. G. R. Gouinlock, 15th Battery, was wounded at the "O.P."

For weeks after the capture of Hill 70, the 2nd Divisional Artillery, in conjunction with other Batteries of the Corps, carried out an aggressive programme of sniping, gassing, and harassing fire—completely subduing the enemy, and assuring our Infantry of undisputed mastery of the situation along the front. About this time Capt. E. Flexman became Major of the 22nd Howitzer Battery, and Capt. J. M. McDonnell, M.C. assumed command of the 16th Battery.

Toward the latter part of September, when the proposed operation against Sallaumines was called off, the 6th Brigade, C.F.A. moved back to Vimy flats, with wagon-lines on the Arras-Souchez Road. The weather had become colder, but as the new "lines" consisted of shacks and covered stables we passed the time comfortably.

Finally, word came through about October 20th that we were to leave for Flanders shortly, and a few days later the 2nd C.D.A. proceeded by daily marches to the new area, establishing wagon-lines along the Poperinghe-Vlamertinghe Road,, about a half mile west of the latter village. Capt· F. G. Bond, M.C. was then in command of the 16th Battery, Capt. J. M. McDonnell being transferred to the 3rd C.D.A. as Brigade Major.

Our Infantry had not yet arrived, but the Batteries were sent into the line immediately, each unit taking over "guns in situ" from an Imperial A.F.A. Brigade, close to the Ypres-Roulers Railway, and northwest of Zonnebeke. The 15th were situated close to Kink Corner, and the 16th between Zonnebeke and Kansas Cross. Close by were units of the 4th C.D.A. Here and there—to relieve the dreariness and desolation of the shell-cratered battlefield—was a concrete "pill-box." Not a sign of vegetation remained, and not a tree. Even the Department Highway from Ypres to Roulers and the railway embankment were blasted beyond recognition. ·Only a pile of broken brick and masonry remained of the neighbouring village of Zonnebeke.

No covering of any kind was possible for the guns· In full view of the enemy our casualties were appalling. Here, the brave A/Cmdr. of the 16th, Capt. F. G. Bond, M.C., was killed. Scores of others, equally brave members of these units, made "The Great Sacrifice." Capt W. G. Wright then assumed command of the 16th Battery.

During the terrible ordeal of our stay in the "Salient" no complaint was heard—nothing but duty mattered. The Canadian Corps was detailed to capture the Passchendaele Ridge, and all ranks determined the task should be accomplished, irrespective of the magnitude of the undertaking.

At 6 a.m. of November 6th, the 6th Brigade, C.F.A. supported the assault of the 6th Canadian Infantry Brigade on Passchendaele, which village was in the centre of "Square 6" on the trench map. On the 1917 Christmas card selected by the 6th Canadian Infantry Brigade there was a "four leaf clover" bearing a "6" on each leaf in commemoration of this extraordinary coincidence.

Capt. W. G. Wright met with an accident November 17th and Capt. R. F. Baker was made Major of the 16th Battery. Lieut. B. B.

McConkey then became acting Captain of the 15th Battery. The Brigade Padre won the M.C. for very gallant work in burying the dead at Hillside Line.

The 15th and 22nd Batteries were continually shelled, and, when the gun crews were not on duty firing, they took refuge in the large "pill-box" close by. Equipped with rows of ammunition boxes around the sides, and a double row down the middle, this place afforded refuge for forty men. All had to sit; there was no place to sleep, but everyone preferred this haven to the open waste outside, where flying fragments of shrapnel and "H.E." swept the whole area. In six days the 15th Battery alone lost 13 guns. Night after night the gun positions were gassed, and the roads and approaches from Ypres heavily shelled and bombed. But for the soft mud our casualties would have been tremendous.

From whatever angle the Battle of Passchendaele is viewed it is equally ghastly to contemplate. Battered in "pill-boxes," surrounded by scores of dead bodies, of both the enemy and our own troops; countless carcasses of decaying horses, strewn along the sides of imperceptible trails called roads; the millions of pounds of ammunition lost in the mud; the hundreds of derelict guns; and the constant stream of broken, bruised, and lacerated humanity made a spectacle too gruesome and terrible to attempt to describe. Every one who passed through this terrible ordeal deserved a Victoria Cross.

Finally, on November 20th, the 6th Brigade was relieved. That night the officers had a dinner at Poperinghe, and at 6 a.m. the next day the Unit marched out of Flanders on its return to Vimy. On arrival the Batteries went direct into action near "The Double Culvert" on Vimy Plain. This sector was now very quiet. Covered standings at La Targette afforded every comfort, and all units settled down to a well earned rest after their strenuous experience in the "Salient."

On December 20th, the Brigade moved out of action to Amettes. The weather had turned very cold, but cozy billets were secured in farms nearby, and all ranks prepared for the Christmas festival. Exercise rides, checking equipment and cleaning up the vehicles were the daily routine. As only one suitable building, the convent school, could be secured in the village for the Christmas dinner, each unit had to draw lots for it, two of the Batteries had their celebration on the 25th, and the other two on the 26th.

®perations, 1918

CHAPTER III

O N December 28th, 1917, the 15th Battery moved to Pernes, as the unit selected for the School of Gunnery there. Good accommodation and covered stables were available, and till February 24th remained on this duty. Rejoining the 6th Brigade, C.F.A. at Marles-les-Mines, reserve gun positions were laid out and constructed on Vimy Ridge.

Finally, on March 18th, the Brigade was back in action at Liévin, with wagon-lines near Boyeffles. All was tense excitement about this time. The big German "drive" commenced on the 21st, and as Vimy was threatened, the 2nd Divisional Artillery was held in reserve. Two days later, our Batteries moved south to Acq, near Mont St. Eloi.

On the 27th, an all-night march took us to Basseux. Hundreds of refugees surged westward, carrying goods in wagons and wheel-barrows, and battle weary Infantry passed to the rear. The enemy were not far off, and the 2nd Canadian Division was assembled in the area to protect Arras from the south. The situation was critical. It was reported that German plans were in readiness to exploit the success of their Infantry.

All day the Brigade "stood-to," awaiting orders. Machine-guns were mounted in front of the gun positions in case of a surprise attack. To the south of us the British Guards Division were heavily engaged. The issue of battle hung in the balance. Toward evening however, news was received that the enemy had met with defeat. The line still held, and Arras was safe. That night the Batteries went into action near Ficheux, and gun teams were kept close by the positions in case of eventualities. Gradually the situation cleared, and trench warfare again set in.

It was not until July 1st that the Infantry of the 2nd Division rejoined the Canadian Corps. When it left the Neuville-Vitasse sector it did so with a splendid record. Holding this front for ninety-two days, during which time many local attacks had been replused, twenty-seven raids carried out and a large number of prisoners, machine-guns, and trench-mortars captured, Sir Arthur Currie declares :—

"The aggressive attitude adopted by this Division at such a critical time and under such adverse conditions, had a most excellent effect on our troops, and it certainly reduced to the lowest point the fighting value of two German Divisions."

During this period Major A. H. Bick left the Brigade and was transferred to the 1st C.D.A. to become Brigade Major. Capt. B. B. McConkey, M.C., who had assumed command of the 15th Battery was wounded May 30th and died the same day in hospital at Doullens. Capt. C. J. Swift then became Acting Major of this unit.

About the end of May, the 6th Brigade, C.F.A. was relieved and moved out of action to Wailly for anti-tank manoeuvres. Many of the men were taken down with "flu"—the epidemic had spread throughout the whole Army and the hospitals and rest camps were full. Luckily only a small proportion of the cases were serious.

After four weeks training at Wailly, the Unit proceeded to Magnicourt, Agny-lez-Duisans, and Savvy-Barlette for Divisional manoeuvres and a rest. All ranks thoroughly enjoyed themselves. Major F. J. Alderson joined the 15th Battery at Magnicourt, July 27th, and three days later the Brigade began its "trek" to an unknown destination far to the south, marching at night.

At last we were to see a war of movement. A big offensive was to be launched by the Fourth British Army, in the vicinity of Amiens.

Passing through Doullens and Ailly-sur-Somme, the Brigade arrived at Longeau, and took cover in the surrounding woods. The whole neighbourhood was crammed with Artillery, Cavalry, and Tanks. After packing up ammunition and camouflaging the guns in masked positions, we eagerly awaited the "zero day." The movement of the Canadian Corps from Arras to Amiens was intended as a surprise for the enemy, and all preparations and details had to be carefully laid out beforehand. None of the Batteries registered; map ranges and corrections had to be computed. The guns had been calibrated a short time before at the Corps Calibration Ranges, and the units went into action in the open, on the night of August 7th-8th, behind Villers-Bretonneux.

At 4.20 a.m. the following morning the battle opened with a terrific barrage of hundreds of guns. To our left the Australians and British were co-operating; to the south of the Corps—the 1st French Army. The 2nd Division, with the 4th Infantry Brigade in the line, had to follow high, open ground over a plateau cut by deep valleys. The resistance was very stiff, but, by 7.20 a.m. Marcelcave had been captured. The 5th Infantry Brigade then followed through to carry on the attack. Our Tanks suffered heavily once the mist had lifted. By early afternoon, Wiencourt and Guillaucourt were taken, after a series of stubborn pitched battles. The 6th Infantry Brigade then came into action, and passed through the 2nd objection to carry the old Amiens Defence Line, by evening. Over 6,000 prisoners had been taken by the Canadian Corps and a record advance of over 16,000 yards made for the day.

As soon as the initial barrage had been fired, the 6th Brigade, C.F.A. moved forward passed Villers-Bretonneux, and took up new positions near Wiencourt. Casualties in the Brigade were very light although Lieut. E. L. Fick (16th Battery) was wounded shortly before "zero." Our guns kept up a formidable harassing fire during the evening, and took on many "opportunity targets." Major Alderson and Major Baker were in close contact with the advancing infantry throughout the operations and rendered valuable assistance all day.

At 11 a.m. on the 9th, the advance was resumed. The 2nd Division, with the 5th and 6th Infantry Brigades in line, capturing Meharicourt and Rosières after heavy fighting, the Australians and 1st and 3rd Canadian Divisions on our flanks conforming with the movement, representing a penetration of nearly four miles.

Hard, stubbor fighting characterized the next few days. Our Infantry had been relieved by the 4th Canadian Division, and were now in Corps Reserve. The guns, however, remained in action, and followed an aggressive programme of harassing fire. Beautiful weather continued, and enemy bombing planes soared over the area each night, searching for suitable targets. Time after time, battery positions and horse lines were located by the enemy machines, and the crashing of bombs caused many casualties.

New positions were occupied near Vrély and Meharicourt, and till the 23rd, when the Brigade was relieved and moved out of action, nothing of importance took place. The Battle of Amiens was now over, and the Canadian Corps was ordered to the Arras sector. The 6th Brigade, C.F.A. then began its march to the north, arriving at Berneville a few days later.

Going into action in front of Beaurains, the Brigade took part in the opening barrage for the Battle of Arras, August 26th. In this operation, the 2nd and 3rd Canadian Divisions captured Wancourt, Guemappe, and Monchy-le-Preux. Stiff opposition was encountered in taking the guns forward. The German Artillery was very active, sweeping our rear and assembly areas with "5.9's" high velocity shells, and gas, Between Wancourt and Chérisy, new positions were occupied, in readiness for the second phase of the operations.

Though the Drocourt-Quéant Line was considered well-nigh impregnable, the impetuous dash and ardour of our attacking Battalions overcame all opposition in their brilliant advance of September 2nd. By evening the high ground overlooking the Canal du Nord had been attained. The Hindenburg System was broken on a wide front.

As soon as the barrage ceased, the 6th Brigade, C.F.A. moved forward and late in the afternoon took up positions between the Bois de Loison and Bois de Bouche, in front of Cagnicourt. From the slope ahead, a clear view could be obtained of the enemy country for miles. For hours a steady sniping and harassing fire was directed on the retiring enemy.

September 2nd! Who will forget that memorable day? With the breaching of the Hindenburg Line, and the crushing defeat of several fresh German Divisions, Ludendorff's last hopes of a successful resistance were shattered.

Throughout the day, enemy machine-gunners and artillerymen fought with great courage, and did not give in, until hopelessly surrounded. Many continued firing to the last, and died at their guns.

German airmen flew low over the lines all day, machine-gunning our Infantry, sweeping the roads and approaches, and bombing our battery positions and horse-lines.

The losses of the 16th Battery were appalling during this action, due to bombing—8 men being killed, 10 wounded, and a large number of animals destroyed and injured.

On the 3rd, as the enemy retired beyond the Canal du Nord, a further advance was made by the Infantry, and the Batteries moved on to the neighbourhood of Buissy.

From then on the German resistance stiffened, and hostile shelling increased, especially in the use of gas. Further artillery preparation was necessary before the attack could be resumed, and, as the enemy positios were considered extremely formidable, Sir Arthur Currie determined to rest his troops before the next operation.

The 6th Brigade, C.F.A. then moved out of action to the vicinity of Hendecourt, guns were recalibrated, and the Units rested and refitted.

The assault on the Canal du Nord was set for September 27th, and, for two or three nights previous all Batteries packed up ammunition to the battle positions near Inchy-en-Artois.

As soon as the barrage commenced, in support of the assault, hostile retaliatory fire fell amongst the guns, the Brigade suffering many casualties. The 16th received especial attention—Lieuts. Sparling, Cochrane, and Jacobs, Sergeants Campbell and Mulligan, and a large number of gunners being wounded.

About noon, of the 27th, the Batteries crossed the canal and went into action north of Quarry Wood. On the following morning a barrage was fired between Haynecourt and Raillencourt, where the 15th Battery encountered heavy machine-gun fire.

In subsequent operations, the guns were continually firing on the enemy and answering "S.O.S." calls. The spires of Cambrai could be clearly seen and behind the German lines, the enemy was busily engaged in destroying war material, and blowing up ammunition dumps. A few days later, the city fell, and the Brigade went into rest on the western edge of the Canal de l'Escaut, in the vicinity of Neuville St. Remy.

The enemy was now in full retreat. Roads had been mined and blown up, and bridges destroyed. Every attempt had been made by the Bosches to delay pursuit.

After the fall of Cambrai, the Canadian Corps, with the exception of the 2nd Division, took over the British positions along the line of the Sensée River. The 2nd Canadian Division moved on Iwuy, and in conjunction with the 49th British Division, captured this strong position after stubborn resistance, on Oct. 11th. In this operation, our Batteries had an opportunity of engaging and dispersing German Tanks. In spite of desperate efforts on the part of the enemy to hold up our advance, Bouchain was captured, October 16th.

Next day the 1st Canadian Division forced a crossing of the Canal du Nord, and the line of the Sensée was evacuated by the enemy. A rapid advance followed, Douai was taken, and town after town, village after village fell into the hands of the Canadians. Denain was captured by the 4th Division on the 20th, and the 2nd Division then went into Corps Reserve.

With the fall of Valenciennes, November 1st, the 2nd Divisional Artillery moved to that city, where all Units remained till the 6th. Our troops then relieved the 4th Canadian Division. With wagon-lines at Onnaing and gun positions down the Mons Road, a barrage was fired in support of an assault on enemy positions along the Franco-Belgian frontier at Quievrechain.

On the 9th and 10th, the Infantry advanced rapidly towards Mons, and our Batteries fired their last shells of the War on the afternoon of November 10th at Frameries. During the night of the 10th-11th, Mons was taken by troops of the 3rd Canadian Division, and at 11 o'clock next morning Armistice went into effect.

At 11.20 a.m. of the 11th, the 6th Brigade, C.F.A. moved into Havré, where our men were greeted with wild enthusiasm by the populace. Fine billets were available here, and all ranks settled down for a well-earned rest after the continual grind of the "Last Hundred Days."

March to the Rhine

CHAPTER IV

ON November 15th, the Brigade proceeded to Houdeng-Aimeries. Shortly after, news was received that the 1st and 2nd Canadian Divisions would march to the Rhine, and at 8.30 a.m. of the 21st, the Batteries commenced the "trek" to Germany.

Day after day, in cold damp weather, the long column moved eastward, resting two days at Gouy-lez-Pietons, where 2 days were spent cleaning vehicles and harness—Sombreffe—over muddy roads via Namur to Champion, where our route, flanked by high rocky cliffs, paralleled the picturesque River Meuse—on to Thon, where some of the men discovered a barge laden with white wine, and fought the "Battle of the Barge" that night—climbed the Ardennes Mountains where we passed discarded enemy lorries and tractors—and on to Havelange and Grandham.

On December 1st, the Brigade pulled into Vaux-Chavanne, 25 kilometres from the German frontier. After two days rest, the column proceeded on to Salm-Chateau, and on the 5th crossed the "border" at 11.55 a.m. All through France and Belgium the towns and villages had been gaily decorated with flags and bunting, but once we crossed into Germany, enthusiasm was replaced by solemnity and quietude. Continuing on through Rodt, Aulder, Cronenburg, Eicherscheid, we arrived at Flerzheim—10 kilometres from Bonn, on the Rhine, December 10th.

Following the Rhine valley to Mehlem, we passed through densely populated districts, and well-cultivated fields. Across the river was a range of craggy heights, and here and there a castle. The beauty of the scene gripped us. The next day was spent in cleaning up for the Triumphal Entry into Bonn.

At 7.30 a.m. on the 13th of December, the Brigade marched to Bonn, passed through the Kaiserplatz, along the avenue past Bonn University and the white statue of Wilhelm I, and via the Markt Platz to the great Rhine Bridge.

Crossing the river at 11.30 a.m., where the Brigade was inspected by Gen. Sir Arthur Currie, Maj.-Gen. Burstall, and Brig.-Gen. Panet, the units continued on to Hangelar. This place was so crowded that the 15th Battery moved to Vilich-Muldorf the next day. We had then reached our permanent "home," as part of the Army of Occupation. All ranks were well billetted, and the horses were in covered stables.

The usual routine for the ensuing period was grooming, harness cleaning, and exercise rides. Every opportunity was given the Batteries to "see the sights." Ror a while, the civilians were openly hostile, but in time became more friendly. Some were very eager to learn the English language, and many of our boys "swaped" German words for our own. War souvenirs were easily procured. Food was good, and though the prices (in marks) seemed very high, meals were cheap when figured in our own currency.

Christmas Day was celebrated in great style. A light snow covered the ground and lent a touch of winter. Every unit in the Brigade held its own dinner. The 15th Battery "Menu" was as follows:—

MENU

SOUP DU SWIFT

ROAST

BEEF A LA DUG-OUT

POULTRY:
CHICKEN SANS CLOTHES

VEGETABLES:
SHRAPNEL POTATOES - CARROTS DU MAIN

CABBAGE A LA GORMAN

SWEETS:
XMAS PUDDING AVEC SAUCE DU PICQUET

EXTRAS:
BEER ALLEMAGNE - TEA A LA PURDIE

CIGARS   CIGARETTES
CRACKERS

15th BATTERY, C.F.A.
C.E.F.
Vilich · Muldorf
Germany   Xmas 1918

Electric trams took our men to Bonn in 10 minutes, passage free. The "See Toos" played to the troops in the big theatre, and the Y.M.C.A. gave free cinema shows. Cologne was not far away, and electric cars were crowded with Canadians daily. It was a simple matter to secure leave of absence for a few days.

Cologne was very interesting. The great Hohenzollen Bridge over the Rhine, with its three magnificent spans—the main one, 187 yards long and 34 yards high—was indeed a massive structure. The Neu Markt and the Heu Markt, beautiful squares, lined with trees and statues, and the wide avenues and boulevards, with grass, and tree-lined down the centre, called "Rings"—Hohenstaufen, Kaiser Wilhelm, Hausa, and the most wonderful of all, Deutscher Ring, laid out in the form of a circle, in the centre of which were three fountains. The civilians seemed well-to-do, and the city quite prosperous.

Finally, on January 28th, 1919, the Brigade, now in charge of Major F. J. Alderson, proceeded to Wahn, and entrained for Belgium. At last we were on the way home! Passing through Huy to Namur, the Units detrained, hooked in, and marched to Mornimont.

We hoped our stay in Belgium would be brief, but we were doomed to disappointment. The weather up to this time had been very cold, but by the end of February and the beginning of March, the fields dried up, and sports were held daily. Meanwhile, all ranks were given leave to visit Brussels, Antwerp, and Paris.

Soon after, our guns, wagons, transport, and horses were taken over by the Belgian Government, and each Unit was required to report shortages of equipment, etc. Boxing bouts and football games were arranged for Divisional Championships. The 6th Brigade, C.F.A. won its contest from the 5th Brigade, C.F.A. by a score of 3 to 1, and in the final Unit Championship, the 15th Battery lost to the 5th Brigade, H.Q.— 0 to 2.

With the advent of April, the Brigade was warned to prepare for evacuation to England. Entraining on the 10th, we proceeded to Le Havre via Charleroi, Mons, Valenciennes, Arras, Acq, and Amiens. After a few days in the rest camp at Le Havre, during which time bathing and clothing parades were held, all units embarked for Southampton, where we arrived on the early morning of the 16th, and proceeded straight to Witley Camp.

The whole Division was concentrated in the Witley area. Medical inspections, checking of accounts and classifying the men for repatrition took up several weeks. Married men with families in England were segregated from the units and concentrated at Buxton. The remainder were given "sailing leave" and saw London and their favourite "haunts" for the last time.

Finally, on the morning of May 13th, the Brigade entrained for Tilbury Docks and sailed for Halifax on the "Minnekahda." After a rather stormy trip, we landed on the 22nd, and were despatched to M.D. No. 2, Toronto, where demobilization took place three days later.

Return to "Civies"

By Hon. Capt. R. F. Thompson, M.C.

NOW that the turmoil of War has passed, and we are back home once more, trying to begin our peace time pursuits from where we left off in 1914, we have time and opportunity to take stock of ourselves and ponder over a few searching questions.

What was it that enabled our "Old Brigade" to play its part so stoutly to the end of the conflict, and in after years send a thrill of pleasure through our hearts when old faces are seen again and old associations renewed? What subtle thing was it that took hundreds of men from all walks of life, in all parts of the country, and welded them into one unified whole whose powerful driving force was the power of the Brigade?

It was the spirit of the men. Yes, in spite of statements to the contrary from materialists, spirit, not mechanics, still continues to be the most potent force in life. It was this spirit of loyalty that made us each feel that the "Fourth" was the finest Field Artillery Brigade that ever went into action. Doubtless there were other Brigades that were good, but the "Fourth" was just a bit better, because it was ours.

We were like blood-brothers in the primitive days of the war, and we shared a comradeship the like of which the world had never seen. Before the larger interests of the Battery or Brigade, selfish interests were forgotten. There was practical community of goods and spirit. The only rivalry was a friendly one in service to the common cause.

Come what may—dangers, suffering, hardships, discomfort, a pleasure they were all in the days work, and were shared by all with supreme good humour. Naturally, we all reserved the privilage to exercise on fitting occasions, the inalienable right of the old soldier to "grouse," but we failed to deceive anyone, even ourselves, by so doing, for we would not have been anywhere else for the world.

We did not, however, lay claim to be plaster "saints" or embryo angels, waiting for the wings to sprout. We knew our weaknesses and so did our comrades, for we lived too close to each other and too near to the grim realities of life for any elaborate cloak of pretense to act as a disguise, even if anyone had wanted to wear it.

But all this has faded into the historic past. Old scenes have changed. For the trench-mats and pavé roads we have the pavements and roads of our own land; for gun-pits or dug-outs we have substituted the office, or factory.

Old comradeships have been broken up. The "Old Brigade" has passed away in body—does its spirit still survive in us? In other words, have we learnt the lesson which the Great Master was trying to teach us, even amid the havoc and carnage of war?—Comradeship in a common Service.

Greater are the natural forces that unite us than the artificial barriers which make for division. The great adventure of War is finished: the equally great adventure of Peace still lies before us, and demands from us those same qualities which made the "Old Fourth" a source of pride to us all.

Courage? Yes. Patience and endurance? Undoubtedly. Discipline and self control? Assuredly. Loyalty and faith? By all means. But above all else, unselfish comradeship with those whom we are now associated in the varied walks of life. May that old spirit never be lost.

Let us penetrate human weaknesses to a unison of those good qualities in human nature which are so often seeking an opportunity to express themselves. Let us not forget that in the days of strain and stress, when the needs of active service made supreme demands, men rose to heights of sublime devotion and self sacrifice of which we never expected them capable.

But there are many of our number who did not return: for them, the War ended all. But did it? True, their ashes rest on foreign soil, but they themselves have gone back to the Lord of all good life, who has found other and broader spheres of service for them.

We remember them with pride and affection—they fought a good fight, they were "faithful unto death" and counted their lives not too dear an offering to pay that those whom they loved might enjoy the blessings of Freedom and Peace.

To all those whom they left behind in the lone circle, we, their comrades of the "Old Brigade," would say they have not died in vain, and we pledge ourselves to be loyal and steadfast to those principles for which they made "the Supreme Sacrifice."

Whatever our task may be in this new day, let us do it with the best that is in us, remembering ever that the guardianship of the traditions of the Fourth Brigade is in our hands. May we play a worthy part!

Appendices

Honour Roll

4th Brigade, C.F.A.

Regimental Number	Rank	Name	Date	Nature
84101	Gnr.	Alton, D. G.	31-10-16	K. in A.
73	Gnr.	Amos, J.	3-5-17	K. in A.
83777	Gnr.	Anderson, B. S.	26-8-17	K. in A.
83125	Gnr.	Archer, W. C.	9-11-17	D. of W.
300523	Dvr.	Armour, W.	15-12-18	D. of D.
339879	Gnr.	Armstrong, E.	17-5-17	D. of W.
	Lieut.	Armstrong, T.—M.M.	18-2-18	D. of W.
36	Dvr.	Ashbourne, R. J.	31-3-16	D. of W.
	Lieut.	Atkin, J. P. H.	4-2-19	D. of D.
84009	Gnr.	Bailey, F.	11-3-16	D. of D.
83361	Sgt.	Bailey, G. T.	24-9-16	D. of W.
83629	Sgt.	Baldwin, E.	4-3-18	K. in A.
1250503	Gnr.	Banbury, L. A.	17-4-17	K. in A.
	Lieut.	Bell, C. H.	30-10-16	D. of W.
90025	Sgt.	Bell, J. G.—M.M.	18-10-17	K. in A.
83785	Gnr.	Bibby, A.	10-11-16	K. in A.
294	Dvr.	Birkett, W. G.	25-8-16	D. of W.
89861	Gnr.	Black, G. S.	23-11-17	D. of W.
90010	Bdr.	Bolton, F. G.	30-10-17	K. in A.
	Capt.	Bond, F. G.—M.C.	29-10-17	K. in A.
302360	Gnr.	Bommer, W.	3-11-17	K. in A.
90075	Gnr.	Booth, H.	20-11-17	D. of W.
84105	Gnr.	Breay, E. C. P.	12-10-18	D. of D.
141349	Dvr.	Brown, T.	12-10-16	Acc. Kld.
339462	Gnr.	Bruford, W. P.	24-10-17	K. in A.
91578	A/Bdr.	Burley, W. F.	9-9-17	D. of W.
342823	Gnr.	Bush, A. R.	5-11-17	K. in A.
2100056	Gnr.	Campbell, J. D.	13-11-17	D. of W.
83636	Dvr.	Campbell, S.	2-3-19	D. of D.
75327	Gnr.	Catchpole, G. H.	11-5-17	K. in A.
83977	Gnr.	Challicom, O.	17-10-16	K. in A.
476592	Gnr.	Chamberlin, A.	6-5-17	D. of W.
	Lieut.	Chaplin, A.	3-5-17	K. in A.
433	Dvr.	Chapman, J.	8-8-18	D. of W.
85295	Gnr.	Charbonneau, T.	24-11-16	K. in A.
84117	Gnr.	Clark, S. N.	8-11-16	K. in A.
613	Dvr.	Clynick, J.	25-11-16	D. of W.
300539	Bdr.	Cobb, S. F.	16-6-17	K. in A.
86902	A/Bdr.	Coleman, W.	5-11-17	K. in A.
43854	Gnr.	Connolly, A.	27-10-16	D. of W.
305514	Gnr.	Coon, R. A.	6-2-18	D. of W.
86017	Gnr.	Cornthwaite, W.	29-10-17	K. in A.
315	Dvr.	Corp, C. N.	8-9-17	K. in A.
84109	Dvr.	Courtier, F. T.	4-9-18	D. of W.
83370	Cpl.	Crocker, F.	8-7-16	D. of D.
41435	Gnr.	Currie, J. A.	23-8-17	D. of W.
83374	Gnr.	Currie, T.	21-4-17	K. in A.
83473	Gnr.	Dalling, W. V.	19-10-16	D. of D.
83379	Cpl.	Daniels, G.	1-10-17	D. of D.
83375	Gnr.	Dawson, E.	2-10-18	D. of D.
104203	Gnr.	Dennison, R.	15-11-17	D. of D.
84120	Gnr.	Donaldson, A.	2-11-16	D. of D.

Regimental Number	Rank	Name	Date	Nature
83377	Bdr.	Douglas, G.	10-5-17	D. of D.
5950	Gnr.	Douglas, R.	3-11-17	D. of D.
303662	Gnr.	Douglas, W.	18-10-17	K. in A.
89876	Cpl.	Downs, J.	30-10-17	K. in A.
83219	Gnr.	Edwards, W. F.	22-9-18	D. of W.
316889	Gnr.	English, T.	28-10-17	K. in A.
87664	Dvr.	Ferguson, A.	2-9-18	K. in A.
83242	Bdr.	Fielding, T.	24-8-18	K. in A.
83384	A/Bdr.	Foster, J. S.	8-5-17	K. in A.
335865	Gnr.	Fowler, L. W.	9-3-18	D. of D.
83227	Bdr.	Fox, H. C.	30-4-16	K. in A.
89179	Gnr.	Gagne, N.	29-9-18	K. in A.
83606	Sgt.	Gailor, C. F.	16-9-15	D. of Inj.
84129	Gnr.	Gatward, R.	28-4-19	D. of D.
84134	Gnr.	Gibbs, O. T.	24-4-16	D. of W.
86915	Cpl.	Gillen, F. C.	7-6-19	D. of D.
	Lieut.	Godwin, C. R. M.	4-4-16	K. in A.
84242	Gnr.	Goldie, T. L.	28-8-16	D. of D.
	Lieut.	Gordon, W. H.	30-10-16	K. in A.
2001054	Gnr.	Hall, F. C.	9-3-18	D. of W.
83153	Gnr.	Halliday, C. G.	29-11-16	D. of D.
84238	Gnr.	Harpin, H. E.	20-10-16	Drowned
83662	Gnr.	Harrison, R. H.	21-4-17	K. in A.
1251011	Gnr.	Harvey, W.	26-10-17	K. in A.
83658	Gnr.	Hately, J.	21-8-17	K. in A.
381	Dvr.	Haylor, J.	4-9-18	D. of W.
83667	Dvr.	Henry, A. H.	31-8-18	K. in A.
337816	Gnr.	Henry, A. H.	4-9-18	D. of W.
83610	Dvr.	Heppell, R.	3-11-17	D. of W.
2085328	Gnr.	Hepworth, G.	6-11-17	D. of W.
339030	Dvr.	Hicks, H.	10-8-18	D. of W.
83247	Gnr.	Hill, F. R.	27-2-17	D. of D.
83669	Gnr.	Hill, J. E.	28-3-16	D. of W.
341143	Gnr.	Hipkiss, C. H.	3-9-18	K. in A.
40531	Gnr.	Hirst, J. T.	3-11-17	K. in A.
83910	Cpl.	Hodges, S.	12-11-18	D. of D.
341811	Gnr.	Hogan, A. J.	10-8-18	K. in A.
86286	Dvr.	Holmes, J.	16-8-18	K. in A.
86919	A/Cpl.	Hook, G. A.	8-5-17	D. of W.
49429	Dvr.	Horton, E.	17-9-16	K .in A.
90065	Bdr.	Hutchison, J. C.	30-9-18	K. in A.
83883	Bdr.	Jackson, J.	3-5-17	K. in A.
83673	A/Sgt.	Johnson, D. H.	19-11-16	D. of W.
87022	Dvr.	Johnstone, D.	11-6-16	D. of W.
86933	Gnr.	Jones, J. M.	27-4-17	K. in A.
338998	Gnr.	Kelly, L.	9-11-17	D. of W.
1262710	Dvr.	Kelly, W. H.	3-9-18	K. in A.
35212	Gnr.	Kerr, K.	8-7-18	D. of D.
90077	Gnr.	Kirkpatrick, J.	26-9-17	K. in A.
300247	Gnr.	Klock, J. M.—M.M.	15-10-18	D. of W.
1251773	Gnr.	Lackey, F. J.	7-11-17	K .in A.
301440	Gnr.	Lafrance, E.	3-9-18	K. in A.
41240	Dvr.	Lake, T.	25-5-16	D. of W.
89904	Gnr.	Lalonde, L.	7-3-19	Acc. Kld.
334128	Gnr.	Last, A.	27-9-18	K. in A.
316932	Gnr	Leitch, R.	30-9-18	K. in A.
84157	Gnr.	Leonard, F. W.	26-4-17	K. in A.
322920	Gnr.	Leonard, R. A.	18-10-17	K. in A.
86943	Gnr.	Line, R.	20-5-17	K. in A.
91461	Gnr.	Little, R. W.	1-6-17	K. in A.
446	Gnr.	Livingstone, W.	14-1-16	K. in A.

Regimental Number	Rank	Name	Date	Nature
89906	Dvr.	Lockey, B.	26-10-18	D. of D.
83679	Gnr.	Longhurst, H.	14-5-17	D. of W.
89912	Gnr	Luckie, W. A.	19-8-18	D. of W.
87029	Gnr.	Lumsden, J.	24-4-17	K. in A.
560	Dvr.	Madden, A.	27-9-18	D. of W.
83695	Gnr.	Mason, J. W.	21-4-17	K. in A.
83415	Gnr.	May, J.	10-3-19	D. of D.
86667	Cpl.	Mayer, E.	4-6-17	K. in A.
84160	Gnr.	Mead, H.	1-5-16	K. in A.
84212	Sgt.	Meadows, J. C.	19-10-16	D. of W.
83690	Dvr.	Merlin, D.	16-9-18	D. of Inj.
83165	Gnr.	Merrey, R. C.	13-6-17	D. of Inj.
89921	Cpl.	Millar, J.	2-7-16	D. of W.
83128	Gnr.	Mitchell, O. J.	27-3-19	D. of D .
83420	Cpl.	Moon, H.	2-6-16	D. of W.
83259	Gnr.	Moore, H. W.	15-8-17	D. of W.
338962	A/Bdr.	Moran, L. J.	16-11-17	D. of W.
348520	Dvr.	Morley, C.	5-9-18	K. in A.
1257816	Gnr.	Morrison, D. E.	27-9-18	K. in A.
347740	Dvr.	Murray, P.	29-10-17	K. in A.
394	Gnr.	Mylan, J	13-6-16	K. in A.
90105	Gnr.	McCallum, D.—M.M.	27-9-18	K. in A.
	Capt.	McConkey, B. B.—M.C.	30-5-18	D. of W.
83992	Gnr.	McCulloch, G.	1-9-18	K. in A.
83151	Gnr.	MacDonald, K. M.	31-5-16	K. in A.
5998	Gnr.	McDonald, W.	27-4-17	K. in A.
87199	Gnr.	MacDuff, G. H.	30-10-17	D. of W.
83918	Gnr.	McFarlane, W. L.	17-9-18	D. of W.
83228	Gnr.	McKinnon, T.	24-6-16	D. of W.
454	Dvr.	McLean, J. W.	30-1-16	D. of W.
345825	Gnr.	McLean, J. D.	3-9-18	K. in A.
86874	Sgt.	McLeod, B.	2-9-18	K. in A.
86665	Sgt.	MacNaughton, J.	5-9-18	D. of W.
1262739	Gnr.	McQueen, J. P.	11-3-18	D. of W.
347509	Gnr.	MacSweeney, M. B.	16-8-17	D. of W.
86965	A/Bdr.	Nickerson, A.	27-4-17	D. of W.
335886	Gnr.	Norman, H. L.	1-5-17	K. in A.
316962	Gnr.	Painter, J. R.	6-10-18	D. of W.
300276	Dvr.	Parker, S. O.	20-10-17	D. of W.
86972	Dvr.	Parks, H.	29-9-18	D. of W.
115	Cpl.	Paterson, J. D.	29-4-17	D. of W.
341155	Gnr.	Perry, H. H.	2-9-18	D. of W.
84243	Gnr.	Pettit, W. H.	24-4-16	K. in A.
336215	Gnr.	Phillopps, E. G.	22-2-19	D. of D.
83610	Sgt.	Pickett, C.	10-4-17	D. of D.
83141	Gnr.	Plato, P.	31-5-16	K. in A.
	Lieut.	Plunkett, E. A. P.	16-7-17	K. in A.
	Major	Powell, V. H. de B.	2-1-18	Died
339792	Gnr.	Quinn, J. B.	3-9-18	D. of D.
2100825	Sig.	Rafuse, J. H.	10-8-18	K. in A.
90018	Dvr.	Rayner, J.	21-6-18	K. in A.
83500	Gnr.	Renfrew, G. A.	7-11-17	K. in A.
83182	Gnr.	Riddell, W. C.	24-8-16	K. in A.
335804	Gnr.	Rideout, R. D.	16-6-17	K. in A.
83712	Dvr.	Ryan, E. C.	19-7-16	D. of W.
86872	Sgt.	Sergeant, C.	27-4-17	D. of W.
83118	Gnr.	Seymour, C. N.	10-11-17	K. in A.
83716	Dvr.	Short, F.	6-9-18	K. in A.
84186	Gnr.	Simon, H. C.	2-4-17	D. of D.
91231	Gnr.	Sinclair, J.	30-10-17	K. in A.
83936	Sgt.	Slack, F. J.	5-6-16	D. of W.
90844	Gnr.	Sladden, A.	22-4-17	K. in A.

Regimental Number	Rank	Name	Date	Nature
197	**Cpl.**	Speirs, W. McV.	28-10-18	K. in A.
	Lieut.	Stairs, K. C.	30-9-18	K. in A.
84188	Cpl.	Stanley, R. C.	27-9-18	K. in A.
83934	A/Cpl.	Staples, A. H.	11-5-17	K. in A.
84031	Gnr.	Staton, S. N.	21-10-16	K. in A.
	Major	Steacy, W. E.	25-11-18	D. of D.
347544	Gnr.	Swift, W. J.	30-4-17	D. of W.
89982	Gnr.	Tabrott, J.	24-10-17	K. in A.
	Capt.	Taylor, G. V.	13-11-16	K. in A.
83160	Bdr.	Taylor, R. M.	8-1-16	K. in A.
413	Gnr.	Thomas, C.	14-1-16	K. in A.
	Lieut.	Thurston, A. M.	26-6-16	K. in A.
83939	Gnr.	Tiernan, A.	31-5-16	D. of W.
1258184	Gnr.	Tobin, E. T.	27-9-18	K. in A.
86862	Gnr.	Tozer, J. T.	2-10-18	D .of W.
	Capt.	Tuck, W. S.	30-10-16	K. in A.
84191	Gnr.	Turner, E.	28-2-16	K. in A.
	Major	Vansittart, G. E.	14-5-16	D. of W.
87051	Dvr.	Waggitt, J. G.	30-7-17	Drowned
	Major	Waldron, S. M.	4-5-17	K. in A.
301502	Dvr.	Walker, E.	28-9-17	D. of Inj.
1250210	Gnr.	Wallace, G. C.	29-9-18	K. in A.
83264	A/Cpl.	Warden, E. A.	16-9-17	D. of Inj.
42763	Cpl.	Wareham, S. B.	11-11-18	K. in A.
84195	Gnr.	Warren, H.	20-3-16	D. of W.
	Lieut.	Watson, C. H.	11-8-18	K. in A.
87019	Gnr.	Watson, C.	20-11-17	D. of W.
83726	Cpl.	Welham, A.	29-9-18	K. in A.
301948	Dvr.	Werley, F. C.	1-11-17	D. of W.
84199	Gnr.	White, T. B.	26-4-17	K. in A.
83732	Gnr.	Whitten, F. S.	19-11-16	K. in A.
1250518	Dvr.	Williamson, B.	4-11-18	K. in A.
37283	Gnr.	Williamson, J.	2-8-18	D. of D.
1251853	Gnr.	Wims, T. P.	26-11-18	D. of D.
83990	Sgt.	Wingfield, G. A.	15-5-17	D. of W.
83454	Gnr.	Wishart, G.	28-1-18	D. of W.
443	Gnr.	Wood, J. S.	27-3-16	D. of W.
	Capt.	Zimmerman, A. L.	20-3-18	Acc. Kld.

Decorations

4th Brigade, C.F.A.

Regimental Number	Rank	Name	Decorations
	Capt.	Aitkens, L. J. B.	M.C., M. in D.
	Lieut.	Alexander, G. B.	M.M.
83355	B.S.M.	Allen, S.	M.M.
86886	Cpl.	Anderson, A.	Croix de Guerre (Belgian)
	Lieut.	Anderson, A. D.	M.M., M. in D.
	Lieut.	Armstrong, T.	M.M.
89667	Cpl.	Armstrong, T. E.	M.M.
	Major	Arnoldi, F. F.	D.S.O. and Bar, Order of St. Stanislaus with Swords,(2nd class) M. in D.
90023	A/Sgt.	Ash, E.	Croix de Guerre
	Capt.	Atkinson, T. J.	M.C.
	Capt.	Auld, J. C.	M.C. and Bar
84207	A/Cpl.	Bagg, V.	M.M.
348986	Gnr.	Baldwin, W.	M.M.
83628	A/Sgt.	Ball, C. D.	M.M.
89616	Dvr.	Bardy, L.	M.M.
83208	Sgt.	Beale, G. A.	M.M.
26527	Gnr.	Beck, C. L.	M.M.
90025	Sgt.	Bell, J. G.	M.M.
83889	Gnr.	Bennett, A.	M. in D.
86695	Gnr.	Bennett, J. T.	M.M.
83891	Cpl.	Bennett, R. S.	M. in D.
	Lieut.	Bennett, R. C.	M.M.
89984	R.S.M.	Birch, E.	D.C.M.
83627	Sgt.	Blackburn, A.	M.M.
83127	Sgt.	Boaden, G.	M.M.
	Capt.	Bond, F. G.	M.C.
	Major	Bovill, K. H.	M.C., M. in D.
86401	Dvr.	Brown, H.	M.M.
89506	Cpl.	Brown, W.	M.M.
87030	A/Bdr.	Bryce, A.	M.M.
90034	Gnr.	Bullis, H. E.	M.M.
1258261	Cpl.	Burke, A. E.	M.M.
	Lieut.	Burrage, J. A. H.	M.M.
319955	Gnr.	Button, P. H.	M.M.
	Lieut.	Cagney, A. F.	M.C., M.M. and Bar
161	Sgt.	Campbell, A.	M.M.
86897	Cpl.	Campbell, J.	M.M.
8185856	F/Sgt.	Champion, J. H.	M.M.
90021	Sgt.	Clarke, G. G.	M. in D.
86647	Sgt.	Clements, E. G.	M.M.
	Lieut.	Cole, D. H.	M.M.
83635	Cpl.	Cole, J. P.	M.M.
83964	A/Sgt.	Coutts, J. R.	M.M.
	Lieut.	Cowan, A. J.	M.C.
83995	Bdr.	Cox, S. H.	M.M.
83186	Cpl.	Crawford, J.	M.M.
	A/Lt. Col.	Culver, A. E.	M.C.
	Lieut.	Davidson, J.	M. in D.
300254	Sig.	Davis, A. R.	M.M.
	Lieut.	Davis, H. J.	M.M.

Regimental Number	Rank	Name	Decorations
83904	Bdr.	Dimond, R.	M.S.M.
	Lieut.	Donnolly, J. T.	D.C.M., **M.M.**
300466	A/Sgt.	Downton, F. H.	M.S.M.
	Major	Drew, G. L.	D.S.O., M. in D.
348967	Gnr.	Ewen, J. D.	M.M.
	Lieut.	Fairbrother, A.	Croix de Guerre (Belgian)
	Capt.	Finney, W. J.	O.B.E., M. in D.
83221	Dvr.	Fitzpatrick, J. B.	M.M.
476606	Cpl.	Gaspard, A. G.	M.M.
86707	Dvr.	Gilbert, J.	M.M.
84131	Bdr.	Gilliland, H. W.	M.M.
	Capt.	Gillis, A. A.	M.C.
	Lieut.	Gillis, C. H.	M.M.
87026	Sgt.	Gordon, A. C.	M.M.
	Lieut.	Gossage, B. F.	M.C.
	Lieut.	Greer, S. R.	M.C.
84135	Dvr.	Griffin, M.	Croix de Guerre
86916	Sgt.	Gunn, R. B.	M.M.
84142	Cpl.	Hale, H.	M.M.
2043506	Sgt.	Hamblin, W. J.	M.M. and Bar
157059	A/Sgt.	Hamilton, W. S.	M.M.
	Lieut.	Hampson, A.	M.S.M.
83397	Sig.	Hann, F. E.	M. in D.
84143	Sgt.	Harris, E. J.	D.C.M.
	Major	Harris, W. E.	M. in D.
261	Bdr.	Head, J. F.	M.M.
303606	Gnr.	Heaton, H.	M.M.
	Major	Hendrie, W. I. S.	M. in D.
	Lieut.	Hill, G. R. L.	M.M.
540018	Sig.	Hilliard, R.	M.M.
316917	Gnr.	Hoshall, W. A.	M.M.
	Lieut.	Humphries, W. G.	M.C.
83955	Bdr.	Jackson, A.	D.C.M., **M.M.**
86930	Cpl.	Jackson, W.	M.S.M.
1668	Spr.	Jacobs, S.	M.M.
34740	Sgt.	James, W. F.	M.S.M.
2040518	Dvr.	Jamieson, A.	Croix de Guerre (Belgian)
342161	Gnr.	Johnston, O. O.	M.M.
83994	Sgt.	Kappler, G. M.	M.M.
	S/Capt.	Kelly, L. St. George	M.C., M. in D.
86934	Gnr.	Kelso, J. L.	M.M.
	Lieut.	Kenneally, J. L.	D.C.M.
	Capt.	Kent, R.	M.C.
316925	Gnr.	King, B.	M.M.
83404	Bdr.	Kirkpatrick, N.	M.M.
300247	Gnr.	Klock, J. M.	M.M.
	Lieut.	Larkin, H. W.	M.C.
55086	A/Sgt.	Law, J.	M.M.
	Capt.	Leather, E. R.	M.C.
83851	Sgt.	Lee, E.	M.M.
	Lieut.	Lewis, A. C.	M. in D.
303601	Bdr.	Lidstone, R. M.	M.M.
83852	Sgt.	Litherland, C.	M.M.
	Capt.	Lovelace, E. J.	M.C., M. in D.
83866	Gnr.	Maloney, C.	M.M.
	Major	Martin, C. K. C.	D.S.O., M. in D
84247	Sgt.	Martin, G. S.	M.M.
	Lieut.	Mason, A. D.	M.C. and Bar, **M.M.**
89916	Sgt.	Mathews, S. G.	M.M. and Bar
	Capt.	Maunder, J. F. C.	M.C., M. in D.
	Lieut.	Merry, F. S.	M.C.
106	Sgt.	Mersereau, B. M.	M.M. and Bar

Regimental Number	Rank	Name	Decorations
1250035	Gnr.	Miller, D.	M.M.
87028	Sgt.	Miller, L. G.	M.M.
90085	Cpl.	Miller, R. C.	M. in D.
83177	Cpl.	Miller, W.	M.M.
	Lieut.	Milne, F. C.	M. in D.
316952	Cpl.	Mitcham, A. J.	M.M.
40073	Sgt.	Moffat, L. C.	M.M.
83619	B.S.M.	Monro, R. S.	M.M., M. in D.
84159	A/Sgt.	Morden, G. A.	M.S.M.
619	Cpl.	Morison, C. K.	M.M.
	Capt.	Morse, F. G.	M.C.
	Capt.	Mortimore, A. R.	M. in D.
83922	Gnr.	Mundell, W. C.	M.S.M., M. in D.
730032	Gnr.	Murray, A.	M.M.
1250626	Gnr.	Murray, J. A.	M.M.
	Lieut.	Murray, W. J. R.	M.M.
83978	B.S.M.	Mylchreest, W.	M.M., M. in D.
84000	Q.M.S.	MacAndrew, J. L.	Croix de Guerre (Belgian)
90105	Gnr.	McCallum, D.	M.M.
1078	Gnr.	McCallum, F. A.	M.M.
	Capt.	McConkey, B. B.	M.C.
84169	Bdr.	McCreith, L. V.	M.M.
	Lieut.	McDonald, A. B.	M. in D.
91679	Bdr.	McIlraith, H. S.	M.M.
	Major	McKechnie, D. W.	D.S.O., M. in D.
	Lieut.	McKenna, V.	M.C.
	Capt.	MacKenzie, J. A.	D.S.O.
	Lieut.	McLaren, D. B.	M.M.
103	B.S.M.	McLaskey, A. W.	M.M.
28772	Sgt.	MacMillan, A.	M.M.
87062	Sgt.	McMillan, C. D.	M.M.
86665	Sgt.	MacNaughton, J.	M.M.
	Major	McSloy, J. I.	D.S.O., M. in D.
86969	Sgt.	O'Boyle, R. F.	M.M.
	Capt.	O'Brien, T. H.	M.C.
	Capt.	O'Halloran, M.	M.C.
	Lieut.	Oliver, R. R.	M.C., M. in D.
342838	Gnr.	O'Neill, M. C.	M.M.
300528	Sgt.	Overs, G.	M.M.
83707	Gnr.	Paget, A. J.	M.M.
	Lieut.	Palmer, F. A.	D.C.M.
84041	Sgt.	Palmer, H. J.	M.M.
397	Sgt.	Phelan, C.	M.S.M., M. in D.
	Lieut.	Phillips, A. H.	M.M., M. in D.
	Major	Powell, V. H. de B.	M.C.
	Lieut.	Purchas, C. M. G.	M.C.
86199	Bdr.	Rait, D.	M.M.
	Capt.	Read, J. E.	M. in D.
	Capt.	Reid, L. A.	M.C.
	Lieut.	Richardson, W. F.	M.M.
86979	Dvr.	Riley, J.	M.M.
83426	B.S.M.	Rimmer, W. B.	D.C.M.
	Major	Robson, S.	D.S.O.
1257803	A/Bdr.	Ross, D. G.	M.M.
	Lt. Col.	Ross, M. N.	D.S.O. and Bar, M. in D.
	Lieut.	Routh, W. B.	M.M.
90073	Sig.	Rowland, W. J.	M.M.
	Lieut.	Rowley, T. H.	M. in D.
805145	Sig.	Samis, J. C.	M. in D.
1260289	Gnr.	Saunders, G. E.	M.S.M.
	Major	Savage, H. M.	D.S.O. and Bar, M. in D.
84220	Sgt.	Schofield, S.	M.M.
	Col.	Sharman, C. H. L.	C.M.G., C.B.E., Order of St. Vladimir (4th class) with Swords

Regimental Number	Rank	Name	Decorations
	Capt.	Shaw, W. E.	M. in D.
	Major	Sifton, C.	D.S.O., M. in D.
	Lieut.	Simmonds, J. F. L.	M.C.
	Lieut.	Smith, C. A.	M.C.
84280	Gnr.	Soulsby, E.	M.M.
86731	Bdr.	Stanbridge, R. R.	M.M.
41340	F/Sgt.	Starkey, J. S.	Croix de Guerre (French)
	Major	Steacy, W. E.	M.C.
	Lt. Col.	Stewart, J. C.	D.S.O., M. in D.
	Lieut.	Stubbs, J. R.	M.C.
86981	B.S.M.	Studdert, P.	D.C.M.
86684	Gnr.	Thom, J.	M.M.
301495	A/Sgt.	Thompson, A.	M.M.
	Hon./Capt.	Thompson, R. F.	M.C.
	Lieut.	Thompson, S.	M. in D.
83773	Sgt.	Tinning, S. E.	M.M.
83487	S/Sgt.	Todd, R.	D.C.M.
	Capt.	Townsley, W. A.	M.C.
	Lieut.	Trewhitt, J. A.	M.C., M.M.
	Major	Vansittart, G. E.	M. in D.
	Capt.	Vernon, W. H.	O.B.E.
83731	Gnr.	Waldron, S. E.	M.M.
	Lieut.	Walter, N. P.	M.M.
89530	Cpl.	Ware, R. H.	M.M. and Bar
42763	Cpl.	Wareham, S. B.	M.M.
84036	Gnr.	Watson, C. E.	M.M.
	Capt.	Webster, H.	M.C., M. in D.
301564	Bdr.	Wiedenhamer, A.	M.M.
84246	Dvr.	West, W. E.	M.M.
	Lieut.	West, W. R.	M.C.
83954	Sgt.	Whall, N.	M.M.
90053	Bdr.	Wheeler, P. W.	M.M. and Bar
91514	Bdr.	Whittaker, J.	M.M.
	Lieut.	Whitehead, F. C.	M.C.
84203	B.S.M.	Whitehead, W. B.	La Medaille d'Honneur avec glaives, en argent.
123123	Gnr.	Wiese, T. E.	M.M.
337926	Gnr.	Wilding, T.	M.M.
	Lieut.	Wilson, G.	M.M.
348757	Gnr.	Wilson, H. A.	M. in D.
	Lieut.	Wilson, S. H.	M.C.
84221	Sgt.	Woods, P.	M.M.
	Major	Wright, W. G.	M.C.
83858	Cpl.	Yardley, T.	D.C.M., M.M.
	Capt.	Zimmerman, A. L.	M. in D.

Nominal Roll

4th Brigade, C.F.A., C.E.F.

Number	Rank	Name	Decorations	Wounded	Disposition	Date
86883	Cpl.	Abbott, G.		29-9-18	Demob.	27-8-19
417	Gnr.	Abbott, W. T.			M.U.	4-3-19
342897	Gnr.	Acton, C. J.			Demob.	27-5-19
83360	Gnr.	Adam, F. R.		9-5-17	M.U.	25-3-20
91574	Gnr.	Adam, G. D.			M.U.	11-7-19
348885	Gnr.	Adams, W. G.			Demob.	29-5-19
1260252	Sgt.	Adderley, F. A.			Demob.	20-12-19
2050686	Gnr.	Agnew, C. H.			Demob.	27-5-19
83776	Gnr.	Aiken, J. M.			M.U.	20-1-19
89859	Cpl.	Aitchison, T. F.		8-11-17	M.U.	10-4-19
2522563	Gnr.	Aitken, E. D.			Demob.	27-5-19
1250733	Gnr.	Aitken, R. .G			Demob.	10-6-19
	Capt.	Aitkens, L. J. B.—M.C., M. in D.		31-7-17	Demob.	30-6-19
	*Lieut.	Aldous, H. N.			S.N.L.R.	15-9-17
83863	Dvr.	Aldridge, H.			Demob.	23-4-19
	*Lieut.	Alexander, G. B.—M.M.		28-9-16	Demob.	26-3-19
83747	Bdr.	Alexander, J.		27-9-18	Demob.	24-9-19
316851	Dvr.	Alford, W.			Demob.	27-5-19
87065	Gnr.	Allan, J. S.			Demob.	21-3-19
	*Lieut.	Allardyce, A. T.		11-10-16	Demob.	16-7-19
339645	Gnr.	Allardyce, W. J.		21-1-18	R.M.S.	11-11-18
84014	Cpl.	Allder, R. C.		27-9-18	Demob.	16-5-19
86871	Q.M.S.	Alldritt, G. F.			Demob.	29-5-19
1250491	Gnr.	Allen, A. F.			Demob.	29-5-19
349666	Gnr.	Allen, B.			Demob.	11-2-19
83882	Dvr.	Allen, C. W.			Demob.	25-7-19
1251113	Gnr.	Allen, G.			Demob.	14-3-19
83355	B.S.M.	Allen, S.—M.M.			Demob.	21-5-19
84101	Gnr.	Alton, D. G.			K.I.A.	31-10-16
1251142	Bdr.	Alton, T. J.		2-11-18	Demob.	5-4-19
73	Gnr.	Amos, J.			K. I. A.	3-5-17
83359	Cpl.	Anchor, H.			M.U.	15-4-18
86886	Cpl.	Anderson, A.—Croix de Guerre (Bel.)			Demob.	15-8-19
83777	Gnr.	Anderson, B. S.			K.I.A.	26-8-17
84102	Sgt.	Anderson, D.		28-10-17	M.U.	29-10-18
87064	A/Cpl.	Anderson, G.		24-4-17	M.U.	14-8-20
34734	**Sgt.	Anderson, J.			Demob.	25-8-19
153348	Gnr.	Anderson, J. E.			Demob.	23-4-19
1258269	Gnr.	Anderson, L. E.		5-6-17	Demob	29-5-19
83862	Sgt.	Andrews, C.		5-5-17	Demob.	18-9-18
83152	Gnr.	Anger, H. F.			Demob.	24-5-19
83623	Gnr.	Antrobus, H.		14-8-17	Demob.	11-8-19
334882	Gnr.	Appleby, F. C.			Demob.	17-8-19
90046	Gnr.	Appleton, H. J.			Demob.	27-5-19
83125	Gnr.	Archer, W. C.		2-11-17	D.of W .	9-11-17
83624	Cpl.	Archibald, J.			Demob.	11-7-19
345817	Gnr.	Armi, W. A.			Demob.	24-6-19
300523	Dvr.	Armour, W.			D.of D.	15-12-18
339879	Gnr.	Armstrong, E.		24-4-17	D.ofW.,UK.	17-5-17
83613	Bdr.	Armstrong, I. E.			M.U.	13-9-18
84253	Gnr.	Armstrong J. F.		24-9-16	Demob.	26-5-19
	*Lieut.	Armstrong, T.—M.M.		4-2-18	D.ofW.	18-2-18
89667	Cpl.	Armstrong, T. E.—M.M.		18-10-17 2-9-18	Demob.	30-5-19
83358	Cpl.	Arnold, H.			Demob.	27-5-19
	Major	Arnoldi, F. F.—D.S.O., Bar, Order St. Stanislas with swords, 2nd class M. in D.			Demob.	17-7-19
90023	A/Sgt.	Ash, E.—Croix de Guerre			Demob.	6-2-19
83888	Dvr.	Ashbrooke, G. R.			Demob.	29-6-19

*Served as O.R. only with 4th Bde., C.F.A.
**C.A.V.C.

Number	Rank	Name	Decorations	Wounded	Disposition	Date
36	Dvr.	Ashburne, R. J.		31-3-16	D.ofW.	31-3-16
83622	Gnr.	Ashford, B.		4-3-18	Demob.	15-4-19
91132	Gnr.	Ashton, J.			Demob.	12-4-19
348946	Dvr.	Ashworth, C. W.			Demob.	23-7-19
	Lieut.	Atkin, J. P. H.			D.ofD.	4-2-19
	Capt.	Atkinson, T. H.—M.C.			Demob.	27-5-19
476579	Bdr.	Atwell, A.		12-11-17	Demob.	21-2-19
	Capt.	Auld, J. C.—M.C., Bar		1-5-16	Demob.	6-1-19
				28-9-18		
91128	Bdr.	Austen, S. H.			Demob.	27-5-19
83357	Gnr.	Austin, A. G.			M.U.	24-3-19
	Lieut.	Avery, C. R.			Demob.	12-3-19
83356	Gnr .	Avis, (R.			M.U.	25-6-18
40327	Gnr.	Barber, W.			A.C.I.A.	14-12-17
84207	A/Cpl.	Bagg, V.—M.M.		27-9-18	Demob.	8-2-19
84009	Gnr.	Bailey, F.			D.ofD.	11-3-16
83361	Sgt.	Bailey, G. T.		24-9-16	D.ofW.	24-9-16
83897	Bdr.	Bailey, H. V.			Demob.	25-5-19
339040	Gnr.	Bailey, P. H.		21-4-17	M.U.	10-7-19
348151	BQMS.	Bailey, E.			Demob.	27-5-19
86892	Gnr.	Baillie, Q.		13-11-17	Demob.	15-8-19
89383	Gnr.	Baird, B.			Demob.	3-4-19
86888	Dvr.	Baird, J.		5-11-17	Demob.	15-3-19
83466	Dvr.	Baird,W. G.			M.U.	22-1-19
300904	Gnr.	Baker, C. B.			M.U.	8-3-18
89651	Gnr.	Baker, S.		24-10-17	Demob.	15-7-19
341135	Gnr.	Baker, T. E.			Demob.	11-7-19
517	Dvr.	Baker, W.		29-9-18	Demob.	27-9-19
83362	Gnr.	Baker, W. R.			M.U.	9-5-18
	Lieut	Balch, R. E.			Demob.	10-5-19
83629	Sgt.	Baldwin, E.		20-10-17	K.I.A.	4-3-18
348986	Gnr.	Baldwin, W.—M.M.		6-11-17	Demob.	28-2-19
83628	A/Sgt.	Ball, C. D.—M.M.			A.C.I.A.	21-9-18
83170	Gnr.	Ball, F. C.		19-6-16	Demob.	25-5-19
89972	Cpl.	Ball, H. G.			Demob.	27-5-19
86896	Cpl.	Bamber, W.			Demob.	5-7-19
1250503	Gnr.	Banbury, L. A.			K.I.A.	17-4-17
87067	Dvr.	Bancroft, H.			Demob.	9-4-19
83218	Dvr.	Bannagan, T.			Demob.	17-5-18
89616	Dvr.	Bardy, Louis—M.M.			Demob.	3-7-19
84215	Gnr.	Barlow, F. C.			M.U.	23-8-18
86894	Gnr.	Barnes, F.		5-4-17	Demob	15-2-19
451394	Dvr.	Barr, F.			Demob.	18-5-19
2043553	Dvr.	Barstow, M.			Demob.	6-6-19
172	Dvr.	Barton, A. F.		29-10-17	Demob.	6-6-19
86893	A/Sgt.	Bassett, W.		16-8-18	Demob.	27-8-19
40372	Dvr.	Bathgate, G.			C.G.	22-9-18
300446	Dvr.	Bateman, J. H.			Demob.	27-5-19
83187	Gnr.	Bayley, H. E.			M.U.	23-1-18
334693	Gnr.	Bayliss, L. P.			Demob.	27-5-19
83208	Sgt.	Beale, G. A.—M.M.			Demob.	28-5-19
83033	Gnr.	Bearman, T.			Demob.	26-5-19
334639	Gnr.	Beattie, C. G.			Demob.	27-5-19
83575	Gnr.	Beauvis, J. A.			Demob.	11-7-19
83498	Gnr.	Beaty, R.			Demob.	9-5-19
26527	Gnr.	Beck, C. L.—M.M.		12-5-15	Demob.	27-5-19
2657101	Gnr.	Becker, A. H.			Demob.	12-4-19
104154	Gnr.	Beeching, S. E.			Demob.	15-2-19
40144	A/Sgt.	Beeching, W. E.		5-5-15	Demob.	21-1-19
339112	Dvr.	Beer, L.			Demob.	14-7-19
339478	Gnr.	Bell, B. R.			M.U.	2-4-18
	Lieut.	Bell, C. H.		3-10-16	D.ofW.	30-10-16
90025	Sgt.	Bell, J. G.—M.M.			K.I.A.	18-10-17
89534	S/Sgt.	Bell J. H.			Demob.	11-10-18
150031	Sgt.	Bell, R. T.		24-4-17	Demob.	29-5-18
				17-10-17		

Number	Rank	Name	Decorations	Wounded	Disposition	Date
84107	Dvr.	Bell, W.			Demob.	25-5-19
248739	Gnr.	Bellefountaine, M.			Demob.	2-6-19
248620	Dvr.	Bellfountain, L.			Demob.	15-6-19
87072	Sgt.	Bemis, F. K.			Demob.	3-3-19
91265	Spr.	Bender, P. H.			Demob.	20-8-19
83742	Gnr.	Benn, S. F.			Demob.	27-5-19
83190	Dvr.	Bennett, A. D.			Demob.	27-5-19
83889	Gnr.	Bennett, A.—M. in D.			Demob.	31-5-19
83740	A/Bdr.	Bennett, G. G.			M.U.	14-3-18
86695	Gnr.	Bennett, J. T.—M.M.			Demob.	17-7-19
83753	Dvr.	Bennett, P. J.		30-9-18	Demob.	19-8-19
83891	Cpl.	Bennett, R. S.—M. in D.			Demob.	31-5-19
	Major	Bennett, R. O. G.—M.C.			Demob.	20-9-19
	Lieut.	Bennett, R. C.—M.M.			Demob.	7-4-19
228006	Bdr.	Bennett, W. R.			Demob.	6-7-19
	Lieut.	Benson, A.		29-10-17	Demob.	19-9-19
552891	Gnr.	Benson, A. H.			Demob.	23-8-19
520	Gnr.	Benson, C. W.			Demob.	29-5-19
432974	Gnr.	Benton, F.			Demob.	18-7-19
89865	Gnr.	Benton, J. G.			Demob.	29-3-19
86055	Gnr.	Berard, A.		15-10-16	M.U.	26-1-18
76	Gnr.	Berton, C.		7-6-18	Demob.	23-1-19
83614	Sgt.	Bescoby, F. H.			T.C.P.S.	16-12-18
83785	Gnr.	Bibby, A.			K.I.A.	10-11-16
317012	Gnr.	Biddle, H. G.			M.U.	18-4-18
48726	Sgt.	Biggs, J.			Demob.	19-8-19
83892	Cpl.	Bing, A.		28-8-18	Demob.	25-5-19
338956	Gnr.	Bingham, F. A.			Demob.	29-1-19
89984	R.S.M.	Birch, E.—D.C.M.			Demob.	27-5-19
84026	Bdr.	Bird, S.		26-9-16		
				1-5-17	Demob.	25-5-19
206	Gnr.	Birkett, F. F. C.			S.C.	24-12-17
294	Dvr.	Birkett, W. G.		25-8-16	D.of W.	25-8-16
315975	Gnr.	Bishop, J. D. C.		16-7-17	M.U.	11-4-18
89861	Gnr.	Black, G. S.		30-10-17	D.of W.	23-11-17
83627	Sgt.	Blackburn, A.—M.M.			Demob.	27-5-19
83507	A/Bdr.	Blackman, H. M.			Demob.	25-8-19
86395	Dvr.	Blackman, W. E.			Demob.	2-5-19
91374	Dvr.	Blackmore, G. W.		8-5-17		
				28-9-18	Demob.	27-5-19
339384	Gnr.	Blair, A.			C.G.	11-4-18
47086	Dvr.	Blake, C. O.			Demob.	6-7-19
341215	Gnr.	Blakey, H. B.			Demob.	27-5-19
	Capt.	Bland, A. G.			Demob.	9-6-19
86490	Dvr.	Blanks, A. J.			Demob.	29-5-19
	*Capt.	Blayney, Y.			Demob.	6-7-19
83127	Sgt.	Boaden, G.—M.M.			Demob.	27-5-19
91263	Gnr.	Boaprey, C. L.			Demob.	27-5-19
751658	Cpl.	Boettger, H. S.			Demob.	11-7-19
86397	Dvr.	Bolland, R.		1-6-17		
				30-9-18	Demob.	1-6-19
90010	Bdr.	Bolton, F. G.			K.I.A.	30-10-17
	Capt.	Bond, F. G.—M.C.		15-6-19	K.I.A.	29-10-17
1251003	Gnr.	Bonell, L. F.			Demob.	16-10-19
302360	Gnr.	Bommer, W.			K.I.A.	3-11-17
349355	A/Sgt.	Booth. F. W.			Demob.	27-2-19
90075	Gnr.	Booth, H.		20-11-17	D.of W.	20-11-17
336913	A/Sgt.	Borque, E. V.			Demob.	3-3-19
1258079	Gnr.	Boutilier, V.			Demob.	17-5-19
	Major	Bovill, K. H.—M.C., M. in D.			Demob.	20-8-19
83755	Dvr.	Bowers, J. J.			Demob.	17-5-19
90170	A/Sgt.	Bowser, G. A.			M.U.	21-1-19
90231	Bdr.	Boyce, H.			Demob.	30-3-19
2163416	Gnr.	Boyd, J. D.			Demob.	1-6-19
84103	Dvr.	Boyle, R.			Demob.	25-5-19
83222	A/Sgt.	Bradley, E.			M.U.	1-2-19

*Served as O.R. with 4th Bde. C.F.A.

Number	Rank	Name	Decorations	Wounded	Disposition	Date
330150	Gnr.	Bradley, F.			Demob.	5-2-19
83626	Bdr.	Bradley, J. H.			Demob.	17-5-19
83001	R.S.M.	Brain, G. S.			M.U.	19-11-18
90164	Gnr.	Brand, J. E.			Demob.	7-2-19
300571	Gnr.	Bray, W. O.			M.U.	1-8-18
83617	Cpl.	Brazier, G. L.		19-11-16	M.U.	9-3-18
84105	Gnr.	Breay, E. C. P.			D.ofD. inCan.	12-10-18
83213	Gnr.	Brelsford, P.			M.U.	4-5-18
83365	Gnr.	Bremmer, W.			Demob.	27-5-19
83123	*Spr.	Brennan, T. F.			Demob.	27-3-19
92945	Gnr.	Breton, L.			Demob.	6-9-19
83123	Cpl.	Brewer, A. E.			Demob.	27-5-19
83942	Gnr.	Brewer, G.			Demob.	28-5-19
83741	Dvr.	Brewer, W.			Demob.	11-7-19
300165	**Sig.	Bridge, N. H.		15-11-16	Demob.	16-6-19
	Lieut.	Bridges, H. A.			Demob.	11-6-19
	Lieut.	Briggs, W. A.		19-8-18 30-10-18	M.U.	10-9-19
84219	Gnr.	Brill, C.		11-9-18 27-9-18	M.U.	7-2-19
83364	Dvr.	Brimmer, F.			Demob.	27-5-19
83189	Bdr.	Brittenden, F.			Demob.	12-8-19
338106	Sig.	Broddy, F. M.		2-10-18	Demob.	27-5-19
83150	Gnr.	Bromley, A. G.		25-4-17	Demob.	24-1-19
	Lieut.	Brooke, H. G.		6-11-17 27-9-18	Demob.	29-5-19
172044	Dvr.	Brookes, A.			Demob.	28-5-19
83496	Gnr.	Brooks, H. F.			Demob.	21-5-19
91136	Dvr.	Brooks, W. W.			Demob.	27-5-19
76129	A/Sgt.	Broome, W. T.			App. F.C., R.A.F.	13-9-18
86890	A/Bdr.	Brophy, D.			Demob.	3-8-19
220252	Dvr.	Brown, A.			Demob.	27-5-19
	Capt.	Brown, A. M.			Demob.	25-1-20
300467	Gnr.	Brown, C. V.			Demob.	17-5-19
301383	Sgt.	Brown, G. W. A.			Demob.	27-5-19
	***Lieut.	Brown, G. K.			Demob.	3-3-19
	Lieut.	Brown, H, D.			Demob.	27-7-19
86401	Dvr.	Brown, H.—M.M.			Demob.	29-5-19
349455	Gnr.	Brown, H.		16-8-18	Demob.	24-2-19
300339	Gnr.	Brown, H. W.			Demob.	27-5-19
83009	Gnr.	Brown, J. L.			To Com.	8-2-16
83366	Dvr.	Brown, R.			S.C.	31-8-17
83518	Gnr.	Brown, S. J.			M.U.	25-11-18
141349	Dvr.	Brown, T.			K. (Acc.)	22-10-16
	Lt./Col.	Brown, W. J.			Demob.	6-5-20
89506	Cpl.	Brown, W.—*		15-8-18	Demob.	24-4-19
339462	Gnr.	Bruford, W. P.			K.I.A.	24-10-17
87030	A/Bdr.	Bryce, A.—M.M.			Demob.	5-11-19
2139026	Gnr.	Buchanan, D.			Demob.	1-6-19
339436	Gnr.	Buchanan, H.			Demob.	20-3-19
84213	S/Sth.	Buckberrough, C. W.			M.U.	10-5-16
84223	*Pte.	Buckland, E. H.			Demob.	10-5-19
85493	Gnr.	Buckner, A.			Demob.	20-5-19
83363	Dvr.	Budd, W.			Demob.	17-7-19
84108	Cpl.	Bull, H. C.		19-8-18	M.U.	17-1-19
1250413	Gnr.	Bull, S. E.			Demob.	29-5-19
83235	S/Sgt.	Bullen, E.			Demob.	25-5-19
90034	Gnr.	Bullis, H. E.—M.M.			Demob.	26-5-19
334915	Dvr.	Bullock, R.			Demob.	27-5-19
83853	Gnr.	Burgess, H.		14-5-17	M.U.	1-4-19
87141	**Sig.	Burgess, W. R.			M.U.	12-12-18

*Last Unit, C.R.T.
**Last unit 4th Div. Sig. Coy.
***Served as O.R. with 4th Bdr. C.F.A.
*C.A.M.C. attached

Number	Rank	Name	Decorations	Wounded	Disposition	Date
1258261	Cpl.	Burke, A. E.—M.M.		3-10-18	Demob.	26-8-19
2557472	Gnr.	Burley, A. H.			Demob.	27-5-19
91578	A/Bdr.	Burley, W. F.		8-9-17	D.ofW.	9-9-17
89507	Bdr.	Burnett, W. B.			M.U.	27-9-18
343150	Gnr.	Burnham, G. E.			Demob.	27-5-19
86889	Gnr.	Burns, J.		31-10-18	Demob.	31-5-19
84003	A/Sgt.	Burns, M. C.		24-5-16	A.F.C.	
					R.A.F.	31-3-18
	Lieut.	Burrage, J. A. H.—M.M.			Demob.	31-5-19
177561	Gnr.	Burrows, S. T.		30-10-17	Demob.	25-1-19
300027	Dvr.	Burton, A.		5-11-16		
				24-8-18	Demob.	22-5-18
337860	A/Sgt.	Burton, C. E.			A.F.C.	
					R.A.F.	2-8-18
87027	Gnr.	Bury, G. M.			Demob.	29-5-19
83224	Gnr.	Busby, E. L.			Demob.	8-8-19
342823	Gnr.	Bush, A. R.			K.I.A.	5-11-17
37417	Gnr.	Butler, J.			Demob.	27-5-19
84234	Gnr.	Butler, W.			Demob.	16-5-19
2085338	Gnr.	Button, F.			M.U.	13-1-19
319955	Gnr.	Button, P. H.—M.M.			Demob.	27-5-19
	Lieut.	Cagney, A. F.—M.C., M.M.Bar		27-4-17		
				2-11-17		
				28-8-18	Demob.	2-6-19
412696	Gnr.	Cairns, J. H.			Demob.	27-5-19
337863	Gnr.	Calbeck, A. G.		2-11-17	Demob.	30-11-18
83220	Cpl.	Calder, C. P.		18-8-18	Demob	21-2-19
90088	Cpl.	Caldwell, G.			Demob.	21-5-19
83770	Bdr.	Calliphronas, C.		21-4-17	Demob.	1-6-19
89156	Gnr.	Callon, T.			M.U.	21-2-19
317039	A/Sgt.	Cameron, H. D.		7-1-18	M.U.	15-3-19
	*Capt.	Cameron, L. W.			Demob.	30-8-19
316863	Cpl.	Cameron, R. C.		27-9-18	Demob.	4-2-19
161	Sgt.	Campbell, A.—M.M.		9-10-16	Demob.	17-5-19
1251523	Bdr.	Campbell, D. D.		2-10-18	Demob.	22-1-19
340177	Gnr.	Campbell, E. D.			Demob.	27-5-19
85926	Dvr.	Campbell, H. R.			M.U.	17-1-19
86897	Cpl.	Campbell, J.—M.M.		29-10-17	Demob.	28-7-19
210056	Gnr.	Campbell, J. D.		13-11-17	D.ofW.	13-11-17
348907	A/Bdr.	Campbell, S. K.			Demob.	27-5-19
83636	Dvr.	Campbell, S.			D.ofD.	2-3-19
334031	Gnr.	Cannon, E. P.		30-9-18	Demob.	27-5-19
349401	Gnr.	Capel, G .R.			Demob.	27-5-19
83244	Gnr.	Card, J.			M.U.	31-3-19
2601906	Gnr.	Carey, G. W.			Demob.	7-6-19
316865	Gnr.	Carey, H. G.			Demob.	5-7-19
349485	Gnr.	Carey, I. A.			Demob.	18-1-19
	A/Capt.	Carley, H. B.			R.inU.K.	17-6-19
22121	Dvr.	Carlile, A. D.			Demob.	21-5-19
2045056	Sig.	Carpenter, F. J.		9-11-17	Demob.	8-7-19
346031	Gnr.	Carpenter, G. E.			Demob.	27-5-19
340896	Gnr.	Carpenter, H. L.			Demob.	11-3-19
316866	Dvr.	Carpenter, W.		19-4-17		
				1-11-18	Demob.	27-5-19
338434	Gnr.	Carr, H.			Demob.	27-5-19
83497	Gnr.	Carr, W. T.			Demob.	13-5-19
84011	Dvr.	Carrick, T.			Demob.	17-9-19
248726	Gnr.	Carrington, G.			Demob.	27-3-19
90015	Sgt.	Carrol, W.		27-9-18	Demob.	14-3-19
	Lt. Col.	Carruthers, G. A.			Surplus	20-12-17
318964	Gnr.	Carson, I. J.		26-10-17	M.U.	18-2-19
64	Gnr.	Carson, J. H.		26-10-17	M.U.	29-1-19
91526	Gnr.	Carter, E.		30-9-18	Demob.	27-5-19
90057	Gnr.	Carter, J.			M.U.	22-1-18
40616	Cpl.	Carter, V. W.		4-10-16	Demob.	30-8-19
89973	Gnr.	Carter, W.			M.U.	31-12-17

*C.A.D.C. att. to 4th Bde. C.F.A.

Number	Rank	Name	Decorations	Wounded	Disposition	Date
	*Lieut.	Casey, E. L.			Demob.	30-4-19
339678	Dvr.	Caspell, E. V.			Demob.	6-4-19
84115	Gnr.	Cassidy, J.			M.U.	8-12-17
533	Gnr.	Castle, J. H.			Demob.	14-5-19
83865	Bdr.	Catchpole, B. E.		7-8-16	Com. in R.F.C.	20-6-17
75327	Gnr.	Catchpole, G. H.			K.I.A.	11-5-17
83867	Gnr.	Catchpole, L. A.			Demob.	30-5-19
83372	Gnr.	Catterall, H.		17-4-16	M.U.	21-10-18
300449	Bdr.	Cavanah, O. O. V.		2-10-16	Demob.	1-4-19
316869	Dvr.	Caveen, F. J.			Demob.	27-5-19
83630	Gnr.	Caveen, T. E.		25-10-16	M.U.	4-10-19
84114	Dvr.	Caveney, J. A.			M.U.	10-4-18
86901	Dvr.	Chalkley, A.		3-9-18	Demob.	31-3-19
83977	Gnr.	Challicom, O.			K.I.A.	17-10-16
83854	S/Sgt.	Challis, J. R.			Demob.	18-8-19
83771	Cpl.	Chalmers, T. D.			Demob.	6-6-19
273364	Dvr.	Chamberlain, A. G.			M.U.	26-11-18
83241	Gnr.	Chamberlain, C.			M.U.	30-9-17
83104	Gnr.	Chamberlain, J. J.			M.U.	6-11-18
83968	A/Sgt.	Chamberlain, J.		29-7-16	M.U.	10-1-19
84	Gnr.	Chamberlain, L. C.		10-11-17	M.U.	26-2-19
476592	Gnr.	Chamberlni, A.		26-4-17	D.ofW.	6-5-17
86858	F/Sgt.	Champion, J. H.—M.M.			Demob.	29-5-19
	Lieut.	Chaplin, A.			K.I.A.	3-5-17
83010	Gnr.	Chapman, A.			M.U.	5-12-15
433	Dvr.	Chapman, J.		8-8-18	D.ofW.	8-8-18
349329	Gnr.	Chaput, R.			Demob.	27-5-19
85295	Gnr.	Charbonneau, T.		2-4-16	K.I.A.	24-11-16
83171	A/Sgt.	Charlton, P.			Demob.	17-1-20
342269	Dvr.	Charsley, R. P.			Demob.	27-5-19
84116	A/Sgt.	Chauncy, R. J.		11-4-17	Demob.	18-8-19
84110	Dvr.	Cheshire, P. R.			Demob.	3-7-19
84240	Bdr.	Chester, W. M.			Demob.	31-3-19
83756	Gnr.	Childs, J. H.			Demob.	30-12-19
87077	Gnr.	Chisholm, C. A.			Demob.	20-2-19
441515	Pte.	Chisholm, W.			M.U.	5-4-19
338388	Dvr.	Choles, W. G.			M.U.	21-8-19
	Lieut.	Chown, W. F.			Demob.	28-5-19
83621	Cpl.	Christian, E.		29-3-18	M.U.	20-2-19
540010	Gnr.	Christie, R. A.			Demob.	27-5-19
	*Lieut.	Christopherson, J.			Demob.	26-4-19
2045027	Dvr.	Chusuk, T.		5-11-17	M.U.	16-9-18
300458	A/Bdr.	Clancy, V. E.			Demob.	26-5-19
83900	Gnr.	Clark, B.		29-10-17	M.U.	10-1-19
83373	Dvr.	Clark, E.		26-5-16 28-1-18 30-9-18	M.U.	3-3-19
83634	Gnr.	Clark, H. G.			M.U.	29-6-18
316	A/Bdr.	Clark, P. M.			Demob.	27-5-19
85289	Gnr.	Clark, P. W.		18-11-17	Demob.	17-1-19
	*Lieut.	Clark, R. L.		18-11-17	Demob.	3-4-19
210	Dvr.	Clark, R. G.			Demob.	27-5-19
84117	Gnr.	Clark, S. N.			K.I.A.	8-11-16
84113	B.S.M.	Clark, W.			Demob.	12-5-19
335824	Bdr.	Clarke, A. B.			Demob.	6-6-19
343809	Sgt.	Clarke, G. C.		6-8-18	Demob.	15-7-19
90021	Sgt.	Clarke, G. G.—M. in D.			Demob.	27-5-19
300810	Gnr.	Clarke, T.		14-11-18	Demob.	5-5-19
521032	Bdr.	Clarke, T. E.			M.U.	11-3-19
300851	Gnr.	Clarkson, G. H.			Demob.	23-1-19
316871	Gnr.	Clarkson, H. W.		19-4-17	M.U.	8-8-18
160878	Dvr.	Clausen, A.			Demob.	31-5-19
84028	Gnr.	Clayton, F. J.		19-11-17	Demob.	25-5-19
83368	Gnr.	Cleaves, H.		30-7-16	Demob.	27-5-19

*Served as O.R. only with 4th Bde., C.F.A.

Number	Rank	Name	Decorations	Wounded	Disposition	Date
	Lieut.	Cleeves, A. C.			Demob.	30-12-18
86647	Sgt.	Clements, E. G.—M.M.		18-10-17	Demob.	14-4-19
86702	Gnr.	Clent, E.		21-1-18	M.U.	15-2-19
84021	Gnr.	Clifford, T.			M.U.	11-1-19
84111	Bdr.	Clough, H. S.		30-8-18	Demob.	25-5-19
613	Dvr.	Clynick, J.		25-11-16	D.ofW.	25-11-16
339419	A/Sgt.	Coates, W. W.			A. F. C. in R.A.F.	21-6-18
300539	Bdr.	Cobb, S. F.			K.I.A.	16-6-17
300721	A/Cpl.	Cochrane, A.		28-10-17	Demob.	12-4-19
86356	Gnr.	Coffin, F. G.			Demob.	29-5-19
258230	Gnr.	Coldwell, E. B.			Demob.	15-6-19
	Lieut.	Cole, D. H.—M.M.		11-8-18	Demob.	23-5-19
86410	Dvr.	Cole, E.			Demob.	29-5-19
83635	Cpl.	Cole, J. T.—M.M.			Demob.	27-5-19
334157	Gnr.	Coleman, L. G. S.			Demob.	27-5-19
86902	A/Bdr.	Coleman, W.			K.I.A.	5-11-17
83252	Gnr.	Colgate, W. G.			Demob.	27-5-19
334245	Sig.	Collins, E. C.			Demob.	27-5-19
83632	Sgt.	Collins, F. W.			Demob.	12-7-19
83129	Cpl.	Collis, A. H.			Demob.	27-5-19
451809	Gnr.	Collis, J. A.			Demob.	28-5-19
84228	Gnr.	Colwell, G. A.		7-10-16	M.U.	20-4-18
125001	Gnr.	Congdon, C. A.			Demob.	15-6-19
91628	Cpl.	Conner, A. N.		6-8-18	M.U.	20-8-19
87058	Cpl.	Conner, C. A.		23-4-18	Demob.	27-5-19
43854	Gnr.	Connolly, A.		12-10-16	D.ofW.	27-10-16
83751	A/Sgt.	Connolly, J. A.			Demob.	17-2-19
1257827	Dvr.	Cook, G.			Demob.	27-5-19
85184	Sgt.	Cook, G. F.		11-8-18	Demob.	27-5-19
248556	Gnr.	Cook, M.			Demob.	17-7-19
84281	Gnr.	Cooke, A. W.			M.U.	31-12-17
335041	Bdr.	Cooke, F. A. E.			Demob.	21-9-19
2044151	Gnr.	Cooksley, J. R. R.			Demob.	27-5-19
305514	Gnr.	Coon,, R. A.		6-2-18	D.ofW.	6-2-18
85856	Gnr.	Cooper, J. P. G.		14-5-17	Demob.	19-8-19
83355	Bdr.	Cooper, W. G. G.		2-10-16	Demob.	11-8-19
1251267	Gnr.	Cope. W. R.			Demob.	27-5-19
83369	Dvr.	Coppley, H.			M.U.	31-8-17
347472	Cpl.	Corbett, J. A.		26-9-18	Demob.	12-7-19
331767	Dvr.	Cormack, G.		21-10-17	Demob.	30-8-19
371	Dvr.	Corn, T.		9-11-16	Demob.	29-5-19
1251636	Dvr.	Cornell, H. M.			Demob.	27-5-19
341827	A/Bdr.	Cornish, A.			Demob.	27-5-19
84035	Gnr.	Cornish, J. S.			Demob.	30-5-19
84118	Dvr.	Cornish, T.			M.U.	26-3-19
86882	Gnr.	Cornish, W. C.		16-7-17	Demob.	29-5-19
86017	Gnr.	Cornthwaite, Wm.			K.I.A.	29-10-17
315	Dvr.	Corp, C. N.			K.I.A.	8-9-17
339033	Gnr.	Corpe, E. H.			Demob.	14-7-19
90198	A/Bdr.	Cosgorve, J.			Demob.	20-5-19
84112	Gnr.	Cosh, M. A.			Demob.	30-6-19
	Lieut.	Cossitt, E. C.			Demob.	28-5-19
788940	Gnr.	Costello, Wm. Peter			Demob.	5-6-19
13861	Gnr.	Cottrell, R. J.		15-5-17 16-9-18	M.U.	1-3-19
321853	A/Sgt.	Couch, L. T.			Demob.	11-2-19
84235	Sgt.	Couling, J. A.		12-11-17	Demob.	25-5-19
84109	Dvr.	Courtier, F. T.		3-9-18	D.ofW.	4-9-18
89975	Dvr.	Cousineau, N.			Demob.	2-6-19
89873	Dvr.	Cousins, J. H.		22-5-17	Demob.	27-5-19
83964	A/Sgt.	Coutts, J. R.—M.M.		18-11-16	M.U.	25-3-19
84020	A/Sgt.	Coutts, S. M.			App. F.C. in R.A.F.	30-8-18
	Lieut.	Cowan, A. J.—M.C.			Demob.	26-6-19

Number	Rank	Name	Decorations	Wounded	Disposition	Date
89870	Gnr.	Cowan, A. R.		5-11-17	Demob.	20-2-19
1250900	Gnr.	Cowell, G. M.			Demob.	30-5-19
1251548	Gnr.	Cowie, W. C.			Demob.	7-1-19
83995	Bdr.	Cox, S. H.—M.M.		5-4-18	M.U.	23-1-19
437324	Dvr.	Craddock, V. O.			Demob.	11-6-19
348428	Sig.	Craig, W. E.		30-9-18		
				4-1-18	M.U.	18-10-19
349038	Gnr.	Crawford, J.			Demob.	6-4-19
83186	Cpl.	Crawford, J.—M.M.			Demob.	25-5-19
504954	Gnr.	Crawford, J.		11-5-17	Demob.	27-5-19
40148	Gnr.	Crawford, J. A.		3-5-15	Demob.	13-5-19
87023	Sgt.	Creighton, L.		19-10-17	Demob.	27-5-19
1251388	Gnr.	Creighton, W. K.			Demob.	31-5-19
345095	Gnr.	Cressey, H. S.			Demob.	27-5-19
83633	Dvr.	Cripps, W. J.		1-5-17	Demob.	3-3-19
83370	- Cpl.	Crocker, F.			D.ofD.	8-7-16
338009	Gnr.	Cronk, S. C.		24-2-18	Demob.	6-6-19
83371	Gnr.	Cropper, J. A.			M.U.	11-3-19
799708	Gnr.	Cruden, J. S.		11-8-18		
				1-10-18	M.U.	25-3-19
	A/Lt. Col.	Culver, A. F.—M.C.			Demob.	13-5-19
	Lieut.	Cumming, A. R.			Demob.	18-9-19
86903	Pte.	Cummings, R.			Demob.	18-9-19
271	Gnr.	Cundiff, A.			Demob.	26-7-19
301165	Gnr.	Curley, J. M. F.			M.U.	13-7-18
41435	Gnr.	Currie, J. A.		22-8-17	D.ofW.	23-8-17
83374	Gnr.	Currie, T.			K.I.A.	21-4-17
	Lieut.	Curtis, N.		8-5-17	M.U.	1-5-18
84236	Dvr.	Cusick, H. W.			Demob.	13-5-19
	Lieut.	Cushing, A. G.		2-5-17	Demob.	17-3-19
83225	**Saddler	Dalby, J. T.			Cess. of W. Pay	8-9-16
83473	Gnr.	Dalling, W. V.			D.ofD. in Can.	19-10-16
85153	Gnr.	Daly, J. E.			M.U.	31-1-18
83640	A/Bdr.	Daly, J.		18-8-18	Demob.	27-3-19
83379	Bdr.	Daniels, A.			K.I.A.	24-9-16
87071	Cpl.	Daniel, G.		1-10-17	D.ofW.	1-10-17
83174	Gnr.	Danvers, J.		8-9-18	M.U.	12-3-19
1260277	Bdr.	Darby, H. J.			Demob.	21-5-19
83901	A/Sgt.	D'Arcy, R.			M.U.	14-1-19
83605	B.S.M.	Darling, J. F.		4-9-17		
				29-10-17	M.U.	9-6-18
2152325	Gnr.	Darrin, L. T.			Demob.	27-5-19
203	Dvr.	Davidson, A.			M.U.	15-1-19
	Lieut.	Davidson, A. R. W.		22-7-17	M.U.	30-11-17
339482	A/Bdr.	Davidson, G. R.			Demob.	29-5-19
	*Lieut.	Davidson, J.—M. in D.		24-4-17	M.U.	24-10-19
				5-10-18		
89878	Gnr.	Davidson, S.			M.U.	16-11-18
83513	Gnr.	Davies, D. G. W.			Com. Imp. Army	12-10-15
83641	Gnr.	Davies, F.			Demob.	26-4-19
348883	Gnr.	Davies, H. A.			Demob.	25-3-19
340898	Gnr.	Davies, L. L.			Demob.	21-1-19
300758	Gnr.	Davies, O. L.		16-10-16	Demob.	6-8-19
300254	Sig.	Davis, A. R.—M.M.		4-11-18	M.U.	15-10-19
344805	Sig.	Davis, F. W.			Demob.	1-4-19
	*Lieut.	Davis, H. J.—M.M.			To Res. Med. S.	23-10-18
336847	Dvr.	Davis, S. P.			M.U.	25-1-19
	Capt.	Daw, P. F.			To Res. Civil O.	16-8-18
83375	Gnr.	Dawson, E.		29-9-18	D.ofW.	2-10-18

**Also served in C.M.P.C., 20-7-17 to 23-12-18.
*Served as O.R. only with 4th Bde., C.F.A.

Number	Rank	Name	Decorations	Wounded	Disposition	Date
335311	Gnr.	Dawson, E. E.			Demob.	27-5-19
84214	Sgt.	Day, A.			M.U.	·20-12-16
636578	Gnr.	Daynard, G. W.			Demob.	27-5-19
83903	Dvr.	Debling, A.			M.U.	27-3-19
348083	Dvr.	Debling, A.		3-9-18	M.U.	18-6-19
83864	Gnr.	Debling, S.			Demob.	9-5-19
335983	Gnr.	Deen, C.			M.U.	16-5-18
338931	Gnr.	Delamatr, H. A.			Demob.	31-7-19
83957	Gnr.	Dennison, H.		31-5-16	M.U.	31-8-17
104203	Gnr.	Dennison, R.		6-11-17	D.ofW.	15-11-17
88	Dvr.	Denniston, L. M.			Demob.	17-5-18
84122	Dvr.	Denton, R. J.			Demob.	23-6-19
343317	Gnr.	Desjardins, C.			Demob.	27-5-19
2001052	Gnr.	Deltor, J. A.			M.U.	8-5-18
83642	Gnr.	Devitt, J.		25-10-16	M.U.	28-5-19
	Lieut.	Dewberry, A. B.			Demob.	10-4-19
343139	Gnr.	Dewolfe, L. A.			Demob.	27-5-19
87020	Gnr.	Dickie, P.			Demob.	15-3-19
340877	Gnr.	Dickson, H. E.			M.U.	15-11-18
84225	Dvr.	Dimmock, G. E.		23-8-16	M.U.	7-9-17
83904	Bdr.	Dimond, R.—M.S.M.			Demob.	15-8-19
84121	Sd|r.	Dingle, C.			Demob.	20-5-19
2085465	Sig.	Dix, F. W. W.			Demob.	27-5-19
84010	*Dvr.	Dixon, H.			M.U.	31-3-16
	Major	Dixon, J.		3-5-17	M.U.	10-2-20
335966	Dvr.	Dixon, M. C.		20-4-17	Demob.	6-6-19
530531	Dvr.	Dixon, T.			Demob.	27-5-19
90055	Dvr.	Dixon, W.			Demob.	27-5-19
83381	Cpl.	Dodd, H. S.			Demob.	5-8-19
476536	Dvr.	Dodd, S.		5-5-17	Demob.	22-6-19
84124	Gnr.	Dodds, V. E.		9-4-17		
				30-8-18	Demob.	29-3-19
337880	Bdr.	Dodge, L. W.		30-10-18	M.U.	28-4-19
	Capt.	Doheny, C. W.		27-1-18	Demob.	26-11-19
34116	Gnr.	Dominy, T. P.		4-9-18	Demob.	12-7-19
89510	Dvr.	Donald, J.			Demob.	4-7-19
84120	Gnr.	Donaldson, A.		31-10-16	D.ofW.	2-11-16
349649	Cpl.	Donaldson, J. T.			Demob.	27-5-19
	**Lieut.	Donnolly, J. T.—D.C.M., M.M.			Demob.	8-4-19
1261185	Gnr.	Doucet, G. S.			Demob.	18-7-19
89879	Dvr.	Doucette, M.			Demob.	20-3-19
349073	A/Bdr.	Douglas, G. K.		22-8-17	Co. Gr.	15-3-18
83377	Bdr.	Douglas, G.		10-5-17	D.ofW.	10-5-17
349074	Gnr.	Douglas, J. W.		26-2-18	Demob.	21-1-19
5950	Gnr.	Douglas, R.		26-3-16		
				3-11-17	D.ofW.	3-11-17
344030	Gnr.	Douglas, N. J.			Demob.	22-5-19
86124	Cpl.	Douglas, R. A.			K.I.A.	18-10-17
303662	Gnr.	Douglas, W.			Demob.	21-11-19
83138	Gnr.	Dow, A. A.			Demob.	17-5-19
91582	Bdr.	Dowell, J.		7-10-16	Demob.	26-5-19
89854	Dvr.	Dowbiggin, E. E.			Demob.	28-5-19
207322	Sig.	Dowd, W. J.			Demob.	27-5-19
	Capt.	Dowding, C. E.		22-9-17	To Res. Civil O.	28-6-18
344131	Gnr.	Downing, T. A.			Demob.	27-5-19
83122	Gnr.	Downward, W.			Demob.	20-8-19
89876	Cpl.	Downs, J.			K.I.A.	30-10-17
300466	A/Sgt.	Downton, F. H.—M.S.M.			Demob.	11-7-19
316886	Dvr.	Dowthwaite, F. S.		1-7-17	Demob.	31-3-19
344027	Gnr.	Doyle, F.			Demob.	27-5-19
83376	Gnr.	Drawbelle, F.			M.U.	19-4-19
	Lieut.	Drew, G. A.		5-5-16	M.U.	(6-6-19
	Major.	Drew, G. L.—D.S.O.,M. in D.			Demob.	10-2-19

*Also served in Special Service Co. from 15-2-17 to 15-10-17.
**Served as O.R. only with 4th Bde., C.F.A.

Number	Rank	Name	Decorations	Wounded	Disposition	Date
304017	Gnr.	Drummond, A.		10-4-17	Demob.	29-3-19
2101012	Sig.	Drury, K. C.			Demob.	11-5-19
340064	Gnr.	Drybrough, R. W.		28-5-17 9-4-18	Demob.	20-1-19
84119	Gnr.	Drysdale, A.			Demob.	27-3-19
83508	Gnr.	Duffield, G. E.			Demob.	3-3-19
83638	Gnr.	Duffy, W.		3-9-18	Demob.	13-3-19
83154	Gnr.	Dufton, J. H.		3-6-16	M.U.	5-7-19
83639	Bdr.	Dugdale, T.			Demob.	27-5-19
83178	Gnr.	Duke, J. H.			Demob.	28-5-19
83905	Gnr.	Duncan, J.			Demob.	24-5-19
317029	Bdr.	Duncan, W. J.			Demob.	27-5-19
1257783	Gnr.	Dunham, F. V. H.			Demob.	6-6-19
344034	Gnr.	Dunlop, P. J.		1-8-18	Demob.	22-5-19
83523	Dvr.	Dunn, A. T.			M.U.	30-1-18
1258262	Dvr.	Dunn, H.		17-8-17	Demob.	11-9-19
83887	Sgt.	Dustan, G. W.			M.U.	31-8-17
83380	Gnr.	Duval, E. C.			Demob.	27-5-19
84123	Gnr.	Duxbury, H.			Demob.	8-2-19
83382	Dvr.	Dyson, G.			Demob.	27-5-19
89802	Dvr.	Eadie, D.			Demob.	26-5-19
83906	Gnr.	Eadie, R.			M.U.	18-6-18
639679	Gnr.	Eagan, J. M.			Demob.	27-5-19
339428	Gnr.	Earl, T. E.		3-6-17	M.U.	12-8-18
2601976	Gnr.	Earsman, K. M.			Demob.	27-5-19
89994	Sig.	Eaton, S.		11-8-18	Demob.	25-8-19
83217	Gnr.	Eatwell, A.			M.U.	30-11-17
83943	Gnr.	Edgar, G.		29-11-17	Demob.	15-7-19
1260248	Gnr.	Edmonds, A. E.			Demob.	27-5-19
304067	Gnr.	Edmondson, R.			Demob.	27-5-19
83907	Dvr.	Edwards, E. L.		8-8-18	Demob.	23-6-19
83142	Dvr.	Edwards, F. H.			Demob.	29-2-19
83219	Gnr.	Edwards, F. W.		8-8-18	D.ofW.	22-9-18
83383	Gnr.	Edwards, G. T.			Demob.	27-5-19
83184	Dvr.	Egglestone, V. H.			Demob.	12-6-19
341876	Dvr.	Elliott, A. C.			Demob.	27-5-19
84025	Gnr.	Elliott, B.			M.U.	11-2-19
2601926	Gnr.	Elliott, L. G.			Demob.	30-7-19
	Lieut.	Elliott, L. H.			Demob.	18-1-19
355	Gnr.	Elliott, R. P.			App. C. I. Army	5-1-18
84126	A/Bdr.	Ellis, F. G.			M.U.	1-8-18
86650	Dvr.	Ellis, W.			Demob.	20-5-19
83664	Gnr.	Ellis, W. A.		22-5-17	Demob.	21-6-19
86907	Bdr.	Ellwood, W. E.			Demob.	12-7-19
83885	S/Sgt.	English, T.			M.U.	13-1-19
316889	Gnr.	English, T.			K.I.A.	28-10-17
83197	Gnr.	Erion, J. A.			Demob.	24-4-19
83646	Dvr.	Erskine, W. L.			Demob.	31-3-19
83645	Dvr.	Esber, G.			M.U.	17-3-17
181	Gnr.	Estey, R. H.		5-10-16	Demob.	15-7-19
87007	Dvr.	Etherden, S. G.			Demob.	29-5-19
428	Dvr.	Evans, F. W.			M.U.	10-3-19
2590878	Dvr.	Ewen, G. W.			Demob.	30-5-19
348967	Gnr.	Ewen, J. D.—M.M.		17-6-17	Demob.	27-5-19
84227	S/Sgt.	Exley, J. W.			Cess. of W. Pay	23-2-17
	*Lieut.	Fairbrother, A.—Bel. Croix de Guerre		17-10-16	Demob.	22-7-19
84005	A/Sgt.	Fairbrother, W.		3-5-17	Demob.	16-3-19
349158	Gnr.	Farrand, J.		18-4-17	M.U.	30-1-18
396891	Gnr.	Farrell, J. S.			Demob.	23-1-19
83012	Gnr.	Faulkner, C.			Demob.	7-8-19
1250041	Sig.	Fawcett, A. E.			Demob.	29-5-19
83648	Gnr.	Fell, R.			Demob.	14-3-19

*Served as O.R. only with 4th Bde., C.F.A.

Number	Rank	Name	Decorations	Wounded	Disposition	Date
86764	Dvr.	Ferguson, A.			K.I.A.	2-9-18
301174	Dvr.	Ferguson, D. J.		.	Demob.	27-5-19
907873	Dvr.	Ferguson, T.			M.U.	21-12-18
316892	Gnr.	Fick, E.			Demob.	23-1-19
317054	Dvr.	Fick, R.			Demob.	27-5-19
91632	Gnr.	Field, C. A.			Demob.	25-1-19
83242	Bdr.	Fielding, T.			K.I.A.	24-8-18
317056	Gnr.	Fife, C. W.			Demob.	27-3-19
40167	Gnr.	Finlayson, R. H.			Demob.	24-8-19
84125	Dvr.	Finch, A.			M.U.	13-2-18
346971	Gnr.	Finn, W. L.			Demob.	13-3-19
	Capt.	Finney, W. J.—O.B.E., M. in D.			Demob.	31-5-20
87025	Gnr.	Firby, H. E.		26-4-17	M.U.	31-12-20
859899	Gnr.	Firby, R. M.			Demob.	9-5-19
84127	Gnr.	Fischer. J. A.			Demob.	15-2-19
342882	Gnr.	Fitzgerald, D. L.		9-11-17	Demob.	27-5-19
26077	Cpl.	Fitzgerald, J.			Demob.	27-5-19
83221	Dvr.	Fitzpatrick, J. B.—M.M.			Demob.	27-5-19
1250566	Dvr.	Flath, W. W.			Demob.	17-5-19
300056	Gnr.	Flegg, E.			Demob.	5-6-19
542366	Gnr.	Fleming, C. R.			Demob.	27-5-19
89978	Dvr.	Fleming, G.			Demob.	29-1-19
343013	Dvr.	Fleming, J.			Demob.	27-5-19
83766	Bdr.	Fleming, R. D.			Demob.	31-3-19
83243	*Spr.	Fletcher, A.			Demob.	23-5-19
1251957	Gnr.	Fletcher, M. C.			Demob.	27-5-19
90145	Gnr.	Flieger, G. A.		28-3-18	Demob.	25-1-19
83433	Cpl.	Flower, A. E.			Demob.	30-8-19
337850	A/Bdr.	Flynn, M. J.			Demob.	27-5-19
84282	Gnr.	Foot, H. G.			Demob.	26-3-19
83649	Gnr.	Forbes, G. B.		30-10-17	M.U.	20-1-19
1251317	Dvr.	Ford, F.			Demob.	31-5-19
83257	Bdr.	Ford, G. K.			Demob.	27-5-19
89885	Gnr.	Ford, W. R.			Demob.	28-5-19
3057167	Gnr.	Forler, H. G.			Demob.	27-5-19
84128	Gnr.	Forrest, H.			Demob.	26-3-19
331632	Sig.	Forsyth, F. P.		27-10-17 11-9-18	Demob.	1-7-19
87038	Dvr.	Forsyth, J. B.			Demob.	25-5-19
316898	Gnr.	Forsyth, N. B.			M.U.	1-11-18
	Capt.	Forsyth, R.		8-5-17	Demob.	28-5-19
	**Capt.	Forsyth, W. W.			M.U.	15-7-19
83386	Sgt.	Foster, R.		30-9-18	M.U.	10-4-20
83384	A/Bdr.	Foster, S. J.			K.I.A.	8-5-17
319939	Dvr.	Foulds, A.		22-4-17	Demob.	8-4-19
	***Capt.	Fowler, C. H.		11-9-18	Demob.	1-4-19
1250685	Gnr.	Fowler, H. A.		24-11-17	Demob.	27-5-19
335865	Gnr.	Fowler, W. L.			D.ofD. in Can.	9-3-18
83227	Bdr.	Fox, C. H.			K.I.A.	30-4-16
1250736	Dvr.	Fraser, A. T.			Demob.	30-5-19
300454	L/Cpl.	Fraser, D. F.			Demob.	12-7-19
476790	Cpl.	Fraser, D.			Demob.	11-6-19
83155	A/Bdr.	Fraser, J.			Demob.	12-7-19
248702	Gnr.	Fraser, J. A.			Demob.	18-4-19
84208	Sgt.	Fraser, R.			Cess. of W. Pay	5-9-16
334558	Gnr.	Freel, W. O.			Demob.	27-5-19
1250821	Gnr.	Freeman, R. W.			Demob.	30-5-19
86908	Gnr.	Freeman, W.			M.U.	16-3-18
83260	S/Sth.	Fry, L.			Cess. of W. Pay	21-11-16

*Last unit C.R.T.
**C.A.V.C., att. 4th Bde., C.F.A.
***C.A.D.C.

Number	Rank	Name	Decorations	Wounded	Disposition	Date
****Lieut.	Fryer, S. T. J.		13-11-16	Surplus	15-9-17
341100	Gnr.	Fugard, R. D.		28-9-18	Demob.	15-2-19
349419	Dvr.	Fullard, C. H.			Demob.	3-7-20
141430	Dvr.	Fullerton, A.		19-10-17	Demob.	27-5-19
226245	Gnr.	Fuller, R. M.		30-9-18	M.U.	3-3-19
90074	Gnr.	Furneaux, W. A.			Demob.	24-5-19
83652	Dvr.	Gabriel, C. L.			Demob.	21-1-19
83974	A/Sgt.	Gabriel, P. E.		26-9-17	Demob.	16-6-19
83655	Cpl.	Gadbsy, L. R.			Demob.	4-7-19
341291	Gnr.	Gage, E.			Demob.	27-5-19
89179	Gnr.	Gagne, N.		13-7-16	K.I.A.	29-9-18
83606	Sgt.	Gailer, F. C.			D.ofInj.	16-9-15
84034	Dvr.	Gailer, G. M.			Demob.	31-7-19
	**Capt.	Galbraith, W. T.			Demob.	12-10-19
83651	F/Sgt.	Gale, A.			Demob.	12-4-19
2100266	Gnr.	Gallagher, E. J.			Demob.	13-7-19
2001301	Cpl.	Galliah, J. J.			Demob.	6-6-19
83788	Dvr.	Galloway, A. W.			M.U.	15-2-19
307694	Gnr.	Galloway, H. H.			Demob.	8-2-19
12	Dvr.	Gamson, S.		1-5-17 11-11-17	Demob.	29-1-19
335065	Gnr.	Garden, G. B.			Demob.	25-4-19
83209	Gnr.	Garlick, W. G. P.			M.U.	24-12-18
83387	Dvr.	Garner, B.			Demob.	6-6-19
342180	Bdr.	Garrison, F. W.			Demob.	27-5-19
40174	Dvr.	Garrison, J.			M.U.	19-2-19
334191	Gnr.	Garrison, J. F.			Demob.	13-4-19
476606	Cpl.	Gaspard, A. G.—M.M.		12-1-17	Demob.	31-1-19
84129	Gnr.	Gatward, Roland			D.ofD.	28-4-19
86917	Gnr.	Gault, H. A.			M.U.	11-3-18
87047	Gnr.	Gay, G. L.			Demob.	28-11-19
337829	Gnr.	Geddes, G. W.			Demob.	27-5-19
83013	Gnr.	German, D. P.			M.U.	10-11-16
40598	Gnr.	Gibbons, C. G.			Demob.	9-5-19
334242	Gnr.	Gibbs, E.			Demob.	27-5-19
84134	Gnr.	Gibbs, O. T.		24-4-16	D.ofW.	24-4-16
	*Capt.	Gibson, C.			Demob.	23-8-19
83784	Gnr.	Gibson, H.		11-6-16	Demob.	1-2-19
349351	Bdr.	Gibson-Pattinson, R.			Demob.	21-5-19
1251613	Gnr.	Gilbert, I. W.		2-5-17	Demob.	27-5-19
86707	Dvr.	Gilbert, J.—M.M.			Demob.	20-5-19
678176	Gnr.	Giles, M. H.			Demob.	27-5-19
84140	Gnr.	Gilham, F.		12-6-18 26-8-18	Demob.	7-2-19
	Lieut.	Gill, E. R.		13-10-16 30-9-18	M.U.	15-3-20
84033	Gnr.	Gill, F. H.			Demob.	25-7-19
86915	Cpl.	Gillen, F. C.			D.ofD.	7-6-19
229466	Gnr.	Gillen, W.			Demob.	4-7-19
83163	Cpl.	Gillespie, A.			Demob.	28-5-19
	A/Maj.	Gilles, A. R.		14-5-17	M.U.	30-11-17
84131	Bdr.	Gilliland, H. W.—M.M.		25-5-17 1-10-18	Demob.	23-4-19
83975	***A/Bdr.	Gillion, W. E.			Demob.	15-7-19
	***Lieut.	Gillis, A. A.—M.C.		13-6-16 11-6-17 20-8-17	Demob.	16-7-19
	****Capt.	Gillis, C. H.—M.M.			Demob.	8-9-19
90002	Gnr.	Gilmartin, W.		22-5-17 1-11-17	M.U.	21-1-19
83246	Gnr.	Gilmore, A.			M.U.	31-12-17

**C.A.V.C., att. 4th Bde. C.F.A.
*C.A.P.C. attached 4th Bde., C.F.A.
***Served in N. Russia with 16th Bde., C.F.A.
****Served as O.R. only with 4th Bde., C.F.A.

Number	Rank	Name / Decorations	Wounded	Disposition	Date
87032	Gnr.	Gilmore, G. C.		M.U.	14-11-18
87018	Dvr.	Gilmour, J.		Demob.	27-6-19
83126	Gnr.	Gilmour, R. P.		Demob.	29-5-19
1250415	Gnr.	Gilmour, W.		Demob.	29-5-19
2040621	Gnr.	Gilroy, A. H.		Demob.	21-8-19
2100448	Gnr.	Girouard, J. A.		Demob.	6-6-19
334240	Sig.	Glass, A. J. E.		Demob.	27-5-19
89888	Dvr.	Gleason, J. P.		M.U.	2-1-19
84132	Gnr.	Glenfield, W.	3-9-18	Demob.	27-2-19
83997	Gnr.	Glennon, W. P.	28-9-16 26-10 17	Demob.	25-5-19
302529	Gnr.	Glover, R.		Demob.	26-7-19
304640	Gnr.	Godkin, F. A.		Demob.	27-5-19
1251415	Gnr.	Godsell, T.		Demob.	31-5-19
	Lieut.	Godwin, C. R. M.		K.I.A.	4-4-16
339191	Gnr.	Gold, W.		Demob.	13-6-19
84242	Gnr.	Goldie, T. L.		D.ofD.	28-8-16
84138	Gnr.	Goldsmith, G. A.		Demob.	26-5-19
	Lieut.	Goldston, R. G.		Demob.	25-3-19
83389	Cpl.	Goldstraw, E.	3-11-16	Demob.	12-8-19
89159	Gnr.	Goodman, A.		Demob.	26-5-19
90171	Cpl.	Goodwin, C. M.		Demob.	21-2-19
83615	Cpl.	Goodwin, R. A.		M.U.	11-3-18
195	Gnr.	Gordon, A. J.	13-8-17	Demob.	29-3-19
87026	Sgt.	Gordon, A. C.—M.M.		Demob.	29-5-19
	Lieut.	Gordon, A. R.	2-9-18	Demob.	31-12-18
254	Gnr.	Gordon, J.	23-5-17	Demob.	30-3-19
349478	Gnr.	Gordon, S. E.		Demob.	27-5-19
	*Lieut.	Gordon, S. H.		Demob.	27-4-19
342878	Gnr.	Gordon, T. E.		Demob.	31-5-19
	*Lieut.	Gordon, W. H.		K.I.A.	30-10-16
83191	F/Sgt.	Gosden, H.		Demob.	27-5-19
	Lieut.	Gossage, B. F.—M.C.		Demob.	26-6-19
342140	Gnr.	Gostenhofer, C. E.	14-8-18	Demob.	30-3-19
84137	A/Bdr.	Gough, E. G.	1-10-18	Demob.	26-3-19
84133	Dvr.	Gough, H.		M.U.	29-4-18
83952	Cpl.	Gould, J. B.	3-10-16	Demob.	25-5-19
83654	Sgt.	Goulder, C C.		Demob.	3-4-19
83609	Cpl.	Gout, G. D. V.		Com. in I. Army	9-7-15
1250230	Dvr.	Gowanlock, G. S.	30-8-17	Demob.	12-7-19
340849	Gnr.	Gracie, G. B.		Demob.	31-5-19
86913	Bdr.	Graham, D.		Demob.	7-8-19
300297	Gnr.	Graham, E. J.		Demob.	20-2-19
2085445	Gnr.	Graham, E. A.	31-10-18	Demob.	13-2-19
91163	Bdr.	Graham, H. W.	19-10-17	Demob.	15-2-19
2152399	Gnr.	Graham, M. B.		Demob.	21-8-19
349131	Gnr.	Graham, S.		Demob.	27-5-19
342857	Gnr.	Grant, D. N.		Demob.	27-5-19
84019	Gnr.	Graham, J. H.	14-5-17 27-9-18	M.U.	21-8-19
429	Gnr.	Grant, L.		Demob.	29-4-19
334153	Dvr.	Grant, R. R.		Demob.	27-5-19
83908	Gnr.	Grant, W.	2-10-16	Demob.	27-5-19
337915	Gnr.	Grasett, E. T.		M.U.	24-7-18
1251953	Gnr.	Gravel, J.		Demob.	27-5-19
349604	Dvr.	Gray, E.		Demob.	28-5-19
343930	Gnr.	Gray, F. W.		Demob.	27-5-19
300372	Cpl.	Gray, G. A.	18-4-17 27-9-18	Demob.	20-3-19
84136	Cpl.	Gray, H. G.	28-8-18	Demob.	26-3-19
337879	Gnr.	Gray, T.	21-4-17	Demob.	15-7-19
50490	Gnr.	Gray, W. H.		M.U.	16-11-18
46486	Gnr.	Green, A. S.	21-5-15	Demob.	15-5-19
183772	Cpl.	Green, C. L.	20-4-16	Demob.	13-3-19

*Served as O.R. only with 4th Bde., C.F.A.

Number	Rank	Name	Decorations	Wounded	Disposition	Date
	Major	Green, J. K. M.			Demob.	5-2-19
342107	Gnr.	Green, J. L.			Demob.	27-5-19
83949	F/Sgt.	Green, R.			Cess. of W. Pay	20-10-16
341073	Sig.	Green, W. R.		10-11-17	Demob.	27-5-19
83103	Gnr.	Greene, E. W.			M.U.	15-6-16
83656	Bdr.	Greenfield, S.		21-4-17	Demob.	17-2-19
349240	Gnr.	Greenleese, E. S.		28-9-18	M.U.	3-4-19
339569	Dvr.	Greenwell, C. W.			Demob.	15-6-19
91342	Gnr.	Greenwell, R.			Demob.	29-3-19
49676	Gnr.	Greenwood, A.			Demob.	23-9-19
	Lieut.	Greenwood, H. F. S.		13-8-17	Demob.	29-8-19
135150	Sig.	Greenwood, R. J.		30-10-17	Demob.	27-5-19
1251483	Gnr.	Greenwood, W. L.			Demob.	27-5-19
243970	Gnr.	Greer, J.			Demob.	5-4-19
	*Lieut.	Greer, S. R.—M.C.		21-10-16	Demob.	31-5-19
	Lieut.	Greey, D. C.		21-10-16	App. to R.A.F.	25-6-17
425	Gnr.	Gregg, J.		14-1-16 8-11-17	Demob.	18-3-19
87034	A/Bdr.	Gregg, P.		20-10-17	Demob.	16-7-19
342076	Gnr.	Gregor, J. R.			Demob.	27-5-19
2152323	Gnr.	Gregory, J. P.			Demob.	27-5-19
317030	Gnr.	Gregory, W.			Demob.	27-5-19
338293	Gnr.	Gregson, W.			Demob.	31-7-19
1054209	Sig.	Greig, A.			Demob.	27-5-19
83388	Gnr.	Grenstead, E.			Demob.	20-5-19
86918	Gnr.	Griffin, B.			Demob.	27-5-19
84135	Dvr.	Griffin, M.—Croix de Guerre		22-3-16 11-9-18	Demob.	25-3-19
1260222	Sig.	Griffin, S. H.			Demob.	11-4-19
317049	Cpl.	Griffiths, H. E.			M.U.	22-1-19
710	Dvr.	Grimes, E. J.			Demob.	27-5-19
1258276	Gnr.	Grimes, W. J.			Demob.	24-9-19
89892	Gnr.	Grimmond, G.			Demob.	11-9-19
84231	Gnr.	Grisdale, J. W.			Demob.	25-5-19
85171	Gnr.	Grundle, D. C.			Demob.	27-5-19
2163311	Bdr.	Grundy, R. A.			Demob.	29-5-19
87070	Dvr.	Gubbins, H.			Demob.	29-5-19
41796	Gnr.	Gulliver, R. A.			M.U.	7-3-18
83121	Gnr.	Gunn, A.			M.U.	6-2-18
86916	Sgt.	Gunn, R. B.—M.M.			Demob.	29-5-19
84209	Sgt.	Gutteridge, A. E.			M.U.	21-12-16
	Lieut.	Gwatkin, R.			Res Vet. Studies	12-9-18
119013	Gnr.	Hack, R. B.		19-11-16	Demob.	13-6-19
89896	A/Bdr.	Hackett, A.			Demob.	23-8-19
83745	Gnr.	Hadden, G.		25-10-16	Demob.	12-6-19
86921	Bdr.	Hagen, P.		3-5-17 3-11-18	Demob.	26-2-19
84142	Cpl.	Hale, H.—M.M.		12-10-16	Demob.	25-5-19
339393	Gnr.	Hall, A. H.			Demob.	2-12-18
2001054	Gnr.	Hall, F. C.		4-3-18	D.ofW.	9-3-18
83603	Sgt.	Hall, H. J.			Demob.	3-6-19
84146	Dvr.	Hall, H. E.			Demob.	19-4-19
83153	Gnr.	Halliday, C. G.		1-2-16	D.ofD.	29-11-16
89641	Gnr.	Hallihan, O.			Demob.	11-7-19
2043506	Sgt.	Hamblin, W. J.—M.M. and Bar			Demob.	29-5-19
339430	Dvr.	Hamilton, A.			Demob.	1-6-19
1250751	Gnr.	Hamilton, A. S.			Demob.	30-5-19
3231963	Gnr.	Hamilton. A. M.			Demob.	27-5-19
91387	Gnr.	Hamilton, H.		16-10-16 1-5-17	M.U.	14-1-18
157059	A/Sgt.	Hamilton, W. S.—M.M.			Demob.	6-2-19
1260595	Gnr.	Hamlyn, R. G.			Demob.	18-5-19

*Served as O.R. only with 4th Bde., C.F.A.

Number	Rank	Name	Decorations	Wounded	Disposition	Date
83754	Dvr.	Hammond, C.			Demob.	27-5-19
	*Lieut.	Hampson, A.—M.S.M.			Demob.	2-9-19
83668	Sgt.	Hancock, A.		11-6-18	Demob.	25-5-19
86019	A/Bdr.	Hancox, E. G.			Demob.	3-6-19
86927	Bdr.	Handyside, N.			Demob.	13-7-19
340890	Bdr.	Hanger, K. H.			Demob.	27-5-19
83761	Gnr.	Hankins, A. E.			Demob.	25-2-19
83397	Sig.	Hann, F. E. —M. in D.			Demob.	27-5-19
84015	Dvr.	Hanna, E.		9-9-18	Demob.	22-7-19
89343	Gnr.	Hannah, A. G.		26-5-18	Demob.	26-5-19
87054	Dvr.	Hanover, F. C.			M.U.	26-11-18
87053	Gnr.	Hanover, W. H.			Demob.	7-1-19
1250349	Bdr.	Hansen, C. A.			Demob.	1-7-19
83203	A/Bdr.	Hansford, W. H.			Demob.	25-5-19
336235	Gnr.	Hanson, E. I.			Demob.	6-6-19
349660	Gnr.	Hanson, H.			Demob.	5-6-19
86657	Sgt.	Hardement, H. P.		4-3-18	Demob.	30-5-19
84042	**Cpl.	Harding, T. R.			Demob.	30-9-19
89515	Gnr.	Hardisty, R. S.			App. F. C. in R.A.F.	24-6-18
83014	Gnr.	Hardman, K.		24-4-17	Demob.	24-4-19
760145	Dvr.	Hargreaves, T. W.			Demob.	17-2-19
83478	Gnr.	Harland, M. F.		8-5-17	Demob.	17-2-19
349921	Dvr.	Harper, T. H.			Demob.	19-3-19
84238	Gnr.	Harpin, H. E.			Drown.	20-10-16
273104	Dvr.	Harrigan, L.			Demob.	8-4-19
84144	Dvr.	Harrington, J.		21-9-16	M.U.	31-3-18
342081	Sig.	Harris, A. G. F.			Demob.	27-5-19
84143	Sgt.	Harris, E. J.—D.C.M.			Demob.	25-5-19
83661	Gnr.	Harris, H.			M.U.	25-1-19
83113	Dvr.	Harris, H.			Demob.	27-3-19
83663	Dvr.	Harris, J.			Demob.	23-4-19
187069	Dvr.	Harris, L.			Demob.	3-4-19
87002	Dvr.	Harris, T.			Demob.	29-5-19
	Major	Harris, W. E.—M. in D.			Demob.	2-4-19
336808	Gnr.	Harrison, A. S. B.		8-4-17	M.U.	13-8-18
89626	***Gnr.	Harrison, G.			Demob.	16-7-19
84004	R.S.M.	Harrison, H.			Demob.	4-4-19
87024	Gnr.	Harrison, L.			M.U.	26-4-19
83662	Gnr.	Harrison, R. H.			K.I.A.	21-4-17
83390	A/Bdr.	Harrow, F.		9-5-17	Demob.	14-3-19
83179	S/M.	Hart, E. W.			Com. in I. Army	19-8-15
829247	Gnr.	Hart, J. G.			Demob.	17-5-19
357	Gnr.	Hartley, J. C.		13-10-15	Demob.	27-8-19
83393	Dvr.	Harvey, A. C.		8-5-17	Demob.	29-5-19
83162	Gnr.	Harvey, J.		25-10-16	M.U.	14-1-19
86920	Sgt.	Harvey, M.			M.U.	22-7-18
1251011	Gnr.	Harvey, W.			K.I.A.	26-10-17
84040	Gnr.	Hastings, F.			M.U.	16-3-17
83658	Gnr.	Hately, J.			K.I.A.	21-8-17
2085323	Gnr.	Hathaway, J. W.			Demob.	8-1-19
316909	Gnr.	Hatton, F. T.			Demob.	19-5-19
301429	***A/Sgt.	Hawkins, F. S.		14-8-17	Demob.	18-10-19
90060	Gnr.	Hawkins, H.		7-9-17	M.U.	3-3-19
40815	Gnr.	Haworth, W.		19-8-17	Demob.	1-4-19
83391	Gnr.	Hayden, E.			Demob.	25-8-19
381	Dvr.	Haylor J.		4-9-18	D.ofW.	4-9-18
83395	Gnr.	Haynes, E.			App. F. C. in R.A.F.	4-10-18
210404	Dvr.	Haynes, J.			Demob.	27-5-19
210409	Gnr.	Haynes, W. A.			Demob.	27-5-19
87069	Dvr.	Head, C.		31-3-16	O. Rqt.	7-7-17

*Served as O.R. only with 4th Bde., C.F.A.
**4th Bde., C.F.A., U.K. only
***Served in N. Russia with 16th Bde., C.F.A.

Number	Rank	Name	Decorations	Wounded	Disposition	Date
261	Bdr.	Head, J. F.—M.M.		**6-7-17**		
				7-9-18	Demob.	31-3-19
339600	Gnr.	Healey, H. A.			Demob.	29-5-19
83665	Gnr.	Heath, L.		20-11-16	M.U.	31-7-17
335812	Gnr.	Heatlie, W. C.			Demob.	6-6-19
303606	Gnr.	Heaton, H.—M.M.		13-10-16		
				4-9-18	Demob.	19-9-19
83522	Gnr.	Heazley, J. L.			Deserter	9-7-15
126420	Gnr.	Hebden, J. W.			Demob.	27-7-19
341061	Gnr.	Hebert, M. C.			Demob.	11-7-19
341062	Gnr.	Helston, H. T.		6-8-18	M.U.	18-2-19
334215	A/Bdr.	Henderson, E. C.			Demob.	27-5-19
338120	Gnr.	Henderson, J. M.			Demob.	27-5-19
316023	Dvr.	Henderson, T. E.			M.U.	21-9-18
	Major	Hendrie, W. I. S.—M. in D.			Demob.	2-6-19
83667	Dvr.	Henry, A. H.			K.I.A.	31-8-18
337816	Gnr.	Henry, A. H.		3-9-18	D.ofW.	4-9-18
86130	Dvr.	Heppell, R.		3-11-17	D.ofW.	3-11-17
90058	Cpl.	Heppleston, A. E.			Demob.	27-5-19
342820	Sig.	Hepton, W. M.			Demob.	30-5-19
2085328	Gnr.	Hepworth, G.		6-11-17	D.ofW.	6-11-17
2042574	Gnr.	Herivel, A. C.			Demob.	11-6-19
90061	Dvr.	Hewitt, H.			Demob.	7-4-19
87033	Bdr.	Hewitt, J.		16-8-18	Demob.	29-5-19
339806	Gnr.	Hewson, A. T.		26-10-17	Demob.	19-2-19
83396	Gnr.	Heys, J.			M.U.	17-2-19
83746	Dvr.	Hickey, C. H.			Demob.	8-4-20
339030	Dvr.	Hicks, H.		10-8-18	D.ofW.	10-8-18
314670	Gnr.	Hie, I.		11-8-18	M.U.	21-3-19
83215	Dvr.	Hill, A. J.			M.U.	31-7-18
83247	*Gnr.	Hill, F. R.			D.ofD.	27-2-17
316912	Gnr.	Hill, F. T.		8-5-17	Demob.	27-5-19
	Lieut.	Hill, G. R. L.—M.M.		1-11-18	Demob.	27-5-19
83669	Gnr.	Hill, J. E.			D.ofW.	28-3-16
89514	A/Sgt.	Hill, L. A.		31-7-17	Demob.	31-5-19
2529	Gnr.	Hill, N. B.			Demob.	29-5-19
343056	Gnr.	Hill, R. E.			Demob.	27-5-19
1251138	Gnr.	Hillhouse, J.			Demob.	27-5-19
540018	Sig.	Hilliard, R.—M.M.		24-2-18	Demob.	27-5-19
2101023	Gnr.	Hines, S.			Demob.	15-6-19
341143	Gnr.	Hipkiss, C. H.			K.I.A.	3-9-18
40531	Gnr.	Hirst, J. T.		22-4-15	K.I.A.	3-11-17
83524	Gnr.	Hirst, J.			Demob.	23-5-19
83111	Gnr.	Hislop, G. W.			Demob.	27-5-19
86220	Gnr.	Hodgert, A.			M.U.	25-3-19
83910	Cpl.	Hodges, S.			D.ofD.	12-11-18
89895	Gnr.	Hodgin, L.			Demob.	27-5-19
83767	A/Sgt.	Hodgson, D. E.		22-5-17	Demob.	15-3-19
304161	Gnr.	Hoey, J. B.			Demob.	27-5-19
341811	Gnr.	Hogan, A. J.			K.I.A.	10-8-18
83666	Dvr.	Hogan, W. L.			Demob.	28-3-19
83781	A/Cpl.	Hoge, B. O.			**Demob.**	**2-12-19**
2044145	Gnr.	Hogg, J. E.		29-9-18	Demob.	19-5-19
349628	Dvr.	Holley, J. F.		2-9-18	Demob.	11-8-19
342103	Gnr.	Holmes, A. H. F.			Demob.	27-5-19
86286	Dvr.	Holmes, J.			K.I.A.	16-8-18
2001024	Gnr.	Holmes, L. T.			Demob.	27-5-19
1250865	Gnr.	Holmes, L.			Demob.	29-5-19
83232	Gnr.	Honess, G.			M.U.	28-1-19
83011	Gnr.	Honeycombe, W. H.			Demob.	27-5-19
200085	Dvr.	Hooey, G. F.			Demob.	1-6-19
86919	A/Cpl.	Hook, G. A.		3-5-17	D.ofW.	8-5-17
1250391	Gnr.	Hooper, G. C.			Demob.	21-3-19
1250392	Gnr.	Hooper, H. W.			Demob.	29-5-19
86922	Gnr.	Hooper, R.			Demob.	14-7-19

*4th Bde., C.F.A., U.K. only

Number	Rank	Name	Decorations	Wounded	Disposition	Date
334237	Dvr.	Hopkins, H. J.			M.U.	22-2-19
476620	Gnr.	Hornby, P. F.			M.U.	31-5-18
2601841	Gnr.	Horne, T. D.			Demob.	20-5-19
2041587	Gnr.	Horning, A. C.		29-9-18	Demob.	8-12-19
83394	Gnr.	Horrocks, W.			Demob.	28-5-19
90299	Cpl.	Horsnell, A.			Demob.	12-9-19
49429	Dvr.	Horton, E.			K.I.A.	17-9-16
335869	Gnr.	Horton, H.			Demob.	6-6-19
316917	Gnr.	Hoshal, W. A.—M.M.		30-9-18	Demob.	4-2-19
83392	A/Cpl.	Hoskins, F. G.			Demob.	18-9-19
311	Gnr.	Hough, G.		27-7-17	M.U.	14-2-18
83194	Gnr.	Houghting, A.			S. Case	28-7-17
301435	A/Bdr.	Hourd, A. P.		21-10 16	Demob.	27-5-19
1250239	Dvr.	Hourd, W. A.			Demob.	27-5-19
339840	Gnr.	Hourston, W. B. S.			M.U.	17-2-19
342346	Dvr.	Housego, A. J.			Demob.	27-5-19
219729	*Q.M.S.	Howarth, G.			Demob.	27-5-19
304694	Sig.	Howe, F. H.			Demob.	1-6-19
809060	Sig.	Howe, M. E.			Demob.	1-6-19
2522354	Gnr.	Howell, C. F.			Demob.	27-5-19
85202	Gnr.	Howell, W. A.			Demob.	27-5-19
3317	Dvr.	Howson, J. W. F.		28-9-15 18-1-16	M.U.	13-3-18
7786	Dvr.	Hoyland, W.			Demob.	20-5-19
83659	Gnr.	Hubbard, F.			M.U.	13-11-15
83953	A/Sgt.	Hubbard, T. S.			Demob.	7-2-19
316918	Gnr.	Hubert, D. R.			M.U.	16-12-18
341887	Gnr.	Hubble, F. R.			M.U.	11-7-18
340901	Dvr.	Huckstep, J. H.			M.U.	25-1-19
84147	Bdr.	Hudson, H. F.			M.U.	31-5-17
84141	Dvr.	Hudson, S. F.		3-9-18	Demob.	25-5-19
349146	Gnr.	Hughes, J.			Demob.	28-5-19
84237	Gnr.	Hughes, P. W.		9-11-17	M.U.	5-3-19
86923	Sgt.	Hughes, R.			Demob.	14-3-19
86924	Dvr.	Hughes, R.			Demob.	30-5-19
300431	Gnr.	Hughes, R. G.			Demob.	5-6-19
2001007	Gnr.	Hugg, A.			Demob.	28-2-19
461	A/Bdr.	Hulbert, A. H.		5-7-17	Demob.	3-4-19
84211	Dvr.	Hummell, J. F.		19-9-16	M.U.	31-8-17
	Lieut.	Humphries, W. G.—M.C.			Demob.	27-3-19
259	**Gnr.	Hunt, A.			Demob.	15-7-19
85310	Dvr.	Hunt, M.			Demob.	15-8-19
	***Capt.	Hunter, A. H.			Demob.	4-1-19
83664	Dvr.	Hunter, J.			Demob.	27-5-19
90062	Bdr.	Hunter, J. C.			Demob.	27-5-19
1251580	Gnr.	Hunter, R. T.		30-9-18	Demob.	13-6-19
2099931	Gnr.	Huntingford, G.		30-9-18	Demob.	6-6-19
340816	Gnr.	Hurst, W. F.			Demob.	12-7-19
83216	Dvr.	Hurst, W.			Demob.	11-1-19
788879	Sig.	Hurteau, J.		31-10-17 10-8-18	Demob.	20-1-19
339791	Gnr.	Hutchins, F. G.			M.U.	13-6-19
83911	Gnr.	Hutchinson, S.		15-5-17	M.U.	21-3-19
83782	Gnr.	Hutchinson, W. M.			Demob.	2-4-19
1251661	Dvr.	Hutchison, B. G.			Demob.	28-5-19
90065	Bdr.	Hutchison, J. C.			K.I.A.	30-9-18
	Capt.	Huycke, E. D.		31-5-16	Demob.	14-5-19
	Lieut.	Huycke, W. F.			Demob.	28-5-19
310839	Gnr.	Hyfield, J. A.		13-1-18 4-11-18	Demob.	27-5-19
83912	Gnr.	Inger, G.			Demob.	24-1-19
916773	Gnr.	Ingle, A.			M.U.	22-1-19
84148	Pte.	Ingham, W.			M.U.	24-4-19

*C.O.C. attached 4th Bde., C.F.A.
**Served in North Russia with 16th Bde., C.F.A.
***C.A.V.C. attached 4th Bde., C.F.A.

Number	Rank	Name	Decorations	Wounded	Disposition	Date
83031	Sgt.	Ingraham, R. E.			Com. I. Army	28-10-15
86929	Bdr.	Ingram, G.			Demob.	21-5-19
339480	Gnr.	Irvine, R. L.		21-1-18	Demob.	14-4-19
2099938	Gnr.	Irving, J. W.			Demob.	6-6-19
	*Col.	Irving, L. E. W.			Demob.	31-8-19
348940	Gnr.	Irwin, J. B.			Demob.	27-5-19
316920	Sgt.	Ives, R. E.			Resume Med. S.	28-11-18
310758	Dvr.	Ivory, G. W.		10-11-17	Demob.	5-7-19
84149	Gnr.	Jack, P.			M.U.	7-5-18
83955	Bdr.	Jackson, A.—D.C.M., M.M.			M.U.	30-7-18
83883	Bdr.	Jackson, J.			K.I.A.	3-5-17
40581	Sgt.	Jackson, M.			Demob.	6-6-19
328933	Dvr.	Jackson, S. C.			Demob.	12-5-19
83913	Gnr.	Jackson, T. C.			M.U.	4-2-19
86930	Cpl.	Jackson, W.—M.S.M.			Demob.	10-8-19
83950	Gnr.	Jacobs, G. A.			Demob.	27-5-19
1668	Spr.	Jacobs, S.—M.M.			Demob.	2-6-19
341933	Gnr.	Jaggard, E. J.			Demob.	8-4-19
83886	Sgt.	Jagger, C.			M.U.	26-1-17
83618	**Gnr.	James, W.			Demob.	9-7-19
34740	***Sgt.	James, W. F.—M.S.M.			Demob.	20-5-19
2040518	Dvr.	Jamieson, A.—Belgian Croix de Guerre			Demob.	15-6-19
87050	Gnr.	Jaques, S.			Demob.	7-7-19
41359	Gnr.	Jardine, J.			Demob.	6-2-19
83672	Gnr.	Jarman, W.		23-9-16	M.U.	25-3-19
83494	Dvr.	Jarrett, S.		1-11-17	Demob.	6-11-18
2522524	Dvr.	Jarvis, E. J.			Demob.	27-5-19
91675	Gnr.	Jensen, C.		24-8-18	M.U.	18-3-19
341206	Gnr.	Jewett, G. B.			Demob.	6-6-19
1260201	S/Sth.	Jinks, E. A.			Demob.	18-9-19
83673	A/Sgt.	Johnson, D. H.		19-11-16	D.ofW.	19-11-16
83914	Gnr.	Johnson, E.		13-9-18	Demob.	27-6-19
334751	Gnr.	Johnson, F. G.			Demob.	27-5-19
1250782	Gnr.	Johnson, J. J.			Demob.	29-7-19
273126	Dvr.	Johnson, J.			Demob.	13-3-19
348504	Gnr.	Johnson, W. A.			Demob.	29-5-19
	Lieut.	Johnston, C. F.			Demob.	11-3-19
86132	Gnr.	Johnston, E.			Demob.	2-6-19
343038	Gnr.	Johnston, G. W. F.			Demob.	27-5-19
83482	Cpl.	Johnston, G. H.		20-7-17	Demob.	30-7-19
349473	Gnr.	Johnston, H. H. P.		9-11-17	Demob.	27-5-19
89004	Sgt.	Johnston, H. B.			Demob.	14-2-19
342161	Gnr.	Johnston, O. O. —M.M.		2-9-18	Demob.	27-5-19
2040596	Pte.	Johnston, P.			Demob.	1-5-19
97	Bdr.	Johnston, W. J.		21-8-17	Demob.	20-3-19
87022	Dvr.	Johnstone, D.		4-6-16	D.ofW.	11-6-16
273864	Dvr.	Johnstone, D. G.			Demob.	27-5-19
86713	A/Bdr.	Johnstone, J. W.		9-11-17	M.U.	2-11-20
83110	Sgt.	Jolley, G. H.			Demob.	28-5-19
83401	Pte.	Jolly, F.		12-3-16	M.U.	4-3-19
83399	Dvr.	Jones, D.			Demob.	29-5-19
83946	A/Cpl.	Jones, F. L.			M.U.	31-12-17
83760	Dvr.	Jones, J. H.			M.U.	20-4-18
86933	Gnr.	Jones, J. M.			K.I.A.	27-4-17
83211	Gnr.	Jones, J. R.			Demob.	9-5-19
301721	Dvr.	Jones, R. N.			Demob.	29-5-19
83671	Cpl.	Jones, W.		7-7-17	Demob.	12-8-19
333899	Bdr.	Jones, W. L.			M.U.	12-12-18
83674	**Gnr.	Jones, W. T.			Demob.	2-6-19
1252000	Dvr.	Jones, W.		5-9-18	M.U.	4-6-19

*Last unit, C.A.M.C.
**4th Bde., C.F.A., U.K. only
***C.A.V.C., Att. 4th Bde.

Number	Rank	Name	Decorations	Wounded	Disposition	Date
346955	Gnr.	Jones, W. V.			Demob.	27-5-19
83102	Gnr.	Jordan, A. E.		25-4-17	Demob.	21-1-19
83149	Gnr.	Jordan, V. W.			Demob.	8-4-19
349599	Gnr.	Jordan, W.			Demob.	27-5-19
475903	Gnr.	Joslyn, J. C.			Demob.	27-5-19
83400	'Gnr.	Judge, W.		24-8-17	Demob.	24-1-19
348502	Gnr.	Jupp, L. R.			Demob.	27-5-19
84150	B.S.M.	Jupp, W.			Demob.	31-3-19
2100692	Pte.	Kaiser, B. R.			Demob.	28-8-19
2611829	Gnr.	Kalbfleisch, A. E.			Demob.	27-5-19
53584	Gnr.	Kane, W. M.			M.U.	30-4-17
83994	Sgt.	Kapples, G. M.—M.M.		28-8-18	M.U.	15-2-19
84206	Gnr.	Kay, C.			Demob.	25-5-19
87043	Gnr.	Kay, S.			Demob.	15-3-19
349624	Gnr.	Keachie, J. G.			Demob.	27-5-19
334154	Gnr.	Kearns, J. S.		26-9-18	Demob.	23-5-19
87186	Gnr.	Kearns, P.		28-9-18	M.U.	24-3-19
462	Cpl.	Keatinge, A. B.		27-9-18	Demob.	11-6-19
232	A/Sgt.	Keeble, E. A.			M.U.	19-8-19
83407	A/Sgt.	Keen, F. J.			App. F. C. in R.A.F.	20-9-18
341049	Gnr.	Kehoe, C. H.		3-9-18	M.U.	6-9-19
339967	Cpl.	Kelley, F. R.			Demob.	16-6-19
2557330	Gnr.	Kelly, C. D.			Demob.	30-8-19
343941	Gnr.	Kelly, D. C.			Demob.	27-3-19
2552329	Dvr.	Kelly, H. A.			Demob.	15-6-19
	S/Capt.	Kelly, L. St. G.—M.C., M. in D.		15-6-15	Demob.	25-6-19
338998	Gnr.	Kelly, L.		27-10-17 9-11-17	D.ofW.	9-11-17
86938	Gnr.	Kelly, W.		22-11-17	Demob.	29-8-19
1262710	Dvr.	Kelly, W. H.			K.I.A.	3-9-18
86934	Gnr.	Kelso, J. L.—M.M.		27-9-18	Demob.	3-3-19
248667	Gnr.	Kemp, C.			Demob.	15-7-19
83466	Gnr.	Kemp, C.		1-6-16 18-8-17	Demob.	5-10-19
40436	Gnr.	Kenna, T. H.		26-4-15	Demob.	9-5-19
	Lieut.	Kenneally, J. L.—D.C.M.		15-9-17	Demob.	28-5-19
89538	Arm.S/S.	Kennedy, J.			Demob.	17-8-19
343022	Gnr.	Kennedy, W. R.			U. Age	22-1-18
	Lieut.	Kennett, F.			Demob.	29-5-19
89901	Bdr.	Kent, C. W.			Demob.	27-5-19
	Capt.	Kent, R.—M.C.			Demob.	28-5-19
40431	Gnr.	Kent, T. R.			M.U.	31-12-17
86936	Whl.	Kenyon, G.			Demob.	6-5-19
48562	Gnr.	Kernan, A.			Demob.	28-5-19
316923	Gnr.	Kernohan, J.			Demob.	12-9-19
	Lieut.	Kerr, A. H.		4-5-17	M.U.	26-12-17
86715	Dvr.	Kerr, J. K.			Demob.	12-2-19
35212	Gnr.	Kerr, K.			D.ofD.	8-7-18
341342	Gnr.	Kerr, R. H.			Demob.	27-5-19
	Lieut	Kerr, W. G.			Res.	30-9-17
89277	Dvr.	Keywood, W.			Demob.	27-5-19
317042	Gnr.	Kidd, H.			Demob.	29-5-19
182	Sgt.	Kierstead, A. B.		13-10-16	M.U.	20-12-17
897792	Gnr.	Killame, D.			Demob.	6-6-19
2043510	Gnr.	Killeen, F. J.		3-9-18	Demob.	27-1-19
41385	Gnr.	Kiloh, A. L.		1-5-15	Demob.	27-5-19
	Lieut.	Kilpatrick, N. O.		31-3-17	Demob.	14-2-19
300288	Dvr.	Kincaid, S. D.			Demob.	27-5-19
300468	Gnr.	Kincaid, W. A. B.		4-11-18	Demob.	3-4-19
316925	Gnr.	King, B.—M.M.		27-9-18	Demob.	14-2-19
1251063	Gnr.	King, H. E.		25-10-17	Demob.	1-6-19
316926	Cpl.	King, J. W.		27-9-18	Demob.	27-5-19
3130139	Gnr.	Kingsborough, B.			Demob.	27-5-19

*4th Bde. C.F.A. in U.K. only.

Number	Rank	Name	Decorations	Wounded	Disposition	Date
334208	Gnr.	Kingsborough, L. J.			Demob.	3-4-19
	Lieut.	Kingsford, G. E.		20-4-16	Demob.	26-8-19
316927	Gnr.	Kinlock, G.			M.U.	30-4-19
2004373	Dvr.	Kirby, S. G.			Demob.	1-6-19
83256	Gnr.	Kirkham, T.			M.U.	23-4-18
90077	Gnr.	Kirkpatrick, J.		18-11-16	K.I.A.	26-9-17
83404	Bdr.	Kirkpatrick, N.—M.M.		3-5-17	Demob.	8-4-19
83405	Gnr.	Kirton, T.			M.U.	3-10 18
300247	Gnr.	Klock, J. M.—M.M.		29-9-18	D.ofW.	15-10-18
85973	Gnr.	Knight, J. P.			Demob.	25-1-19
304509	Gnr.	Knowles, C. W.		2-11-17	M.U.	19-11-18
4383	Sgt.	Koehler, C. H.			Demob.	22-3-20
84151	Sgt.	Kohl, J. A.		30-8-18	M.U.	19-8-19
411104	Sgt.	Koyl, E. G.			Demob.	13-2-17
2152473	Gnr.	Kukkola, I.			Demob.	13-2-19
84158	Dvr.	Lacey, H.			Demob.	15-4-19
83999	Gnr.	Lacey, W. M.			M.U.	15-4-18
345875	Dvr.	LaChance, J.			Demob.	27-5-19
40212	Gnr.	LaChapelle, B.		24-5-15	Demob.	15-7-19
1251773	Gnr.	Lackey, F. J.			K.I.A.	7-11-17
86932	Bdr.	Ladner, L.			Demob.	31-3-19
301440	Gnr.	LaFrance, E.		3-5-17	K.I.A.	3-9-18
333926	Gnr.	Laidlaw, H. L.		28-2-18	Demob.	28-2-19
	*Major	Laidlaw, W. C.			Demob.	23-6-19
300479	A/Cpl.	Laing, N. W.			Demob.	11-2-19
83677	A/Sgt.	Lainson, R. D.			Demob.	7-2-19
89910	Dvr.	LaJeunesse, A.			Demob.	24-1-19
41240	Dvr.	Lake, T.		25-5-16	D.ofW.	25-5-16
335114	Gnr.	Laking, C. C.			Demob.	27-5-19
89904	Gnr.	Lalonde, L.			Kld. (A)	7-3-19
315985	Gnr.	Lamb, C. L.			Demob.	27-5-19
302500	Gnr.	Lamb, H. K.			Demob.	27-5-19
835652	Gnr.	Lamb, J. H. T.			Demob.	18-10-19
86869	Gnr.	Lane, A. V.			Demob.	26-7-19
83876	Pte.	Langbridge, W.			Demob.	26-2-19
342985	Gnr.	Langdon, A. F.			Demob.	27-5-19
334564	Gnr.	Langford, G. W.		1-10-18	Demob.	27-5-19
83016	Dvr.	Langlands, A.			Demob.	27-5-19
345841	Dvr.	LaPointe, H.			Being a Minor	6-8-18
	Lieut.	Larkin, H. W.—M.C.			Demob.	27-5-19
386	Gnr.	Larkin, H.		7-4-16 28-4-17 28-9-18	Demob.	2-4-19
305669	Dvr.	Larmer, W. E.			Demob.	27-5-19
2115655	Dvr.	Larson, A.			Demob.	15-5-19
303680	Gnr.	Larter, R. W.			M.U.	19-6-19
334128	Gnr.	Last, A.			K.I.A.	27-9-18
83117	Dvr.	Last, W.			Demob.	27-5-19
345929	Gnr.	Latham, K.			Being a Minor	27-2-18
55877	A/Sgt.	Laurence, S.			Demob.	14-7-19
345923	Dvr.	Lauvray, L.			Being a Minor	6-6-18
343071	Gnr.	Lauell, F. M.			Demob.	27-5-19
300350	Gnr.	Lavery, J.			Demob.	24-8-19
55086	A/Sgt.	Law, J.—M.M.			Demob.	3-4-19
19598	Gnr.	Lawless, L. R.		3-6-16 25-7-17 1-11-18 2-9-18	Demob.	8-4-19
83409	Cpl.	Lawrence, J.			Demob.	8-3-19
	**Lieut.	Lawrie, D. J.		29-9-18	Demob.	19-2-19
340804	Gnr.	Lawrie, J.			M.U.	10-5-18
86663	Gnr.	Lawrie, R.		19-10-17	Demob.	31-1-19

*C.A.M.C. att. 4th Bde., C.F.A.
**Served as O.R. only with 4th Bde., C.F.A.

Number	Rank	Name	Decorations	Wounded	Disposition	Date
2591129	Gnr.	Lawson, H.			Demob.	9-7-19
	Major	Lawson, H. H.			Demob.	9-8-19
83413	Gnr.	Lawson, W.		30-9-18	Demob.	24-1-19
86944	Gnr.	Laxton, C.			Demob.	24-6-19
316929	Sig.	Layton, L. G.		1-11-18	Demob.	27-5-19
316930	Gnr.	Layton, N. H.			M.U.	14-1-19
86438	Cpl.	Lea, J.			Demob.	29-5-19
86664	Gnr.	Leadley, J.		1-6-17 29-9-18	M.U.	25-1-19
	Capt.	Leather, E. R.—M.C.			Demob.	18-3-19
	*Lieut.	Leathers, F. J.		26-4-17	Demob.	14-3-19
86941	Gnr.	Lebaron, B.			Demob.	6-2-19
89907	Gnr.	Leclerc, L.			Demob.	31-5-19
307768	Dvr.	Leconte, F. C.			Demob.	27-5-19
89805	Gnr.	Lee, C.			Demob.	28-2-19
166	Bdr.	Lee, C. F.		24-8-18	Demob.	11-2-19
83851	Sgt.	Lee, E.—M.M.			Demob.	25-5-19
2045015	Gnr.	Lee, H.			Demob.	28-8-19
	**Capt.	Lee, R. M.			Demob.	12-8-19
83106	Dvr.	Lee, T. F.			Demob.	9-5-19
248644	Dvr.	Leech, E.		8-5-17	Demob.	19-9-19
83006	Sgt.	Leech, F. W.			To Com. Med. S.	18-2-16
2152498	Gnr.	Leech, H. W.			Demob.	27-5-19
84218	Gnr.	Leech, J.			M.U.	10-3-18
	Lieut.	Lees, A. G.			Demob.	25-11-18
298	A/Cpl.	Lees, R. G.			Demob.	28-2-19
83017	Gnr.	Legge, G. B.			Com. in R.A.F.	11-10-15
83516	Gnr.	Legge, W. H.			Com. in R.N.V.R.	8-10-15
83408	A/Sgt.	Leighton, S. S.			M.U.	25-2-19
89913	Bdr.	Leishman, K.			Demob.	28-6-19
316932	Gnr.	Leitch, R.			K.I.A.	30-9-18
83462	Q.M.S.	Leith, J.			M.U.	6-5-18
83916	Cpl.	Lammond, W. J.		27-9-18	Demob.	3-4-19
310868	Gnr.	Lennox, A. E.			Demob.	16-6-19
84157	Gnr.	Leonard, F. W.			K.I.A.	26-4-17
322920	Gnr.	Leonard, R. A.			K.I.A.	18-10-17
444514	Gnr.	Lerette, F. A.			Demob.	10-4-19
83175	Bdr.	Leroy, W. J.			Demob.	28-5-19
83857	***Gnr.	Leslie, W.			M.U.	16-4-18
84153	***Gnr.	Letheren, F. C.			M.U.	28-1-19
83682	Sgt.	Lewington, G. E.			Demob.	16-10-19
	*Lieut.	Lewis, A.C.—M. in D.			Demob.	8-4-19
84154	Gnr.	Lewis, F. A.			M.U.	11-7-16
83018	Gnr.	Lewis, H. J.			Demob.	12-8-19
83240	Sgt.	Lewis, J. M.			Demob.	27-5-19
2327482	Gnr.	Lewis, W. J.			Demob.	27-5-19
850441	Sig.	Liddle, G. A.		27-9-18	Demob.	27-5-19
303601	Bdr.	Lidstone, R. M.—M.M.			Demob.	31-5-19
83969	Gnr.	Lightfoot, J. H. T.			M.U.	10-5-18
1251200	Gnr.	Lillico, R. S. B.			Demob.	30-7-19
1251133	Gnr.	Lindeman, F.			Demob.	1-6-19
339287	Gnr.	Lindgren, S.			M.U.	27-3-19
161	Cpl.	Lindop, G.		1-3-15	M.U.	13-6-18
192051	Sig.	Lindsay, H.			Demob.	26-8-19
83168	Sig.	Lindsay, T. R.			Demob.	29-5-19
186770	Gnr.	Line, J. H.			Demob.	30-5-19
86943	Gnr.	Line, R.			K.I.A.	20-5-17
91595	Dvr.	Lines, A.			Demob.	6-6-19
348966	Gnr.	Lingard, F. C.			Demob.	27-5-19
476550	Gnr.	Lister, A.			Demob.	30-7-19

*Served as O.R. only with 4th Bde., C.F.A.
**C.A.V.C. att. 4th Bde. C.F.A.
***Served in U.K. only with 4th Bde., C.F.A.

Number	Rank	Name	Decorations	Wounded	Disposition	Date
339903	A/Sgt.	Lister, O. L.		11-8-18	Demob.	4-2-19
83852	Sgt.	Litherland, C.—M.M.			M.U.	6-2-19
	Lieut.	Little, P. M.			Demob.	27-5-19
91461	Gnr.	Little, R. W.			K.I.A.	1-6-17
316935	Dvr.	Littlejohn, E. H.			Demob.	27-5-19
316051	Cpl.	Livingston, H. A.		13-5-17		
				22-4-18	Demob.	27-5-19
446	Gnr.	Livingstone, W.			K.I.A.	14-1-16
340100	Gnr.	Lloyd, T. A. C.			Demob.	29-9-19
301671	Gnr.	Lloyd, T. J.			Demob.	24-2-19
90017	Spr.	Lock, J. W. K.			Demob.	16-6-19
84156	Gnr.	Lockard, R.			Demob.	25-5-19
83410	Sgt.	Locke, F.		9-8-18	Demob.	24-1-19
89906	Dvr.	Lockey, B.			D.ofD.	26-10-18
334395	Dvr.	Lockwood, G. C.			Demob.	27-5-19
321	Gnr.	Loftus, R.			M.U.	17-2-19
83877	BQMS.	Loftus, W. J.			Demob.	11-8-19
339708	Gnr.	Long, L. T.		3-9-18	Demob.	15-4-19
83679	Gnr.	Longhurst, H.		26-4-17	D.ofW.	14-5-17
83680	Gnr.	Loosemore, R.			Demob.	11-4-19
90256	Gnr.	Lorette, G. A.			Demob.	18-8-19
90255	Dvr.	Lorette, P.			Demob.	7-4-19
	Capt.	Lorimer, N. H.			Demob.	27-5-19
1251269	Gnr.	Louden, C. H.			Demob.	1-6-19
344136	Gnr.	Loucks, D. A.			Demob.	27-5-19
	Capt.	Lovelace, E. J.—M.C., M. in D.			M.U.	20-2-19
157624	Gnr.	Lovett, G. H.			M.U.	1-8-18
159760	Gnr.	Lovett, P. J.			Demob.	27-5-19
304079	Dvr.	Low, D. A.			Demob.	27-5-19
83488	Gnr.	Lowe, C. M.			M.U.	13-5-16
83412	Gnr.	Lowe, F.		1-11-18	M.U.	7-3-19
1251994	Gnr.	Lowe, T.			Demob.	27-5-19
83411	Gnr.	Lowry, W. J.		3-11-15		
				8-5-17	Demob.	15-2-19
	Lieut.	Lucas, H. G.			Demob.	29-8-19
41331	Dvr.	Lucas, W.		4-5-15	Demob.	28-5-19
89912	Gnr.	Luckie, W. A.		10-8-18	D.ofW.	19-8-18
444514	Gnr.	Luke, A. M.		24-11-15		
				6-4-16		
				29-3-17	M.U.	23-10-18
85976	Bdr.	Luke, H. W.		30-9-17	M.U.	6-8-19
83140	A/Cpl.	Lukey, E. R.		25-2-16		
				17-8-18	M.U.	31-1-20
87029	Gnr.	Lumsden, J.			K.I.A.	24-4-17
83681	Gnr.	Lumsden, P. V.			Com. Imp.	
					Army	8-10-15
83678	Sgt.	Lunn, W. C.			M.U.	5-3-19
301673	Gnr.	Lunney, W. G.			Demob.	24-2-19
94155	Dvr.	Luscombe, J. C. E.			M.U.	30-11-17
2341422	Gnr.	Lyall, T. F.			Demob.	27-5-19
90069	Gnr.	Lyddon, J. L.			M.U.	13-2-19
142620	Gnr.	Lynes, J. H.		19-10-17		
				28-9-18	Demob.	24-9-19
335316	Gnr.	Maben, G. C.			Demob.	27-5-19
85250	Dvr.	Mack, W. A.		13-1-16	Demob.	27-5-19
86955	Bdr.	Mackie, C.			Demob.	30-5-19
83691	*Gnr.	Macklem, G.			M.U.	8-3-19
86956	Gnr.	Macklem, P. P.			Demob.	27-8-19
560	Dvr.	Madden, A.		27-9-18	D.ofW.	27-9-18
83688	Gnr.	Madill, R. G.		19-11-16	M.U.	12-3-18
87041	Cpl.	Maguire, P.			M.U.	21-6-20
2040562	Gnr.	Maher, J. W.			Demob.	22-2-19
84007	Cpl.	Main, G. E.			Demob.	25-5-19
349716	Dvr.	Mainwaring, J. E.			Demob.	27-5-19

*U.K. only with 4th Bde., C.F.A.

Number	Rank	Name	Decorations	Wounded	Disposition	Date
83944	Gnr.	Majury, J.		29-6-18		
				10-8-18	M.U.	31-5-19
341120	Gnr.	Malcolm, W. J.			Demob.	27-5-19
348911	A/Cpl.	Mallaby, G. P.		31-10-17	Demob.	22-1-19
83866	*Gnr.	Maloney, C.—M.M.		14-5-17	Demob.	15-7-19
529276	Gnr.	Maltby, T.			Demob.	22-9-19
1251840	Dvr.	Manhire, R. L.			Demob.	27-5-19
84167	Dvr.	Mann, A. E.		21-9-16		
				13-11-16	M.U.	30-10-18
89359	Gnr.	Mann, A.			Demob.	4-4-19
349597	Gnr.	Mann, R. C.			Demob.	4-7-19
343098	Gnr.	Mann, R.			Demob.	22-5-19
316948	Dvr.	Manser, F.			Demob.	27-5-19
90082	Cpl.	Manson, J.			Demob.	23-3-19
3055621	Gnr.	Mapes, C. E.			Demob.	27-5-19
21	Gnr.	Marcus, J. A.			Demob.	15-2-19
339758	Gnr.	Marentette, E. W.			Demob.	29-3-19
85106	Gnr.	Marginson, A.			Demob.	8-4-19
83985	Sgt.	Marriner, J. L.			M.U.	31-12-17
83874	Gnr.	Marsh, B. F.		10-8-17	ReE-n. in	
					Amer. A.	28-8-18
84216	**Sgt.	Marsh, C. H.			M.U.	14-1-18
522751	***Cpl.	Marsh, H. B.			Demob.	26-5-19
400008	***Pte.	Marsh, R. H.			Demob.	25-8-19
342359	Gnr.	Marshall, J. A.			Demob.	27-5-19
341360	Gnr.	Marshall, J. L.			Demob.	27-5-19
341341	Sig.	Marshall, W. V.			Demob.	17-5-19
89919	Gnr.	Marsolais, J.			Demob.	27-5-19
2152381	Gnr.	Martin, A. A.			Demob.	19-2-19
83034	Gnr.	Martin, A.		31-10-17	Demob.	27-5-19
	Major	Martin, C. K. C.—D.S.O., M. in D.			Demob.	6-7-19
301135	Dvr.	Martin, C. S.		12-9-18	Demob.	13-2-19
84247	Sgt.	Martin, G. S.—M.M.			M.U.	11-1-19
83223	Gnr.	Martin, H.		7-4-18		
				9-8-18	Demob.	17-2-19
83230	Gnr.	Martin, J.		23-9-18	M.U.	17-4-19
1251585	Bdr.	Martin, J. W.		20-10-17	Demob.	8-7-19
282	Gnr.	Martin, R. K.			Demob.	16-5-19
83694	Dvr.	Martyn, A. W.			M.U.	6-11-18
89608	Bdr.	Mason, A. C.			Demob.	11-8-19
	****Lieut.	Mason, A. D.—M.C., Bar, M.M.			Demob.	2-4-19
111571	Spr.	Mason, B. C.			Demob.	15-3-19
83695	Gnr.	Mason, J. W.			K.I.A.	21-4-17
1257951	Gnr.	Mason, J. R.			Demob.	27-5-19
	*****Lieut.	Massey, R. H.		14-5-16		
				7-6-16	Demob.	12-5-19
2650714	Gnr.	Masterman, J. B.			Demob.	27-5-19
1251440	Dvr.	Matheson, A.			Demob.	15-6-19
86948	Gnr.	Mathews, C. E.			Demob.	13-4-19
239126	Gnr.	Matthews, F. G.			Demob.	2-6-19
	Lieut.	Matthews, F. J.			Demob.	3-1-19
15156	Cpl.	Matthews, M. H.			Demob.	13-5-19
89916	Sgt.	Matthews, S. G.—M.M., Bar			Demob.	27-5-19
302223	Dvr.	Matthews, V.			Demob.	27-5-19
83875	Gnr.	Mattinson, H. E.			Cess. of	
					W. Pay	1-11-16
	Capt.	Maunder, J. F. C.—M.C., M. in D.			Demob.	16-6-19
89793	Sgt.	Maxwell, A. D.			Demob.	25-5-19
340971	Bdr.	Maxwell, C. C.			Demob.	27-5-19
83514	Dvr.	May, F.		2-4-16	Demob.	26-8-19
83415	Gnr.	May, J.		15-2-17	D.ofD.	10-3-19

*Served in N. Russia with 16th Bde., C.F.A.
**Served in U.K. only with 4th Bde., C.F.A.
***C.A.M.C. att. to 4th Bde., C.F.A.
****Served in France as O.R., with 4th Bde., C.F.A.
*****Served with Amm. Col., in Siberia

Number	Rank	Name	Decorations	Wounded	Disposition	Date
	*Lieut.	Mayberry, F. C.		26-9-16	Demob.	23-4-19
86667	Cpl.	Mayer, E.		13-10-16	K.I.A.	4-6-17
341094	Gnr.	Mayer, J. M.		10-8-18	Demob.	27-5-19
86668	Gnr.	Mayo, W. J.		1-4-16		
				26-10-17	Demob.	28-1-19
84160	Gnr.	Mead, H.			K.I.A.	1-5-16
84212	Sgt.	Meadows, J. C.		12-10-16	D.ofW.	19-10-16
90130	Cpl.	Meaney, D. J.			Demob.	27-3-19
42539	Gnr.	Mearns, A. J.			M.U.	7-3-19
317041	A/Sgt.	Medland, T. M.			Demob.	3-2-19
83503	Dvr.	Meeson, T.			M.U.	4-1-17
42542	Dvr.	Meiklejohn, R.			Demob.	27-5-19
300168	Gnr.	Melanson, J. H		30-10 17	M.U.	16-7-19
87035	Gnr.	Melhuish, E.			Demob.	29-5-19
85340	Gnr.	Melhuish, H.			Demob.	29-3-19
86961	Bdr.	Mellis, R.			Demob.	5-4-19
1251510	Gnr.	Melville, L. R.		28-9-18	M.U.	25-8-19
344994	Gnr.	Melvin, W.			Demob.	14-10-19
83921	**Gnr.	Menary, J.		10-11-17	M.U.	26-11-19
83880	***Gnr.	Menzie, H. H.			M.U.	27-2-19
83690	Dvr.	Merlin, D.			D.ofI.	16-9-18
83165	Gnr.	Merrey, R. C.			D.ofI.	13-6-17
	Major	Merritt, W. H.			Demob.	22-3-19
	Lieut.	Merry ,F. S.—M.C.			Demob.	31-7-19
106	Sgt.	Mersereau, B. M. —M.M., Bar			Demob.	27-5-19
	*Lieut.	Mewburn, J. S.			Demob.	25-4-19
87046	Dvr.	Middleton, C.			Demob.	31-5-19
83135	Bdr.	Might, G.			Demob.	8-8-19
341952	Gnr.	Miles, S. G.		12-4-18	Demob.	25-5-19
89921	Cpl.	Millar, J.		2-7-16	D.ofW.	2-7-16
	Lieut.	Millard, R. T.		27-9-18	Demob.	14-7-19
1250035	Gnr.	Miller, D.—M.M.		2-9-18	Demob.	17-2-19
86953	Dvr.	Miller, E.		5-11-17	Demob.	17-2-19
645512	Gnr.	Miller, G. E.		4-11-18	Demob.	1-6-19
1251157	Gnr.	Miller, H. J.		25-10-17	Demob.	19-9-19
1251960	Gnr.	Miller, J. D.		6-11-18	Demob.	1-4-19
87028	Sgt.	Miller, L. G.—M.M.			Demob.	29-5-19
334464	Gnr.	Miller, M. L.			Demob.	17-3-19
83468	Cpl.	Miller, P. J.			Demob.	21-5-19
90085	Cpl.	Miller, R. C.—M. in D.		6-4-16		
				16-9-16	Demob.	28-5-19
339996	Gnr.	Miller, T. C.		12-8-18	Demob.	25-1-19
83177	Cpl.	Miller, W.—M.M.		11-4-17	Demob.	19-8-19
331738	Gnr.	Miller, W. A.			Demob.	1-6-19
	Lieut.	Miller, W. J.			Demob.	28-5-19
83101	BQMS.	Mills, G. A.			Demob.	4-7-19
348211	Sgt.	Millwood, F. J.			Com. in I. Army	11-8-18
83261	Gnr.	Milne, A. J.			Com. in I. Army	3-10-15
	*Lieut.	Milne, F. C.—M. in D.			Demob.	11-10-19
87061	Gnr.	Milne, G. R.		30-10-16		
				26-10-17	Demob.	20-12-18
340174	Sig.	Milson, W. A.			Demob.	27-5-19
1251438	Gnr.	Milton, J.			Demob.	8-4-19
273	Gnr.	Minter, W.		6-12-16		
				2-6-18	Demob.	7-8-19
316952	Cpl.	Mitcham, A. J.—M.M.		27-9-18	Demob.	29-3-19
159150	Pte.	Mitchell, H.			M.U.	6-3-19
117	Gnr.	Mitchell, H. L.		2-11-17	M.U.	25-6-19
	Lieut.	Mitchell, J. A.			Demob.	12-2-19
86954	Gnr.	Mitchell, J. B.			Demob.	8-1-19
3181044	Gnr.	Mitchell, J. B.			Demob.	2-6-19

*Served as O.R. only with 4th Bde., C.F.A.
**Served in N. Russja with 16th Bde., C.F.A.
***Served in U.K. only with 4th Bde., C.F.A.

Number	Rank	Name	Decorations	Wounded	Disposition	Date
55897	Gnr.	Mitchell, L. W.			Demob.	2-8-19
83128	Gnr.	Mitchell, O. J.			D.ofD.	27-3-19
83920	Dvr.	Mitchell, R. G.			Demob.	30-7-19
40073	Sgt.	Moffat, L. C.—M.M.			Demob.	27-5-19
2327634	Gnr.	Moffatt, W. W. C.			Demob.	27-5-19
83414	Dvr.	Molen, A.			Demob.	4-7-19
83019	Gnr.	Mollison, R. W.			App. Com. in R.F.A.	20-12-15
83505	Gnr.	Monkman, R.			Demob.	28-5-19
83619	B.S.M.	Monro, R. S.—M.M., M. in D.		25-10-16 1-6-17	Demob.	27-5-19
84252	Gnr.	Montague, J. J.			Demob.	8-8-19
84001	Gnr.	Montieth, A. S.			Demob.	21-5-19
	Lieut.	Montieth, W. B.			Demob.	31-7-19
444	Gnr.	Montgomery, N.			Demob.	13-7-19
83420	Gnr.	Moon, H.		2-6-16	D.ofW.	2-6-16
336174	Gnr.	Moore, F. M.			Demob.	15-3-19
90873	Gnr.	Moore, G. J.		2-7-16 24-9-16	M.U.	15-5-18
40453	Sgt.	Moore, G.		10-10-16	Demob.	27-5-19
83259	Gnr.	Moore, H. W.		15-8-17	D.ofW.	15-8-17
339486	Gnr.	Moore, J.			Demob.	2-6-19
83692	Gnr.	Moore, J.			M.U.	2-10-16
1260208	Gnr.	Moore, J. R.			Demob.	20-3-19
83114	Dvr.	Moore, R.			Demob.	25-5-19
83687	Pte.	Moore, S. E.			M.U.	18-1-19
334540	Dvr.	Moore, S. S.			Demob.	27-5-19
338355	Gnr.	Moore, W. L.			Demob.	27-5-19
83448	Gnr.	Moore, W.			S. Case	1-6-17
84161	Dvr.	Moore ,W. S.		24-4-17	M.U.	15-1-19
86194	Gnr.	Moors, J. W.		1-6-17 6-9-17	M.U.	31-1-18
1250071	Gnr.	Moran, C. H.		14-8-18	Demob.	3-3-19
338962	A/Bdr.	Moran, L. J.		11-11-17	D.ofW.	16-11-17
84159	A/Sgt.	Morden, G. A.—M.S.M.		13-11-16 4-5-17 29-10-17	Demob.	25-5-19
2557447	Gnr.	Morden, H. H.			Demob.	29-5-19
84222	Gnr.	Moreton, C.		3-9-18	Demob.	25-5-19
89520	Spr.	Morgan, A. R.			Demob.	6-7-19
84162	Dvr.	Morgan, C. F.			M.U.	31-12-17
619	Cpl.	Morison, C. K.—M.M.			Demob.	29-5-19
618	Gnr.	Morison, W. R.			Demob.	29-5-19
348520	Dvr.	Morley, C.			K.I.A.	5-9-18
304378	Dvr.	Morley, F. C.		20-8-18	M.U.	21-2-19
315899	Dvr.	Morley, P. H.			Demob.	27-5-19
338144	Gnr.	Morran, D. A.			Demob.	27-5-19
83156	Gnr.	Morris, G. A.			Demob.	4-7-19
1257816	Gnr.	Morrison, D. E.			K.I.A.	27-9-19
83693	Gnr.	Morrison, E.		25-10-16	M.U.	31-12-18
89253	Gnr.	Morrison, G.		22-7-16 27-7-17	Demob.	19-3-19
83980	Gnr.	Morrison, J.			Deserter	31-7-15
83982	Gnr.	Morrison, J. A.			Demob.	29-5-19
83996	Gnr.	Morrison, J. T.		14-5-17	Demob.	28-5-19
1251290	Gnr.	Morrison, J. R.			Demob.	31-5-19
90063	Gnr.	Morrisey, J. J.			Over age	15-10-17
87031	Dvr.	Morrow, J. M.			Demob.	14-4-19
	Capt.	Morse, F. G.—M.C.			Demob.	1-4-19
339740	Dvr.	Morten, J. F. D.			Demob.	15-5-19
	*Capt.	Mortimore, A. R.—M. inD.			To Perm. Force	31-5-20
83416	Dvr.	Morton, T.			Demob.	25-5-19
217	Gnr.	Moxon, W. H.			M.U.	23-5-18
89078	Gnr.	Moylan, W. J.			Demob.	17-5-19

*C.A.M.C. Att. 4th Bde., C.F.A.

Number	Rank	Name	Decorations	Wounded	Disposition	Date
1251262	Gnr.	Muir, W.			Demob.	31-5-19
	Major	Muirhead, R. G.			M.U.	25-6-18
84166	Sgt.	Mulcahy, W.			M.U.	14-4-19
341226	Gnr.	Mulvenna, R.			Demob.	12-7-19
91803	Gnr.	Mummett, M.			Demob.	11-5-19
84165	Gnr.	Munday, R. H.			Demob.	8-1-19
83922	Gnr.	Mundell, W. C. —M.S.M., M. in D.			Demob.	25-5-19
83133	Gnr.	Munks, F.		30-7-17	M.U.	20-7-18
83137	Gnr.	Munro, W.		30-9-18	Demob.	1-5-19
84233	Dvr.	Murfin, B. J.			M.U.	22-5-17
321905	Gnr.	Murphy, E. A.			Demob.	21-3-19
86135	Cpl.	Murray, A.			Demob.	20-8-19
730032	Gnr.	Murray, A.—M.M.		6-11-17 2-10-18	M.U.	21-10-19
3056813	Gnr.	Murray, G. H.			Demob.	27-5-19
83417	Sgt.	Murray, H.		30-9-18	Demob.	27-5-19
1250626	Gnr.	Murray, J. A.—M.M.		31-7-17 4-9-18	Demob.	18-5-19
1251399	Gnr.	Murray, J. C.			Demob.	6-6-19
347740	Dvr.	Murray, P.			K.I.A.	29-10-17
469295	Gnr.	Murray, W. A.			Demob.	15-6-19
	*Lieut.	Murray, W. J. R.—M.M.			Demob.	8-4-19
85347	Pte.	Musicant, A.		4-3-18	Demob.	20-3-19
340903	Gnr.	Mustard, G. A.			Demob.	26-5-19
2601934	Gnr.	Murtie, F. L.			Demob.	27-5-19
394	Gnr.	Mylan, J.			K.I.A.	13-6-16
57697	Dvr.	Mylchreest, A. E.			Demob.	20-8-19
83978	B.S.M.	Mylchreest, W.—M.M., M. in D.			Demob.	25-5-19
84168	Dvr.	Myles, J. P.			Demob.	12-5-19
337937	Gnr.	Myles, T. C.		14-8-18	Demob.	20-10 19
84000	Q.M.S.	MacAndrew, J. L.—Bel. C. de G.			Demob.	25-5-19
	*Lieut.	McArthur, G. C.		7-9-17	Demob.	23-8-19
	**Capt.	MacBeth, W. L. C.			Demob.	1-3-19
	*Lieut.	McBride, C. A.			Demob.	19-5-19
85346	Gnr.	McBride, J.			M.U.	5-11-18
90105	Gnr.	McAllum, D.—M.M.			K.I.A.	27-9-18
1078	Gnr.	McAllum, F. A.—M.M.			Demob.	10-3-19
341067	Dvr.	McAllum, M.			Demob.	27-5-19
83783	Dvr.	McCarthy, C.		11-8-18	Demob.	23-5-19
317956	Gnr.	McCarthy, H. A.			Demob.	30-3-19
349536	Dvr.	McCartney, H. S.			Demob.	27-5-19
335922	Gnr.	McCartney, H. H.			Demob.	24-4-19
83254	Dvr.	McCarty, A. V.		20-5-17	M.U.	16-7-19
84170 ***Bdr.		McCaulley, E. E.			M.U.	13-2-18
327896	Dvr.	McClelland, T.			Demob.	30-5-19
	Lieut.	McClintock, G. A.		29-4-15 22-9-16 6-11-17	Demob.	2-6-19
349612	Gnr.	McCloskey, J. J.			Demob.	28-5-19
2522398	Sig.	McClurg, A. H.			Demob.	5-6-19
89523	Gnr.	McCollough, A.			Demob.	20-9-19
	Capt.	McConkey, B. B.—M.C.		29-5-18	D.ofW.	30-5-18
349625	Gnr.	MacConnell, I. G. C.			Demob.	31-5-19
84037	Gnr.	MacCormack, A. M.		18-11-16	Com. in R.A.F.	20-9-18
83971	Cpl.	MacCormack, S.			K.I.A.	6-10-16
341554	Gnr.	McCormick, W. H.			Demob.	27-5-19
1250309	Gnr.	McCoy, J.			Demob.	12-6-19
87214	Gnr.	McCready, K.			Demob.	4-4-19
84169	Bdr.	McCreith, L. V.—M.M.		31-10-17	Demob.	12-2-19
301184	Dvr.	McCuish, A.			Demob.	15-6-19
83992	Gnr.	McCulloch, G.			K.I.A.	1-9-18
1250753	Gnr.	McCullough, W.			Demob.	31-5-19
342276	Gnr.	McCullum, N. L.		27-9-18	Demob.	22-5-19

*Served as O.R. only with 4th Bde., C.F.A.
**C.A.M.C. att 4th Bde., C.F.A.
***U.K. only with 4th Bde., C.F.A.

Number	Rank	Name	Decorations	Wounded	Disposition	Date
331735	Dvr.	McClymont, J.		1-6-17	Demob.	27-5-19
83941	Sgt.	McDermott, J.		26-9-16	M.U.	20-10-19
	**Lieut.	McDonald, A. B.—M. in D.		26-10-16	Demob.	25-5-19
83185	Dvr.	McDonald, A.			M.U.	26-2-18
86931	Gnr.	McDonald, C.			Demob.	13-7-19
86952	Gnr.	McDonald, C. M.			Demob.	17-6-19
304102	Dvr.	McDonald, G.		22-5-16	Demob.	23-4-19
86035	Bdr.	MacDonald, G. W.		21-10-17	Demob.	15-6-19
85756	Gnr.	MacDonald, G. D.		6-5-18	Demob.	13-5-19
301675	Dvr.	MacDonald, H.			Demob.	30-5-19
89353	Dvr.	McDonald, J.			Demob.	20-9-19
2605880	Gnr.	McDonald, J. A.		1-11-18	Demob.	30-3-19
83151	Gnr.	MacDonald, K. M.			K.I.A.	31-5-16
345859	Gnr.	MacDonald, L.			Demob.	27-5-19
87055	Dvr.	McDonald, N.			Demob.	5-7-19
83418	Gnr.	MacDonald, N.			Demob.	27-5-19
784115	Dvr.	McDonald, N. C.			Demob.	12-7-19
90054	BQMS.	MacDonald, W. J.			Demob.	27-5-19
5998	Gnr.	McDonald, W.		3-6-16	K.I.A.	27-4-17
91471	Dvr.	MacDonald, W. L.		12-10-16	Demob.	7-4-19
1250555	Cpl.	Mc.Dougall, D.			M.U.	21-7-19
87199	Gnr.	MacDuff, G. H.		30-10-17	D.of W.	30-10-17
338415	Gnr.	McFarlane, C. H.			Demob.	27-5-19
335196	Gnr.	McFarlane, E. W.			Demob.	27-5-19
83918	Gnr.	McFarlane, W. L.		7-9-18	D.of W.	17-9-18
348825	Gnr.	McGahey, A. E.		29-9-18	M.U.	19-2-19
318961	Gnr.	McGeer, J. A.			Demob.	14-7-19
83686	Gnr.	McGibbon, H. B.			Demob.	12-4-19
393	Gnr.	McGilp, A. F.		6-4-16		
				14-11-17	Demob.	3-1-19
1250554	Gnr.	McGregor, D.			Demob.	31-5-19
339406	Gnr.	McGuire, J. S.		21-11-17	Demob.	27-5-19
83860	Gnr.	McGunigal, L.			Demob.	25-5-19
345036	Gnr.	McIlquham, H. C.			Demob.	27-5-19
91679	Bdr.	McIlraith, H. S.—M.M.		16-4-17	Demob.	27-5-19
71190	Bdr.	McIntosh, J.		2-10-18	Demob.	27-5-19
2601994	Gnr.	MacKintosh, S. W.			Demob.	27-5-19
255739	Gnr.	McKaig, D. A.			Demob.	1-6-19
2101016	Gnr.	McKay, A. J.			Demob.	11-4-19
87052	Dvr.	McKay, D. E.			Demob.	30-5-19
333984	Gnr.	McKay, G.			Demob.	27-5-19
84164	*Dvr.	McKay, J. R.			M.U.	3-4-19
1251030	Gnr.	McKay, R. S.		3-10-18	Demob.	31-5-19
	***Major	McKechnie, D. W.—D.S.O., M. in D.			Demob.	28-5-19
348996	L/Cpl.	McKee, D. J.			Demob.	8-6-19
316945	Gnr.	McKee, S.			Demob.	23-6-19
338131	Sig.	McKendry, W. N.			Demob.	27-5-19
	Lieut.	McKenna, V.—M.C.			Demob.	3-6-19
	**Capt.	MacKenzie, A. E.			Demob.	8-7-19
343833	Gnr.	MacKenzie, D.			Demob.	24-1-19
317013	Sgt.	McKenzie, I. C.			M.U.	3-3-19
	****Capt.	Mackenzie, J. A.—D.S.O.		10-8-18		
				28-8-18	Demob.	1-8-19
	***Capt.	MacKenzie, J. W.			Demob.	3-9-19
	Lieut.	MacKenzie, R. J.		11-8-18	M.U.	4-6-20
89880	Gnr.	McKenzie-Davies, R.			Demob.	29-5-19
87217	Bdr.	McKeown, J.			Demob.	26-5-19
349813	Gnr.	McKeown, J. W.			Demob.	27-5-19
	***Capt.	McKinnon, C. J.			Demob.	19-9-19
3131101	Gnr.	McKinnon, E.			Demob.	27-5-19
335993	Dvr.	McKinnon, L. C. W.			Demob.	24-2-19
83228	Gnr.	McKinnon, T.		24-6-16	D.of W.	24-6-16
1250572	Gnr.	MacKnight, R. O.		2-10-18	Demob.	19-2-19

*Served under name of Munroe, J.
**Served as O.R. only with 4th Bde., C.F.A.
***C.A.M.C. Att. 4th Bde., C.F.A.

Number	Rank	Name	Decorations	Wounded	Disposition	Date
	*Lieut.	McLaren, D. B.—M.M.			Demob.	15-9-19
50491	**Cpl.	McLaren, J. G.			Demob.	27-5-19
103	B.S.M.	McLaskey, A. W.—M.M.		30-10-17	Demob.	27-5-19
	Lieut.	MacLatchy, E. B.		29-10-16	Surplus	10-9-17
40676	L/Cpl.	McLaughlin, W. R.			M.U.	31-1-20
248470	Gnr.	McLean, A. R.			Demob.	22-5-19
41421	B.S.M.	McLean, J. D.			M.U.	19-7-16
1250152	Bdr.	McLean, J. D.			Demob.	29-5-19
454	Dvr.	McLean, J. W.		14-1-16	D.ofW.	30-1-16
345825	Gnr.	McLean, J. D.			K.I.A.	3-9-18
340363	Gnr.	McLean, T. J.			Demob.	6-7-19
340062	Gnr.	McLennan, J. F.			M.U.	20-6-18
86874	Sgt.	McLeod, B.			K.I.A.	2-9-18
83419	Gnr.	MacLeod, C. A.			Demob.	21-1-19
301190	Gnr.	MacLeod, M.		10-8-18	Demob.	15-6-19
89522	Gnr.	McLeod, M. R.			M.U.	5-2-18
2552304	Dvr.	MacLeod, M. E.			Demob.	15-6-19
2601978	Gnr.	McLeod, N. H.			Demob.	27-5-19
2522512	Gnr.	McMahon, J. E.			Demob.	27-5-19
28772	Sgt.	MacMillan, A.—M.M.		25-4-15 8-8-18	Demob.	26-7-19
87062	Sgt.	McMillan, C. D.—M.M.			Demob.	20-2-19
336173	Gnr.	McNair, A. J.			Demob.	9-7-19
83689	Bdr.	McNair, G. G.		14-5-17	Demob.	25-5-19
301464	Bdr.	McNaught, A. B.			Demob.	27-5-19
86665	Sgt.	MacNaughton, J.—M.M.		21-8-17 3-9-18	D.ofW.	5-9-18
301206	Gnr.	McNeil, N. K.		27-9-18	M.U.	28-2-19
1258176	Bdr.	MacNeill, V. H.			Demob.	11-7-19
1260316	Dvr.	McNeill, J. D.			Demob.	6-4-19
86960	Dvr.	MacPherson, D.		16-7-17	M.U.	21-11-18
	Capt.	MacPherson, J. S.			Demob.	24-9-19
84210	Gnr.	MacPherson, P. M.		3-9-18	M.U.	19-6-19
317033	Sgt.	MacPherson, W. J.			Demob.	27-5-19
349031	Gnr.	McQuaig, H.			Demob.	20-3-19
1262739	Gnr.	McQueen, J. P.		19-8-17 4-3-18	D.ofW.	11-3-18
2021783	Dvr.	McRae, A.			Demob.	30-7-19
86949	Bdr.	McShane, W. J.		28-5-17	M.U.	7-11-18
	Major	McSloy, J. I.—D.S.O., M. in D.			Demob.	28-5-19
347509	Gnr.	MacSweeney, M. B.		11-8-17	D.ofW.	16-8-17
287	Gnr.	Narraway, P. R.		6-10-16 7-9-18	M.U.	21-2-19
89360	Gnr.	Nash, D.		12-1-17	M.U.	6-5-19
1257845	Gnr.	Nash, J. R.			M.U.	4-11-18
89923	Dvr.	Neita, A. W.			Demob.	27-5-19
83528	Dvr.	Nelson, J. G.		28-9-18	Demob.	27-3-19
89283	Gnr.	Nesbitt, C.		1-10-18	M.U.	7-4-19
83923	Gnr.	Nesbitt, F.			Demob.	11-5-19
343904	Gnr.	Neville, J. L.			M.U.	5-6-19
	*Lieut.	Neville, M. H.			Demob.	12-4-19
	Lieut.	Newcombe, W. A.		23-2-17	Demob.	15-7-19
2591236	Gnr.	Newkiak, A. J.			Demob.	27-5-19
341998	Gnr.	Newman, R. B.			Demob.	27-5-19
434242	Gnr.	Newton, A.			Demob.	28-3-19
87021	Pte.	Nicholas, S. J.		17-10-16	M.U.	15-2-18
300156	Gnr.	Nicholls, H. A.		6-2-18	M.U.	13-1-19
316956	Dvr.	Nicholls, J. R.			Demob.	27-5-19
91202	Gnr.	Nicholson, A.			Demob.	28-2-19
2650677	Sig.	Nicholson, G. H.			Demob.	29-5-19
86965	A/Bdr.	Nickerson, A.		27-4-17	D.ofW.	27-4-17
300105	Cpl.	Nidd, P. A.			Demob.	4-6-19
339102	Gnr.	Nimmo,, W. E. W.			M.U.	6-5-19

*Served as O.R. only with 4th Bde., C.F.A.
**C.A.M.C. att. to 4th Bde., C.F.A.

Number	Rank	Name	Decorations	Wounded	Disposition	Date
90084	Gnr.	Niven, W. E.		12-10-16		
				28-10-16	Demob.	14-7-19
348156	Gnr.	Nixon, E.			Demob.	6-7-19
83198	Pte.	Nixon, H.			M.U.	11-10-18
83699	Gnr.	Noble, G. R.		2-9-18		
				4-11-18	Demob.	27-3-19
83199	*Gnr.	Noden, F.			M.U.	30-1-17
348908	Gnr.	Nodwell, E. W.			Demob.	27-5-19
338337	Gnr.	Nolan, F. J.			Demob.	27-5-19
300174	Gnr.	Nolan, R.			Demob.	11-4-19
89924	Dvr.	Nolet, A.			Demob.	12-6-19
84029	Gnr.	Norcott, T. G.		18-10-17	Demob.	7-5-19
335886	Gnr.	Norman, H. L.			K.I.A.	1-5-17
83697	Cpl.	Norris, W. A.		2-9-18	Demob.	28-8-19
334601	Dvr.	Northgraves, J.			Demob.	27-5-19
86967	Gnr.	Nunn, E. J.			Demob.	21-8-19
86964	Gnr.	Nutkins, F.			Demob.	20-5-19
10684	Dvr.	Nutt, E.			Demob.	16-6-19
340410	Gnr.	Oakes, C. S.			Demob.	27-5-19
459	Dvr.	Oakley, J. H.			M.U.	19-2-19
161105	Gnr.	Oaks, A. W.			Demob.	30-5-19
86969	Sgt.	O'Boyle, R. F.—M.M.			Demob.	29-5-19
2040628	Gnr.	O'Brien, D. L.			Demob.	6-6-19
	Capt.	O'Brien, T. H.—M.C.			Demob.	13-6-19
300392	A/Sgt.	O'Connor, L. J.			Demob.	8-4-19
335892	Gnr.	O'Connor, P. R.			Demob.	6-6-19
	**Lieut.	O'Dell, J. H.			Demob.	5-1-19
344853	Gnr.	Ogilvie, W. G.			Demob.	27-5-19
	Capt.	O'Halloran, M.—M.C.		22-10-16	Demob.	26-5-19
2100796	Sig.	Oicle, L. M.			Demob.	25-7-19
1251404	Gnr.	O'Leary, M. P.			Demob.	10-8-19
34714	***Sgt.	Oliver, H. R.			Demob.	2-7-19
83701	Sgt.	Oliver, H. T.		22-7-17	Demob.	27-5-19
	****Lieut.	Oliver, R. R.—M.C., M. in D.		30-10-17	Demob.	30-3-19
301159	Bdr.	Oliver, W. F.			Demob.	15-6-19
83970	Cpl.	Ollerenshaw, E.			Demob.	8-8-19
339885	Gnr.	O'Loughlin, E. L.		19-4-17	M.U.	31-1-18
	****Capt.	O'Neil, I. L.			Demob.	21-8-19
89927	Dvr.	O'Neill, F.			Demob.	27-5-19
83465	Gnr.	O'Neill, F.		8-5-17	M.U.	2-10-18
7820	Gnr.	O'Neill, J.		31-10-18	Demob.	27-5-19
5122	Cpl.	O'Neill, J. L.		4-11-18	Demob.	6-6-19
342838	Gnr.	O'Neill, M. C.—M.M.		29-9-18	Demob.	31-7-19
83265	Cpl.	O'Neill, R. A.			Demob.	27-5-19
317026	Sgt.	Orchard, R. C.			Demob.	12-4-19
83147	Gnr.	Ostrander, J.		20-11-17	Demob.	3-2-19
83702	Gnr.	Oswald, H. D.		10-11-16		
				12-7-17	M.U.	11-3-19
1251189	A/Sgt.	Ottewell, C. P.			Demob.	21-2-19
83145	Sgt.	Ough, C. R.			Demob.	14-1-19
300528	Sgt.	Overs, G.—M.M.			Demob.	27-5-19
334423	Sig.	Owens, G. E.			Demob.	28-5-19
1263209	Dvr.	Owens, J. F.			Demob.	2-6-19
83263	Gnr.	Padgett, H.		5-5-16	M.U.	10-3-19
84175	Q.M.S.	Page, T. H.			Demob.	12-5-19
83707	Gnr.	Paget, A. J.—M.M.		23-5-16		
				25-8-17	Demob.	27-5-19
316962	Gnr.	Painter, J. R.		30-9-18	D.ofW.	6-10-18
84030	Bdr.	Palframan, W. J.		18-8-17		
				27-9-18	Demob.	21-3-19

*Served in U.K. only with 4th Bde., C.F.A.
**Served in N. East with C.A.M.C.
***C.A.V.C. attached 4th Bde., C.F.A.
****Served as O.R. only with 4th Bde., C.F.A.

Number	Rank	Name	Decorations	Wounded	Disposition	Date
258123	A/Sgt.	Palmen, C. E. G.			Demob.	4-2-19
	Lieut.	Palmer, F. A.—D.C.M.		15-10-17	Demob.	11-4-19
84041	Sgt.	Palmer, H. J.—M.M.			Demob.	14-3-19
2043572	Dvr.	Palmer, P.		4-3-18	Demob.	30-5-19
341352	Dvr.	Palombo, D.			Demob.	22-9-19
345193	Gnr.	Pannanman, A.		31-10-18	Demob.	10-3-19
	*Lieut.	Panter, J. S.			Demob.	17-9-19
86723	Dvr.	Park, J.			Demob.	23-5-19
83988	Gnr.	Parker, E. G.			M.U.	31-1-18
83515	Gnr.	Parker, J.			Demob.	27-5-19
84172	Dvr.	Parker, J. L.		16-4-16	M.U.	19-4-18
114	Dvr.	Parker, R. M.		19-12-16 6-11-17	Demob.	17-5-19
2044121	Gnr.	Parker, R. L.			Demob.	27-7-19
300276	Dvr.	Parker, S. A.		20-10-17	D.ofW.	20-10-17
83987	Dvr.	Parker, W. H.			Demob.	27-5-19
	*Lieut.	Parkinson, N. F.		3-5-17	Ser. No Long. R.	8-7-18
86972	Dvr.	Parks, H.		24-3-16 28-9-18	D.ofW.	29-9-18
150190	Cpl.	Parry, J.		26-4-17	M.U.	20-8-18
83708	Gnr.	Parsons, A. E. D.		21-9-16	Demob.	20-2-19
83951	Sgt.	Parsons, R. R.		2-10-16	Demob.	16-3-19
2152416	Gnr.	Parsons, S. J.			Demob.	27-5-19
83960	Gnr.	Partridge, C.		2-5-17	Demob.	28-5-19
86675	Gnr.	Partridge, H.		4-10-18	M.U.	27-3-19
243295	Gnr.	Partridge, I. O.			Demob.	27-5-19
83251	Gnr.	Pass, W. E.			Demob.	27-5-19
83423	Gnr.	Paterson, A. P.			Demob.	28-5-19
115	Cpl.	Paterson, J. D.		28-4-17	D.ofW.	29-4-17
89931	**Dvr.	Patterson, E.		30-9-16	Demob.	11-9-19
335249	Gnr.	Patterson, F. A.			Demob.	23-5-19
83422	Bdr.	Patterson, J.			M.U.	31-8-17
83709	Gnr.	Patterson, J.			M.U.	26-2-18
86971	Bdr.	Patterson, J. S.		14-1-18	Demob.	27-3-19
89286	Gnr.	Patterson, T. G.			Demob.	27-5-19
83258	Gnr.	Patterson, W.		27-9-18	Demob.	27-5-19
40475	Sgt.	Patteson, E.		3-5-15 28-5-17	M.U.	9-6-18
1251219	Gnr.	Pattison, A. E.		27-9-18	Demob.	31-5-19
83763	Bdr.	Paupst, F.		25-5-16	Demob.	11-2-19
83495	Sgt.	Payne, T.		12-11-16	Demob.	27-5-19
2041555	Gnr.	Peake, V. I. F.			Demob.	6-6-19
398	Dvr.	Pearcy, F. W.			Demob.	1-6-19
86457	Cpl.	Pearson, J.		2-6-17 26-10-17	Demob.	27-8-19
83173	Gnr.	Peat, J.			M.U.	25-2-19
83148	Sgt.	Peel, P. W.			Demob.	2-4-19
83431	Cpl.	Pegg, H.			M.U.	2-5-19
400843	***Pte.	Pell, B.			Un. Age	29-11-17
344887	Dvr.	Pelletier, A. A.			Demob.	23-7-19
	Lieut.	Penno, E. F. L.		28-2-18 3-9-18	Demob.	10-7-19
1261179	A/Sgt.	Pentz, L.			Demob.	5-11-19
83226	A/Sgt.	Peren, G. S.			Com. in R.A.F.	6-10-15
87008	Gnr.	Perkin, F. R.		7-10-16	M.U.	30-3-17
339582	Gnr.	Perkins, J. J.			Demob.	14-7-19
301745	Sgt.	Perkins, W. B.		8-4-17 28-3-18	Demob.	4-1-19
343059	Gnr.	Perrett, A. V.			Demob.	27-5-19
576	Cpl.	Perrin, F. H.			Demob.	26-5-19
83928	Gnr.	Perrins, J. E.			Demob.	25-5-19
338431	Gnr.	Perry, A. S.			Demob.	12-7-19

*Served as O.R. only with 4th Bde., C.F.A.
**Served in N Russia with 16th Bde., C.F.A.
***C.A.M.C. Att. 4th Bde., C.F.A.

Number	Rank	Name	Decorations	Wounded	Disposition	Date
341155	˙ Gnr.	Perry, H. H.		2-9-18	D.of W.	2-9-18
83250	Gnr.	Petrie, J.			M.U.	11-12-17
84243	Gnr.	Pettit, W. H.			K.I.A.	24-4-16
249811	Gnr.	Pew, W. H.			Demob.	6-6-19
86229	A/Bdr.	Phair, G.			Demob.	29-5-19
397	Sgt.	Phelan, C.—M.S.M., M. in D.			Demob.	28-5-19
83925	Gnr.	Philip, F. D.			Demob.	24-5-19
	*Lieut.	Phillipps, A. H.—M.M., M. in D.			Demob.	11-11-19
336215	Gnr.	Phillips, E. G.			D.of D.	22-2-19
84038	Dvr.	Phillips, J. M.			Com. Imp. Army	13-9-15
86263	Cpl.	Phillips, W.			Demob.	19-9-19
89930	Gnr.	Picard, W.			Demob.	22-5-19
340392	Gnr.	Pickard, F.			Demob.	27-5-19
301725	Dvr.	Picken, J. W.		2-9-18	Demob.	29-5-19
83610	Sgt.	Pickett, C.			D.of D.	10-4-17
339008	Dvr.	Pickworth, H. D.		9-5-17	Demob.	27-5-19
85108	Gnr.	Pignotiello, J.			M.U.	2-5-17
	Lieut.	Pilgrim, E. W.		4-11-18	Demob.	22-3-19
54	Cpl.	Pilley, J. W.		22-7-17	M.U.	25-7-18
83706	Gnr.	Pinder, J. E. C.			Demob.	21-7-19
83421	A/Bdr.	Pinney, S.			Demob.	7-8-19
83926	Gnr.	Piper, T.		30-8-18	Demob.	27-4-19
84174	Sgt.	Pipes, J.			M.U.	25-9-17
84226	Gnr.	Pitt, C. H.		18-1-18 4-9-18	M.U.	28-8-19
83141	Gnr.	Plato, P.			K.I.A.	31-5-16
83132	Bdr.	Platts, J.		20-4-17	Demob.	26-5-19
333946	**Gnr.**	Plewes, V. R.			Demob.	27-5-19
304677	**Gnr.**	Plewes, W. J.			Demob.	4-5-19
	Lieut.	Plunkett, E. A. P.		24-4-17	K.I.A.	16-7-17
83517	**Gnr.**	Pollard, T.		3-6-16	M.U.	10-2-17
2487409	Gnr.	Poole, A. E.			Demob.	13-7-19
342181	Gnr.	Pope, G. H.		16-8-18	M.U.	25-3-20
84171	Sgt.	Pope, R. H.		12-10-16	M.U.	17-6-18
161184	Gnr.	Port, L.			M.U.	13-8-19
2100762	Sig.	Porter, J. L.			Demob.	6-6-19
341186	Gnr.	Potter, H. A.			Demob.	27-6-19
1251968	Dvr.	Poulter, N.			Demob.	27-5-19
84176	Gnr.	Poulton, R. W.			Demob.	11-5-19
	Lieut.	Powell, A. W. F.			Demob.	5-7-19
84177	**Gnr.	Powell, J. E.		28-8-17	Demob.	28-4-19
	Major	Powell, V. H. de B.—M.C.		6-10-16 10-9-17	Died	2-1-18
2353321	A/Bdr.	Powers, A. D. J.			Demob.	27-5-19
91649	Sgt.	Preece, G.		30-9-18	Demob.	30-7-19
338291	Gnr.	Prescott, C. B.			Demob.	2-4-19
89791	Dvr.	Presley, H.			Demob.	14-3-19
83506	A/Cpl.	Preston, J. W.			Demob.	20-9-19
522809	Gnr.	Preston, R. A.		24-10-17	Demob.	26-3-19
2152548	Dvr.	Preston, W.			Demob.	27-5-19
89935	Gnr.	Price, A. H.			Demob.	14-1-20
83965	Dvr.	Price, C.			Demob.	17-9-19
86970	Gnr.	Price, C. S.		3-11-17	M.U.	15-4-19
83927	Gnr.	Price, G.		20-9-18	Demob.	10-2-19
	Lieut.	Price, W. J.			Demob.	18-7-19
1251604	Gnr.	Priest, A. D.			Demob.	27-5-19
2045040	A/Bdr.	Priest, K.			Demob.	27-5-19
341269	Gnr.	Pringle, E. E.		2-9-18	M.U.	25-1-19
1251301	Gnr.	Probert, A.			Demob.	17-8-19
	***Lieut.	Proctor, W. D.			Demob.	4-4-19
83131	Dvr.	Pullin, F. G.		26-11-15 9-5-17	Demob.	30-3-19

*C.O.C. att. served as O.R only with 4th Bde., C.F.A.
**Served in U.K. only with 4th Bde., C.F.A.
***Served as O.R. only with 4th Bde., C.F.A.

Number	Rank	Name	Decorations	Wounded	Disposition	Date
	Lieut.	Purchas, C. M. G.—M.C.		25-4-17	Demob.	1-1-19
84012	Gnr.	Purdie, J. C.		15-10-17	Demob.	25-5-19
83607	Sgt.	Purdon, C. H.		4-5-17	Demob.	29-8-19
83464	Cpl.	Pursell, G. A.			Demob.	27-5-19
453	Dvr.	Purvis, G.		25-5-17	Demob.	24-4-19
83196	Dvr.	Puttock, J.			M.U.	17-5-16
339546	Gnr.	Pyle, A.			Demob.	27-5-19
84224	Gnr.	Quelch, W.			M.U.	22-7-18
340876	Dvr.	Quigley, A. J.			Demob.	28-7-19
339792	Gnr.	Quinn, J. B.		24-8-18	D.ofD.	3-9-18
83022	Dvr.	Radford, H. E.			Demob.	6-6-19
532343	*Pte.	Rae, A.			Demob.	29-5-19
	**Capt.	Rae, C. A.			Demob.	3-9-19
2100825	Sig.	Rafuse, J. H.			K.I.A.	10-8-18
86026	Bdr.	Raine, H. G.		8-1-18	Demob.	31-3-19
86199	Bdr.	Rait, D.—M.M.			Demob.	29-5-19
341396	Gnr.	Ralphs, T. W.			Demob.	19-2-19
336092	Gnr.	Ralston, J. J.			Demob.	27-5-19
3810	Gnr.	Ramsay, F. K.			Demob.	26-8-19
19138	Gnr.	Ramsay, T. C.			Demob.	18-5-19
86975	Gnr.	Rand, C. T.		26-4-17	Demob.	30-1-19
90081	Dvr.	Rawlings, A.			Demob.	29-5-19
90018	Dvr.	Rayner, J.			K.I.A.	21-6-18
	Capt.	Read, J. E.—M. in D.		15-1-17	M.U.	26-7-18
86458	Gnr.	Rean, C. H.			Demob.	23-5-19
333944	Dvr.	Reardon, C. W.			Demob.	27-5-19
343299	Gnr.	Reardon, D. W.			Demob.	27-5-19
84183	A/Sgt.	Reason, F.			M.U.	27-3-19
83033	***Sgt.	Reason, V. W.			Demob.	11-7-19
	**Capt.	Reddick, J. W.			Demob.	17-7-19
	Lieut.	Reddy, E. B. F.		4-9-18	Demob.	30-12-18
337899	Gnr.	Redman, E. H.			Demob.	27-5-19
83958	Gnr.	Redmond, J.			Demob.	26-5-19
	Lieut.	Redmond, L. J. H.			Demob.	4-1-19
1251009	Gnr.	Reed, G. W. H.			Demob.	29-8-19
333945	Gnr.	Reed, H. M.			Demob.	27-5-19
2327625	Gnr.	Reed, N. H.			Demob.	27-5-19
348980	Sig.	Reesor, P. J.		22-7-17	Demob.	16-6-19
336817	Pte.	Reid, E. D.			Demob.	1-4-19
2327323	Sig.	Reid, G. C.		27-9-18	Demob.	11-3-19
	Capt.	Reid, L. A.—M.C.			Demob.	4-8-19
1250759	Gnr.	Reid. R. H.			Demob.	5-6-19
336816	Gnr.	Reid, V. J.			Demob.	18-2-19
83500	Gnr.	Renfrew, G. A.			K.I.A.	7-11-17
192710	Gnr.	Renfrew, W. G.			Demob.	6-7-19
342332	Gnr.	Revie, D. W. W.			Demob.	18-9-19
344975	Gnr.	Rew, T.			Demob.	22-4-19
2043027	Gnr.	Reynolds, E.			Demob.	31-5-19
2327617	Gnr.	Reynolds, H.			Demob.	5-6-19
2049665	Gnr.	Rhude, W.			Demob.	15-6-19
85781	Gnr.	Rice, A. J.			Demob.	2-5-19
83780	****Dvr.	Rice, M. B.			M.U.	28-12-16
89601	Gnr.	Rice, T. H.			Demob.	11-8-19
87045	Cpl.	Rice, W. H.		17-3-17	M.U.	11-1-19
83183	Gnr.	Richards, D. C.			M.U.	16-3-19
336155	Gnr.	Richards, G. W.			Demob.	15-6-19
89765	Gnr.	Richards, H.			Demob.	22-5-19
83714	Bdr.	Richardson, C. H.			M.U.	29-11-18
84178	Dvr.	Richardson, H. J.			to R.F.C.	10-3-17
84184	****A/Bdr.	Richardson, I.			M.U.	1-3-19

*C.A.M.C. Att. 4th Bde., C.F.A.
**Served as O.R. only with 4th Bde., C.F.A.
***C.A.D.C. att. 4th Bde., C.F.A.
****U.K. only 4th Bde., C.F.A.

Number	Rank	Name	Decorations	Wounded	Disposition	Date
	Lieut.	Richardson, W. F.—M.M.		5-10-16	Demob.	3-6-19
	*Major	Richmond, L. A.			Demob.	10-7-19
300118	Dvr.	Ricketts, L. S.		16-9-16		
				5-11-17	Demob.	28-2-19
316968	Cpl.	Riddell, W. A.		29-9-18	Demob.	10-3-19
83182	Gnr.	Riddell, W. C.			K.I.A.	24-8-16
335804	Gnr.	Rideout, R. D.			K.I.A.	16-6-17
83105	Dvr.	Ridgway, R.		30-10-16	Demob.	11-6-19
1250134	Gnr.	Ridout, T.			Demob.	29-5-19
2522388	Gnr.	Rielly, C. T.		2-9-18	Demob.	27-5-19
86977	Gnr.	Riley, G. T.			Demob.	23-8-19
86979	Dvr.	Riley, J.—M.M.			Demob.	30-5-19
83521	A/Sgt.	Rimmer, H.		13-4-17	Demob.	23-9-19
83430	A/RSM	Rimmer, N. B.		15-5-16	M.U.	31-12-17
83426	B.S.M.	Rimmer, W. B.—D.C.M.		16-11-16	M.U.	5-3-17
50493	*A/Sgt.	Rippon, N. E.			Demob.	6-2-19
83427	Gnr.	Rippon, T.		8-5-17	Demob.	17-2-19
334338	Dvr.	Riseborough, W. J.			Demob.	27-5-19
83429	Dvr.	Ritchey, J.			Demob.	31-5-19
86743	Sig.	Ritchie, R.			Demob.	5-7-19
2152490	Gnr.	Roach, E. A.			Demob.	27-5-19
87001	Gnr.	Robb, N.		23-2-18	Demob.	12-2-19
85421	A/Cpl.	Robbins, H. J.			Demob.	23-8-19
83107	Gnr.	Robbins, S. H.		30-9-16	M.U.	9-11-18
83255	Dvr.	Roberge, P.			Demob.	17-5-19
300158	Gnr.	Roberge, W.			Demob.	17-5-19
339111	Gnr.	Roberts, A. R.			Demob.	24-5-19
83930	Dvr.	Roberts, H.			Demob.	28-3-19
83193	Dvr.	Roberts, R. H.		22-4-17	M.U.	6-5-18
83234	Far.				Cess. of	
	Sgt.	Roberts, R.			W. Pay	30-10-16
83249	A/Bdr.	Roberts, S. R.		11-7-16	Demob.	23-4-19
84283	Gnr.	Roberts, V. F.			M.U.	6-2-19
86027	Gnr.	Robertson, J.			Demob.	29-5-19
83608	Gnr.	Robertson, J. M.			Com. in	
					I. Army	6-10-15
90080	Gnr.	Robertson, R. T.		30-9-18	Demob.	21-5-19
83108	Dvr.	Robins, T. E.			M.U.	10-12-16
87059	Dvr.	Robinson, E.		6-9-17	M.U.	18-6-19
83204	Gnr.	Robinson, G. W.			M.U.	6-2-19
1251601	Gnr.	Robinson, H. A.			Demob.	11-7-19
	Lieut.	Robinson, H. K.			Demob.	4-7-19
249201	Dvr.	Robinson, W.		23-2-17	Demob.	28-5-19
86873	A/Sgt.	Robson, C.			Demob.	14-2-19
	Major	Robson, S.—D.S.O.			Demob.	28-6-19
84182	A/Sgt.	Rogers, F. W.			Demob.	10-5-19
316972	Sig.	Rogerson, J. E.			Demob.	27-5-19
83139	Gnr.	Roland, R.			Demob.	26-5-19
1251597	Gnr.	Rolland, H. S.		7-8-17		
				9-11-17	Demob.	12-5-19
83959	Gnr.	Roope, G. A.		6-11-16		
				2-10-18	Demob.	3-4-19
1263202	Gnr.	Rooth, A.			Demob.	12-6-19
84252	**Gnr.	Roper, E. G.			Demob.	25-4-19
339343	Gnr.	Rose, H. A.			Demob.	3-8-19
339465	Cpl.	Rose, H. K.			Demob.	1-6-19
342193	Gnr.	Rose, N. A.			Demob.	7-8-19
341808	Dvr.	Rosevear, W. J.			Demob.	27-5-19
83202	Dvr.	Ross, D.			Demob.	1-2-19
1257803	A/Bdr.	Ross, D. G.—M.M.			Demob.	17-7-19
83428	Gnr.	Ross, G. G.			Demob.	9-5-19
2001227	Gnr.	Ross, G. B.			Demob.	15-6-19
84017	Gnr.	Ross, H.			Demob.	8-8-19

*C.A.M.C. att. 4th Bde., C.F.A.
***U.K. only 4th Bde., C.F.A.

Number	Rank	Name	Decorations	Wounded	Disposition	Date
342911	Gnr.	Ross, J. E.			Demob.	27-5-19
83200	Cpl.	Ross, J.		22-7-16	M.U.	31-1-18
	Lt. Col.	Ross, M. N.—D.S.O., Bar, M. in D.		1-10-18	Demob.	21-8-19
84016	Dvr.	Ross, R.			Demob.	28-5-19
349901	Dvr.	Ross, W.			Demob.	6-7-19
476561	Gnr.	Rosson, R. J.			Demob.	27-5-19
	Lieut.	Routh, W. B.—M.M.		16-9-16	Demob.	17-5-19
91487	Dvr.	Rowden, S. C.			Demob.	18-8-19
90056	Cpl.	Rowe, T.			Demob.	27-5-19
84181	A/Bdr.	Rowland, J.		31-10-16	M.U.	31-3-18
90073	Sig.	Rowland, W. J.—M.M.			Demob.	21-6-19
	Lieut.	Rowley, T. H.—M. in D.			Demob.	7-4-19
83201	Gnr.	Rowntree, I.			Demob.	3-4-19
86001	Gnr.	Roy, F.			Demob.	14-9-19
1258272	Gnr.	Roy, I.			Demob.	16-5-19
333861	Gnr.	Rumball, F. H.			Demob.	27-5-19
345963	Gnr.	Runions, Z.			Demob.	12-7-19
83931	A/Sgt.	Ruse, R.			Demob.	26-7-19
121	Gnr.	Russell, A.			Demob.	14-7-19
84180	*Gnr.	Russell, H. G.		24-5-16 30-7-17	Demob.	3-3-19
83711	*Cpl.	Russell, P.			Demob.	25-4-19
300436	Dvr.	Russell, R. G.			Demob.	28-5-19
77064	Dvr.	Ruth, H. V.			Demob.	20-2-19
2043044	Gnr.	Rutherford, M. R.			Demob.	6-7-19
310710	A/Bdr.	Rutherford, T. N.			Demob.	31-5-19
84179	A/Bdr.	Rutherford, W. J.			M.U.	31-12-17
438844	Gnr.	Rutledge, E.			Demob.	8-3-19
83712	Dvr.	Ryan, E. C.		19-7-16	D.ofW.	19-7-16
	Capt.	Ryan, J. R.		9-12-17	M.U.	14-4-18
91556	A/Bdr.	Ryder, J. L.		4-3-18 30-9-18	Demob.	27-5-19
90189	Dvr.	Sabean, J.			Demob.	27-5-19
83463	Dvr.	Sage, E.			Demob.	29-5-19
89370	Sig.	Sale, F. W.			Demob.	11-7-19
91229	Gnr.	Salisbury, G.		28-3-16	Demob.	29-5-19
86680	Gnr.	Salter, J. R.			M.U.	17-1-18
805145	Sig.	Samis, J. C.—M. in D.			Demob.	27-5-19
1262714	Gnr.	Sampson, A.		23-4-17	Demob.	13-4-19
300782	Gnr.	Sampson, G. S.			Demob.	5-6-19
83441	Dvr.	Sanders, S.			Demob.	21-5-19
338916	Gnr.	Sanderson, S.			Demob.	18-3-19
84190	Dvr.	Sanderson, W.		6-10-16	M.U.	31-5-18
1260289	Gnr.	Saunders, G. E. —M.S.M.			Demob.	7-3-19
89941	Gnr.	Sauve, A.			Demob.	27-5-19
89948	Gnr.	Sauve, O.			Demob.	18-2-19
	Major	Savage, H. M.—D.S.O., Bar, M. in D.		24-8-18	Demob.	8-4-19
348745	Gnr.	Scammell, P. F.			Demob.	30-7-19
1250180	Gnr.	Scarrow, A. O.			Demob.	11-6-19
83437	Cpl.	Scearce, A. W.			M.U.	30-6-17
300406	Gnr.	Schofield, F. L.			M.U.	31-12-17
84220	Sgt.	Schofield, S.—M.M.		1-10-16	Demob.	25-5-19
84185	Sgt.	Schofield, W.		2-10-16 10-9-18	M.U.	25-3-19
83442	Sgt.	Scott, A.			Demob.	27-3-19
	Lieut.	Scott, C. O.			Demob.	2-6-19
334625	Gnr.	Scott, G. S.			Demob.	27-5-19
341375	Gnr.	Scott, H. C.			Demob.	27-5-19
300195	Dvr.	Scott, J.			Deserter	4-12-18
83491	Gnr.	Scott, J. O.			M.U.	21-7-16
2353319	Sig.	Scott, N. C.			Demob.	4-7-19
87042	Gnr.	Scott, W. J.			Demob.	21-5-19
83479	Dvr.	Scott, W.			M.U.	17-1-19
339607	Gnr.	Sears, C. A.			Demob.	8-4-19

*U.K. only with 4th Bde., C.F.A.

Number	Rank	Name	Decorations	Wounded	Disposition	Date
	*Lieut.	Sears, E. D.		1-11-18	Demob.	10-11-19
348352	Dvr.	Seddon, F. C.			Demob.	23-6-19
83967	Bdr.	Sedgwick, H.		25-9-16	M.U.	7-2-18
1257866	Bdr.	Seely, C. R.		27-9-18	Demob.	27-5-19
83480	A/Sgt.	Segre, B. H.		26-3-16	App. Com.	
					I. Army	12-7-18
89943	Dvr.	Selway, G. R.			Demob.	27-5-19
86872	Sgt.	Sergeant, C.		27-4-17	D.of W.	27-4-17
91831	Dvr.	Service, J. R.		3-5-17	Demob.	27-5-19
349869	Dvr.	Seward, N. W.			Demob.	27-5-19
83118	Gnr.	Seymour, C. N.		1-6-16	K.I.A.	10-11-17
341831	Gnr.	Shanahan, J.			Demob.	27-5-19
341872	Gnr.	Shanahan, W. G.			Demob.	27-5-19
	Col.	Sharman, C. H. L.—C.M.G.., C.B.E., O. of St. Vladimir 4th Cl. with S.		18-5-15	Demob.	14-8-19
340406	Gnr.	Sharp, D. C.		30-9-18	Demob.	5-4-19
5343	A/Bdr.	Sharpe, J.			Demob.	12-7-19
2100460	Gnr.	Sharpe, F. N.			Demob.	27-5-19
84189	Sgt.	Sharratt, L.			Demob.	25-5-19
83124	Gnr.	Shave, P. L.			M.U.	28-11-18
83873	**Gnr.	Shaw, E. J.		1-9-16	M.U.	27-11-17
86726	Gnr.	Shaw, J. C.		19-10-17		
				31-10-18	Demob.	20-5-19
41785	Gnr.	Shaw, W.			M.U.	30-4-18
	Capt.	Shaw, W. E. V.—M. in D.		23-10-17	Demob.	29-5-19
83023	Gnr.	Sheekey, R.		11-11-16	M.U.	17-4-18
184	Gnr.	Shennan, A. H.		11-10-16	Demob.	7-8-19
6072	Dvr.	Shepherd, H. T.			M.U.	12-4-18
87063	Bdr.	Shepherd, W. N.		24-7-18	Demob.	19-5-19
1251285	Bdr.	Sheppard, A. C.			Demob.	4-6-19
322971	Gnr.	Sherred, S. C.			Demob.	27-5-19
308641	Sig.	Sherwood, L. B.			Demob.	17-5-19
80060	Gnr.	Shinnan, A.			Demob.	31-5-19
83749	Gnr.	Shipley, G. H.			M.U.	30-9-17
234	Dvr.	Shipton, E. H.		21-4-17	Demob.	27-5-19
1251707	Gnr.	Shone, G. H.			Demob.	9-7-19
86146	Sgt.	Shoobert, W. A.			Demob.	29-5-19
2043123	Gnr.	Shore, W. J.			Demob.	22-5-19
83716	Dvr.	Short, F.			K.I.A.	6-9-18
334903	Gnr.	Shrimpton, G. P.			Demob.	11-7-19
83146	Gnr.	Sibley, P. E.			M.U.	31-12-17
2022490	Gnr.	Siddall, H. S.			Demob.	1-6-19
	Major	Sifton, C.—D.S.O., M. in D.		7-11-16		
				9-8-18		
				4-9-18	Demob.	28-5-19
83493	Cpl.	Simmonds, R.			Demob.	21-3-19
	*Lieut.	Simmons, J. F. L.—M.C.		9-4-17	Demob.	5-5-19
84186	Gnr.	Simon, H. C.			D.of D.	2-4-17
	Lieut.	Simonds, W. F.			Demob.	5-8-19
3181001	Gnr.	Simpson, A. B.			Demob.	15-6-19
338143	Sig.	Simpson, H. H.		2-11-18	Demob.	27-5-19
307693	Gnr.	Simpson, J.		10-8-18	M.U.	1-4-18
86005	Gnr.	Simpson, J. B.		12-10-16		
				2-11-17		
				30-9-18	Demob.	27-9-19
339628	Gnr.	Simpson, D. D.		3-9-18	Demob.	19-2-19
303690	Gnr.	Simpson, P.			Demob.	27-8-19
	Lt. Col.	Simpson, W.			M.U.	4-12-19
348140	Dvr.	Simpson, W.			Demob.	28-6-19
345050	Gnr.	Sinclair, G.			Demob.	27-3-19
84245	Dvr.	Sinclair, H. C.			Demob.	25-5-19
91231	Gnr.	Sinclair, J.			K.I.A.	30-10-17

*Served as O.R. only with 4th Bde., C.F.A.
**Served in U.K. only with 4th Bde., C.F.A.

Number	Rank	Name	Decorations	Wounded	Disposition	Date
83030	Cpl.	Sinclair, R. B.			Com. in I. Army	4-10-15
301960	Gnr.	Sinclair, W.			Demob.	27-5-19
345033	Dvr.	Sinnett, R. L.			Demob.	27-5-19
2522481	Gnr.	Sinton, N. R.			Demob.	27-5-19
83719	Gnr.	Sisley, A. J. S.			Com. in I. Army	31-12-16
90087	Sig.	Skinner, A.			Demob.	31-7-19
1057413	Gnr.	Skinner, S. D.			Demob.	28-5-19
316979	Gnr.	Skippen, W. J.			Demob.	27-5-19
345847	Gnr.	Skuce, E. D.			Demob.	22-5-19
83936	Sgt.	Slack, F. J.		5-6-16	D. of W.	5-6-16
90844	Gnr.	Sladden, A.			K.I.A.	22-4-17
1251410	Gnr.	Smail, E. C.			Demob.	31-5-19
90845	Dvr.	Small, S.		6-5-17	M.U.	1-2-18
475287	A/Cpl.	Smart, F. A.			Demob.	3-2-19
89533	A/Bdr.	Smart, W. W.		1-5-17	M.U.	24-5-18
2601932	Gnr.	Smillie, W.			Demob.	1-6-19
316980	Gnr.	Smith, A. H.			Demob.	28-5-19
86730	Dvr.	Smith, A. T.			Demob.	30-5-19
92994	Bdr.	Smith, A.			Demob.	28-7-19
83112	Cpl.	Smith, B.		25-8-16	M.U.	25-1-18
2522537	Gnr.	Smith, C.			Demob.	27-5-19
875445	Gnr.	Smith, C.			Demob.	6-6-19
	*Lieut.	Smith, C. A.—M.C.		28-10-17	Demob.	31-3-19
83445	Sgt.	Smith, E. J.			M.U.	31-7-19
	*Lieut.	Smith, F. L.			Demob.	6-7-19
1258249	Dvr.	Smith, F. T.			Demob.	16-6-19
83787	Dvr.	Smith, G.			Demob.	27-3-19
	Lieut.	Smith, G. L.			Demob.	28-5-19
341832	Dvr.	Smith, H. J.			Demob.	27-5-19
339616	Gnr.	Smith, H. W.		31-10-17	Demob.	3-6-19
590	Gnr.	Smith, J.		13-8-17	Demob.	27-5-19
301488	Cpl.	Smith, J.		20-10-17 2-10-18	Demob.	18-2-19
83212	S/Sgt.	Smith, J. C.			Demob.	4-7-19
83166	Cpl.	Smith, J.			Demob.	11-7-19
343083	Gnr.	Smith, L. F.			Demob.	27-5-19
3032531	Gnr.	Smith, M.			M.U.	9-11-18
83157	Gnr	Smith, R.			M.U.	30-4-18
313970	Gnr.	Smith, R.		11-5-17	M.U.	4-2-19
339842	Dvr.	Smith, R. K.		8-5-17	Demob.	27-5-19
862903	Gnr.	Smith, R. J.			Demob.	28-8-19
344129	Gnr.	Smith, V. R.			Demob.	27-5-19
83722	Gnr.	Smith, W.		3-5-17	M.U.	13-9-19
2557336	Gnr.	Smith, W. B.			Demob.	21-5-19
476567	A/Sgt.	Smith, W. H.			Demob.	12-6-19
3055877	Gnr.	Smith, W. H.			Demob.	27-5-19
83470	Gnr.	Smith, W. J.		11-10-16	Demob.	27-3-19
1251445	Gnr.	Smith, W. P.			Demob.	31-5-19
89952	Gnr.	Smithers, G. T.			Demob.	6-2-19
2601931	Gnr.	Smyth, H. S.			Demob.	27-5-19
605	Gnr.	Snelgrove, H.			M.U.	23-8-18
83002	A/Sgt.	Snelgrove, R. A.			App. Com. I. Army	30-4-18
1251207	Gnr.	Snider, E. C.			Demob.	2-8-19
342179	Gnr.	Snyder, E. L.			Demob.	23-4-19
340962	Dvr.	Somerville, K. R.			Demob.	27-5-19
339900	Gnr.	Sommerville, W. L.		3-9-18	Demob.	7-8-19
84280	Gnr.	Soulsby, E.—M.M.		3-5-17	M.U.	27-3-19
89950	Gnr.	Southan, E. J.			Demob.	7-4-19
1260285	Gnr.	Sowerbutts, C.			Demob.	14-3-19
3055607	Gnr.	Spafford, L.			Demob.	27-5-19
40257	L/Cpl.	Sparham, H. A.			Demob.	14-5-19

*Served as O.R. only with 4th Bde., C.F.A.

Number	Rank	Name	Decorations	Wounded	Disposition	Date
687679	Dvr.	Sparks, W. J.			Demob.	27-6-19
316984	*Gnr.	Spearn, W. A.		1-10-18	M.U.	9-4-19
524418	Pte.	Speed, C. R. S.			M.U.	20-5-18
128	Sgt.	Speight, S.		3-9-18	Demob.	23-1-19
197	Cpl.	Speirs, W. M.		27-1-18	K.I.A.	28-10-18
1258123	Gnr.	Spence, H.			Minor	12-7-18
89944	Sgt.	Spencer, A. W.			Demob.	3-11-19
334483	Gnr.	Spencer, G. R.			Demob.	27-3-19
43651	Gnr.	Spicer, J. H.		12-11-17	Demob.	15-2-19
2040663	Gnr.	Spires, J.			Demob.	6-6-19
84187	Cpl.	Spooner, W. S.		2-10-16	Demob.	9-5-19
83757	Gnr.	Spratt, S.		4-9-18	Demob.	4-2-19
83207	Dvr.	Spriggs, P.			Demob.	8-11-19
83723	Dvr.	Springer, E. F.			M.U.	9-3-17
83765	Dvr.	Sproule, W. R.			M.U.	30-6-17
86985	Gnr.	Squires, M.		12-11-17	Demob.	13-5-19
300563	Gnr.	Stainsby, W. R.		19-5-16	M.U.	28-4-19
669401	Gnr.	Stainton, M. M.			Demob.	27-5-19
	**Lieut.	Stairs, K. S.			K.I.A.	30-9-18
84249	Gnr.	Stamp, C. H.		21-9-16	Demob.	26-3-19
15177	Gnr.	Stanbridge, P. C.		29-4-15 17-4-16 2-6-17	Demob.	6-8-19
86731	Bdr.	Stanbridge, P. C.		24-11-16 21-1-18	Demob.	30-6-19
86202	A/Sgt.	Stanford, K.		12-5-17	Demob.	21-3-19
84188	Cpl.	Stanley, R. C.			K.I.A.	27-9-18
83934	A/Cpl.	Staples, A. H.			K.I.A.	11-5-17
314695	S/Sth.	Staples, C. R.		3-9-18	Demob.	27-5-19
349737	Dvr.	Staples, H. H.			Demob.	27-5-19
270240	Gnr.	Stapleton, C.		28-9-18	M.U.	12-12-19
341129	Gnr.	Starke, K. M.			Demob.	27-5-19
41340	Far.Sgt.	Starkey, J. S.—French Croix de G.			Demob.	24-8-19
349016	Gnr.	Starr, F. A. E.		30-10-17	Demob.	15-7-19
83935	Cpl.	Starr, W. T.			Demob.	27-5-19
1251711	Dvr.	Stars, J. F.			M.U.	6-1-19
84031	Gnr.	Staton, S. N.			K.I.A.	21-10-16
2522485	Gnr.	St. Denis, H.			Demob.	2-7-19
	Major.	Steacy, W. E.—M.C.		25-11-17	D.ofD.	25-11-18
83961	Sgt.	Stebbing, C. D.			M.U.	8-3-17
1250874	Gnr.	Stedman, E. F.			Demob.	30-5-19
1251794	Gnr.	Stephens, A. C.			Demob.	24-1-19
90341	Dvr.	Stephenson, E.			Demob.	30-3-19
1251264	Gnr.	Sterling, G. W.			Demob.	14-6-19
343155	Gnr.	Sterns, H. D.			Demob.	15-6-19
161182	Gnr.	Stevenson, G. A.		30-10-17	M.U.	7-2-19
83205	Gnr.	Stevenson, W.			Demob.	21-5-19
83769	A/Sgt.	Stewart, A.			Demob.	13-11-19
2522426	Gnr.	Stewart, D. K. M.			Demob.	20-9-19
336063	Gnr.	Stewart, E. A.			Demob.	11-4-19
	Lt. Col	Stewart, J. C.—D.S.O., M. in D.		12-4-17	Demob.	9-4-19
89528	***Sgt.	Stewart, J. H.			Demob.	27-5-19
300134	A/Sgt.	Stewart, K. A.		17-4-17 19-10-17	Demob.	7-2-19
1251002	Gnr.	Stewart, K. P.			M.U.	14-7-18
83253	Whr.	Stewart, R.			Demob.	29-5-19
335295	Gnr.	Stewart, R.			Demob.	27-5-19
89527	Gnr.	Stitt, W.		31-7-17	M.U.	11-3-19
316986	Gnr.	Stogdill, G. W.		8-5-17	Demob.	27-5-19
	**Lieut.	Stokes, H. E.		3-11-15	Demob.	29-5-19
2341494	Gnr.	Stokes, H. D.			Demob.	27-5-19
344105	Gnr.	Stokes, J. F.			Demob.	31-5-19
83601	R.S.M.	Stone, A.			Demob.	23-12-18

*C.A.M.C. attached
**Served as O.R. with 4th Bde., C.F.A.
***C.A.V.C. att. to 4th Bde., C.F.A.

Number	Rank	Name	Decorations	Wounded	Disposition	Date
83435	Gnr.	Storer, E.			M.U.	21-10-16
2557419	Gnr.	Strachan, S. R.			Demob.	1-6-19
342986	Gnr.	Stratton, S.		8-8-18	Demob.	27-5-19
2601939	Gnr.	Strong, J. C.			Demob.	1-6-19
83976	Gnr.	Strong, W. J.		1-5-17	Demob.	15-7-19
344916	Cpl.	Stuart, C. H.			**Demob.**	27-5-19
1251321	Gnr.	Stubbs, H.			Demob.	27-5-19
	Lieut.	Stubbs, J. R.—M.C.			Demob.	1-6-19
86981	B.S.M.	Studdert, P.—D.C.M.			Demob.	29-5-19
2040516	Dvr.	Stultz, H. H.		4-11-17	Demob.	6-6-19
83443	Dvr.	Sullivan, A.			Demob.	6-6-19
1251242	Gnr.	Sullivan, C. L.		10-8-18	Demob.	20-2-18
86982	Cpl.	Sullivan, D.			Demob.	29-5-19
83721	'*Cpl.	Sullivan, J.		25-9-16 8-8-17	Demob.	23-4-19
83748	Gnr.	Summerhill, W. J.			Demob.	30-3-19
90222	Dvr.	Summers, J. T.			Demob.	6-6-19
1251744	Gnr.	Sutherland, A. J.			Demob.	27-5-19
340327	Gnr.	Sutherland, A.			Demob.	24-6-20
89942	Dvr.	Sutherland, W. J.		26-4-17 28-9-18	Demob.	3-1-19
1251377	Gnr.	Swallow, C. H.			Demob.	25-4-19
83439	Dvr.	Swan, J.			Demob.	27-5-19
	**Lieut.	Swann, H. F.			M.U.	28-9-18
	Major	Swift, C. J.		3-5-17	Demob.	25-5-19
347544	Gnr.	Swift, W. J.		30-4-17	D.ofW.	30-4-17
339595	Gnr.	Sykes, S. M.			Demob.	1-6-19
840	Gnr.	Symington, H, E.		7-9-18	Demob.	26-4-19
83526	Dvr.	Symons, R. C.			M.U.	31-8-17
89982	Gnr.	Tabrett, J.			K.I.A.	24-10-17
340404	Dvr.	Tanner, C. A.			Demob.	27-5-19
84192	Cpl.	Tansley, J. E.			Demob.	11-9-19
83237	S/Sgt.	Tapson, G. C.			Demob.	14-7-19
301365	Cpl.	Tart, B. R.			Demob.	29-5-19
1250879	Gnr.	Tarzwell, W. L.			Demob.	18-9-19
347555	Dvr.	Taschereau, R. H.			Demob.	21-6-19
150226	Dvr.	Taylor, A. G.			Demob.	20-2-19
	***Capt.	Taylor, D. B.			Demob.	20-9-19
2522310	Gnr.	Taylor, F. M.			Demob.	27-5-19
	Capt.	Taylor, G. V.			K.I.A.	13-11-16
316987	Sgt.	Taylor, H. J.			M.U.	31-3-19
90041	Dvr.	Taylor, J.			Demob.	21-3-19
342252	Dvr.	Taylor, J. H.			Demob.	27-5-19
238048	Dvr.	Taylor, L.			Demob.	26-5-19
83160	Bdr.	Taylor, R. M.			K.I.A.	8-1-16
90014	Gnr.	Taylor, W. A.		11-8-18	Demob.	29-3-19
91239	Gnr.	Teer, A. G.			Demob.	1-6-19
1251897	Gnr.	Tees, F. A.			Demob.	27-5-19
83937	A/Sgt.	Terry, A. G.		14-5-17	Demob.	26-4-19
86178	Gnr.	Tetlow, H.		2-9-18	Demob.	5-7-19
	Lt. Col.	Thackray, R. G.		20-3-15	Demob.	1-10-19
86989	Dvr.	Thebo, B.			Demob.	2-8-19
86684	Gnr.	Thom, J.—M.M.		12-5-17	Demob.	5-4-19
413	Gnr.	Thomas, C.			K.I.A.	14-1-16
301993	Bdr.	Thomas, D. G.		11-8-18	M.U.	26-9-19
83236	Gnr.	Thomas, E.			M.U.	21-2-19
83447	Gnr.	Thomas, G.			M.U.	20-9-16
89502	Sgt.	Thomas, H. W.			Demob.	2-6-19
340455	Gnr.	Thompson, A.			Demob.	27-5-19
301495	A/Sgt.	Thomson, A.—M.M.			Demob.	26-2-19
84229	*Dvr.	Thompson, D.			Demob.	16-1-19
317032	Bdr.	Thompson, G. F.			Demob.	11-7-19

*Served in U.K. only with 4th Bde., C.F.A.
**Served as O.R. only with 4th Bde., C.F.A.
***C.A.P.C. attached to 4th Bde., C.F.A.

Number	Rank	Name	Decorations	Wounded	Disposition	Date
312011	Gnr.	Thompson, J. A.			Demob.	27-8-19
340842	Dvr.	Thompson, J. R.			Demob.	27-5-19
348330	Dvr.	Thompson, R. A.		9-5-17	Demob.	2-4-19
	*H/Capt.	Thompson, R. F.—M.C.			Demob.	13-1-19
1250043	Gnr.	Thompson, R. J.		1-3-18	Demob.	20-2-19
	**Lieut.	Thompson, S.—M. in D.			Demob.	12-5-19
343016	Gnr.	Thomson, D. B.			Demob.	27-5-19
302286	Gnr.	Thomson, E.		6-9-18	Demob.	27-3-19
83446	Gnr.	Thomson, J.			Demob.	27-5-19
343912	Gnr.	Thomson, J. M.		1-8-18	Demob.	2-7-19
343201	Dvr.	Thomson, S. R.			Demob.	27-5-19
84006	Cpl.	Thomson, T.			Demob.	26-5-19
86021	Gnr.	Thornton, V.		29-9-18	Demob.	18-2-19
83026	Pte.	Thorp, G. J.			Demob.	11-6-19
83728	Gnr.	Thorpe, C. H.		26-5-16 7-10-16 3-11-17	Demob.	31-5-19
83158	Gnr.	Threader, J.		1-11-17	M.U.	15-2-19
	*** Lieut.	Thurston, A. M.			K.I.A.	26-6-16
83939	Gnr.	Tiernan, A.		31-5-16	D.ofW.	31-5-16
83206	Gnr.	Tiffney, S.		29-10-17	M.U.	27-10-20
84193	***Gnr.	Tighe, G.			M.U.	19-1-18
521182	Gnr.	Tildesley, C. W.			Demob.	28-3-19
83773	***Sgt.	Tinning, S. E.—M.M.			Demob.	27-3-19
316993	Gnr	Titterington, J.			M.U.	12-4-18
1258184	Gnr.	Tobin, E. T.			K.I.A.	27-9-18
2601925	Gnr.	Todd, G. R.			Demob.	1-6-19
343068	Sig.	Todd, K.			Demob.	29-7-19
83487	S/Sgt.	Todd, R.—D.C.M.			Demob.	11-6-19
86988	Dvr.	Todd, T. H.			Demob.	29-5-19
90263	Gnr.	Tomilson, A. E.		19-5-17	Demob.	6-6-19
83181	Bdr.	Tomlinson, H.			Demob.	27-3-19
83444	B.S.M.	Toms, G.		3-5-17	M.U.	19-4-18
83449	Dvr.	Towler, A. E.			M.U.	27-1-19
316995	Gnr.	Towner, E. L.			Demob.	27-5-19
	Capt.	Townsley, W. A.—M.C.			Demob.	12-4-19
341951	Dvr.	Toy, H. F.			M.U.	23-6-19
	'**Lieut.	Toy, M. H.			App. to R.F.C.	23-8-17
86862	Gnr.	Tozer, J. T.		2-10-18	D.ofW.	2-10-18
83938	Gnr.	Trays, G.		2-10-16 27-11-17 7-9-18	Demob.	25-5-19
83027	Gnr.	Trebilcock, J. A.			Com. in I. Army	11-10-15
	**Lieut.	Trewhitt, J. A.—M.C., M.M.		2-9-18	Demob.	28-7-19
597	Bdr.	Trimm, J. C. R.		2-7-17 27-9-18	Demob.	29-5-19
476570	Gnr.	Trotter, W.			Demob.	20-5-19
83471	Sgt.	Troubridge, F. R.			M.U.	31-12-17
83176	Gnr.	Trow, G. A.		3-9-18	M.U.	2-6-19
89956	Sgt.	Trudeau, A. J.		28-11-17 28-3-18	Demob.	7-4-19
341882	Gnr.	Truscott, G. E.			M.U.	13-12-18
2522492	Dvr.	Tuck, F.			Demob.	28-5-19
83727	Bdr.	Tuck, P. E.		7-5-16	M.U.	10-12-17
	Capt.	Tuck, W. S.			K.I.A.	30-10-16
86987	Dvr.	Tucker, W.			M.U.	31-8-20
339392	Gnr.	Tufts, E. L.			Demob.	1-6-19
86475	Gnr.	Tullock, J.		23-4-17	Demob.	26-5-19
83602	Q.M.S.	Turnbull, A. R.			M.U.	12-6-16
343864	Dvr.	Turnbull, W. T.			Demob.	27-5-19
83451	Sgt.	Turner, A.			Demob.	6-6-19

*Chaplain attached 4th Bde., C.F.A.
**Served as O.R. only with 4th Bde., C.F.A.
***C.A.M.C. att. 4th Bde., C.F.A.

Number	Rank	Name	Decorations	Wounded	Disposition	Date
835454	Gnr.	Turner, C. H.		27-2-18	Demob.	15-7-19
84191	Gnr.	Turner, E.			K.I.A.	28-2-16
83779	Gn.r	Turner, F.			M.U.	27-1-19
336891	Gnr.	Turner, J.			Demob.	27-5-19
339939	Gnr.	Turner, T.		19-4-17	Demob.	27-5-19
89710	Sgt.	Tuthill, J. C.			Demob.	26-5-19
83450	Gnr.	Twidale, H.			Demob.	27-5-19
83453	Cpl.	Underwood, H.		23-8-17	Demob.	27-3-19
83878	Sgt.	Ungar, E. B.			To Con. V. Stud.	17-1-19
83452	Gnr.	Usher, A. S.		4-11-16	Demob.	26-5-19
89378	Gnr.	Valin, C. H.			Demob.	23-4-19
	*Capt.	Valiquet, M. U.			Demob.	28-4-19
1251191	Gnr.	Vallary, G. L. F.			Demob.	27-5-19
337889	A/Bdr.	Vallentyne, H. J.			Demob.	27-5-19
83620	Sgt.	Vallillee, J. E.		27-9-18	Demob.	15-9-19
83109	Gnr.	Van Alstine, H. E.			M.U.	26-8-18
	Major	Vansittart, G. E.—M. in D.		14-5-16	D.ofW.	14-5-16
83119	Gnr.	Varcoe, W. R.		17-5-18	Demob.	18-1-19
85439	**Gnr.	Vaughan, E. G.		11-5-16	Demob.	15-7-19
87290	Gnr.	Vere, J.		2-9-18	Demob.	18-2-19
2100944	Gnr.	Verge, W. B.			Demob.	14-8-19
	***Capt.	Vernon, W. H.—O.B.E.			M.U.	26-4-20
83945	Gnr.	Vice, J.			M.U.	26-1-18
89097	Gnr.	Vickers, F.			Demob.	24-6-19
84194	****Bdr.	Vincent, J. W. L.			Demob.	11-5-19
349143	Sig.	Vincent, R. G.		3-9-18	Demob.	4-7-19
86042	Dvr.	Vincent, S. R.			Demob.	20-6-19
86478	Bdr.	Voice, T.			Demob.	30-8-19
	***Lieut.	Vokes, A. L.		1-4-18	Demob.	26-2-19
	Lieut.	Vooght, R. C.		28-9-18	Demob.	1-6-19
86991	Cpl.	Waddington, H.		1-6-17	Demob.	20-5-19
342864	Gnr.	Wade, C. A. G.			Demob.	27-5-19
87051	Dvr.	Waggitt, J. G.			Drowned	30-7-17
83733	A/Sgt.	Wainwright, A. L.			Demob.	3-1-19
341820	Gnr.	Waite, F. N.			Demob.	5-6-19
83458	Gnr.	Waite, W.			Demob.	12-8-19
2557498	Gnr.	Waldron, R. C.			Demob.	27-5-19
83731	Gnr.	Waldron, S. E.—M.M.			Demob.	8-2-19
	Major	Waldron, S. M.			K.I.A.	4-5-17
86993	Dvr.	Walker, C. M.			Demob.	20-5-19
301502	Dvr.	Walker, E.			D.of I.	28-9-17
72	Gnr.	Walker, J.		26-4-17	Demob.	25-4-19
90160	Gnr.	Walker, J.			Demob.	14-1-19
89379	Gnr.	Walker, J. R.			Demob.	27-5-19
1250210	Gnr.	Wallace, G. C.			K.I.A.	29-9-18
1251016	Gnr.	Wallace, J. S.			Demob.	26-5-19
84032	Bdr.	Wallace, W. W.		26-5-16	M.U.	31-8-17
690727	Gnr.	Wallington, J.		23-7-17	Demob.	4-7-19
84203	Gnr.	Wallis, A. S. J.			Demob.	22-9-19
2327357	Gnr.	Walmsley, J. A. M.			Demob.	27-5-19
83735	Gnr.	Walsh, S.			M.U.	31-7-17
83195	Dvr.	Walter, H.		28-10-17	Demob.	27-5-19
	***Lieut.	Walter, N. P.—M.M.			Demob.	21-5-19
86877	A/Bdr.	Walters, C. W.			Demob.	12-5-19
415	Gnr.	Walters, F. A.		29-10-17	M.U.	6-12-18
84200	Gnr.	Walters, O. W.			Demob.	4-7-19
83143	Gnr.	Walters, W. F.			Demob.	15-9-19
83233	Gnr.	Ward, A.		6-10-16	Demob.	12-7-19

*C.A.M.C. att. to 4th Bde., C.F.A.
**Served with 16th Bde., C.F.A., in N. Russia
***Served as O.R. only with 4th Bde., C.F.A.
****U.K. only with 4th Bde., C.F.A.

Number	Rank	Name	Decorations	Wounded	Disposition	Date
83422	Sadlr.	Ward, J. W. T.			Cess. of W. Pay	1-10-16
83264	A/Cpl.	Warden, E. A.			D.ofI.	16-9-17
89530	Cpl.	Ware, R. H.—M.M., Bar		17-11-16	Demob.	8-6-19
42763	*Cpl.	Wareham, S. B.—M.M.		26-10-17	K.I.A.	11-11-18
83467	Dvr.	Waring, A.			Demob.	27-5-19
89968	Gnr.	Waring, S.			Demob.	31-3-19
681211	Gnr.	Warnes, A.		28-10-17	Demob.	11-2-19
84195	Gnr.	Warren, H.		28-2-16	D.ofW.	20-3-16
300520	Gnr.	Warren, J. H.			Demob.	3-7-19
339999	Gnr.	Wass, P. M.			Demob.	15-6-19
150236	Bdr.	Watson, A.			Demob.	13-4-19
84036	Gnr.	Watson, C. E.—M.M.			Demob.	4-7-19
	Lieut.	Watson, C. H.			K.I.A.	11-8-18
87019	Gnr.	Watson, C.		6-11-17	D.ofW.	20-11-17
2100785	Gnr.	Watson, D. C.			Demob.	24-1-19
86550	Gnr.	Watson, G.			Demob.	17-2-19
338202	Sig.	Watson, G. A.			Demob.	27-5-19
322867	A/Bdr.	Watson, H. L.			Demob.	27-5-19
83459	Dvr.	Watson, W.			Demob.	29-5-19
416	Dvr.	Watt, E.			Demob.	29-5-19
86995	Gnr.	Watt, J. C.			M.U.	18-6-18
318951	Gnr.	Watters, J. A.			Demob.	27-5-19
83116	Gnr.	Watts, A. G.			Demob.	2-4-19
337875	Gnr.	Waugh, H. S.		17-3-17 5-6-17	M.U.	20-1-19
319907	A/Bdr.	Weagant, H. W.			Demob.	27-5-19
84196	Gnr.	Wearne, H.			App. Com. in I. Army	24-10-17
335884	Gnr.	Weatherby, G. M.			Demob.	27-5-19
33611	Gnr.	Weatherby, J. M.			Demob.	27-5-19
86875	Bdr.	Weatherhead, R. C.			Demob.	27-5-19
83180	Sgt.	Weaver, E. F.		1-9-18	Demob.	25-5-19
85397	Gnr.	Weaver, W.		1-6-17	Demob.	2-6-19
150239	Dvr.	Webb, C. J.			Demob.	25-6-19
340225	Gnr.	Webb, W. J.			Demob.	5-6-19
1250178	Gn.r	Webster, F. J.		25-5-17 26-8-18	Demob.	30-5-19
	Capt.	Webster, H.—M.C., M. in D.		29-3-17 12-10-16	Demob.	27-5-19
339377	Gnr.	Webster, J. M.			M.U.	1-10-19
345994	Gnr.	Weegar, R. I.			Demob.	12-7-19
301564	Bdr.	Weidenhamer, A.—M.M.			Demob.	29-5-19
83192	Gnr.	Weir, A. V.			Demob.	6-7-19
83726	Cpl.	Welham, A.			K.I.A.	29-9-18
48810	**A/Sgt.	Weller, N. F.			M.U.	21-2-19
	***Capt.	Wells, C. A.			Demob.	29-5-19
83004	S/Sgt.	Wells, M. H.			Com. in I. Army	8-6-16
317000	A/Bdr.	Wellwood, G. R.		25-8-18	Demob.	27-5-19
89961	Dvr.	Welsh, J.			Demob.	16-1-19
2022405	Gnr.	Welte, R. M.			Demob.	4-6-19
83461	Dvr.	Wenham, W.		8-5-17	Demob.	27-5-19
300340	Gnr.	Wenn, W. G. T.		21-4-17	Demob.	31-7-19
301948	Dvr.	Werley, F. C.		1-11-17	D.ofW.	1-11-17
317001	Gnr.	West, P. E.			Demob.	9-7-19
84246	Dvr.	West, W. E.—M.M.		2-5-17	Demob.	7-4-19
	Lieut.	West, W. R.—M.C.		11-1-17 29-9-18	M.U.	18-3-19
	*Lieut.	Wesmore, A. E. L.		17-4-17	Demob.	17-7-19
317002	Gnr.	Weston, G. E.			Demob.	27-5-19
83954	Sgt.	Whall, N.—M.M.			Demob.	21-3-19

*Served in N. Russia with 16th Bde., C.F.A.
**C.A.V.C. att. 4th Bde., C.F.A.
***Served as O.R. only with 4th Bde., C.F.A.

Number	Rank	Name	Decorations	Wounded	Disposition	Date
84197	Bdr.	Whalley, J.			Demob.	27-5-19
83611	A/Cpl.	Wharton, A. J.		26-9-16	M.U.	2-8-19
1251402	Gnr.	Wharton, R.			Demob.	14-1-19
51471	Gnr.	Wheatley, A.			M.U.	28-9-18
90053	Bdr.	Wheeler, P. W.—M.M. and Bar		29-9-18	Demob.	27-5-19
83774	Bdr.	Wheelock, C. H.			App. Com. I. Army	10-10-17
91514	Bdr.	Whitaker, J.—M.M.		24-4-17	M.U.	29-1-18
845574	Gnr.	Whitbourne, A.		2-11-18	M.U.	9-7-19
83238	Gnr.	White, A.			M.U.	18-2-19
317005	Gnr.	White, A. E.			M.U.	25-3-19
300401	Gnr.	White, C. T.		8-7-17	M.U.	16-9-20
89988	Gnr.	White, J. C.		29-9-18	Demob.	27-5-19
111519	Dvr.	White, O. M.			M.U.	16-2-18
90043	Dvr.	White, T.			Demob.	27-5-19
84199	Gnr.	White, T. B.			K.I.A.	26-4-17
334661	Gnr.	White, T. W.			Demob.	27-5-19
83134	Cpl.	White, W. M.			Demob.	17-9-19
	Lieut.	Whitehead, F. C.—M.C.			Demob.	3-6-19
83460	Dvr.	Whitehead, W.		29-12-15	M.U.	31-3-19
84203	B.S.M.	Whitehead, W. B.—La Medaille d'Honneur avec glaives, en argent		29-10-17	Demob.	2-9-19
83737	Dvr.	Whitham, G.			Demob.	23-5-19
83456	Dvr.	Whiting, M.			Demob.	20-2-19
47418	Gnr.	Whitney, P.			Demob.	13-8-19
83732	Gnr.	Whitten, F. S.			K.I.A.	19-11-16
341812	Gnr.	Whitten, F. T.		13-8-17	Demob.	27-5-19
84201	A/Sgt.	Whittle, H.			Demob.	31-7-19
276122	Sig.	Whyte, A. D.			Demob.	30-5-19
463384	Gnr.	Whyte, J.			M.U.	28-2-18
123123	Gnr.	Wiese, T. E.—M.M.			Demob.	28-5-19
83966	*Gnr.	Wilcock, W. S.			Demob.	15-7-19
91256	Gnr.	Wilcockson, J.			M.U.	14-1-19
337926	Gnr.	Wilding, T.—M.M.			Demob.	29-5-19
2740	Gnr.	Wildman, A.		1-10-18	Demob.	5-7-19
342115	Gnr.	Wilkinson, J. A.			Demob.	27-5-19
83115	Gnr.	Wilkinson, J. B.			Demob.	12-5-19
	**Lieut.	Wilkinson, W. A.			Demob.	31-3-19
84278	Dvr.	Williams, A. F.			Demob.	9-5-19
348720	Cpl.	Williams, F. J.			Demob.	27-5-19
84039	Gnr.	Williams, G. H.			M.U.	11-2-19
273	Gnr.	Williams, J. A.			Demob.	15-6-19
2099960	Gnr.	Williams, J.			Demob.	6-6-19
84027	Gnr.	Williams, M. G.		7-9-18	Demob.	25-5-19
86484	Gnr.	Williams, O. T.			Demob.	29-8-19
83455	Dvr.	Williams, P. C.			Demob.	27-5-19
83028	Gnr.	Williams, R. E.			Demob.	23-5-19
84008	Gnr.	Williams, R. J.		30-9-18	Demob.	26-7-19
	**Lieut.	Williams, S. E.			Demob.	28-4-19
83612	Cpl.	Williams, T. J.			Com. in I. Army	10-9-15
1250518	Dvr.	Williamson, B.			K.I.A.	4-11-18
37283	Gnr.	Williamson, J.			D.ofD.	2-8-18
2085406	Gnr.	Willoughby, F. D.			Demob.	27-5-19
339690	Gnr.	Wills, N. C. K.		27-9-18	Demob.	2-6-19
252	Gnr.	Wills, R. G.		3-11-17	Demob.	2-4-19
	**Lieut.	Wilson, G.—M.M.			Demob.	27-2-19
2044111	Bdr.	Wilson, G. B.			Demob.	2-6-19
348757	Gnr.	Wilson, H. A.—M. in D.			Demob.	27-5-19
343062	Gnr.	Wilson, J. M.			Demob.	27-5-19
89529	Gnr.	Wilson, J. W.			Demob.	20-9-19
	**Lieut.	Wilson, M. A.			Demob.	26-8-19
2044074	Bdr.	Wilson, N. E.			Dembo.	28-8-19

*Served in N. Russia with 16th Bde., C.F.A.
**Served as O.R. only wtih 4th Bde., C.F.A.

Number	Rank	Name	Decorations	Wounded	Disposition	Date
348758	Dvr.	Wilson, N. L.		4-11-17		
				4-10-18	Demob.	27-5-19
	Lieut.	Wilson, S. H.—M.C.			Demob.	28-5-19
83940	Dvr.	Wiltshire, F. W.			Demob.	27-5-19
1251853	Gnr.	Wims, T. P.			D.ofD.	
					U.K.	26-11-18
83120	A/Cpl.	Windrum, J. S. D.			Demob.	17-5-19
83990	Sgt.	Wingfield, G. A.			D.ofW.	15-5-17
83752	Gnr.	Winslow, W. D.			Demob.	13-11-19
349003	Gnr.	Winters, E. E.			Demob.	30-7-19
90279	Gnr.	Wiseman, P. P.		27-10-17	Demob.	1-2-19
83454	Gnr.	Wisheart, G.		28-1-18	D.ofW.	28-1-18
69	Cpl.	Withers, S. J.		16-8-18	M.U.	22-8-19
334966	Gnr.	Wolfe, C.			Demob.	30-7-19
83738	Sgt.	Wood, D. C.		28-2-18	Demob.	27-5-19
1260226	Gnr.	Wood, E.		7-9-18	Demob.	18-3-19
83734	Gnr.	Wood, H. R.		30-10-18	Demob.	27-3-19
443	Gnr.	Wood, J. S.		27-3-16	D.ofW.	27-3-16
83869	*Gnr.	Woods, G.		11-5-17	Demob.	24-4-19
84221	Sgt.	Woods, P.		29-10-17		
				27-9-18	M.U.	24-3-19
528986	**Pte.	Wollard, F. W.			Demob.	24-4-19
84251	Gnr.	Wolley, H. H.		7-5-17	M.U.	28-1-19
317028	Gnr.	Wootton, W. G.			M.U.	4-5-18
84248	Gnr.	Worcester, G. D.			Minor, Am.	
					Citizen	8-9-16
244	Dvr.	Wright, A. J.			Demob.	29-5-19
349621	Gnr.	Wright, F. S.			Demob.	27-5-19
83136	Bdr.	Wright, H. O.		25-9-16		
				14-4-17	Demob.	25-5-19
349424	Gnr.	Wright, R. S.			Demob.	27-2-19
	Major	Wright, W. G.—M.C.		24-9-16	M.U.	31-1-20
84198	Gnr.	Wyper, J.			Demob.	12-3-19
83858	Cpl.	Yardley, T.—D.C.M., M.M.		31-5-16	M.U.	11-2-20
322914	Gnr.	Yeager, A. J.			Demob.	31-12-18
318030	Gnr.	Yorke, J. L.		6-6-17	Demob.	27-5-19
1250807	Gnr.	Young, A. R.			Demob.	30-5-19
335231	Gnr.	Young, H. A.			Demob.	27-5-19
340053	Dvr	Young, W.			Demob.	12-7-19
2040637	Gnr.	Yuill, D. B.			Demob.	16-6-19
346028	Gnr.	Yule, A. D. W.			Demob.	27-5-19
	Capt.	Zimmerman, A. L.—M.in D.			Killed (accid.)	20-3-18
1250828	Gnr.	Zimmerman, S. O.			Demob.	4-6-19

*Served in U.K. only with 4th Bde., C.F.A.
**C.A.M.C. att. to 4th Bde., C.F.A.

14th Battery, C.F.A.

DESIGNATION	BDE.	DIV.	FROM	TO	NO. OF GUNS	PLACE
14th Battery	4th	2nd	25-11-14		4-18 pr.	Toronto England France

Authority for formation— Privy Council Orders 2067/2068.d/6-8-14, and Privy Council Order 2831.d/7-11-14. Published in G.O. 36.d /15-3-15.

Mobilization authorized— 4-11-14

Mobilized at— Toronto, Ont. (M.D.No.2)

Formed from— 7th (St. Catharines Battery, C.F.A. (C.M.) 9th (Toronto) Battery, C.F.A. (C.M.)

Entrained for Overseas— 19-5-15 Toronto,Ont.

Embarked for England— 20-5-15 Montreal, S.S.Missanabie

Arrived England— 29-5-15 Plymouth

Disembarked— 30-5-15 Devonport

Arrived— 31-5-15 Westenhanger Camp, Shorncliffe Area

Proceeded on— 29-8-15 To Trawsfynydd, Wales, for live shell practice

Returned on— 5-9-15 To Westenhanger Camp, Shorncliffe Area

Left England for France— 14-9-15 Southampton

Arrived France— 15-9-15 Havre

(Absorbed in France by 19th and 27th Batteries, C.F.A., on 18-3-17

Disbanded by— Privy Council Order 3417.d/7-1-18. Published in G.O. 82.d/1-6-18

Memory perpetuated as— 14th (Midland) Field Battery, C.A. Headquarters, Cobourg, Ont.

14th Battery, C.F.A.

DESIGNATION	BDE.	DIV.	FROM	TO	NO. OF GUNS	PLACE
14th Battery	4th	2nd	25-11-14		4-18 pr.	Toronto England France

Authority for formation—	Privy Council Orders 2067/2068.d/6-8-14, and Privy Council Order 2831.d/7-11-14. Published in G.O. 36.d /15-3-15.
Mobilization authorized—	4-11-14
Mobilized at—	Toronto, Ont. (M.D.No.2)
Formed from—	7th (St. Catharines Battery, C.F.A. (C.M.) 9th (Toronto) Battery, C.F.A. (C.M.)
Entrained for Overseas—	19-5-15 Toronto,Ont.
Embarked for England—	20-5-15 Montreal, S.S.Missanabie
Arrived England—	29-5-15 Plymouth
Disembarked—	30-5-15 Devonport
Arrived—	31-5-15 Westenhanger Camp, Shorncliffe Area
Proceeded on—	29-8-15 To Trawsfynydd, Wales, for live shell practice
Returned on—	5-9-15 To Westenhanger Camp, Shorncliffe Area
Left England for France—	14-9-15 Southampton
Arrived France—	15-9-15 Havre
	(Absorbed in France by 19th and 27th Batteries, C.F.A., on 18-3-17
Disbanded by—	Privy Council Order 3417.d/7-1-18. Published in G.O. 82.d/1-6-18
Memory perpetuated as—	14th (Midland) Field Battery, C.A. Headquarters, Cobourg, Ont.

15th Battery, C.F.A.

DESIGNATION	BDE.	DIV.	FROM	TO	NO. OF GUNS	PLACE
15th Battery	4th	2nd	Dec./14	22-5-16	4-18 pr.	Toronto Shorncliffe England France
15th Battery	6th	2nd	22-5-16	19-3-17	4-18 pr.	France
15th Battery	6th	2nd	19-3-17		6-18 pr.	France

(By addition of One Section from 28th Battery, C.F.A.)

Authority for formation—	Privy Council Orders 2067/2068.d/6-8-14, and Privy Council Order 2831.d/7-11-14. Published in G.O. 36.d /15-3-15
Mobilization authorized—	4-11-14
Mobilized at—	Toronto,Ont. (M.D.No.2)
Formed from—	9th (Toronto) Battery, C.F.A. (C.M.) 4th (Hamilton) Battery, C.F.A. (C.M.)
Entrained for Overseas—	28-5-15 Toronto, Ont.
Embarked for England—	29-5-15 Montreal, S.S. Northland
Arrived England—	8-6-15 Plymouth
Arrived—	7-8-15 Westenhanger Camp, Shorncliffe Area
Proceeded on—	29-8-15 To Trawsfynydd, Wales, for live shell practice
Returned on—	5-9-15 To Westenhanger Camp, Shorncliffe Area
Left England for France—	14-9-15 Southampton
Arrived France—	15-9-15 Havre
Left France for England—	14-4-19
Arrived England—	15-4-19
Left England for Canada—	14-5-19 Tilbury, S.S. Minnekahda
Arrived Canada—	22-5-19 Halifax
Demobilized—	25-5-19 Toronto, (M.D.No.2)
Disbanded by—	Privy Council Order 2561.d/23-10-20. Published in G.O.191.d/1-11-20
Memory perpetuated as—	15th Field Battery, C.A. Headquarters, Toronto Ont.

15th Battery, C.F.A.

DESIGNATION	BDE.	DIV.	FROM	TO	NO. OF GUNS	PLACE
15th Battery	4th	2nd	Dec./14	22-5-16	4-18 pr.	Toronto Shorncliffe England France
15th Battery	6th	2nd	22-5-16	19-3-17	4-18 pr.	France
15th Battery	6th	2nd	19-3-17		6-18 pr.	France
(By addition of One Section from 28th Battery, C.F.A.)						

Authority for formation—	Privy Council Orders 2067/2068.d/6-8-14, and Privy Council Order 2831.d/7-11-14. Published in G.O. 36.d /15-3-15
Mobilization authorized—	4-11-14
Mobilized at—	Toronto,Ont. (M.D.No.2)
Formed from—	9th (Toronto) Battery, C.F.A. (C.M.) 4th (Hamilton) Battery, C.F.A. (C.M.)
Entrained for Overseas—	28-5-15 Toronto, Ont.
Embarked for England—	29-5-15 Montreal, S.S. Northland
Arrived England—	8-6-15 Plymouth
Arrived—	7-8-15 Westenhanger Camp, Shorncliffe Area
Proceeded on—	29-8-15 To Trawsfynydd, Wales, for live shell practice
Returned on—	5-9-15 To Westenhanger Camp, Shorncliffe Area
Left England for France—	14-9-15 Southampton
Arrived France—	15-9-15 Havre
Left France for England—	14-4-19
Arrived England—	15-4-19
Left England for Canada—	14-5-19 Tilbury, S.S. Minnekahda
Arrived Canada—	22-5-19 Halifax
Demobilized—	25-5-19 Toronto, (M.D.No.2)
Disbanded by—	Privy Council Order 2561.d/23-10-20. Published in G.O.191.d/1-11-20
Memory perpetuated as—	15th Field Battery, C.A. Headquarters, Toronto Ont.

16th Battery, C.F.A.

DESIGNATION	BDE.	DIV.	FROM	TO	NO. OF GUNS	PLACE
16th Battery	4th	2nd	5-11-14	April/15	4-12 pr.	London, Ont.
16th Battery	4th	2nd	April/15	22-5-16	4-18 pr.	London, Ont.
						Guelph, Ont.
						Shorncliffe
						England
						France
16th Battery	6th	2nd	22-5-16	19-3-17	4-18 pr.	France
16th Battery	6th	2nd	19-3-17		6-18 pr.	France

(By addition of one Section from 28th Battery, C.F.A.)

Authority for formation—	Privy Council Orders 2067/2068.d/6-8-14 and Privy Council Order 2831.d/7-11-14. Published in G.O.36.d /15-3-15.
Mobilization authorized—	4-11-14
Mobilized at—	London, Ont. (M.D.No.1)
Moved on—	January, 1915, to Guelph, Ont.
Formed from—	16th (How.) Battery, C.F.A. (C.M.), Guelph, Ont. 6th (London) Battery, C.F.A (C.M.), London, Ont. 30th Battery, C.F.A. (C.M.)
Entrained for Overseas—	19-5-15, Guelph, Ont.
Embarked for England—	20-5-15 Montreal, S.S. Missanabie
Arrived England—	29-5-15 Plymouth
Disembarked—	30-5-15 Devonport
Arrived—	31-5-15 Westenhanger Camp, Shorncliffe Area.
Proceeded on—	29-8-15 To Trawsfynydd, Wales, for live shell practice
Returned on—	5-9-15 To Westenhanger Camp, Shorncliffe Area
Left England for France—	14-9-15 Southampton
Arrived France—	15-9-15 Havre
Left France for England—	
Arrived England—	
Left England for Canada—	14-5-19 Tilbury, S.S. Minnekahda
Arrived Canada—	22-5-19 Halifax
Demobilized—	25-5-19 London, Ont. (M.D.No.1)
Disbanded by—	Privy Council Order 2561.d/23-10-20. Published in G.O.191.d/1-11-20.
Memory perpetuated as—	16th Field Battery, C.A. Headquarters, Guelph, Ont.

19th Battery, C.F.A.

DESIGNATION	BDE.	DIV.	FROM	TO	NO. OF GUNS	PLACE
19th Battery	5th	2nd	Nov./14	17-3-17	4-18 pr.	Winnipeg, Man. England France
19th Battery	5th	2nd	17-3-17	21-6-17	6-18 pr.	France
(By addition of one Section from 14th Battery, C.F.A.)						
19th Battery	5th	4th	21-6-17		6-18 pr.	France

Authority for formation—	Privy Council Orders 2067/2068.d/6-8-14 and Privy Council Order 2831.d/7-11-14. Published in G.O.36.d /15-3-15.
Mobilization authorized—	4th November, 1914
Mobilized at—	Winnipeg, Man. (M.D.No.10)
Formed from—	38th Battery, C.F.A. (C.M.)
Entrained for Overseas—	5-8-15 Winnipeg.
Embarked for England—	9-8-15 Halifax, S.S. Metagama
Sailed—	10-8-15
Arrived England—	18-8-15 Plymouth
Arrived—	19-8-15 Otterpool Camp, England
Left England for France—	18-1-16 Southampton
Arrived France—	19-1-16 Havre
Left France for England—	
Arrived England—	
Left England for Canada—	19-5-19 Southampton, S.S. Aquitania
Arrived Canada—	25-5-19 Halifax
Demobilized—	28-5-19 Toronto, Ont. (M.D.No.2)
Disbanded by—	Privy Council Order 2561.d/23-10-20. Published in G.O.191.d/1-11-20.
Memory perpetuated as—	19th Field Battery, C.A. Headquarters, Winnipeg, Man.

27th Battery, C.F.A.

DESIGNATION	BDE.	DIV.	FROM	TO	NO. OF GUNS	PLACE
27th Battery	7th	2nd	1-3-15	Aug./15	4-12 pr.	Montreal, P.Q. Valcartier, P.Q.
27th Battery	7th	2nd	Nov./15	18-3-17	4-18 pr.	England France
27th Battery	4th	2nd	18-3-17		6-18 pr.	France

(By the addition of one Section from 14th Battery)

Authority for formation—	Privy Council Orders 2067/2068.d/6-8-14 and Privy Council Order 2831.d/7-11-14. Published in G.O.36.d /15-3-15.
Mobilization authorized—	1st March, 1915
Mobilized at—	Montreal, P.Q. (M.D.No.4)
Recruited in—	Montreal and District
Moved on—	8-6-15 To Valcartier, P.Q.
Embarked for England—	8-8-15 Halifax, S.S. Metagama
Sailed—	9-8-15
Arrived England—	18-8-15 Plymouth
Arrived—	19-8-15 Otterpool Camp, England
Moved on—	25-9-15 To Westenhanger Camp, England
Left England for France—	17-1-16 Southampton, S.S. Viper
Arrived France—	18-1-16 Havre
Left France for England—	25-4-19 Havre
Arrived England—	26-4-19 Southampton
Left England for Canada—	19-5-19 Southampton, S.S. Aquitania
Arrived Canada—	25-5-19 Halifax
Demobilized—	27-5-19 Montreal (M.D.No.4)
Disbanded by—	Privy Council Order 2561.d/23-10-20. Published in G.O.191.d/1-11-20.
Memory perpetuated as—	27th Field Battery, C.A. (How.) Headquarters, Montreal, P.Q.

28th Battery, C.F.A.

DESIGNATION	BDE.	DIV.	FROM	TO	NO. OF GUNS	PLACE
28th Battery	7th	2nd	1-3-15	Aug./15	4-12 pr.	Fredericton, N.B. Valcartier, P.Q.
28th Battery	7th	2nd	Nov./15	19-3-17	4-18 pr.	England France

Authority for formation—	Privy Council Orders 2067/2068.d/6-8-14 and Privy Council Order 2831.d/7-11-14. Published in G.O.36.d /15-3-15.
Mobilization authorized—	1st March, 1915
Mobilized at—	Fredericton, N.B. (M.D.No.6)
Recruited in—	Maritime Provinces
Moved on —	8-7-15 To Valcartier, P.Q.
Embarked for England—	8-8-15 Halifax, S.S. Metagama
Sailed—	9-8-15
Arrived England—	18-8-15 Plymouth
Arrived—	19-8-15 Otterpool Camp, England
Moved on—	25-9-15 To Westenhanger Camp
Left England for France—	17-1-16 Southampton, S.S. Viper
Arrived France—	18-1-16 Havre
	(Absorbed in France by 15th and 16th Batteries on 19-3-17)
Disbanded by—	Privy Council Order 2561.d/23-10-20. Published in G.O.191.d/1-11-20.
Memory perpetuated as—	28th (Newcastle) Field Battery, C.A. (Auty.G.O.83.d/1-10-27)

29th (How.) Battery, C.F.A.

DESIGNATION	BDE.	DIV.	FROM	TO	NO. OF GUNS	PLACE
29th (How.) Battery	8th	2nd	17-9-15	Nov./15	4-4.5	Otterpool Camp, England
21st (How.) Battery	6th	2nd	Nov./15	22-5-16	4-4.5	England France
21st (How.) Battery	7th	2nd	22-5-16	19-3-17	6-4.5	France
21st (How.) Battery	4th	2nd	19-3-17	21-6-17	6-4.5	France
(By addition of one Section from 83rd Battery, C.F.A.)						
21st (How.) Battery	4th	4th	21-6-17		6-4.5	France

Authority for formation—

Mobilization authorized— 7-9-15

Mobilized at— Otterpool Camp, England

Moved on— 17-11-15 To St. Martin's Plain, England

Formed from— Personnel in Artillery Depot, England

Left England for France— 18-1-16 Southampton

Arrived France— 19-1-16 Havre

Left France for England—

Arrived England—

Left England for Canada— 19-5-19 Southampton, S.S. Aquitania

Arrived Canada— 25-5-19 Halifax

Demobilized— 28-5-19 Toronto (M.D.No.2)

Disbanded by— Privy Council Order 2561.d/23-10-20. Published in G.O.191.d/1-11-20.

Memory perpetuated as— 21st Field Battery, C.A. (How.). Headquarters, Saskatoon, Sask.

(See also 21st Battery, C.F.A., organized in Canada)

Table of Commanding Officers

4th Brigade, C.F.A.

C.O.	TEMP. ACTUAL C.O.	FROM	TO	REMARKS
Lt. Col W. J. Brown		25-11-14	18-7-16	To England
Lt. Col. C. H. L. Sharman		18-7-16	17-12-16	On leave and in command 6th Bde., C.F.A. from 31-12-16
"	Maj. A. Ripley	17-12-16	20-1-17	
"		20-1-17	22-2-17	To England on course
Lt. Col. J. S. Stewart, D.S.O.	Lt. Col. J. S. Stewart, D.S.O.	22-2-17	16-3-17	
		13-3-17	19-3-17	To England
		19-3-17	12-6-17	On Leave
"	Maj. J. C. Stewart	12-6-17	24-6-17	
"		24-6-17	11-7-17	Temp. C.R.A. 4th Div.
"	Maj. M. N. Ross	11-7-17	23-7-17	
"		23-7-17	21-9-17	On leave
"	Maj. M. N. Ross, D.S.O.	21-9-17	1-10-17	
"	Maj. A. F. Culver	1-10-17	4-10-17	
"		4-10-17	8-11-17	Att. 4th Div.
"	Maj. M. N. Ross, D.S.O.	8-11-17	29-11-17	
Lt. Col. M. N. Ross, D.S.O.		29-11-17	7-12-17	To England on course and ass. command 3rd C.D.A.
"	Maj. G. L. Drew, D.S.O.	7-12-17	19-7-18	
"		19-7-18	12-8-18	
"	Maj. J. I. McSloy, D.S.O.	12-8-18	17-2-19	On leave
"		17-2-19	19-3-19	
"		19-3-19	Demob.	

13th Battery, C.F.A.

Major G. S. Rennie	Ass. com. (Canada)	16-11-14
	Rel. on being trans. to C.A.M.C.	11-2-15
Major G. E. Vansittart	Ass. com. (Canada)	11-2-15
	Rel. (Died of Wounds)	14-5-16
Major G. L. Drew	Ass. com.	14-5-16
D.S.O. 10-1-17	Rel. evac. sick	22-5-17
Major C. Sifton, Jr.,	Ass. com.	22-5-17
D.S.O. 2-12-18	Rel.	
(Temp. maj. 10-7-17	Proceeded to Eng. with unit	20-4-19)

14th Battery, C.F.A.

Maj. W. H. Merritt	Ass. com. (Canada)	6-11-14
	Rel.	21-5-16
Maj. S. M. Waldron	Ass. com.	21-5-16
	To 6th Bde., C.F.A.	19-3-17

(Battery absorbed 18-3-17)

15th Battery, C.F.A.

Maj. L. E. W. Irving, D.S O.	Ass. com. (Canada)	4-12-14
	Rel.	14-9-15
Maj. F. F. Arnoldi, D.S.O.	Ass. com.	14-9-15
	Rel.	29-11-16
?	?	29-11-16
?	?	14-12-16
Capt. C. J. Swift	Ass. com.	14-12-16
	Rel.	17-3-17
Maj. S. M. Waldron	Ass. com.	17-3-17
	Rel. (Killed in action)	4-5-17
Maj. A. H. Bick, D.S.O.	Ass. com.	4-5-17
	Rel. (to be B.M. 1st C.D.A.)	30-4-18
Capt. B. B. McConkey, M.C.	Ass. com.	9-5-18
	Rel. (Died of wounds)	30-5-18
Capt. (A/Maj.) Swift	Ass. com.	30-5-18
	Rel.	25-7-18
Maj. F. J. Alderson, D.S.O.	Ass. com.	25-7-18
	Rel. to be A/Lt. Col. whilst Com. 6th Bde., C.F.A., 1-3-19 to 15-4-19	1-3-19

NOTE: Ass. com.—Assumed command.
Rel.—Relinquished command.

16th Battery, C.F.A.

Maj. W. Simpson	Ass. com. (Canada)	8-12-14
	Rel.	April 1916
Capt. A. M. Brown	Temp. com.	April 1916
	Rel.	June 1916
Maj. G. L. Drew	Temp. com.	June 1916
	Rel.	July 1916
Maj. J. Dixon	Ass. com.	July 1916
	Rel. (wounded)	3-5-17
Maj. E. Flexman	Ass. com.	3-5-17
	Rel.	14-8-17
Capt. J. M. McDonnell, M.C., 4-6-17	Temp. com.	14-8-17
	(Rel. to be B.M. 3rd C.D.A.)	22-10-17
Capt. F. G. Bond, M.C., 26-7-17	Temp. com.	22-10-17
	Rel. (Killed in action 29-10-17)	29-10-17
Capt. (A./Maj.) W. G. Wright, M.C., 18-7-17	Ass. com.	29-10-17
	Rel.	17-11-17
Maj. R. F. Baker, D.C.M., 5-8-15	Ass. com.	17-11-17
	Rel.	Demob.

19th Battery, C.F.A.

Lt. Col. G. A. Carruthers	Ass. com. (Canada)	Nov. 1914
	Rel. (To Eng. Sick)	3-8-16
Maj. A. F. Culver, M.C., 27-10-17	Ass. com.	3-8-16
	Rel. (S.O.S. to Eng.)	14-12-17
Capt. E. P. P. Armour	Ass. com.	14-12-17
	(Rel. to B.C.s. course, Eng.)	13-3-18
Maj. S. Robson	Ass. com.	13-3-18
	(Rel. to be B.M. 5th C.D.A.)	19-6-18
Maj. W. E. Steacy, M.C., 2-4-19	Ass. com.	19-6-18
	Rel. (to command 7th Bty.)	15-10-18
Maj. W. G. Wright	Ass. com.	15-10-18
	Rel.	12-3-19
Maj. N. A. Thompson, M.C. and Bar, 3-16-18, 5-3-19	Ass. com.	12-3-19
	Rel.	Demob.

NOTE: Ass. com.—Assumed command.
Rel.—Relinquished command.

21st Battery, C.F.A.

Maj. W. G. Scully   **Ass. com. (Canada)**   Nov. 1914

Battery absorbed into Reserve Bde. on arrival Eng., 6-3-15.

21st How. Bty. C.F.A.

Organized in England and Known as 29th (How. Bty. till Nov., 1915)

Maj. A. G. L. McNaughton	Ass. com. (Eng.)	7-9-15
	Rel.	17-3-16
Maj. M. N. Ross, D.S.O., 26-7-17	Ass. com.	17-3-16
	Rel. to com. 4th Bde. C.F.A.	29-10-17
Capt. (A./Maj.) L. J. B. Aitkens, M.C., 14-11-16	Ass. com.	29-10-17
	Rel.	16-3-18
Maj. J. S. B. MacPherson	Ass. com.	16-3-18
	Rel.	15-4-18
Maj. J. I. McSloy, D.S.O., 1-1-17	Ass. com.	15-4-18
	Rel.	Demob.

27th Battery C.F.A.

Map. J. B. Payne	Ass. com. (Canada)	1-3-15
	Rel. (in Eng.)	24-10-15
Maj. J. C. Stewart	Ass. com.	24-10-15
	(Evac. sick)	3-12-16
Capt. (A./Maj.) J. E. Read	Ass. com.	3-12-16
	Rel.	15-1-17
Maj. J. C. Stewart	Res. com.	15-1-17
	Rel. (to com. 8th Army Bde)	12-7-17
Maj. J. I. McSloy	Ass. com.	12-7-17
	Rel. (to Canada)	24-12-17
Capt. J. F. C. Maunder, M.C., 4-2-18	Ass. com.	24-12-17
	Rel.	11-2-18
Maj. J. K. M. Greene	Ass. com.	11-2-18
	Rel. (To Canada)	20-1-19
Maj. L. St. G. Kelly, M.C., 1-1-18	Ass. com.	20-1-19
	Rel.	5-3-19

NOTE: Ass. com.—Assumed command.
Rel.—Relinquished command.

THE GREENWAY PRESS
PRINTERS AND PUBLISHERS
312-18 ADELAIDE ST. WEST, TORONTO

www.ingramcontent.com/pod-product-compliance
Lightning Source LLC
Chambersburg PA
CBHW060838100426
42814CB00016B/416/J